Conversion in Reverse:

How the Ethos of Americanism Converted Catholics

by Thomas A. Droleskey, Ph.D.

Table of Contents

Introduction

The precepts of filial piety as found in the Fourth Commandment and the precepts of the Natural Law (those moral laws that exist in the nature of things and are knowable, albeit imperfectly, by human reason) require us to love the country in which we have been born or have chosen to make our home by means of naturalization.

True love of one's country, however, is not a mere expression of empty, emotionally-laden sentimentality. True love of one's country is an act of the will (that property of the human soul by which we make choices), which must be exercised in accord with what is good. And the true good of one's nation is her Catholicization, that is, that its government documents and civic officials, both elected and appointed, recognize that the Catholic Church is the one and only true Church founded by God Himself, Who has given her the Indirect Power over the temporal affairs of men to provide them with the infallible teaching and supernatural helps necessary to foster the common temporal good in light of man's Last End: the possession of the glory of the Beatific Vision of God the Father, God the Son and God the Holy Ghost for all eternity in Heaven.

Pope Leo XIII, writing in *Sapientiae Christianae*, January 10, 1890, explained that the love of one's country is indeed a duty of the Natural Law. We must, however, love God as He has revealed Himself to us exclusively through His Catholic Church above all else, being ready to die for the sake of Him and His Holy Church if the civil state requires of us things as citizens that are repugnant to our citizenship in Heaven by virtue of having been incorporated as members of the Mystical Body of Christ at the time of our Baptism:

> 4. It cannot be doubted that duties more numerous and of greater moment devolve on Catholics than upon such as are either not sufficiently enlightened in relation to the Catholic faith, or who are entirely unacquainted with its doctrines. Considering that forthwith upon salvation being brought out for mankind, Jesus Christ laid upon His Apostles the injunction to "preach the Gospel to every creature," He imposed, it is evident, upon all men the duty of learning thoroughly and believing what they were taught. This duty is intimately bound up with the gaining of eternal salvation: "He that believeth and is baptized shall be saved; but he that believeth not, shall be condemned."(2) **But the man who has embraced the Christian faith, as in duty bound, is by that very fact a subject of the Church as one of the children born of her, and becomes a member of that greatest and holiest body, which it is the special charge of the Roman Pontiff to rule with supreme power, under its invisible head, Jesus Christ.**

> 5. Now, if the natural law enjoins us to love devotedly and to defend the country in which we had birth, and in which we were brought up, so that every good citizen hesitates not to face death for his native land, very much more is it the urgent duty of Christians to be ever quickened by like feelings toward the Church. For the Church is the holy City of the living God, born of God Himself, and by Him built up and established. Upon this earth, indeed, she accomplishes her pilgrimage, but by instructing and guiding men she summons them to eternal happiness. We are bound, then, to love dearly the country whence we have received the means of enjoyment this mortal life affords, but we have a much more urgent obligation to love, with ardent love, the Church to which we owe the life of the soul, a life that will

endure forever. For fitting it is to prefer the good of the soul to the well-being of the body, inasmuch as duties toward God are of a far more hallowed character than those toward men.

6. Moreover, if we would judge aright, the supernatural love for the Church and the natural love of our own country proceed from the same eternal principle, since God Himself is their Author and originating Cause. Consequently, it follows that between the duties they respectively enjoin, neither can come into collision with the other. We can, certainly, and should love ourselves, bear ourselves kindly toward our fellow men, nourish affection for the State and the governing powers; **but at the same time we can and must cherish toward the Church a feeling of filial piety, and love God with the deepest love of which we are capable. The order of precedence of these duties is, however, at times, either under stress of public calamities, or through the perverse will of men, inverted**. For, instances occur where the State seems to require from men as subjects one thing, and religion, from men as Christians, quite another; and this in reality without any other ground, than that the rulers of the State either hold the sacred power of the Church of no account, or endeavor to subject it to their own will. Hence arises a conflict, and an occasion, through such conflict, of virtue being put to the proof. The two powers are confronted and urge their behests in a contrary sense; to obey both is wholly impossible. No man can serve two masters,(3) for to please the one amounts to contemning the other.

7. **As to which should be preferred no one ought to balance for an instant. It is a high crime indeed to withdraw allegiance from God in order to please men, an act of consummate wickedness to break the laws of Jesus Christ, in order to yield obedience to earthly rulers, or, under pretext of keeping the civil law, to ignore the rights of the Church; "we ought to obey God rather than men."**(4) This answer, which of old Peter and the other Apostles were used to give the civil authorities who enjoined unrighteous things, we must, in like circumstances, give always and without hesitation. No better citizen is there, whether in time of peace or war, than the Christian who is mindful of his duty; **but such a one should be ready to suffer all things, even death itself, rather than abandon the cause of God or of the Church**. (Pope Leo XIII, *Sapientiae Christianae*, January 10, 1890.)

Most Catholics in the world today, including those in the United States of America, have never heard of this simple reiteration of Catholic truths. Indeed, this writer, having spent his childhood in the baby-boom era of the 1950s in a throughly secularized household where talk of politics and current e v e n t s was heard almost exclusively at the dinner table, had never read the great Social Encyclical Letters that our true popes issued in the Nineteenth and early Twentieth Centuries to combat the rise of a civil state that they knew, having been founded upon false naturalistic (the belief that it is possible for men to view themselves and the events of the world by merely natural means without a reliance upon the Deposit of Faith that Our Blessed Lord and Saviour Jesus Christ has entrusted exclusively to His Catholic Church for Its eternal safekeeping and infallible explication) premises, was in the midst of degenerating into a new form of tyranny that had begun to sanction licentiousness under cover of law and would, over the course of time, become as tyrannical as had been the pagan states of antiquity and ape, quite ironically, the despotic exercise of monarchical power that arose in the wake of the Protestant Revolution, begun by Father Martin Luther in Wittenberg, Germany, on October 31, 1517, to make citizens its slaves.

Catholics in the United States of America have been subjected to nationalism (the idolization of one's country and its myths above all else) instead of the true concept of patriotism as taught by Holy Mother Church from the time of arrival of the first Catholic colonists in Maryland in 1634. There was an accommodation by the first American bishops to the prevailing ethos of naturalism that was destined to eat away at the *sensus Catholicus* (the supernatural "common sense," if you will, that we have by means of our Baptism and Confirmation) to such an extent that most Catholics in the United States of America today view the Holy Faith through the eyes of the world rather than viewing the world through the eyes of the Holy Faith.

Pope Leo XIII, writing an Apostolical Letter, *Testem Benevolentiae Nostrae*, to James Cardinal Gibbons, an Americanist who was the Archbishop of Baltimore, Maryland, from October 3, 1877, to March 24, 1921, explained that the ethos of a pluralistic nation (that is, one wherein can be found a multiplicity of false religious sects, all manner of erroneous philosophical and social beliefs, materialism, naturalism, religious indifferentism) had already caused the expression of the Catholic Faith to be watered down to a certain extent in order to appear "non-threatening" to the Protestant majority.

Pope Leo understood that the dangers facing Catholics in this country at the end of the Nineteenth Century were far more insidious than others that Catholics of previous times had faced. That is, it is relatively easy to recognize and to oppose open attacks upon the Holy Faith waged by those intent on destroying It and persecuting Its adherents. It is far more difficult to recognize subtle attacks on the Faith in a land that appears to be generically "Christian" but is actually poisonous to the spiritual and temporal good of all men, Catholics and non-Catholics alike:

> **The underlying principle of these new opinions is that, in order to more easily attract those who differ from her, the Church should shape her teachings more in accord with the spirit of the age and relax some of her ancient severity and make some concessions to new opinions.** Many think that these concessions should be made not only in regard to ways of living, but even in regard to doctrines which belong to the deposit of the faith. They contend that it would be opportune, in order to gain those who differ from us, to omit certain points of her teaching which are of lesser importance, and to tone down the meaning which the Church has always attached to them. **It does not need many words, beloved son, to prove the falsity of these ideas if the nature and origin of the doctrine which the Church proposes are recalled to mind. The Vatican Council says concerning this point: "For the doctrine of faith which God has revealed has not been proposed, like a** philosophical invention to be perfected by human ingenuity, but has been delivered as a divine deposit to the Spouse of Christ to be faithfully kept and infallibly declared. Hence that meaning of the sacred dogmas is perpetually to be retained which our Holy Mother, the Church, has once declared, nor is that meaning ever to be departed from under the pretense or pretext of a deeper comprehension of them." -Constitutio de Fide Catholica, Chapter iv.

> We cannot consider as altogether blameless the silence which purposely leads to the omission or neglect of some of the principles of Christian doctrine, for all the principles come from the same Author and Master, "the Only Begotten Son, Who is in the bosom of the Father."-John I, 18. They are adapted to all times and all nations, as is clearly seen from the words of our Lord to His apostles: "Going, therefore, teach all nations; teaching them to

observe all things whatsoever I have commanded you, and behold, I am with you all days, even to the end of the world."-Matt. xxviii, 19. Concerning this point the Vatican Council says: "All those things are to be believed with divine and catholic faith which are contained in the Word of God, written or handed down, and which the Church, either by a solemn judgment or by her ordinary and universal magisterium, proposes for belief as having been divinely revealed."-Const. de fide, Chapter iii.

Let it be far from anyone's mind to suppress for any reason any doctrine that has been handed down. Such a policy would tend rather to separate Catholics from the Church than to bring in those who differ. There is nothing closer to our heart than to have those who are separated from the fold of Christ return to it, but in no other way than the way pointed out by Christ.

The rule of life laid down for Catholics is not of such a nature that it cannot accommodate itself to the exigencies of various times and places. (VOL. XXIV-13.) The Church has, guided by her Divine Master, a kind and merciful spirit, for which reason from the very beginning she has been what St. Paul said of himself: "I became all things to all men that I might save all."

History proves clearly that the Apostolic See, to which has been entrusted the mission not only of teaching but of governing the whole Church, has continued "in one and the same doctrine, one and the same sense, and one and the same judgment," -- Const. de fide, Chapter iv.

But in regard to ways of living she has been accustomed to so yield that, the divine principle of morals being kept intact, she has never neglected to accommodate herself to the character and genius of the nations which she embraces.

Who can doubt that she will act in this same spirit again if the salvation of souls requires it? In this matter the Church must be the judge, not private men who are often deceived by the appearance of right. In this, all who wish to escape the blame of our predecessor, Pius the Sixth, must concur. **He condemned as injurious to the Church and the spirit of God who** guides her the doctrine contained in proposition lxxviii of the Synod of Pistoia, "that the discipline made and approved by the Church should be submitted to examination,   as if the Church could frame a code of laws useless or heavier than human liberty can bear."

But, beloved son, in this present matter of which we are speaking, there is even a greater danger and a more manifest opposition to Catholic doctrine and discipline in that opinion of the lovers of novelty, according to which they hold such liberty should be allowed in the Church, that her supervision and watchfulness being in some sense lessened, allowance be granted the faithful, each one to follow out more freely the leading of his own mind and the trend of his own proper activity. They are of opinion that such liberty has its counterpart in the newly given civil freedom which is now the right and the foundation of almost every secular state. (Pope Leo XIII, Apostolical Letter to James Cardinal Gibbons, *Testem Benevolentiae Nostrae*, January 22, 1899.)

Pope Leo XIII explained near the end of his Apostolical Letter to James Cardinal Gibbons that he feared that at least some of the American bishops did indeed desire the American model of the religiously pluralistic civil state, which has been so praised by the "popes" of the conciliar church, to be adopted by the Church herself as the means of "reconciling" herself to the "modern" world:

> For it [an adherence to the condemned precepts of Americanism] **would give rise to the suspicion that there are among you some who conceive of and desire the Church in America to be different from what it is in the rest of the world.** (Pope Leo XIII, Apostolical Letter to James Cardinal Gibbons, *Testem Benevolentiae Nostrae*, January 22, 1899.)

Despite all of the great heroism exhibited by Catholic clergy, religious and the laity in the midst of overt hostility to the Holy Faith in the Nineteenth Century on the part of many Protestants and Freemasons, despite the commitment of many of the American bishops prior to the death of Pope Pius XII on October 9, 1958, to build Catholic schools and to establish hospitals and orphanages and institutions without number to care for the poor and the immigrants and to defend the many of the doctrines of the Faith without flinching, despite the fact that there was a thriving Catholic intellectual life by the end of the Nineteenth Century, and despite the fact that millions of people converted to the Faith over the course of time, all of these truly notable and most laudatory accomplishments stood to be–and have been in fact–wiped away by the very false premises upon which the nation was founded. There has been, you see, a process, at first slow and imperceptible, of a "conversion in reverse" that was set in motion from the Seventeenth Century that has resulted in full-scale apostasy on the part of so many alleged Catholic bishops and priests and religious, an apostasy that is shared by so many of the lay faithful.

There is also, of course, a great deal of confusion of principles in the minds of so many Catholics in the United States of America today. There is so much confusion that it is not uncommon for Catholics to find themselves using phrases that contradict each other and that seek to "resolve" social problems by making advertence to every secular or naturalistic solution available rather than taking seriously these simple words of Pope Saint Pius X, found in *Notre Charge Apostolique*, August 15, 1910:

> The same applies to the notion of Fraternity which they found on the love of common interest or, beyond all philosophies and religions, on the mere notion of humanity, thus embracing with an equal love and tolerance all human beings and their miseries, whether these are intellectual, moral, or physical and temporal. **But Catholic doctrine tells us that the primary duty of charity does not lie in the toleration of false ideas, however sincere they may be, nor in the theoretical or practical indifference towards the errors and vices in which we see our brethren plunged, but in the zeal for their intellectual and moral improvement as well as for their material well-being. Catholic doctrine further tells us that love for our neighbor flows from our love for God,** Who is Father to all, and goal of the whole human family; and in Jesus Christ whose members we are, to the point that in doing good to others we are doing good to Jesus Christ Himself. Any other kind of love is sheer illusion, sterile and fleeting.

> Indeed, we have the human experience of pagan and secular societies of ages past to show that concern for common interests or affinities of nature weigh very little against the passions

and wild desires of the heart. No, Venerable Brethren, there is no genuine fraternity outside Christian charity. Through the love of God and His Son Jesus Christ Our Saviour, Christian charity embraces all men, comforts all, and leads all to the same faith and same heavenly happiness. . . .

Here we have, founded by Catholics, an inter-denominational association that is to work for the reform of civilization, an undertaking which is above all religious in character; **for there is no true civilization without a moral civilization, and no true moral civilization without the true religion: it is a proven truth, a historical fact**. (Pope Saint Pius X, *Notre Charge Apostolique*, August 15, 1910.)

The sad truth is, of course, that most Catholics alive today do not understand the fact that Catholicism is the one and only foundation of personal and social order. Nothing else. And it is precisely the fact that the modern civil state is founded upon a rejection of this belief that all has fallen into decay, a decay whose scope and magnitude has been expedited and magnified by the admitted "reconciliation" of the conciliar church with the very anti-Incarnational principles of Modernity that have been condemned repeatedly by our true popes.

The subjects of this three volume book are divided as follows:

Volume I:

1. To provide an overview of the immutable teaching of the Catholic Church concerning her doctrine of the Social Reign of Christ the King and the true nature of the civil state;

2. To provide a brief, thumbnail summary of salvation history from the time of Special Creation to Our Blessed Lord and Saviour Jesus Christ's Incarnation, Nativity, Hidden Years, Public Life and Ministry, Passion, Death, Resurrection and Ascension. We cannot understand contemporary problems if we do not understand them in the light of supernatural truths concerning the very purpose of our existence and the ravages caused by Original Sin and our own Actual Sins;

3. A review of the birth of Holy Mother Church and her missionary work from the time of Pentecost Sunday to the collapse of the Roman Empire in the West at the time of the barbarian invasions at the beginning of the Fifth Century A.D. In contrast to the ethos of the first bishops of the United States of America, the first bishops of the Catholic Church confronted a hostile culture and sought to convert it rather than making their accommodations to it;

4. A rather protracted study of the growth of the Faith in the Middle Ages and how the Faith was exemplified and the Social Reign of Christ the King embodied in the lives of various saints. This section reviews the glories of Christendom in which the Social Reign of Christ the King was exercised, albeit never perfectly and all too frequently marked by conflicts between avaricious,   power-hungry potentates who believed themselves to be the equal to, if not the superior of, Christ the King and of his true and legitimate Vicars here on earth, the popes;

5. A brief examination of the decline of Christendom and the rise of the Renaissance with its   recrudescence of the sophistries of Greek antiquity that made possible the triumph of the

rationalism of the Protestant Revolution;

6. To explain the nature of the principal strains of Protestantism, demonstrating how the devil used the Protestant Revolution to overthrow the Social Reign of Christ the King, thereby creating the religious, political and philosophical environment that created the exercise of unchecked monarchical power that shaped the distorted view of a monarchy held by many of the founders of the United States of America;

7. To provide a summary of the spread of the Social Reign of Christ the King in the Americas, particularly in the aftermath of Our Lady's apparition to Juan Diego in December of 1531, focusing also on the missionary work of the North American Martyrs, who sought to Catholicize the northern regions of the North American continent;

8. To provide a brief history of the hostility to Catholics, then a tiny fragment of the population, in the English-speaking colonies that were located on the Atlantic seaboard of what became the United States of America;

9. A summary of the some of the rationalistic philosophical strains that influenced the founding and subsequent development of the government of the United States of America;

10. A summary of the accommodations made by the first Bishop of Baltimore and thus of the United States of America, John Carroll, to the prevailing spirit of Declaration of Independence and the Constitution as though each were an expression of and perfectly compatible with the truths of the Catholic Faith;

Volume II

11. A review of the Declaration of Independence and the principles of the Constitution of the United States of America, each examined in light of the social encyclical letters and an understanding of the inherent flaws at the foundation of their texts;

12. To provide a review of the legal, political and social hostility visited upon Catholics by Protestants, Masons, nativists and others in the wake of the first massive wave of Irish immigration to the United States in the decades before the War between the States;

13. To assess the rise of a distinct party of American bishops, the Americanists, who were opposed to the solemn proclamation of the doctrine of the Immaculate Conception of the Blessed Virgin Mary by Pope Pius IX in the Papal Bull *Ineffabilis Deus*, on December 8, 1854, *The Syllabus of Errors* that he promulgated on December 8, 1864, the solemn proclamation of doctrine of papal infallibility at the [First] Vatican Council in *Pastor Aeternus* on July 18, 1870, and the possible appointment of a papal nuncio (ambassador) to the United States of America;

14. To discuss the active involvement of Catholics, especially those of immigrant stock, in the Democratic Party to provide themselves with a means of upward social, economic and political mobility at a time when all other temporal avenues of advancement were closed to them, thus creating to this day, at least in the minds and hearts of so many American Catholics,

the belief that we "solve" social problems by means of adhering to this or that organized crime family of naturalism   (political parties);

15.	To explain that the caste of career politicians has been hostile to Our Blessed Lord and Saviour Jesus Christ, the King of all men and all nations, providing Catholics and non-Catholics alike with nothing other than bombast and policies that are bound to fail time and time again because they are based upon one false premise after another;

16.	A thorough review of papal injunctions against the modern civil state and the manner in which the American bishops ignored these injunctions, making the issuance of *Testem Benevolentiae Nostrae* necessary, especially in light of the active spread of the Americanist heresy by the part of American bishops and bishops;

17.	Opposition to and support for American involvement in the Spanish-American War and World War I.;

18.	Woodrow Wilson's antipathy towards the Catholic Faith and his willingness to let Catholics in Mexico die at the hands of the Masonic revolutionaries he supported;

19.	The rise of a national bishops' bureaucratic apparatus that began to operate as a mouthpiece for the Democratic Party by the time of the administration of President Franklin Delano Roosevelt in the 1930s;

20.	The candidacy of New York Governor Alfred Emmanuel Smith as a perfect expression of the heresy of Americanism;

21.	World War II and the postwar era: the rise of the John Birch Society as an expression of political ecumenism committed to the spread of the Americanist ethos as the antidote to Communism and one world governance;

22.	Efforts on the part of bishops and theologians to push the Americanist agenda in the 1940s and 1950s in the realm of liturgy, doctrine and morals;

Volume III

23.	The triumph of the Americanist spirit at the "Second" Vatican Council and the rise of a false church that was shaped as much by the currents that flowed into the Tiber from the Potomac as from the Rhine;

24.	The rise of a caste of Catholics in public life who have maintained their "good standing" in what appears to be the Catholic Church despite their support for one evil after another;

25.	The infestation of theological, liturgical and moral predators in the ranks of the conciliar clergy;

26.   The collapse of even the personal piety that was maintained despite the Americanist ethos because of the graces of true Masses offered according to the Immemorial Mass of Tradition as church buildings were erected as shrines to the Modernist spirit of conciliarism that is an expression in many ways of Jansenism that was at the root of the building (and "renovation") of Basilica of the National Shrine of the Assumption of the Blessed Virgin Mary in Baltimore, Maryland;

Our Lady's Fatima Message as the hope for the restoration of the Church and thus of the Social Reign of Christ the King.

This book does not purport to be a definitive history of the life of Catholics in the United States of America.

No, this book is an effort to provide an overview of salvation history and the life of the Church in the Middle Ages as a means to contrast that era of Christendom with the influences wrought by the uncritical acceptance of the ideas of Modernity in the life of Catholics in the United States of America. It is the goal of three volume series to explain how this uncritical acceptance of the ideas of Modernity and the trends of popular culture were opposed to the Sacred Deposit of Faith and thus has made impossible the realization of a just social order as it has impeded the Church's mission to sanctify and save souls.

Readers of my **www.Christorchaos.com** website will note that there is a lot of material that has been drawn from my articles. However, this book is not a compilation of articles. There is much new textual material in the book. The previously published material has been written over the years with a view to obviating the need to rewrite it all again when the time came to put together this present three volume set. And, of course, the previously published material is now presented in a context linking it to other material, providing readers with a ready resource to use without having to do random searches on my website.

It is as a Catholic first and a citizen of the United States second that this writer has approached the subject as it is impossible to be a good citizen of one's nation unless one is first a citizen of Heaven by virtue of being a member of the Catholic Church who is striving to cooperate with the graces won for him on the wood of the Holy Cross by the shedding of every single drop of the Most Precious Blood of the Divine Redeemer, Christ the King, that flows into his heart and soul through the loving hands of Our Lady, she who is the Mediatrix of All Graces.

This book is thus dedicated to the reestablishment of the Social Reign of the Sacred Heart of Jesus through the Sorrowful and Immaculate Heart of Mary. And this book could not have been completed without the constant love, patience, support and encouragement that I receive each day from my dear wife, Sharon, whose love of the Most Blessed Trinity as the consecrated slave of Our Lady's Sorrowful and Immaculate Heart is so very inspirational, and our beloved daughter, Lucy Mary Therese Norma. I am so grateful to God for the family with which I have been blessed and it is our goal, despite our own individual faults, with my own being the most exaggerated and most intractable, to climb the heights of sanctity together by enfolding ourselves to the tender mercies of the Most Sacred Heart of Jesus through the Sorrowful and Immaculate Heart of Mary.

Chapter I
A Short Catechism of the Social Reign of Christ the King

We must view all things in the world through the supernatural eyes of the Holy Faith.

As most Catholics do not do so, however, being immersed in the activities of the world, it is necessary to provide answers to basic questions, thereby assisting readers who are reading this material for the first time with a framework to use for understanding the subjects covered in the succeeding chapters. This review will also assist those who are familiar with this material, having read it on this writer's <u>**www.Christorchaos.com**</u> website, to use as a ready reference without having to go to their "bookmarks" on the internet.

Part I: The Social Reign of Christ the King

1) What are the principles that must govern human life, both individually and collectively in civil society?

There are limits that exist in the nature of things beyond which men have no authority or right to transgress, whether acting individually or collectively in the institutions of civil governance.

2) Who has revealed these principles and do they bind all men in all circumstances, including those of civil governance?

There are limits that have been revealed positively by God Himself in his Divine Revelation, that bind all men in all circumstances at all times, binding even the institutions of civil governance.

3) What is the nature of the concept of hierarchy in family and social life?

A divinely-instituted hierarchy exists in man's most basic natural unit of association: the family. The father is the head of the family and governs his wife and children in accord with the binding precepts of the Divine positive law and the natural law. Children do not have the authority to disobey the legitimate commands of their parents. Parents do not have the authority to issue illegitimate and/or unjust commands.

4) How is this concept of authority demonstrated in the life of the Holy Family?

Our Lord Himself became Incarnate in Our Lady's virginal and immaculate womb, subjecting Himself to the authority of His creatures, obeying his foster-father, Saint Joseph, as the head of the Holy Family, thus teaching us that all men everywhere must recognize an ultimate authority over them in their social relations, starting with the family.

5) What institution has been instituted by God Himself to transmit His teaching infallibly until the end of time?

Our Lord instituted the Catholic Church, founding it on the Rock of Peter, the Pope, to be the means by which His Deposit of Faith is safeguarded and transmitted until the end of time.

6) Must all men and all nations submit to the teaching authority of the Catholic Church?

Yes. The Catholic Church is the mater, mother, and magister, teacher, of all men in all nations at all times, whether or not men and nations recognize this to be the case.

7) Who has the authority to proclaim the truths of the Catholic Church?

The Pope and the bishops of the Church have the solemn obligation to proclaim nothing other than the fullness of the truths of the Faith for the good of the sanctification and salvation of men unto eternity and thus for whatever measure of common good in the temporal realm, which the Church desires earnestly to promote, can be achieved in a world full of fallen men.

8) Is it possible for men to live virtuously as citizens of a country without striving for sanctity as citizens of Heaven?

No, it is not possible for men to live virtuously as citizens of any country unless they first strive for sanctity as citizens of Heaven, noting that natural virtues can give the *appearance* of a well-ordered individual as that person commits offenses against the Divine Positive Law that he does not accept or about which he is ignorant.

That is, it is not possible for there to be true order in any nation over the course of the long term if men do not have belief in, access to, and cooperation with sanctifying grace, which equips them to accept the truths contained in the Deposit of Faith and to obey God's commands with diligence in every aspect of their lives without exception.

9) Was there ever a period in history when the rulers of nations understood this teaching and attempted to implement it?

Yes, the rulers of Christendom (that era also called the Middle Ages, roughly a period of a little over a thousand years from the time of the collapse of the Roman Empire in the West to the rise of the Protestant Revolt), came to understand, although never perfectly and never without conflicts and inconsistencies, that the limits of the Divine positive law and the natural law obligated them to exercise the powers of civil governance with a view towards promoting man's temporal good in this life so as to foster in him his return to God in the next life. In other words, rulers such as Saint Louis IX, King of France, knew that they would be judged by Our Lord at the moment of their Particular Judgments on the basis of how well they had fostered those conditions in their countries that made it more possible for their subjects to get to Heaven.

10) Who are some of the other rulers of the Middle Ages who ruled in light of man's Last End?

Some of the other rulers of the Middle Ages who ruled their realms in light of man's Last End were Saint Edward the Confessor of England, Saint Henry (King of Bavaria and then Holy Roman Emperor), Saint Stephen of Hungary, Saint Elizabeth of Hungary, King Alfred the Great of Wessex, Saint Casimir, Prince of Poland, and Saint Wenceslaus of Bohemia, among many others. Latter day exemplars of the Social Reign of Christ the King have been King John Sobieski of Poland (Seventeenth Century) and Gabriel Garcia Moreno, President of Ecuador in the Nineteenth Century.

11) How did these rulers subordinate themselves to the Catholic Church in the exercise of their civil rule?

The rulers of Christendom accepted the truth that the Church had the right, which she used judicially after exhausting her Indirect Power over civil rulers by proclaiming the truths of the Holy Faith, to interpose herself in the event that a civil ruler proposed to do something or had indeed done something that violated grievously the administration of justice and thus posed a grave threat to the good of souls.

12) How can one define the Social Kingship of Jesus Christ?

The Social Kingship of Jesus Christ may be defined as the right of the Catholic Church to see to it that the binding precepts of the Divine Positive Law and the Natural Law are the basis of the actions of civil governance and that those who exercise civil power keep in mind man's Last End. This means that the civil state must recognize the Catholic Church as the true Church founded by God Himself and that she possesses the Indirect Power to interpose herself with its officials by means of preaching and teaching and exhortation in order to prevent actions contrary to the good of souls from being undertaken and/or to warn about or apply sanctions when edicts and ordinances contrary to God's laws are made and enforced.

13) Are you saying that each civil state in the world has the obligation to recognize the Catholicism as the true religion?

It is not "my" teaching that I proclaim on my website and in this book but the immutable teaching of the Catholic Church that teaches that each civil state has the obligation to recognize her with the favor and the protection of the laws. Pope Leo XIII, writing to the American bishops in *Longiqua Oceani*, January 6, 1895, explained that the "separation of Church and State" that existed in the United States is not the model for the rest of the world:

> Yet, though all this is true, it would be very erroneous to draw the conclusion that in America is to be sought the type of the most desirable status of the Church, or that it would be universally lawful or expedient for State and Church to be, as in America, dissevered and divorced. The fact that Catholicity with you is in good condition, nay, is even enjoying a prosperous growth, is by all means to be attributed to the fecundity with which God has endowed His Church, in virtue of which unless men or circumstances interfere, she spontaneously expands and propagates herself; but she would bring forth more abundant fruits if, in addition to liberty, she enjoyed the favor of the laws and the patronage of the public authority. (Pope Leo XIII, *Longiqua Oceani*, January 6, 1895.)

14) What passage from a papal encyclical letter best summarizes this teaching and that of the Social Reign of Christ the King?

The passage from a papal encyclical letter that best summarizes the Catholic Church's immutable teaching on the Social Reign of Christ the King is found in Pope Saint Pius X's *Vehementer Nos*, February 11, 1906:

> **That the State must be separated from the Church is a thesis absolutely false, a most pernicious error**. Based, as it is, on the principle that the State must not recognize any religious cult, it is in the first place guilty of a great injustice to God; for the Creator of man is also the Founder of human societies, and preserves their existence as He preserves our own. We owe Him, therefore, not only a private cult, but a public and social worship to honor Him. Besides, this thesis is an obvious negation of the supernatural order. It limits the action of the State to the pursuit of public prosperity during this life only, which is but the proximate object of political societies; and it occupies itself in no fashion (on the plea that this is foreign to it) with their ultimate object which is man's eternal happiness after this short life shall have run its course. **But as the present order of things is temporary and subordinated to the conquest of man's supreme and absolute welfare, it follows that the civil power must not only place no obstacle in the way of this conquest, but must aid us in effecting it.** The same thesis also upsets the order providentially established by God in the world, which demands a harmonious agreement between the two societies. Both of them, the civil and the religious society, although each exercises in its own sphere its authority over them. It follows necessarily that there are many things belonging to them in common in which both societies must have relations with one another. **Remove the agreement between Church and State, and the result will be that from these common matters will spring the seeds of disputes which will become acute on both sides; it will become more difficult to see where the truth lies, and great confusion is certain to arise.** Finally, this thesis inflicts great injury on society itself, for it cannot either prosper or last long when due place is not left for religion, which is the supreme rule and the sovereign mistress in all questions touching the rights and the duties of men. **Hence the Roman Pontiffs have never ceased, as circumstances required, to refute and condemn the doctrine of the separation of Church and State.** Our illustrious predecessor, Leo XIII, especially, has frequently and magnificently expounded Catholic teaching on the relations which should subsist between the two societies. "Between them," he says, "there must necessarily be a suitable union, which may not improperly be compared with that existing between body and soul.-"Quaedam intercedat necesse est ordinata colligatio (inter illas) quae quidem conjunctioni non immerito comparatur, per quam anima et corpus in homine copulantur." He proceeds: "Human societies cannot, without becoming criminal, act as if God did not exist or refuse to concern themselves with religion, as though it were something foreign to them, or of no purpose to them.... As for the Church, which has God Himself for its author, to exclude her from the active life of the nation, from the laws, the education of the young, the family, is to commit a great and pernicious error. -- "Civitates non possunt, citra scellus, gerere se tamquam si Deus omnino non esset, aut curam religionis velut alienam nihilque profuturam abjicere.... Ecclesiam vero, quam Deus ipse constituit, ab actione vitae excludere, a legibus, ab institutione adolescentium, a societate domestica, magnus et perniciousus est error. (Pope Saint Pius X, *Vehementer Nos*, February 11, 1906.)

15) What other encyclical letters can you cite here in which I can find these points explained as

part of the patrimony of the Catholic Church?

Pope Gregory XVI's *Mirari Vos*, August 15, 1832; Pope Pius IX's *Quanto Conficiamur Moerore*, August 10, 1863, and *Quanta Cura*, December 8, 1864; Pope Leo XIII's *Humanum Genus*, August 20, 1884, *Immortale Dei*, November 1, 1885, *Libertas*, June 20, 1888, *Sapientiae Christianae*, January 10, 1890, *Rerum Novarum*, May 15, 1891; *Custodi Di QuellaFede*, December 8, 1892, *Testem Benevolentiae Nostrae*, January 22, 1899, *Tametsi Futura Prospicientibus*, November 1, 1900, *A Review of His Pontificate*, March 19, 1902; Pope Saint Pius X's *Vehementer Nos*, February 11, 1906 and *Notre Charge Apostolique*, August 15, 1910; Pope Pius XI's *Ubi Arcano Dei Consilio*, December 23, 1922, *Quas Primas*, December 11, 1925, *Divini Illius Magistri*, December 31, 1929; *Casti Connubii*, December 31, 1931, *Quadragesimo Anno*, May 15, 1931, *Mit Brennender Sorge*, March 17, 1937, and *Divini Redemptoris*, March 19, 1937.

16) Can a Catholic dissent from the Social Teaching of the Catholic Church concerning the necessity of praying and working for the confessional Catholic civil state and the restoration of the Social Reign of Christ the King?

No. One must adhere to everything contained in these encyclical letters. Pope Pius XI made this clear in *Ubi Arcano Dei Consilio*, December 23, 1922:

> Many believe in or claim that they believe in and hold fast to Catholic doctrine on such questions as social authority, the right of owning private property, on the relations between capital and labor, on the rights of the laboring man, on the relations between Church and State, religion and country, on the relations between the different social classes, on international relations, on the rights of the Holy See and the prerogatives of the Roman Pontiff and the Episcopate, on the social rights of Jesus Christ, Who is the Creator, Redeemer, and Lord not only of individuals but of nations. In spite of these protestations, they speak, write, and, what is more, act as if it were not necessary any longer to follow, or that they did not remain still in full force, the teachings and solemn pronouncements which may be found in so many documents of the Holy See, and particularly in those written by Leo XIII, Pius X, and Benedict XV.
>
> **There is a species of moral, legal, and social modernism which We condemn, no less decidedly than We condemn theological modernism.**
>
> **It is necessary ever to keep in mind these teachings and pronouncements which We have made; it is no less necessary to reawaken that spirit of faith, of supernatural love, and of Christian discipline which alone can bring to these principles correct understanding, and can lead to their observance.** This is particularly important in the case of youth, and especially those who aspire to the priesthood, so that in the almost universal confusion in which we live they at least, as the Apostle writes, will not be "tossed to and fro, and carried about with every wind of doctrine by the wickedness of men, by cunning craftiness, by which they lie in wait to deceive." (Ephesians iv, 14) (Pope Pius XI, *Ubi Arcano Dei Consilio*, December 23, 1922.)

Pope Pius XII emphasized in *Humani Generis*, August 12, 1950, that one is bound to accept the teaching contained in papal encyclical letters as such teaching is but a reiteration of the perennial teaching of the Catholic Church:

> Nor must it be thought that what is expounded in Encyclical Letters does not of itself demand consent, since in writing such Letters the Popes do not exercise the supreme power of their Teaching Authority. For these matters are taught with the ordinary teaching authority, of which it is true to say: "He who heareth you, heareth me"; and generally what is expounded and inculcated in Encyclical Letters already for other reasons appertains to Catholic doctrine. But if the Supreme Pontiffs in their official documents purposely pass judgment on a matter up to that time under dispute, it is obvious that that matter, according to the mind and will of the same Pontiffs, cannot be any longer considered a question open to discussion among theologians. (Pope Pius XII, *Humani Generis*, August 12, 1950.)

Pope Pius XII reiterated the immutable nature of Catholic Social Teaching in 1958, just three months before his death:

> Assuming false and unjust premises, they are not afraid to take a position which would confine within a narrow scope the supreme teaching authority of the Church, claiming that there are certain questions -- such as those which concern social and economic matters -- in which Catholics may ignore the teachings and the directives of this Apostolic See.
>
> This opinion -- it seems entirely unnecessary to demonstrate its existence -- is utterly false and full of error because, as We declared a few years ago to a special meeting of Our Venerable Brethren in the episcopacy:
>
>> "The power of the Church is in no sense limited to so-called 'strictly religious matters'; but the whole matter of the natural law, its institution, interpretation and application, in so far as the moral aspect is concerned, are within its power.
>>
>> "By God's appointment the observance of the natural law concerns the way by which man must strive toward his supernatural end. The Church shows the way and is the guide and guardian of men with respect to their supernatural end."
>
> This truth had already been wisely explained by Our Predecessor St. Pius X in his Encyclical Letter Singulari quadam of September 24, 1912, in which he made this statement: "All actions of a Christian man so far as they are morally either good or bad -- that is, so far as they agree with or are contrary to the natural and divine law -- fall under the judgment and jurisdiction of the Church."
>
> Moreover, even when those who arbitrarily set and defend these narrow limits profess a desire to obey the Roman Pontiff with regard to truths to be believed, and to observe what they call ecclesiastical directives, they proceed with such boldness that they refuse to obey the precise and definite prescriptions of the Holy See. They protest that these refer to political affairs because of a hidden meaning by the author, as if these prescriptions took their origin from some secret conspiracy against their own nation. (Pope Pius XII, *Ad Apostolorum Principis*, June 29, 1958.)

17) May a Catholic claim that he is privately opposed to certain evils, such as abortion, while supporting them under the cover of civil law and in the various aspects of popular culture?

No, he may not. Pope Leo XIII made this clear in *Immortale Dei*, November 1, 1885:

> Hence, lest concord be broken by rash charges, let this be understood by all, that the integrity of Catholic faith cannot be reconciled with opinions verging on naturalism or rationalism, the essence of which is utterly to do away with Christian institutions and to install in society the supremacy of man to the exclusion of God. **Further, it is unlawful to follow one line of conduct in private life and another in public, respecting privately the authority of the Church, but publicly rejecting it; for this would amount to joining together good and evil, and to putting man in conflict with himself; whereas he ought always to be consistent, and never in the least point nor in any condition of life to swerve from Christian virtue.** (Pope Leo XIII, *Immortale Dei*, November 1, 1885.)

Pope Pius XI explained in *Casti Connubii*, December 29, 1930, that those in public life who support the surgical dismemberment of the innocent preborn in their mothers' womb face a strict accounting before their Divine Judge, Christ the King:

> Those who hold the reins of government should not forget that it is the duty of public authority by appropriate laws and sanctions to defend the lives of the innocent, and this all the more so since those whose lives are endangered and assailed cannot defend themselves. Among whom we must mention in the first place infants hidden in the mother's womb. **And if the public magistrates not only do not defend them, but by their laws and ordinances betray them to death at the hands of doctors or of others, let them remember that God is the Judge and Avenger of innocent blood which cried from earth to Heaven."** (Pope Pius XI, *Casti Connubii*, December 30, 1930.)

18) Does the Catholic Church teach that men must follow a particular form of government?

No. The Church, as a loving and wise mother, recognizes that individual men have great latitude to form specific institutional arrangements of civil governance that are suitable to the peculiar characteristics of their own nations and national experiences. She only insists that each civil government recognize her as the true religion and that its policies seek to foster those conditions that promote the sanctification and salvation of the souls of its citizens. Pope Leo XIII noted this precise point in *Immortale Dei*:

> Therefore, when it is said that the Church is hostile to modern political regimes and that she repudiates the discoveries of modern research, the charge is a ridiculous and groundless calumny. Wild opinions she does repudiate, wicked and seditious projects she does condemn, together with that attitude of mind which points to the beginning of a willful departure from God. But, as all truth must necessarily proceed from God, the Church recognizes in all truth that is reached by research a trace of the divine intelligence. And as all truth in the natural order is powerless to destroy belief in the teachings of revelation, but can do much to confirm

it, and as every newly discovered truth may serve to further the knowledge or the praise of God, it follows that whatsoever spreads the range of knowledge will always be willingly and even joyfully welcomed by the Church. She will always encourage and promote, as she does in other branches of knowledge, all study occupied with the investigation of nature. In these pursuits, should the human intellect discover anything not known before, the Church makes no opposition. She never objects to search being made for things that minister to the refinements and comforts of life. So far, indeed, from opposing these she is now, as she ever has been, hostile alone to indolence and sloth, and earnestly wishes that the talents of men may bear more and more abundant fruit by cultivation and exercise. Moreover, she gives encouragement to every kind of art and handicraft, and through her influence, directing all strivings after progress toward virtue and salvation, she labors to prevent man's intellect and industry from turning him away from God and from heavenly things.

All this, though so reasonable and full of counsel, finds little favor nowadays when States not only refuse to conform to the rules of Christian wisdom, but seem even anxious to recede from them further and further on each successive day. Nevertheless, since truth when brought to light is wont, of its own nature, to spread itself far and wide, and gradually take possession of the minds of men, We, moved by the great and holy duty of Our apostolic mission to all nations, speak, as We are bound to do, with freedom. Our eyes are not closed to the spirit of the times. We repudiate not the assured and useful improvements of our age, but devoutly wish affairs of State to take a safer course than they are now taking, and to rest on a more firm foundation without injury to the true freedom of the people; for the best parent and guardian of liberty amongst men is truth. "The truth shall make you free." (Pope Leo XIII, *Immortale Dei*, November 1, 1885.)

19) What does the Catholic Church teach about liberty?

The Catholic Church teaches us that authentic liberty is that natural condition of human being wherein he is able to choose after what is good and true in accordance with the precepts of Divine Revelation and the dictates of right reason. Liberty is not "license," that is unrestrained physical freedom. No one is morally "free" to do everything he desires to do. One is only morally "free" to do what is right. Error has no rights. God grants no civil "right," whether in the Divine Positive Law or the Natural Law, to adherents of false religions to propagate their beliefs openly. God does not want the souls for whom He shed every single drop of His Most Precious Blood on the wood of the Holy Cross to be confused by the open dissemination of error:

But a much more grave, and indeed very bitter, sorrow increased in Our heart - a sorrow by which We confess that We were crushed, overwhelmed and torn in two - from the twenty-second article of the constitution in which We saw, not only that "liberty of religion and of conscience" (to use the same words found in the article) were permitted by the force of the constitution, but also that assistance and patronage were promised both to this liberty and also to the ministers of these different forms of "religion". There is certainly no need of many words, in addressing you, to make you fully recognize by how lethal a wound the Catholic religion in France is struck by this article. For when the liberty of all "religions" is indiscriminately asserted, by this very fact truth is confounded with error and the holy and immaculate Spouse of Christ, the Church, outside of which there can be no salvation, is set on a par with the sects of heretics and with Judaic perfidy itself. **For when favour and patronage is promised even to the sects of heretics and their ministers, not only their persons, but also their very errors, are tolerated and fostered: a system of errors in which is contained that fatal and never sufficiently to be deplored HERESY which, as St. Augustine says** (de Haeresibus, no.72), **"asserts that all heretics proceed correctly and tell the truth: which is so absurd that it seems incredible to me."** (Pope Pius VII, *Post Tam Diuturnas*, April 29, 1814.)

This shameful font of indifferentism gives rise to that absurd and erroneous proposition which claims that liberty of conscience must be maintained for everyone. It spreads ruin in sacred and civil affairs, though some repeat over and over again with the greatest impudence that some advantage accrues to religion from it. **"But the death of the soul is worse than freedom of error,"** as Augustine was wont to say. When all restraints are removed by which men are kept on the narrow path of truth, their nature, which is already inclined to evil, propels them to ruin. Then truly "the bottomless pit" is open from which John saw smoke ascending which obscured the sun, and out of which locusts flew forth to devastate the earth. Thence comes transformation of minds, corruption of youths, contempt of sacred things and holy laws -- in other words, a pestilence more deadly to the state than any other. Experience shows, even from earliest times, that cities renowned for wealth, dominion, and glory perished as a result of this single evil, namely immoderate freedom of opinion, license of free speech, and desire for novelty.

Here We must include that harmful and never sufficiently denounced freedom to publish any writings whatever and disseminate them to the people, which some dare to demand and promote with so great a clamor. We are horrified to see what monstrous doctrines and prodigious errors are disseminated far and wide in countless books, pamphlets, and other writings which, though small in weight, are very great in malice. We are in tears at the abuse which proceeds from them over the face of the earth. Some are so carried away that they contentiously assert that the flock of errors arising from them is sufficiently compensated by the publication of some book which defends religion and truth. Every law condemns deliberately doing evil simply because there is some hope that good may result. Is there any sane man who would say poison ought to be distributed, sold publicly, stored, and even drunk because some antidote is available and those who use it may be snatched from death again and again?

The Church has always taken action to destroy the plague of bad books. This was true even in apostolic times for we read that the apostles themselves burned a large number of books. It may be enough to consult the laws of the fifth Council of the Lateran on this matter and the Constitution which Leo X published afterwards lest "that which has been discovered advantageous for the increase of the faith and the spread of useful arts be converted to the contrary use and work harm for the salvation of the faithful." This also was of great concern to the fathers of Trent, who applied a remedy against this great evil by publishing that wholesome decree concerning the Index of books which contain false doctrine."We must fight valiantly," Clement XIII says in an encyclical letter about the banning of bad books, "as much as the matter itself demands and must exterminate the deadly poison of so many books; for never will the material for error be withdrawn, unless the criminal sources of depravity perish   in flames." Thus it is evident that this Holy See has always striven, throughout the ages, to condemn and to remove suspect and harmful books. The teaching of those who reject the censure of books as too heavy and onerous a burden causes immense harm to the Catholic people and to this See. They are even so depraved as to affirm that it is contrary to the principles of law, and they deny the Church the right to decree and to maintain it. (Pope Gregory XVI, *Mirari Vos*, August 15, 1832.)

But, although we have not omitted often to proscribe and reprobate the chief errors of this kind, yet the cause of the Catholic Church, and the salvation of souls entrusted to us by God, and the welfare of human society itself, altogether demand that we again stir up your pastoral solicitude to exterminate other evil opinions, which spring forth from the said errors as from a fountain. Which false and perverse opinions are on that ground the more to be detested, because they chiefly tend to this, that that salutary influence be impeded and (even) removed, which the Catholic Church, according to the institution and command of her Divine Author, should freely exercise even to the end of the world -- not only over private individuals, but over nations, peoples, and their sovereign princes; and (tend also) to take away that mutual fellowship and concord of counsels between Church and State which has ever proved itself propitious and salutary, both for religious and civil interests.

For you well know, venerable brethren, that at this time men are found not a few who, applying to civil society the impious and absurd principle of "naturalism," as they call it, dare to teach that "the best constitution of public society and (also) civil progress altogether require that human society be conducted and governed without regard being had to religion any more than if it did not exist; or, at least, without any distinction being made between the true religion and false ones." And, against the doctrine of Scripture, of the Church, and of the Holy Fathers, they do not hesitate to assert that "that is the best condition of civil society, in which no duty is recognized, as attached to the civil power, of restraining by enacted penalties, offenders against the Catholic religion, except so far as public peace may require." From which totally false idea of social government they do not fear to foster that erroneous opinion, most fatal in its effects on the Catholic Church and the salvation of souls, called by Our Predecessor, Gregory XVI, an "insanity," viz., that "liberty of conscience and worship is each man's personal right, which ought to be legally proclaimed and asserted in every rightly constituted society; and that a right resides in the citizens to an absolute liberty, which should be restrained by no authority whether ecclesiastical or civil, whereby they may be able openly and publicly to manifest and declare any of their ideas whatever, either by word of mouth, by the press, or in any other way." But, while they rashly affirm this, they do not think and consider that they are preaching "liberty of perdition;" and that "if human arguments are always allowed free room for discussion, there will never be wanting men who will dare to resist truth, and to trust in the flowing speech of human wisdom; whereas we know, from the very teaching of our Lord Jesus Christ, how carefully Christian faith and wisdom should avoid this most injurious babbling."

And, since where religion has been removed from civil society, and the doctrine and authority of divine revelation repudiated, the genuine notion itself of justice and human right is darkened and lost, and the place of true justice and legitimate right is supplied by material force, thence it appears why it is that some, utterly neglecting and disregarding the surest principles of sound reason, dare to proclaim that "the people's will, manifested by what is called public opinion or in some other way, constitutes a supreme law, free from all divine and human control; and that in the political order accomplished facts, from the very circumstance that they are accomplished, have the force of right." **But who, does not see and clearly perceive that human society, when set loose from the bonds of religion and true justice, can have, in truth, no other end than the purpose of obtaining and amassing wealth, and that (society under such circumstances) follows no other law in its actions, except the unchastened desire of ministering to its own pleasure and interests**? (Pope Pius IX, *Quanta Cura*, December 8, 1864.)

So, too, the liberty of thinking, and of publishing, whatsoever each one likes, without any hindrance, is not in itself an advantage over which society can wisely rejoice. On the contrary, it is the fountain-head and origin of many evils. **Liberty is a power perfecting man, and hence should have truth and goodness for its object. But the character of goodness and truth cannot be changed at option. These remain ever one and the same, and are no less unchangeable than nature itself. If the mind assents to false opinions, and the will chooses and follows after what is wrong, neither can attain its native fullness, but both must fall from their native dignity into an abyss of corruption. Whatever, therefore, is opposed to virtue and truth may not rightly be brought temptingly before the eye of man, much less sanctioned by the favor and protection of the law**. A well-spent life is the only way to heaven, whither all are bound, and on this account the State is acting against the laws and dictates of nature whenever it permits the license of opinion and of action to lead minds astray from truth and souls away from the practice of virtue. **To exclude the Church, founded by God Himself, from the business of life, from the making of laws, from the education of youth, from domestic society is a grave and fatal error. A State from which religion is banished can never be well regulated; and already perhaps more than is desirable is known of the nature and tendency of the so-called civil philosophy of life and morals. The Church of Christ is the true and sole teacher of virtue and guardian of morals. She it is who preserves in their purity the principles from which duties flow, and, by setting forth most urgent reasons for virtuous life, bids us not only to turn away from wicked deeds, but even to curb all movements of the mind that are opposed to reason, even though they be not carried out in action**. (Pope Leo XIII, *Immortale Dei*, November 1, 1885.)

In other words, no one has any right to jeopardize the salvation of his own soul or those of others by publishing or speaking things contrary to the teaching of the Catholic Church and thus offensive to God and injurious to the souls for whom He shed every single drop of His Most Precious Blood on the wood of the Holy Cross.

20) What if one lives in a "pluralist" nation such as the United States of America where the Catholic Church does not exercise the Social Reign of Christ the King?

Holy Mother Church does not expect the impossible from her children. She recognizes that we live in concrete circumstances that have fallen far from the ideal of her immutable teaching. She does expect her children to *know* her teaching and to pray and to work for its realization in their own lives, recognizing that the conversion of nations starts with the conversion of families.

Pope Leo XIII made a similar point in *Libertas Praestissimum*, June 20, 1888:

> Yet, with the discernment of a true mother, the Church weighs the great burden of human weakness, and well knows the course down which the minds and actions of men are in this our age being borne. For this reason, while not conceding any right to anything save what is true and honest, she does not forbid public authority to tolerate what is at variance with truth and justice, for the sake of avoiding some greater evil, or of obtaining or preserving some greater good. God Himself in His providence, though infinitely good and powerful, permits evil to exist in the world, partly that greater good may not be impeded, and partly that greater evil may not ensue. In the government of States it is not forbidden to imitate the Ruler of the world; and, as the authority of man is powerless to prevent every evil, it has (as St. Augustine says) to overlook and leave unpunished many things which are punished, and rightly, by Divine Providence. **But if, in such circumstances, for the sake of the common good (and this is the only legitimate reason), human law may or even should tolerate evil, it may not and should not approve or desire evil for its own sake; for evil of itself, being a privation of good, is opposed to the common welfare which every legislator is bound to desire and defend to the best of his ability. In this, human law must endeavor to imitate God, who, as St. Thomas teaches, in allowing evil to exist in the world, "neither wills evil   to be done, nor wills it not to be done, but wills only to permit it to be done; and this is good." This saying of the Angelic Doctor contains briefly the whole doctrine of the permission of evil.**
>
> **But, to judge aright, we must acknowledge that, the more a State is driven to tolerate evil, the further is it from perfection; and that the tolerance of evil which is dictated by political prudence should be strictly confined to the limits which its justifying cause, the public welfare, requires. Wherefore, if such tolerance would be injurious to the public welfare, and entail greater evils on the State, it would not be lawful; for in such case the motive of good is wanting.** And although in the extraordinary condition of these times the Church usually acquiesces in certain modern liberties, not because she prefers them in themselves, but because she judges it expedient to permit them, she would in happier times exercise her own liberty; and, by persuasion, exhortation, and entreaty would endeavor, as she is bound, to fulfill the duty assigned to her by God of providing for the eternal salvation of mankind. **One thing, however, remains always true -- that the liberty which is claimed for all to do all things is not, as We have often said, of itself desirable, inasmuch as it is contrary to reason that error and truth should have equal rights.** (Pope Leo XIII, *Libertas Praestantissimum*, June 20, 1888.)

21) Why have I never heard this before?

There are many reasons, the chief of which being that most, although certainly not all, American bishops and priests in the Nineteenth and Twentieth Centuries have sought to subordinate the Catholic Faith to the naturalist precepts of the American founding rather than to proclaim the Social Reign of Christ the King.

22) Does Our Blessed Lord and Saviour Jesus Christ expect to be recognized as the King of

men and their nations?

Yes. Consider this very succinct summary provided by the late Louis-Edouard-François-Desiré Cardinal Pie, who was the Bishop of Poitiers, France, from 1849 to 1880:

> "If Jesus Christ," proclaims Msgr. Pie in a magnificent pastoral instruction, "if Jesus Christ Who is our light whereby we are drawn out of the seat of darkness and from the shadow of death, and Who has given to the world the treasure of truth and grace, if He has not enriched the world, I mean to say the social and political world itself, from the great evils which prevail in the heart of paganism, then it is to say that the work of Jesus Christ is not a divine work. Even more so: if the Gospel which would save men is incapable of procuring the actual progress of peoples, if the revealed light which is profitable to individuals is detrimental to society at large, if the scepter of Christ, sweet and beneficial to souls, and perhaps to families, is harmful and unacceptable for cities and empires; in other words, if Jesus Christ to whom the Prophets had promised and to Whom His Father had given the nations as a heritage, is not able to exercise His authority over them for it would be to their detriment and temporal disadvantage, it would have to be concluded that Jesus Christ is not God". . . .

> "To say Jesus Christ is the God of individuals and of families, but not the God of peoples and of societies, is to say that He is not God. To say that Christianity is the law of individual man and is not the law of collective man, is to say that Christianity is not divine. To say that the Church is the judge of private morality, but has nothing to do with public and political morality, is to say that the Church is not divine."

In fine, Cardinal Pie insists:

> "Christianity would not be divine if it were to have existence within individuals but not with regard to societies."

Part II: Attacks Upon the Social Kingship of Jesus Christ: Naturalism and Judeo-Masonry

Starting with the period known as the Renaissance, which began in the late-Fourteenth Century and gave "rebirth" to the beliefs of some of the pagans of Greek antiquity, the Social Kingship of Jesus Christ has been under attack. One of the cornerstones of this attack is something called Naturalism, as will be explained presently.

1) What is Naturalism?

Naturalism is that approach to human life wherein all human activity is reduced to the merely natural level as attempts are made to "resolve" human problems without referencing the Deposit of Faith that Our Blessed Lord and Saviour Jesus Christ has entrusted exclusively to the Catholic Church and without relying upon the Sanctifying Grace He won for us by the shedding of every single drop of His Most Precious Blood on the wood of the Holy Cross and that flows into our hearts and souls by the working of the Holy Ghost in the sacraments through the loving hands of Our Lady, the Mediatrix of All Graces.

2) Why is Naturalism wrong?

Naturalism is wrong because it reduces the truths of the Catholic Faith to a matter of complete indifference in the lives of individual men and in the lives of nations, convincing men that they can pursue "happiness" in their own lives and "order" in the lives of their nations without referencing the Incarnation of the Second Person of the Blessed Trinity made Man in His Most Blessed Mother's Virginal and Immaculate womb by the power of the Holy Ghost and without subordinating their thoughts, words and actions at all times to the Deposit of Faith (that is, to the totality of Sacred Revelation by means of Sacred Scripture and Apostolic or Sacred Tradition) He has entrusted exclusively to the Catholic Church for its eternal safekeeping and infallible explication.

3) You mean to say that there is no merely natural way to look at or to seek to "resolve" the problems of the world?

Precisely. As Pope Saint Pius X noted in *Singulari Quadam*, September 24, 1912:

> Accordingly, We first of all declare that all Catholics have a sacred and inviolable duty, both in private and public life, to obey and firmly adhere to and fearlessly profess the principles of Christian truth enunciated by the teaching office of the Catholic Church. In particular We mean those principles which Our Predecessor has most wisely laid down in the encyclical letter "Rerum Novarum." We know that the Bishops of Prussia followed these most faithfully in their deliberations at the Fulda Congress of 1900. You yourselves have summarized the fundamental ideas of these principles in your communications regarding this question.

> These are fundamental principles: No matter what the Christian does, even in the realm of temporal goods, he cannot ignore the supernatural good. Rather, according to the dictates of Christian philosophy, he must order all things to the ultimate end, namely, the Highest Good. All his actions, insofar as they are morally either good or bad (that is to say, whether they agree or disagree with the natural and divine law), are subject to the judgment and judicial office of the Church. All who glory in the name of Christian, either individually or collectively, if they wish to remain true to their vocation, may not foster enmities and dissensions between the classes of civil society. On the contrary, they must promote mutual concord and charity. The social question and its associated controversies, such as the nature and duration of labor, the wages to be paid, and workingmen's strikes, are not simply economic in character. Therefore they cannot be numbered among those which can be settled apart from ecclesiastical authority. "The precise opposite is the truth. It is first of all moral and religious, and for that reason its solution is to be expected mainly from the moral law and the pronouncements of religion."

4) What, then, causes the problems of the world and how can they be resolved?

Each of the problems we find in the world are caused by Original Sin and by the Actual Sins of men. There is no way to "resolve" problems that are caused by fallen human nature. Human beings can, however, ameliorate, that is, lessen, the extent of the problems of the world by their daily cooperation with Sanctifying Grace to climb the heights of sanctity, avoiding the near occasions of sin and seeking to keep uppermost in their minds at all times the simple fact that they could face the moment of their Particular Judgments when they least expect it. Human beings must also cooperate with Actual Grace to respond to the promptings of the Holy Ghost to be diligent in their daily prayers and to perform their daily duties for the greater honor and glory of God as the consecrated slaves of Our Lady's Sorrowful and Immaculate Heart.

5) You mean to say that there is no "political" or "philosophical" way to address social problems absent the conversion of men and their nations to the Catholic Faith?

Yes. We must seek to restore all things in Christ, the phrase from Saint Paul's Epistle to the Ephesians that Pope Saint Pius X took as his motto and which he summarized very well in *Notre Charge Apostolique*, August 15, 1910:

> But, on the contrary, by ignoring the laws governing human nature and by breaking the bounds within which they operate, the human person is lead, not toward progress, but towards death. This, nevertheless, is what they want to do with human society; they dream of changing its natural and traditional foundations; they dream of a Future City built on different principles, and they dare to proclaim these more fruitful and more beneficial than the principles upon which the present Christian City rests.

> No, Venerable Brethren, We must repeat with the utmost energy in these times of social and intellectual anarchy when everyone takes it upon himself to teach as a teacher and lawmaker- the City cannot be built otherwise than as God has built it; society cannot be setup **unless the Church lays the foundations and supervises the work; no, civilization is not something yet to be found, nor is the New City to be built on hazy notions; it has been in existence and still is: it is Christian civilization, it is the Catholic City. It has only to be set up and restored continually against the unremitting attacks of insane dreamers, rebels and miscreants**. omnia instaurare in Christo.

6) What are some of the consequences of naturalism?

The principal consequences of naturalism involve the gradual descent of a nation into barbarism as more and more people lose sight of the true purpose of human existence, that is, to know, love and to serve God as He has revealed Himself exclusively through the Catholic Church and thus to spend all eternity with Him in Heaven after having died in a state of Sanctifying Grace as a member of the Catholic Church.

Pope Leo XIII discussed this in *Tametsi Futura Prospicientibus*, November 1, 1900:

> From this it may clearly be seen what consequences are to be expected from that false pride which, rejecting our Saviour's Kingship, places man at the summit of all things and declares that human nature must rule supreme. And yet, this supreme rule can neither be attained nor even defined. The rule of Jesus Christ derives its form and its power from Divine Love: a holy and orderly charity is both its foundation and its crown. Its necessary consequences are the strict fulfilment of duty, respect of mutual rights, the estimation of the things of heaven above

those of earth, the preference of the love of God to all things. But this supremacy of man, which openly rejects Christ, or at least ignores Him, is entirely founded upon selfishness, knowing neither charity nor selfdevotion. Man may indeed be king, through Jesus Christ: but only on condition that he first of all obey God, and diligently seek his rule of life in God's law. By the law of Christ we mean not only the natural precepts of morality and the Ancient Law, all of which Jesus Christ has perfected and crowned by His declaration, explanation and sanction; but also the rest of His doctrine and His own peculiar institutions. Of these the chief is His Church. Indeed whatsoever things Christ has instituted are most fully contained in His Church. Moreover, He willed to perpetuate the office assigned to Him by His Father by means of the ministry of the Church so gloriously founded by Himself. On the one hand He confided to her all the means of men's salvation, on the other He most solemnly commanded men to be subject to her and to obey her diligently, and to follow her even as Himself: "He that heareth you, heareth Me; and he that despiseth you, despiseth Me" (Luke x, 16). Wherefore the law of Christ must be sought in the Church. Christ is man's "Way"; the Church also is his "Way"-Christ of Himself and by His very nature, the Church by His commission and the communication of His power. Hence all who would find salvation apart from the Church, are led astray and strive in vain.

As with individuals, so with nations. These, too, must necessarily tend to ruin if they go astray from "The Way." The Son of God, the Creator and Redeemer of mankind, is King and Lord of the earth, and holds supreme dominion over men, both individually and collectively. "And He gave Him power, and glory, and a kingdom: and all peoples, tribes, and tongues shall serve Him" (Daniel vii., 14). "I am appointed King by Him . . . I will give Thee the Gentiles for Thy inheritance, and the uttermost parts of the earth for Thy possession" (Psalm ii., 6, 8). Therefore the law of Christ ought to prevail in human society and be the guide and teacher of public as well as of private life. Since this is so by divine decree, and no man may with impunity contravene it, it is an evil thing for the common weal wherever Christianity does not hold the place that belongs to it. **When Jesus Christ is absent, human reason fails, being bereft of its chief protection and light, and the very end is lost sight of, for which, under God's providence, human society has been built up. This end is the obtaining by the members of society of natural good through the aid of civil unity, though always in harmony with the perfect and eternal good which is above nature. But when men's minds are clouded, both rulers and ruled go astray, for they have no safe line to follow nor end to aim at**. (Pope Leo XIII, *Tametsi Futura Prospcientibus*, November 1, 1900.)

7) Who are the chief supporters of naturalism in the world?

The chief supporters of naturalism adhere to a line of beliefs promoted by what is called Judeo-Masonry, although not all naturalists are adherents of the Talmud or belong to Masonic lodges. It is enough for the "organized forces of naturalism" to convince men, especially those who are Catholics, that it is unimportant for men, either individually or collectively in civil society, to adhere to a specific religious creed to live a "meaningful" and "prosperous" life and to live together as "brothers" in the midst of society.

Pope Leo XIII noted this in *Humanum Genus*, April 20, 1884:

What We have said, and are about to say, must be understood of the sect of the Freemasons taken generically, and in so far as it comprises the associations kindred to it and confederated with it, but not of the individual members of them. There may be persons amongst these, and not a few who, although not free from the guilt of having entangled themselves in such associations, yet are neither themselves partners in their criminal acts nor aware of the ultimate object which they are endeavoring to attain. In the same way, some of the affiliated societies, perhaps, by no means approve of the extreme conclusions which they would, if consistent, embrace as necessarily following from their common principles, did not their very foulness strike them with horror. Some of these, again, are led by circumstances of times and places either to aim at smaller things than the others usually attempt or than they themselves would wish to attempt. **They are not, however, for this reason, to be reckoned as alien to the masonic federation; for the masonic federation is to be judged not so much by the things which it has done, or brought to completion,** *as by the sum of its pronounced opinions*.

Now, the fundamental doctrine of the naturalists, which they sufficiently make known by their very name, is that human nature and human reason ought in all things to be mistress and guide. Laying this down, they care little for duties to God, or pervert them by erroneous and vague opinions. For they deny that anything has been taught by God; they allow no dogma of religion or truth which cannot be understood by the human intelligence, nor any teacher who ought to be believed by reason of his authority. And since it is the special and exclusive duty of the Catholic Church fully to set forth in words truths divinely received, to teach, besides other divine helps to salvation, the authority of its office, and to defend the same with perfect purity, it is against the Church that the rage and attack of the enemies are principally directed.

In those matters which regard religion let it be seen how the sect of the Freemasons acts, especially where it is more free to act without restraint, and then let any one judge whether in fact it does not wish to carry out the policy of the naturalists. By a long and persevering labor, they endeavor to bring about this result -- namely, that the teaching office and authority of the Church may become of no account in the civil State; and for this same reason they declare to the people and contend that Church and State ought to be altogether disunited. By this means they reject from the laws and from the commonwealth the wholesome influence of the Catholic religion; and they consequently imagine that States ought to be constituted without any regard for the laws and precepts of the Church. (Pope Leo XIII, *Humanum Genus*, April 20, 1884.)

8) What does naturalism teach about religion?

As Pope Leo XIII noted in the passage cited above from *Humanum Genus*, naturalism teaches that anything concerning God is a matter of "opinion," which is why popular references to "God" and "faith" and "freedom" by careerist politicians of both major political parties in the United States of America signify nothing whatsoever. God can only be understood as He has revealed Himself through His true Church, the Catholic Church, founded upon the Rock of Peter, the Pope. Ultimately, the religious indifferentism (the belief that one religion is as good as another) results in the triumph of atheism or agnosticism as the lowest common denominators in civil society.

Pope Leo XIII made this point in *Immortale Dei*:

> To hold, therefore, that there is no difference in matters of religion between forms that are unlike each other, and even contrary to each other, most clearly leads in the end to the rejection of all religion in both theory and practice. And this is the same thing as atheism, however it may differ from it in name. **Men who really believe in the existence of God must, in order to be consistent with themselves and to avoid absurd conclusions, understand that differing modes of divine worship involving dissimilarity and conflict even on most important points cannot all be equally probable, equally good, and equally acceptable to God**. (Pope Leo XIII, *Immortale Dei*, November 1, 1885.)

9) How does naturalism undermine the precepts of morality?

Naturalism undermines the precepts of morality by convincing men that they are the ultimate arbiters of right and wrong, resulting in the triumph of what is called moral relativism as the foundation of personal lives and public policy.

10) What is moral relativism?

Moral relativism is the belief that the morality of human actions is determined by the relative conditions of time, circumstance, place and motives of the actor(s). Moral relativism, therefore, contends that there are no laws that are absolutely true that govern the conduct of human behavior.

11) Can you explain why moral relativism is wrong?

Moral relativism is wrong because it violates the basic precepts of right reason, which inform us that there must be truth (defined on the merely natural level as a phenomenon that exists in the nature of things and that does not depend upon human acceptance for its binding force or validity) and that truth of its nature is absolute, universal and eternal. Cicero, a pagan philosopher in Rome in the First Century before Christ, explained the nature of moral truth known from reason alone, the Natural Law, as follows:

> True law is right reason conformable to nature, universal, unchangeable, eternal, whose commands urge us to duty, and whose prohibitions restrain us from evil. Whether it enjoins or forbids, the good respect its injunctions, and the wicked treat them with indifference. This law cannot be contradicted by any other law, and is not liable either to derogation or abrogation. Neither the senate nor the people can give us any dispensation for not obeying this universal law of justice. It needs no other expositor and interpreter than our own conscience. It is not one thing at Rome, and another at Athens; one thing to-day, and another to-morrow; but in all times and nations this universal law must forever reign, eternal and imperishable. It is the sovereign master and emperor of all beings. God himself is its author, its promulgator, its enforcer. And he who does not obey it flies from himself, and does violence to the very nature of man. And by so doing he will endure the severest penalties even if he avoid the other evils which are usually accounted punishments. (Cicero, *The Republic*.)

Cicero had it almost entirely correct. Almost. He was wrong in asserting that the Natural Law does not need any "other expositor and interpreter than our own conscience." He lived before the Incarnation and before the founding of the true Church upon the Rock of Peter, the Pope. Cicero thus did not know that man does need an interpreter and expositor of the natural law, namely, the Catholic Church. Apart from this, however, Cicero understood that God's law does not admit of abrogations by a vote of the people or of a "representative" body, such as the Roman Senate in his day or the United States Congress or state legislatures, *et al.* in our own day.

12) Is there anything logically inconsistent about moral relativism?

Yes. Moral relativism contends that there are no absolute moral norms or laws, which is itself an absolute statement and therefore a contradiction of the contention that nothing is absolutely true.

13) What are some of the other consequences of naturalism?

Some of the other consequences of naturalism include the following far from exhaustive ideologies and "philosophies" with thumbnail definitions of each:

"Positivism," the contention that something is true because it has been asserted as being true;

"Materialism," the acquisition and retention of wealth and material goods as the ultimate end of human existence;

"Utilitarianism," the belief that public policy must be founded on the principle of the "greatest good for the greatest number," meaning that "inconvenient" or "useless" human lives may be "engineered," either passively or aggressively, out of existence;

"Pragmatism," the belief that social problems must be resolved on a "practical" basis without regard to a consideration of "root causes";

"Egalitarianism," the belief that there are no divinely-instituted distinctions among men in society, starting with a rejection of the authority vested in the hierarchy of the Church (which is also known as "anti-clericalism");

"Feminism," the assertion that there are no distinctions ordained by God between the sexes and that women have the "right" to do everything that men can do in society;

"Evolutionism," the rejection of Special Creation of man by God and his subsequent Fall from Grace in the Garden of Eden and replacing it with a belief that life evolved over billions of years, thus convincing man that truth itself evolves over time and that there are no fixed standards by which one can judge human behavior;

"Majoritarianism," the belief, drawn, although in different ways, from John Locke and Jean-Jacques Rousseau, that public policy is determined by the will of the majority in society at any given time;

"Liberalism," the political ideology that contends that it is possible for a majority of reasonable men to devise social structures to improve social conditions by the light of their own unaided reason;

"Conservatism," an amalgamation of different philosophies that have one thing in common: a rejection of the necessity of men and their nations to subordinate themselves to the Social Teaching of the Catholic Church;

"Libertarianism," the belief that the civil government has only a limited role to play in the restriction of the behavior of its citizens;

"Socialism," a term used to describe any number of specific politico-economic systems that reject, to one degree or another, the private ownership of property and places the control of the major means of production in the hands of the state while imposing confiscatory taxation in order to "redistribute" wealth according to the decisions made by the socialist elite;

"Communism," the ultimate form of socialism that contends it is possible for all clash among men to cease once private property is confiscated and the wealth derived therefrom distributed equitably amongst the workers according to the principle of "from each according to his ability and to each according to his need;"

"Nationalism," the exaltation of the myths of one's nation above love of God as He has revealed Himself exclusively through the Catholic Church;

"Statism," the exaltation of the state as being endowed with the properties of infallibility and invincibility in its domestic and international policies, which must be obeyed at all times without criticsm by the citizenry;

"Fascism," very much related to statism, seeks to orchestrate politics and the national economy and popular culture to the honor and glory of the state (private property might be permitted in a fascist state, only subject to state-imposed restrictions; corporate enterprises not controlled directly by the state must produce what the state demands and according to the price control established by the state);

"Secularism," which is simply another name for naturalism.

14) Apart from the organized forces of Judeo-Masonry, who is chiefly responsible for naturalism?

The devil. The devil hates Our Lord and His Holy Catholic Church. He hates Our Lady and the cult of the saints. He wants to convince man today that he can remake the world without Christ the King and Mary our Immaculate Queen just as he convinced Adam and Eve that they could like unto "gods" if they only ate of the fruit from the Tree of the Knowledge of Good and Evil that God had forbidden them to eat.

Part III: The Attacks Upon the Social Reign of Christ the King from Protestantism and the Modern State

1) Is Protestantism an attack on the Social Reign of Christ the King?

The Protestant Revolt is, as was described so well by Father Denis Fahey in *The Mystical Body of Christ in the Modern World*, a revolution against the Divine Plan that God has instituted to effect man's return to Him through the Catholic Church. It is but another attack of the devil upon Christ the King and Mary our Immaculate Queen.

2) How does Protestantism attack the Social Reign of Christ the King?

There are many strains of Protestantism, each of which attacks the Social Reign of Christ the King.

First, the Lutheran strain of Protestantism attacks the Social Reign of Christ the King by its insistence that Our Lord did not create a visible, hierarchical Church to sanctify or to govern men, either individually or socially. The denial of the visible, hierarchical church meant that individuals no longer had the sure guidance of the Catholic Church as to how to live their lives and that civil rulers no longer had to answer to a pope or a local bishop if he did things contrary to the good of souls. This opened the way to unbridled monarchical despotism in European kingdoms and principalities where potentates sided with Luther, giving rise to our own modern totalitarianism. Individual licentiousness and civil despotism are the logical results of a world where the Catholic Church is no longer recognized and obeyed as the true teacher and sole sanctifier of man.

Martin Luther himself said that a prince may be a Christian but that his religion should not influence how he governs, giving rise to the contemporary notion of "separation of Church and state," condemned repeatedly by Popes in the Nineteenth and early Twentieth Centuries.

Father Denis Fahey explained this in *The Mystical Body of Christ in the Modern World*:

> The tide of revolt which broke away from the Catholic Church had the immediate effect of increasing the power of princes and rulers in Protestant countries. The Anabaptists and the peasants in Germany protested in the name of 'evangelical liberty,' but they were crushed. We behold the uprise of national churches, each of which organizes its own particular form of religion, mixture of supernatural and natural elements, as a department of State. The orthodox Church in Russia was also a department of State and as such exposed to the same evils. National life was thus withdrawn from ordered subjection to the Divine Plan and the distinction laid down by our Divine Lord Himself, between the things that are God's and the things that are Caesar's, utterly abolished. Given the principle of private judgment or of individual relation with Christ, it was inevitable that the right of every individual to arrange his own form of religion should cause the pendulum to swing from a Caesarinism supreme in Church and State to other concrete expressions of 'evangelical liberty.' One current leads to the direction of indefinite multiplication of sects. Pushed to its ultimate conclusion, this would give rise to as many churches as there are individuals, that is, there would not be any church at all. As this is too opposed to man's social nature, small groups tend to coalesce.

The second current tends to the creation of what may be termed broad or multitudinist churches. The exigencies of the national churches are attenuated until they are no longer a burden to anybody. The Church of England is an example of this. As decay in the belief of the Divinity of Jesus continues to increase, the tendency will be to model church organization according to the political theories in favour at the moment. The democratic form of society will be extolled and a 'Reunion of Christendom,' for example, will be aimed at, along the lines of the League of Nations. An increasing number of poor bewildered units will, of course, cease to bother about any ecclesiastical organization at all. . . . .

The first [political] result was an enormous increase in the power of the Temporal Rulers, in fact a rebirth of the pagan regime of Imperial Rome. The Spiritual Kingship of Christ, participated in by the Pope and the Bishops of the Catholic Church being no longer acknowledged, authority over spiritual affairs passed to Temporal Rulers. They were thus, in Protestant countries, supposed to share not only in His Temporal Kingship of Christ the King, but also in His spiritual Kingship. As there was no Infallible Guardian of order above the Temporal Rulers, the way was paved for the abuses of State Absolutism. The Protestant oligarchy who ruled England with undisputed sway, from Charles the Second's time on, and who treated Ireland to the Penal Laws, may be cited, along with that cynical scoundrel, Frederick of Prussia, as typical examples of such rulers. Catholic monarchs, like Louis XIV of France and Joseph II of Austria, by their absolutist tendencies and pretensions to govern the Catholic Church show the influence of the neighboring Protestant countries. Gallicanism and Josephism are merely a revival of Roman paganism. . . .

The rejection by Luther of the visible Catholic Church opened the door, not only to the abuses of absolute rulers, supreme in Church and State, but soon led to an indifference to all ecclesiastical organizations. As faith in the supernatural life of grace and the supernatural order grew dim and waned, the way was made smooth for the acceptance of Freemasonry. The widespread loss of faith in the existence of the supernatural life and the growing ignorance of the meaning of the Redemption permitted the apostles of Illuminism and Masonry to propagate the idea that the true religion of Jesus Christ had never been understood or been corrupted by His disciples, especially by the Church of Rome, the fact being that only a few sages in secret societies down the centuries had kept alive the true teaching of Jesus Christ. According to this 'authentic' teaching our Saviour had not established a new religion, but had simply restored the religion of the state of nature, the religion of the goodness of human nature when left to itself, freed from the bonds and shackles of society. Jesus Christ died a martyr for liberty, put to death by the rulers and priests. Masons and revolutionary secret societies alone are working for the true salvation of the world. By them shall original sin be done away with and the Garden of Eden restored. But the present organization of society must disappear, by the elimination of the tyranny of priests, the despotism of princes and the slavery resulting from national distinctions, from family life and from private property." (Father Denis Fahey, *The Mystical Body of Christ in the Modern World*.)

Second, Martin Luther believed that the Bible was the sole source of Divine Revelation, rejecting the 1,500 years of belief in Apostolic or Sacred Tradition as other source of Divine Revelation, and he believed that each individual was his own "interpreter of the Bible." He thus planted the seeds of contemporary deconstructionism, which reduces all written documents to the illogical and frequently mutually contradictory private judgments of individual readers, by rejecting the Catholic Church as the repository and explicator of the Deposit of Faith, making the "private judgment" of individuals with regard to the Bible supreme. If mutually contradictory and inconsistent interpretations of the Bible can stand without correction from a supreme authority instituted by God, then it is an easy thing for all written documents, including a Constitution that makes no reference at all to the God-Man or His Holy Church, to become the plaything of whoever happens to have power over its interpretation.

Although the Anglicanism strain of Protestantism differs from the Lutheran strain in some areas, Anglicanism is founded on a specific rejection of the role of the Catholic Church in its exercise of the Social Reign of Christ the King, arrogating the "headship" of the "church" to the King (or Queen) of England. This resulted quite specifically in the rise of monarchical absolutism in England. Over 72,000 Catholics who remained faithful to Rome after King Henry VIII's revolt (largely over his own personal lust) against the Catholic Church were executed on Henry's orders between 1534 and his death in 1547. Monarchical absolutism in England has been replaced over the centuries by majoritarian absolutism as exercised by the House of Commons of the United Kingdom's Parliament.

Perhaps even more influential than the Lutheran and Anglican strains of Protestantism have been the false, heretical precepts of John Calvin:

> 1. Along with Martin Luther, John Calvin rejected the truth that Our Blessed Lord and Saviour Jesus Christ founded a visible, hierarchical Church upon the Rock of Peter, the Pope.

> 2. The absence of a visible, hierarchical Church meant that each individual believer was "equal" to other believers. Those who "presided" at liturgies were merely the representatives of the rest of the "community," in whose name and by whose selection they served in their "leading" capacities.

> 3. Calvin's warfare against a belief in the visible, hierarchical Church and his belief in the strict equality of all believers resulted in a vicious spirit of anticlericalism that unleashed a violent wave of assaults against Catholic priests in Switzerland and The Netherlands and France (See the appendices about the life and the martyrdom of Saint Fidelis of Sigmaringen and the Martyrs of Gorkum, victims each of the bloody band of men known as Calvinists, men who are actually disciples of the devil). The Calvinist spirit of anticlericalism is widespread in the world today, reflected most especially in the text of the Texas Declaration of Independence, March 1, 1836:

>> When the Federal Republican Constitution of their country [Mexico], which they have sworn to support, no longer has a substantial existence, and the whole nature of their government has been forcibly changed, without their consent, from a restricted federative republic, composed of sovereign states, to a consolidated central military despotism, in which every interest is   disregarded but that of the army and the priesthood, both the eternal enemies of civil liberty, the everready minions of power, and the usual instruments of tyrants. (Texas Declaration of Independence, March 2, 1836.)

4. John Calvin believed that man is evil. That is, Calvin believed that man is totally corrupted by Original Sin. The Catholic Church teaches us that man is wounded by Original Sin, not totally corrupted. Those who are regenerated in the Baptismal font by having Original Sin flooded out of their souls and the very inner life of the Most Blessed Trinity flooded into their souls by means of Sanctifying Grace suffer from the vestigial after-effects of Original Sin, the darkened intellect and the weakened will and the overthrowing of the delicate balance between our higher, rational faculties and our lower, sensual passions in favor of the lower passions. Those so regenerated are not totally corrupted by Original Sin. Man is a good being who has a flawed nature that is inclined to commit evil. This is quite an important distinction that was rejected by John Calvin.

5. John Calvin believed that men were predestined by an arbitrary "God" to Heaven or Hell. Nothing that any man did on the face of this earth could change the face of his predestination to Heaven or Hell. In other words, the human being did not have a free will by which to choose to cooperate with the graces won for him on Calvary by the shedding of every single drop of Our Blessed Lord and Saviour Jesus Christ's Most Precious Blood that flow into our hearts and soul through the loving hands of Our Lady, she who is the Mediatrix of All Graces.

6. John Calvin believed that the purpose of civil government was to separate the "saved" from the "damned." That is, the civil government had the obligation to weed out the "undesirables," those who the arbitrary God had destined for Hell from all eternity. Obviously, the Catholic Church teaches us that God alone is the final judge of the subjective state of souls and that, barring private revelations given to genuine mystics or a declaration by the authority of the Catholic Church as she declares solemnly and infallible that a certain person is in Heaven, we do not know what happens to a given soul at the time of death. We do not know whether a particular person who was known as a notorious sinner or as an arch-heretic was given the grace to make a perfect Act of Contrition.

7. The basis upon which John Calvin believed that those in the civil government could separate the "saved" from the "damned" was the degree of their material success here on earth. John Calvin believed that material success was a sign of "divine election." Thus it is that we have the Calvinist "work ethic" as those who subscribe to Calvin's warped, heretical views of God and man work hard not to give honor and glory to the Most Holy Trinity through the Immaculate Heart of Mary but to show to others that they are "saved" by virtue of their material "success" in this passing, mortal vale of tears.

It is this seventh point, flowing from all of the rest, that has provided the foundation for the modern economic system that has forced man off of the land and dehumanized him as he has been made a slave of "material success" by the captains of industry and banking.

Calvinism, which is little more than Talmudic Judaism with a slight Christian gloss, has engendered all manner of economic abuses, not the least of which is the contemporary practice of usury (for a good discussion of how the Catholic Church has never changed her teaching on usury, please see The Church and Usury and The Red Herring of Usury), founded in the belief that men may ignore the binding precepts of the Divine Positive Law and the Natural Law in order to be "successful" in this   world. The injustices engendered by this amoral, naturalistic view of the world helped to encourage   open atheists and anti-Theists, such as Karl Marx and Vladimir Lenin, to postulate an utopian system of naturalism based upon a materialistic view of man that denied his supernatural essence. The   diabolical lie of Marxism-Leninism is but the logical consequence of John Calvin's materialistic view of man that denied that there could be an Omnipotent and Omniscient God Who created rational beings with free wills to choose for or against Him as He has revealed Himself to us through His true Church.

Father Fahey elaborated on the effects of Protestantism, especially the warmed over version of Talmudic Judaism that is Calvinism, in *The Mystical Body of Christ in the Modern World*:

> It was, however, the Calvinistic doctrine on predestination and the signs by which a man's divine election could be recognized, which specially favored the advent of the unlimited competition, unscrupulous underselling and feverish advertising of the present day. In his able work, from which a passage has already been quoted, Professor O'Brien shows that it was in the peculiarly British variety of Calvinism, known as Puritanism, that all the Calvinist   doctrines of succession life as a sign of man's predestination, of the respect and veneration due to wealth, had their fullest development.

>> "When all is said and done, Calvinism remains the real nursing-father of the civic industrial capitalism of the middle classes. . . . Since the aggressively active ethic inspired by the doctrine of predestination urges the elect to the full development of his God-given powers, and offers him this a sign by which he may assure himself of his election, work becomes rational and systematic. In breaking down the motive of ease and enjoyment, asceticism lays the foundation of the tyranny of work over men . . . production for production's sake is declared to be a commandment of religion." (Father Denis Fahey, *The Mystical Body of Christ in the Modern World.*)

This has great application in every aspect of contemporary life. Most people work not for the honor and glory of God, thus giving Him the fruit of their labors as the consecrated slaves of His Most Blessed Mother's Sorrowful and Immaculate Heart, but for the sake of "success," to gain what is considered to be financial "wealth" and earthly "success" as ends that justify each and every method used to achieve such success. This has been the Calvinist "contribution" to the world, so enshrined in the ethos of the "American dream," which eschews the Holy Poverty of the Holy Family of Nazareth and of such great saints as Saint Francis of Assisi and his helper and fellow adorer of the Most Blessed Sacrament, Saint Clare of Assisi. Father Fahey quoted Gilbert Keith Chesterton's observation about the insidious influence of that wretched people known as the Puritans (or Pilgrims) in a footnote on page sixteen of The Mystical Body of Christ in the Modern World: "The Americans have established a Thanksgiving Day to celebrate the fact that the Pilgrim Fathers reached America. The English might very well establish another Thanksgiving Day to celebrate the happy fact that the Pilgrim Fathers left England."

3) How did naturalism and Protestantism influence the founding of the United States of America?

The sons of the so-called Enlightenment, influenced by the multifaceted and inter-related consequences of the errors of the Renaissance and the Protestant Revolt, brought forth secular nations that contended the source of governing authority was the people. Ultimately, all references to "God" were in accord with the Freemasonic notion of a "supreme intelligence" without any recognition of the absolute necessity of belief in and acceptance of the Incarnation and of the Deposit of Faith as it has been given to Holy Mother Church for personal happiness and hence all social order.

The founders of the United States of America did not believe that it was necessary to refer all things in civil life to Christ the King as He had revealed Himself through His true Church, believing that men would be able to pursue "civic virtue" by the use of their own devices and thus maintain social order in the midst of cultural and religious pluralism. This leads, as Pope Leo XIII noted of religious indifferentism, to the triumph of the lowest common denominator, that is, atheism.

4) What is the principal defect, therefore, of the Constitution of the United States of America?

As the Constitution of the United States of America admits of no authority higher than its own words, it, like the Bible for a Protestant (as mentioned above), is utterly defenseless when the plain meanings of its words are distorted and used to advance ends that its framers would have never thought imaginable, no less approved in fact.

This is but the secular version of Antinomianism: the belief advanced by those who took the logic of Luther's argument of being "saved by faith alone" to its inexorable conclusion that one could live a wanton life of sin and still be saved. Luther himself did not see where the logic of his rejection of Catholic doctrine would lead and fought against the Antinomians.

In like manner, you see, the Constitutionalists and Federalists of today do not see that what is happening today in Federal courts, including the Supreme Court of the United States, is the inexorable result of a Constitution that rejects Christ the King and the Catholic Church. These Constitutionalists and Federalists will fight time and time again like Sisyphus pushing the bolder up a hill. They will always lose because they cannot admit that the thing they admire, the Constitution, is the proximate problem that has resulted in all of the evils they are trying to fight.

5) Are you saying that the founders of the United States of America had evil intentions?

Intentions are irrelevant. What matters is the truth or the falsity of the ideas that men possess. It is not true that men can organize themselves socially without referencing the true Faith and by permitting false religions to propagate their false beliefs openly.

6) What is wrong with giving each "religion" the ability to speak publicly to win adherents to its cause?

God gives "rights," not men. To assert that adherents of false religions possess a civil "right," no less a "right" from God Himself, to propagate their false beliefs openly is false. It is to blaspheme God.

As noted, before this assertion of a nonexistent "right" is different than the toleration of the existence of false religions in a Catholic country and of the private practice of their false worship. It is also different from the concessions that Holy Mother Church has had to make for her children who live in non-Catholic countries and in those Catholic lands where the common good might require a toleration of offensive speech. In point of truth, however, the spread of heresy is an act of blasphemy against Our Lord, Who does not want the souls for whom He shed every single drop of His Most Precious Blood confused about Who He is and what He has revealed and how they are to be happy here in this life as a prelude to eternal happiness in Heaven.

7) Has the Catholic Church condemned the "religious liberty" enshrined in the First Amendment to Constitution of the United States of America?

Many times. Please see the quotations cited above from Pope Pius VII's *Post Tam Diuturnas*, Pope Gregory XVI's *Mirari Vos* and Pope Pius IX's *Quanta Cura*.

8) Are you saying that the Catholic Church condemns the form of government created in the Constitution of the United States of America?

No. As noted above, the Church can adapt to any particular form of government. She does insist, however, that she be recognized by the civil government as the true religion and that her right to intervene with civil officials as a last resort after the exhausting of her Indirect Power of teaching and preaching and exhortation be acknowledged in a civil state's organic documents and/or a concordat with the Holy See. Everything else is left to the free judgment of men, who are nevertheless bound to pursue their actions in the civil realm in light of their eternal destiny, noting that it has been Holy Mother Church's preference for men to organize themselves around the monarchical principle as it reflects the monarchy of Christ the King over them and their nations.

Our true popes have made concessions to rise of what is called the republican form of self-rule (in which certain numbers of citizens are elected by others to serve, usually for fixed terms, in public office, which is not the same thing as a democracy, which, understood in its true meaning, is a form of government wherein those eligible to participate in civic affairs assemble to make laws, electing others to serve as administrators in their stead if necessary), while careful to note the inherent dangers in governments so organized. Our true popes have warned us that "democracy," broadly understood today as synonymous with a republican form of government is only one type of government, not the only type, and certainly not the best type:

Pope Saint Pius X made this point in *Notre Charge Apostolique*, August 15, 1910, which condemned the philosophies of The Sillon in France that shaped the beliefs that have been expressed by the heads of the conciliar church since October 28, 1958:

> Indeed, the Sillon proposes to raise up and re-educate the working class. But in this respect the principles of Catholic doctrine have been defined, and the history of Christian civilization bears witness to their beneficent fruitfulness. Our Predecessor [Pope Leo XIII] of happy memory re-affirmed them in masterly documents, and all Catholics dealing with social questions have the duty to study them and to keep them in mind. He taught, among other things, that "Christian Democracy must preserve the diversity of classes which is assuredly the attribute of a soundly constituted State, and it must seek to give human society the form

and character which God, its Author, has imparted to it." Our Predecessor denounced "A certain Democracy which goes so far in wickedness as to place sovereignty in the people and aims at the suppression of classes and their leveling down." At the same time, Leo XIII laid down for Catholics a program of action, the only program capable of putting society back onto its centuries old Christian basis. But what have the leaders of the Sillon done? Not only have they adopted a program and teaching different from that of Leo XIII (which would be of itself a singularly audacious decision on the part of laymen thus taking up, concurrent with the Sovereign Pontiff, the role of director of social action in the Church); but they have openly rejected the program laid out by Leo XIII, and have adopted another which is diametrically opposed to it. Further, they reject the doctrine **recalled by Leo XIII on the essential principles of society; they place authority in the people, or gradually suppress it and strive, as their ideal, to effect the leveling down of the classes. In opposition to Catholic doctrine, therefore, they are proceeding towards a condemned ideal**. . . .

The Sillon places public authority primarily in the people, from whom it then flows into the government in such a manner, however, that it continues to reside in the people. But Leo XIII absolutely condemned this doctrine in his Encyclical "Diuturnum Illud" on political government in which he said:

"Modern writers in great numbers, following in the footsteps of those who called themselves philosophers in the last century, declare that all power comes from the people; consequently those who exercise power in society do not exercise it from their own authority, but from an authority delegated to them by the people and on the condition that it can be revoked by the will of the people from whom they hold it. Quite contrary is the sentiment of Catholics who hold that the right of government derives from God as its natural and necessary principle." Admittedly, the Sillon holds that authority - which first places in the people - descends from God, but in such a way: "as to return from below upwards, whilst in the organization of the Church power descends from above downwards."

But besides its being abnormal for the delegation of power to ascend, since it is in its nature to descend, Leo XIII refuted in advance this attempt to reconcile Catholic Doctrine with the error of philosophism. For, he continues: "It is necessary to remark here that those who preside over the government of public affairs may indeed, in certain cases, be chosen by the will and judgment of the multitude without repugnance or opposition to Catholic doctrine. But whilst this choice marks out the ruler, it does not confer upon him the authority to govern; it does not delegate the power, it designates the person who will be invested with it."

For the rest, if the people remain the holders of power, what becomes of authority? A shadow, a myth; there is no more law properly so-called, no more obedience. The Sillon acknowledges this: indeed, since it demands that threefold political, economic, and intellectual emancipation in the name of human dignity, the Future City in the formation of which it is engaged will have no masters and no servants. All citizens will be free; all comrades, all kings. A command, a precept would be viewed as an attack upon their freedom; subordination to any form of superiority would be a diminishment of the human person, and obedience a disgrace. Is it in this manner, Venerable Brethren, that the traditional doctrine of the Church represents social relations, even in the most perfect society? Has not every community of people, dependent and unequal by nature, need of an authority to direct their activity towards the common good and to enforce its laws? And if perverse individuals are to be found in a community (and there always are), should not authority be all the stronger as the selfishness of the wicked is more threatening? Further, - unless one greatly deceives oneself in the conception of liberty - can it be said with an atom of reason that authority and liberty are incompatible? Can one teach that obedience is contrary to human dignity and that the ideal would be to replace it by "accepted authority"? Did not St. Paul the Apostle foresee human society in all its possible stages of development when he bade the faithful to be subject to every authority? Does obedience to men as the legitimate representatives of God, that is to say in the final analysis, obedience to God, degrade Man and reduce him to a level unworthy of himself? Is the religious life which is based on obedience, contrary to the ideal of human nature? Were the Saints - the most obedient men, just slaves and degenerates? Finally, can you imagine social conditions in which Jesus Christ, if He returned to earth, would not give an example of obedience and, further, would no longer say: "Render to Caesar the things that are Caesar's and to God the things that are God's"?

Teaching such doctrines, and applying them to its internal organization, the Sillon, therefore, sows erroneous and fatal notions on authority, liberty and obedience, among your Catholic youth. The same is true of justice and equality; the Sillon says that it is striving to establish an era of equality which, by that very fact, would be also an era of greater justice. Thus, to the Sillon, every inequality of condition is an injustice, or at least, a diminution of justice? **Here we have a principle that conflicts sharply with the nature of things, a principle conducive to jealously, injustice, and subversive to any social order. Thus, Democracy alone will bring about the reign of perfect justice! Is this not an insult to other forms of government which are thereby debased to the level of sterile makeshifts**? Besides, the Saloonists once again clash on this point with the teaching of Leo XIII. In the Encyclical on political government *[Immortale Dei]* which We have already quoted, they could have read this: "Justice being preserved, it is not forbidden to the people to choose for themselves the form of government which best corresponds with their character or with the institutions and customs handed down by their forefathers."

And the Encyclical alludes to **the three well-known forms of government**, thus implying that justice is compatible with any of them. And does not the Encyclical on the condition of the working class state clearly that justice can be restored within the existing social set-up - since it indicates the means of doing so? Undoubtedly, Leo XIII did not mean to speak of some form of justice, but of perfect justice. **Therefore, when he said that justice could be found in any of the three aforesaid forms of government, he was teaching that in this respect Democracy does not enjoy a special privilege. The Saloonists who maintain the opposite view, either turn a deaf ear to the teaching of the Church or form for themselves an idea of justice and equality which is not Catholic.** (Pope Saint Pius X, *Notre Charge Apostolique*, August 15, 1910.)

In other words, the words found at the beginning of the Constitution of the United States of America, "We, the People," tell a lie as sovereignty does not reside in the people, who are but contingent creatures whose bodies are destined one day for the corruption of the grave until the Last Day at the General Judgment of the Living and the Dead, must be submissive to God in all of their actions, whether personal and social, and recognize that He alone is the Sovereign of men and their nations, not them.

This means that a true realization of the concept of "democracy" as outlined by Pope Leo XIII in *Diurturnum Illud*, June 29, 1881, and reiterated by Pope Saint Pius X is almost impossible in a pluralist society such as the United States of America, where there exists a welter of differing ideas and beliefs that are supposed to result in discovery of a "common ground" on various issues.

Consider Pope Leo XIII's discussion of this matter in *Diuturnum Illud*:

> Those who believe civil society to have risen from the free consent of men, looking for the origin of its authority from the same source, say that each individual has given up something of his right,(15) and that voluntarily every person has put himself into the power of the one man in whose person the whole of those rights has been centered. **But it is a great error not to see, what is manifest, that men, as they are not a nomad race, have been created, without their own free will, for a natural community of life. It is plain, moreover, that the pact which they allege is openly a falsehood and a fiction, and that it has no authority to confer on political power such great force, dignity, and firmness as the safety of the State and the common good of the citizens require. Then only will the government have all those ornaments and guarantees, when it is understood to emanate from God as its August and most sacred source**. (Pope Leo XIII, *Diurturnum Illud*, June 29, 1881.)

We are only witnessing the logical degeneration of the false premises of Modernity.

9) Do secular, naturalist talk show hosts and commentators have anything of value to offer us?

No. Nothing. Naturalism is divided into false "opposition" camps of the "left" and the "right." This is a gigantic diversion from the devil to waste our time and to expend needless energy on projects that can never solve or even ameliorate a single social problem. The saints did not need to "consult" secular, naturalist talk show hosts to know how to order their lives and to know how to order the lives of societies. Neither do we.

10) Isn't the conversion of the United States of America to the Catholic Faith impossible?

Nothing is impossible with God, is it? Catholicism thrived in much of what is now the land of the United States of America long before English-speaking peoples came to displace the natives who had been converted to Catholicism in many instances. Our Lady appeared to Juan Diego on Tepeyac Hill to effect the conversion of all of the Americas to the Catholic Faith.

11) How do we convert a nation to the true Faith?

One soul at a time, starting with our own by means of cooperating with the graces sent to us by Our Lady each day, and one family at a time. We may be able only to plant the seeds for the conversion of a nation. Those seeds may not take root and flower for many years. It took several centuries for the first Christendom to arise from the ashes of the Roman Empire and the pillaging of various barbaric tribes. Even though we may very well be in "end times" as the Mystical Body of Christ suffers the Passion and Death of her Divine Redeemer in the Church Militant, we must nevertheless continue the work of seeking converts.

We do this by enthroning our homes to the Most Sacred Heart of Jesus and to the Sorrowful and Immaculate Heart of Mary.

We do this as a family by trying to get to the daily offering of the Immemorial Mass of Tradition, offered by true bishops and true priests who make no concessions to conciliarism or to the "legitimacy' of the false shepherds who belong to the counterfeit church of conciliarism.

We do this by spending time together as a family before the Most Blessed Sacrament in prayer, if only once or twice a week.

We do this by praying at least one set of mysteries of Our Lady's Most Holy Rosary every day in the home as a family.

We do this by avoiding the near occasions of sin, especially by refusing to participate in any "cultural" enterprise that propagandizes in behalf of naturalism, if not openly attacks the true Faith.

We do this by consecrated ourselves to Our Blessed Lord and Saviour Jesus Christ through the Sorrowful and Immaculate Heart of Mary, seeking to fulfill as far as is within our own ability do so Our Lady's Fatima Message in our family lives.

Unlike naturalists, you see, Catholics do not look for the "results" of their prayers and good works and mortifications and penances and humiliations and sufferings and fastings and almsgiving and sacrifices. They simply strive to remain faithful each day to the fullness of the Catholic Faith, understanding that the Social Teaching of the Catholic Church is part of the Deposit of Faith and thus falls under the charism of infallibility of her Ordinary Magisterium.

We should think of the totality of the Deposit of Faith, including the Social Teaching of the Catholic Church, the next time that we pray the Act of Faith:

> O my God, I firmly believe that Thou art one God, in three Divine Persons, Father, Son and Holy Ghost: I believe that Thy Divine Son became Man, and died for our sins, and that He will come to judge the living and the dead. I believe these and all the truths which the Holy Catholic Church teaches, because Thou hast revealed them, Who can neither deceive nor be deceived. Amen.

With Father Miguel Augustin Pro, S.J., and the Cristeros in Mexico to whom he brought the Sacraments, who uttered the battle cry of "Viva Cristo Rey!", we must always lift high the banner of Christ the King, remembering these stirring words of Pope Pius XI, contained in *Quas Primas*, December 11, 1925:

We firmly hope, however, that the feast of the Kingship of Christ, which in future will be yearly observed, may hasten the return of society to our loving Savior. It would be the duty of Catholics to do all they can to bring about this happy result. Many of these, however, have neither the station in society nor the authority which should belong to those who bear the torch of truth. **This state of things may perhaps be attributed to a certain slowness and timidity in good people, who are reluctant to engage in conflict or oppose but a weak resistance; thus the enemies of the Church become bolder in their attacks. But if the faithful were generally to understand that it behooves them ever to fight courageously under the banner of Christ their King, then, fired with apostolic zeal, they would strive to win over to their Lord those hearts that are bitter and estranged from him, and would valiantly defend his rights**.

Moreover, the annual and universal celebration of the feast of the Kingship of Christ will draw attention to the evils which anticlericalism has brought upon society in drawing men away from Christ, and will also do much to remedy them. While nations insult the beloved name of our Redeemer by suppressing all mention of it in their conferences and parliaments, we must all the more loudly proclaim his kingly dignity and power, all the more universally affirm his rights. (Pope Pius XI, *Quas Primas*, December 11, 1925.)

Chapter II
As the World Was Prepared For the Coming of Its Redeemer

As noted in the previous chapter, the gradual triumph of statism here in the United States of America, as well as elsewhere in the Western world, is the inevitable result, proximately speaking, of the overthrow of the Social Reign of Christ the King wrought by the Protestant Revolt and institutionalized by the complex inter-related, multifaceted forces of naturalistic ideologies and philosophies that can be termed properly as Judeo-Masonry. It is the goal of both Talmudic Judaism and its close ally, Freemasonry, to eliminate belief in the simple fact that human life, both individually and collectively, must be centered in a recognition of the fact that the Word, the very Second Person of the Most Blessed Trinity, became Incarnate in the Virginal and Immaculate Womb of His Most Blessed Mother by the power of the Third Person of the Most Blessed Trinity, God the Holy Ghost. There is no need, according to the lords of Modernity in the world and of Modernism in the counterfeit church of conciliarism, to subordinate all human activity to the binding precepts of the Deposit of Faith that Our Blessed Lord and Saviour Jesus Christ entrusted exclusively to His Catholic Church for its eternal safekeeping and infallible explication. It is "enough," according to the these enemies of the Social Kingship of Our Lord Jesus Christ and the Queenship of Our Lady, for men of "good will" to work together as "brothers" as they put aside denominational differences that should never get in the way of the pursuit of the common temporal good.

No, it is not enough for the true God of Divine Revelation for men to put aside any article of His Deposit of Faith as irrelevant to personal and social order as Catholicism is the one and only foundation of such order. Our Lord did not become Incarnate and die on the wood of the Holy Cross and rise again from the dead on Easter Sunday so that men could be content in a fuzzy belief in some generic concept of God or in a belief that mere natural virtue is enough to provide for the common temporal good. Our Lord did not become Incarnate and die on the wood of the Holy Cross and rise again from the dead on Easter Sunday so that men could organize themselves collectively without referencing First and Last Things, without acknowledging the authority that He has vested to Holy Mother Church to sanctify and to teach men in all that pertains to the good of their immortal souls.

No, it is not enough for the true God of Divine Revelation for men to seek to promote the common temporal good without recognizing that Holy Mother Church, judiciously and in measured ways that are proportionate to the gravity of the matters at hand following the discharge of her Indirect Power of teaching, preaching and exhortation, interpose herself directly with civil authorities when the good of souls demands her mother intervention. Tyranny--whether of one person or a political party or military junta or some other kind of junta or even of the "majority"--*must* result over the course of time when the ability of Holy Mother Church to serve as a check upon the unrestrained exercise of civil power is rejected as either imprudent or entirely unnecessary. It is one of the most telling tragedies of Modernity that naturalists all across the ideological divide have been joined by Catholics all across the vast expanse of the ecclesiastical divide into believing that Catholicism is not the one and only foundation of personal order, that men can "solve" seemingly intractable social problems   that have their remote causes in Original Sin and their proximate causes in the revolution against the Social Reign of Christ the King and the rise of economic systems and methods of world governance that are in direct opposition to the Holy Faith and thus to the good of souls.

Time Itself Is Divided by the Incarnation

One cannot appreciate the depths to which the modern civil state, including that of the United States of America, is radically opposed to the truth of the Incarnation and thus must be an enemy of the good of souls wrought by the Second Person of the Blessed Trinity made Man in His Most Blessed Mother's Virginal and Immaculate Womb.

True history can be viewed only through the eyes of the Holy Faith, which is why we must live every moment of our lives in the shadow of the Holy Cross as we recognize that everything that happens to us and in the world occurs within the Providence of God. It is only through the eyes of the Holy Faith that we can come to see the world more clearly as it is for love of God and thus to divest ourselves of beliefs and attitudes that are impediments to our own sanctification and thus obstacles to the pursuit of the common temporal good, which is dependent upon personal sanctity.

Father Denis Fahey provided an explication of the meaning of true history in *The Mystical Body of Christ in the Modern World*:

> History is concerned with individual and contingent facts. In order to discern the supreme causes and laws of the events which historians narrate, we must stand out from, and place ourselves above these events. To do this with certainty one should, of course, be enlightened by Him Who holds all things in the hollow of His hand. Unaided human reason cannot even attempt to give an account of the supreme interests at stake in the world, for the world, as it is historically, these interests are supernatural.
>
> Human reason strengthened by faith, that is, by the acceptance of the information God has given us about the world through His Son and through the Society founded by Him, can attempt to give this account, though with a lively consciousness of its limitations. It is only when we shall be in possession of the Beatific Vision that the full beauty of the Divine Plan which is being worked out in the world will be visible to us. Until then, we can only make an imperfect attempt at what is not the philosophy, but the theology of history. The theologian who has the Catholic Faith is in touch with the full reality of the world, and can therefore undertake to show, however feebly and imperfectly, the interplay of the supreme realities of life.
>
> The philosopher, as such, knows nothing about the reality of the divine life of Grace, which we lost by the Fall of our First Parents, and nothing of the Mystical Body of Christ through which we receive back that life. **The philosophy of history, if it is to be true philosophy, that is, knowledge by supreme causes, must therefore be rather the theology of history. Yet how few, even among those who have the Catholic Faith, think of turning to the instructions and warnings issued by the representatives of our Lord Jesus Christ on earth, when they wish to ascertain the root causes of the present chaotic condition of the world!** (Father Denis Fahey, *The Mystical Body of Christ in the Modern World*.)

Thus it is that the work of this writer has attempted to provide readers with access to the papal encyclical letters on Holy Mother Church's Social Teaching as they, having studied true history, are reliable teachers concerning what happens to men and their nations when the Incarnation of Christ the King in the Virginal and Immaculate Womb of Mary our Immaculate Queen becomes a matter of indifference and then, by logical succession, of mockery and scorn by men and their nations. We are witnessing at the present time the consequences of the rejection of the Catholic Faith as the sole foundation of personal and social order.

To understand the rise of Christendom in the First Millennium as it reached its zenith in the Thirteenth Century before the rise of the Renaissance in the latter part of the Fourteenth Century and the Protestant Revolution in the Sixteenth Century, one needs to review some of the basics of salvation history. This is necessary in order to provide a summary of salvation history from Genesis to Our Lord's Ascension into Heaven to grasp how little most people around us understand about the very purpose of their lives and the remote and proximate causes of all personal and social problems.

From Genesis to the Incarnation

Life and death. Each of us is born to die. But the passage of a body from conception to physical death is only part of the story of a human life. Every human being has a rational, immortal soul that God infuses into him at the moment of his conception. That soul is the animating principle of the human body. It is the state of the soul which determines where the body will spend eternity after the Second and Final Coming of Our Lord at the end of time. And it was to make it possible for all souls to live in the glory of the Beatific Vision of Father, Son, and Holy Ghost that Our Lord endured His fearful Passion and Death.

Our Blessed Lord and Saviour Jesus Christ, the Second Person of the Blessed Trinity made Man, is the New Adam. His death on the Cross put an end to the power of sin and death forever. His perfect obedience to the Father's will canceled out the disobedience of the first Adam in the Garden of Eden. The shedding of His Most Precious Blood on Calvary paid back the blood-debt that finite beings owed their Infinite Creator. His forty hours in the tomb prior to His Resurrection on Easter Sunday give us the hope of eternal joy. He underwent His death so that we could live. Yet nearly 2,000 years after He instituted the New and Everlasting Covenant of the New Passover from death to life, so few of His followers truly understand how they are to fashion everything in their lives--and in that of their societies--in light of the mysteries of our redemption.

There is a simple explanation for the fact that most people in the world today, including so many Catholics, especially those attached to the structures of the conciliar church, do not understand the mysteries of salvation: they have never been instructed in them. If people do not understand what happened in the Garden of Eden, then they will have no understanding of their own identity as fallen creatures in need of redemption. And if they do not understand their identity as fallen creatures in need of redemption, then they will look to everything except the true religion instituted by Our Lord at the Last Supper to save them from the problems of the world. Like many of the people of Our Lord's time who were looking for a political or secular savior, so are many people today looking for their salvation in all of the wrong places, especially in politics, politicians, political parties, ideologies, and in government programs.

The truth of the matter is, of course, that the Triune God--the Infinite Being, the Uncreated Good, the Uncaused Cause--created both the invisible and the visible worlds out of love. He is a community of love consisting of three Divine Persons, each with His own distinctive identity and mission. The love of each of the Persons of the Blessed Trinity for each other is meant of its nature to be bestowed on others. He created the angels, pure spirits possessing an intellect and a will, out of love. And He created human beings out of love. But God's love is not an act of sentimentality. Not at all. God's love is an act of the Divine Will. He created angels and men out of love so that they would love Him, their First and Last End. He willed their good, which is the possession of His glory for all eternity.

However, God created angels and men as free beings. He wanted his creatures to choose to serve Him out of love, a return of love to Love Himself. Although He knew that certain of the angels, headed by Lucifer, would make an irrevocable choice against Him, God bestowed a free will upon angels in order to show forth His omnipotence. He wanted to teach men that it was the misuse of free will that caused the rebellion of Lucifer. And He wanted to teach them that it was Lucifer's hatred of Him that would impel the fallen angel to lead them to misuse their free wills against Him.

Satan hates God. He knows God and he hates Him. "Non serviam est!" ("I will not serve!") is the devil's motto. Our ancient adversary knows God, hates Him, and refuses to serve Him, the very antithesis of the purpose of human existence, which is, naturally, to know, to love, and to serve God here on earth in order to be happy with Him for all eternity in Heaven. The devil hates us because we are made in the image and the likeness of the One he hates, namely, God. That is why he wants to deceive us into mimicking him by disobeying God and serving ourselves--to the detriment of ourselves and those around us. The Master of Lies and the Prince of Darkness was permitted by God to tempt our first parents, Adam and Eve, in the Garden of Eden.

Adam and Eve had been created by God and placed in a world of Original Innocence. They possessed the preternatural gifts of a perfect human nature, one unspotted by sin. They had a superior intellect and a superior will. And they had a delicate balance between their higher rational faculties and their lower sensual passions. Adam and Eve were in harmony with God, and they were in harmony with each other. They were in harmony with the natural world. There was work without sweat and painless child-birth. The Gates of Heaven were opened to them.

God commanded only two things from our first parents. He asked them to love Him in return for all that He had bestowed upon them, including life itself. And He commanded them not to eat of the fruit of the Tree of the Knowledge of Good and Evil. He knew full well that they would succumb to the allure of the tempter. But He wanted the human race to understand that His love for us is so perfect that He will never force Himself upon us. He wants us to choose to love Him of our own free wills. And He wants us to realize how the misuse of our free wills leads to unhappiness and misery, that we are utterly lost without Him and His Holy Church. He wanted us to know that our souls face eternal death without Him.

The Devil appealed to Eve's pride when he manifested himself as a serpent in the Garden of Eden. He wanted Adam and Eve to be robbed of their birthright of the possession of the vision of God in Heaven. He wanted them to be in a state of war with God and with each other. He wanted them to live lives of despair. He wanted them to hate God as he did.

Eve, the Mother of the Living, did as the serpent wanted, eating of the fruit of the Tree of the Knowledge of Good and Evil, believing that she would be like unto God, knowing all things. Her act of prideful disobedience tied shut the Gates of Heaven. Adam did as she had requested, and his act of disobedience irreparably wounded human nature itself. Original Sin entered the world. Adam and Eve lost the preternatural gifts that had been bestowed upon them by God at their creation. Their intellects were darkened and their wills weakened. The delicate balance between their higher rational faculties and their lower sensual passions was overthrown in favor of the passions. All of the problems of the world--death, disease, injustice, war, poverty, work with sweat, painful childbirth, hatred, gluttony, envy, lust, anger, pride--descended upon the human race. Man had disobeyed the Infinite Being.

God did not abandon His creatures, however. He knew that He would personally enter human history to redeem them, to make it possible for men to overcome the effects of original sin and actual sin in the world if they cooperated with the graces He would win for them on the wood of the Holy Cross. "O happy fault, O necessary sin, which made possible so great a Redeemer," the Easter Exultet proclaims. Yes, the felix culpa of Adam and Eve made it possible for us to know how much God loved us, that the Father would send His only-begotten Son to be made flesh in the virginal and immaculate womb of our Blessed Mother.

In the mystery of His Divine Providence, God wanted to prepare the human race for the Redemption. He works in His time, not ours, something that we have to be reminded of all times, especially in light of the difficulties Holy Mother Church is facing at the early beginnings of the Third Millennium. All of the pages of the Old Testament point to the First Coming of Our Lord. They detail how meticulously God prepared His Chosen People for His own entry into human history in order to redeem the human race.

The Book of Genesis tells us that God chose Abram, a nomadic sheep herder, to be the father in faith of many people. Elongating his name to Abraham, God made a covenant with Abraham, as he had with Noah at the time of the flood. God promised to give Abraham, whose old wife Sarah was beyond her child-bearing years, descendants as numerous as the sands on the seashore or the stars in the sky. Why did he choose Abraham? Why did He choose the Hebrew people to be the instrument by which He would prepare the whole of mankind for the redemption? That is a mystery. There is no human explanation for it. Why did God favor Abel's offering over Cain's? Again, a mystery. But it was in God's ineffable Providence to choose Abraham, the patriarch who is invoked in The Roman Canon as our "father in faith," to build up a people singularly his own.

In a foreshadowing of the Redemption itself, God asked Abraham to sacrifice his long-awaited son, Isaac, on a pyre of wood. Abraham did not know why God was asking him to do such a thing. But He trusted in the word of God. God had asked him to make a sacrifice of his son. Who was he to deny the request? He trusted that God had some greater design beyond human comprehension. And by showing his desire to obey God without question and without delay, Abraham proved himself to be faithful. The sacrifice he was asked to make was a foreshadowing of how the Father had planned to redeem us by offering His only Son on the wood of the Holy Cross.

Catholics are the spiritual descendants of Abraham. His physical descendants formed the Twelve Tribes of Israel, which were sold into slavery in Egypt through Joseph, the son of Jacob, the son of Isaac, the son of Abraham. The Hebrew people spent 440 years in cruel slavery in Egypt, symbolic of the captivity of the human race to the Devil by means of original sin (and also symbolic of each person's captivity to the Devil prior to receiving the Sacrament of Baptism). They grumbled and they complained, wondering when their liberation would occur. Many of them thought that God had abandoned them.

God showed his favor on the Hebrews when He chose Moses to lead them out of their captivity to the Promised Land. It was to Moses that God definitively revealed Himself as the one and only God (Abraham believed that he had been visited by the true God, but he and the Hebrews remained polytheistic until God spoke to Moses face-to-face). Although he considered himself to be ill-equipped to speak to the oppressor of his people, the Pharaoh, he accepted the assignment that God had given him to lead his people to freedom. As one of the several foreshadowings of Our Lord found in the Old Testament, Moses was the one with whom God established the Covenant of the Old Dispensation, the one that would last until Our Lord established His New and Everlasting Covenant at the Last Supper.

The Covenant of the Old Dispensation was inaugurated with the first Passover, an event recounted in The Book of Exodus. The Hebrew people sprinkled the blood of lambs on their doorposts so that the angel of death would "pass over" their houses as every first-born male in Egypt was struck dead. As St. Paul noted in his Letter to the Hebrews, the blood of animals can save no one. But the use of the blood of lambs during the first Passover was a foreshadowing of the fact that each of us is now signed with the Most Precious Blood of the Lamb of God, He Who takes away the sins of the world, Our Lord and Savior Jesus Christ. And the ritual Passover meal was symbolic of the Eucharist, the fruit of the eternal Sacrifice offered to the Father by the Son on the wood of the Cross--re-presented to us in an unbloody manner today in every sacrifice of the Mass.

Led by a column of fire at night and by a cloud during the day, Moses marched the Chosen People to the Red Sea, where they were to cross over to commence their desert journey to the Promised Land. The parting of the waters of the Red Sea was a real event in the history of salvation. But we participated in that parting of the waters when we were baptized. For just as the Pharaoh and his army were swallowed up by the waters of the Red Sea when Moses used his staff to signal the wall of water to come crashing down upon them, so is it the case that the Devil and his minions are swallowed up by the waters stirred up in the baptismal font. We are freed from captivity to him just as the Chosen People were freed from their captivity to the Pharaoh.

Human nature being what it is, however, the Chosen People did not remain grateful to God for long. They grumbled about the harsh conditions of the desert, muttering that they were better off in slavery to the Egyptians. Are we any better? Having been freed from captivity to original sin, how many of us patiently endure the crosses that we are asked to bear? How many of us slowly give ourselves back to the service of the Devil by slipping into venial sins over and over again? How many of us excuse our own spiritual sloth, satisfied with doing the minimum, satisfied with giving First and Last Things only a passing thought now and then? How many of us feel enslaved by our baptismal calling and not by sin?

The desert journey of our spiritual ancestors is symbolic of several things. It is in the first place symbolic of the desert journey of life. We are called to wander in this vale of tears without grumbling. We are called to be faithful in the midst of great trials. We are called to be satisfied with the true manna come down from Heaven, the Eucharist, and to long for no other food. And we are called to realize that the Ten Commandments are written on the flesh of our hearts, being content to worship the true God Who has Revealed Himself entirely in the Person of Our Lord.

The Chosen People worshiped the Golden Calf while Moses was receiving the Ten Commandments. They grumbled so loudly about the manna that had come down from Heaven that God sent them quail to feed them. They got sick of the quail! Their grumbling at the waters of Meribah and Massah resulted in their being bitten by seraph serpents. Many of them died. They repented of their grumbling, being healed by looking at the bronze serpent Moses had made. He lifted high the bronze serpent to heal the people of the wounds they had suffered from the seraph serpents. We are called to look upon Our Lord, Who was lifted high on the Cross to heal us of the wounds caused by our sins.

Although Moses died before the Jews entered the land of Canaan (a result of his having complained about the stiff-necked people God had entrusted to his leadership), the desert journey was completed in forty years. But it was a short time thereafter that they began to worship false gods. Their leaders frequently were most concerned about pursuing the political lusts of their heart rather than being faithful to the Mosaic covenant. Even King David, chosen from the fields to shepherd God's chosen flock, became drunk with his own power and influence for a time, forgetting Who it was Who had chosen him to be king.

This is true, of course, even in our own day. Those who should know the true faith serve the false gods of public opinion and personal political expediency. Materialism and hedonism are rationalized as being consonant somehow with the faith. Both the spirit and the letter of the law written on the flesh of our hearts are ignored. The consequences of all of this in our day are eerily similar to those which faced the Jews: social disarray and anarchy. Over and over again, though, God spoke to the Chosen People through the Prophets--and through all of the events of their history. Micah, Amoz, Hosea, Nathan, Gad, Daniel, Isaiah, Ezekiel, and Jeremiah were among the prophets God used to speak about the coming of the Messias. But there are none so blind as those who refused to see. As Scripture tells us, they had eyes but could not sea, ears but could not hear. The Chosen People expected the Messias would liberate them from political bondage, never more so than when they were suffering under the cruel oppression imposed by their Roman occupiers. It was as though they had learned almost nothing from the Exodus or the Babylonian captivity. No, they were still looking for the political Messias. And aren't many people looking for such a Messias today?

There are few passages in the Old Testament which describe the sort of Messias that would redeem the human race more telling than those found in Chapters 52 and 53 of the Book of the Prophet Isaias:

> "See, my servant shall prosper, he shall be raised high and greatly exalted. Even as many were amazed at him--so marred was his look beyond that of man, and his appearance beyond that of mortals--so shall he startle many nations, because of him kings shall stand speechless; for those who have not been told shall see, those who have not heard shall ponder it.

> "Who would believe what we have heard? To whom has the arm of the Lord been revealed? He grew up like a sapling before him, like a shoot from the parched earth; there was in him no stately bearing to make us look at him, nor appearance that would attract us to him. He was spurned and avoided by men, a man of suffering, accustomed to infirmity, one of those from whom men hide their faces, spurned, and we held him in no esteem.

"Yet it was our infirmities that he bore, our sufferings that he endured, while we thought of him as stricken, as one smitten by God and afflicted. But he was pierced for our offenses, crushed for our sins; upon him was the chastisement that makes us whole, by his stripes we were healed. We had all gone astray like sheep, each following his own way; but the Lord laid upon him the guilt of us all.

"Though he was harshly treated, he submitted and opened not his mouth; like a lamb led to the slaughter or a sheep before the shearers, he was silent and opened not his mouth. Oppressed and condemned, he was taken away, and who would have thought any more of his destiny? When he was cut off from the land of the living, and smitten for the sin of his people, a grave was assigned him among the wicked and a burial place with evildoers, though he had done no wrong nor spoken any falsehood. [But the Lord was pleased to crush him in infirmity.]

"If he gives his life as an offering for sin, he shall see his descendants in a long life, and the will of the Lord shall be accomplished through him. Because of his affliction he shall see the light in fullness of days; through his suffering, my servant shall justify many, and their guilt he shall bear. Therefore I will give him his portion among the great, and he shall divide the spoils with the mighty, because he surrendered himself to death and he was counted among the wicked; and he shall take away the sins of many, and win pardon for their offenses" (Is. 52:13-15; 53:1-12).

Jeremiah wrote:

"Behold, the days are coming, says the Lord, when I will raise up a righteous shoot to David; as king he shall reign and govern wisely, he shall do what is just and right in the land. In his days Judah shall be saved, Israel shall dwell in security. This is the name they give him: 'The Lord our justice'" (Jer. 23:5-6).

Ezekiel prophesied of the Good Shepherd:

"For thus the Lord God: I myself will look after and tend my sheep. As a shepherd tends his flock when he finds himself among his scattered sheep, so will I tend my sheep. I will rescue them from every place where they were scattered when it was cloudy and dark. I will lead them out from among the peoples and gather them from the foreign lands; I will bring them back to their own country and pasture them upon the mountains of Israel. In good pastures will I pasture them, and on the mountain heights of Israel shall be their grazing ground. There they shall lie down on good grazing ground, and in rich pastures shall they be pastured on the mountains of Israel. I myself will pasture my sheep; I myself will give them rest, says the Lord God. The lost I will seek out, the strayed I will bring back, the injured I will bind up, the sick I will heal [but the sleek and the strong I will destroy], shepherding them rightly" (Ez. 35:11-16)

The new Israel, the new Zion, as we know, is the Church. It is through her that Our Lord shepherds us to the true Promised Land of Heaven. And it was to give birth to her from His Wounded Side on the wood of the Holy Cross that He personally entered human history at the Incarnation, fulfilling all of the promises that had been made about Him in the Law and in the Prophets.

Chapter III
God Personally Enters Human History, Thereby Changing It
Forever

Our Lady, having been preserved from all stain of Original and Actual sin when she was conceived in her mother's womb, became the singular vessel of honor through which the Logos, the Word, would enter human history. Denying Himself nothing of the human experience save sin, Our Lord condescended to spend nine months in the tabernacle of Our Lady's virginal and immaculate womb. The world was expecting the Savior to manifest Himself thunderously from a mountainside. But He came as a helpless embryo, unseen to the human eye. He came to do His Father's will. He came to offer Himself up as the blood-offering in propitiation for our own sins. But He came in such a way as to reveal Himself gradually to the creatures He was about to redeem. He wanted us to have faith in Him.

It was complete trust in the word of God that prompted Our Lady to undertake the arduous trip to the hill country of Judah to visit her cousin, Elizabeth, who in her old age was expecting the last of the Old Testament prophets, St. John the Baptist. The unborn John leapt for joy when he heard the voice of the Mother of God pierce his ears in his mother's womb. It was at that moment that John was cleansed of all original sin, enabling him to serve as the pure precursor of the Lamb of God who would take away the sins of the world.

Prompted by God the Holy Ghost, Our Lady proclaimed the Magnificat, which is recited (or, more accurately, which should be recited) at Evening Prayer by every priest and deacon and religious in the world.

> "My soul magnifies the Lord, and my spirit rejoices in God my Savior; because he has regarded the lowliness of his handmaid; for behold, henceforth all generations shall call me blessed; because he who is mighty has done great things for me, and holy is his name; and his mercy is from generation to generation to those who fear him. He has shown might with his arm, he has scattered the proud in their conceit of their heart. He has put down the mighty from their thrones, and has exalted the lowly. He has filled the hungry with good things, and the rich he has sent away empty. He has given help to Israel, his servant mindful of his mercy. Even as he spoke to fathers--to Abraham and to his posterity forever" (Lk. 1:46-55).

The promise made to Abraham was being fulfilled. And when Our Lady's time had arrived, she and St. Joseph made their way to Bethlehem, the City of David, where the prophet Micah had prophesied that the Messias would be born. There was no room for Our Lord in the inn on the night of his birth. Is there any room for Him in the inns of our hearts? In the life of our society? In our politics, our government, our laws, our entertainment?

The re-creation of the world, which had begun at the Incarnation, reached a turning point when Our Lord was born in the stable in the cave in Bethlehem. Born in the wood of the manger to die on the wood of the Cross. Yes, born in a manger, a feeding trough, only to make the instrument of His execution the true manger from which we would be fed His very Body, Blood, Soul, and Divinity. Born amidst the manure of the barn animals to die atop the dung heap known as Calvary. Born in anonymity to die in ignominy, considered a criminal and a blasphemer by all but a handful of people. Born in poverty to die in poverty. Born in obedience to the Father's will to do the Father's will, indeed, to be the Father's will for us all. Given birth painlessly by Our Lady only to watch her writhe in great pain as she gave birth to us as the adopted sons and daughters of God at the foot of the Cross.

Our Lord's Most Holy Face radiated all of the glory of His Sacred Divinity when He lay in the crib in Bethlehem. Our souls once radiated His glory when we were baptized, freed from our captivity to the Devil. But our sins marred that Most Holy Face, making it almost unrecognizable by the time St. Veronica wiped It as He walked on the Via Dolorosa on the road to Calvary. The Cross hovered over Bethlehem. For it was to bear the Cross that Our Lord made his humble entrance in the City of David.

The great and the powerful hated Our Lord almost from the moment He was born. Herod the Great. Herod the Tetrarch. Pontius Pilate. The Pharisees. The Sadducees. The Sanhedrin. And even after His Death and Resurrection, many of the great and the powerful hated Him and His Holy Church with a vengeance. Nero. Diocletian. Trajan. Henry VIII. Cromwell. Marx. Freud. Lenin. Hitler. Stalin. The Freemasons. Mao. Deng. Clinton. Bush 41 and Bush 43. Obama. All other naturalists. He was born to be a sign of contradiction, as Simeon prophesied to Our Lady at the Presentation. And He was to   die as a sign of contradiction.

Each one of us is called to be a sign of contradiction. Our Lord told us that we would be hated as He was hated. He told us that we would be persecuted as He was persecuted. He told us that we would be handed over to kings and governors on His account. All will hate us because of His Name, He said. He was hated from the moment of His birth. He is hated today.

The hatred of Herod the Great was so great that He ordered the slaughter of the Holy Innocents in his quest to destroy the Infant King, Our Lord. But it was not yet His time. The Holy Family fled to Egypt, the very place where the Chosen People from whom Our Lord had taken His Sacred Humanity were enslaved for 440 years, living there for a year and one-half. Rich in symbolism, the Redeemer left His exile in Egypt to return to Nazareth, where He spent nearly thirty years living anonymously, doing the work of a manual laborer, redeeming all things about our ordinary existence.

Each of us lives an ordinary existence. It is in that ordinary existence that we prove ourselves to be friends or enemies of Our Lord and His Holy Church. Do we bear our share of the hardship which the Gospel entails? Do we seek to sanctify every moment of our lives? Do we live in the consciousness of the Divine Presence, always keeping in mind that we could be called home to give an account of our lives at any moment? Do we fulfill the duties of our states-in-life with joy and punctuality? Our Lord did. If it was good enough for Him, it should be good enough for we grumblers as we stumble about in our own desert journey of life.

Our Blessed Lord and Saviour Jesus Christ, the Second Person of the Most Blessed Trinity through Whom all things were made, submitted Himself in humility to the authority of His foster-father, Good Saint Joseph, and His Most Blessed Mother. Although He was their Creator and Redeemer, He obeyed them, teaching us that we must obey all duly constituted authority, starting with our parents, in all things that do not pertain to sin. Sinful commands must not be obeyed.

Our Blessed Lord and Saviour Jesus Christ loved His foster-father, learning from him the intricate work of a skilled carpenter. While Our Blessed Lord and Saviour Jesus Christ knew all things as God, He still had to learn how to *do* those things as man that He had ordained as God to be done by men. Our Blessed Lord and Saviour Jesus Christ therefore submitted Himself to the tutelage of Saint Joseph to learn the trade by which He would earn a living for Himself and His Blessed Mother after Saint Joseph died. Saint Joseph was in the sublime position of teaching God, Who subjected Himself in humility to the teaching authority of His foster-father.

Imagine the daily joy and peace and serenity that surrounded the Holy Family. Saint Joseph and Our Lady were always in the Presence of God Himself. Although there are various private revelations about the nature of the Holy Family's life, Sacred Scripture is as silent about the events of the Hidden Years in Nazareth as Saint Joseph himself. There is a reason for this silence: Our Blessed Lord and Saviour Jesus Christ was teaching us that each of us will grow up in a family. Those of us who marry and are blessed with children are to replicate in our own lives the joy and peace and serenity of the Holy Family of Nazareth day in and day out, fulfilling the duties of our state-in-life without complaint and without delay. Husbands and fathers must see in Saint Joseph the perfect model of what it is to be the head of one's household, intent on developing the manly Catholic virtues of patience and charity and courage and perseverance exhibited to their highest degree in the person of Saint Joseph.

As the model of patience and joy, Saint Joseph did not complain about anything. Indeed, Sacred Scripture records not one word ever uttered by Saint Joseph. He was the just and silent man of the House of David as he faithfully carried out God's will for him each and every day, doing ordinary things extraordinarily well for the love of the Father in the presence of the Son Himself. He is the model of artisans and laborers, a man who pursued excellence as befits a child of God. He wanted nothing more than to use the talents he had been given for God's greater glory, knowing that he had been chosen from all eternity to participate in events that would lead to the Redemption. He, a man who worked with wood, had the privilege of serving the One Who would use the wood of the Cross as the instrument of redeeming mankind.

Saint Joseph suffered along with Our Lady when the Child Jesus stayed behind in Jerusalem to answer questions being posed to him by the doctors of the law. The fright in his heart was palpable when he discovered that his foster-Son was not in their company. His relief was visible when his foster-Son was found. His acceptance of God's will about this event was total. Not a word of complaint. He knew that his foster-Son had to be about His Heavenly Father's business once he heard this from the mouth of the One to Whom he gave love, clothing, shelter and instruction.

How fitting it is that Saint Joseph, who was the head of the Holy Family of Nazareth, is the Patron of the Universal Church. We need to invoke his intercession more faithfully for the needs of Holy Mother Church. For just as Saint Joseph protected the Infant Jesus and Our Lady during their flight to Egypt, so, too, has Our Blessed Lord and Saviour Jesus Christ entrusted to His foster-father the protection of His Mystical Body, the Church, here on earth. So too does he watch over our priests, who are called to imitate his virtue of chastity by denying themselves their biological fatherhood in order to be the spiritual father of others. Saint Joseph is very close to priests and wants them to keep their purity unstained by anything. He wants them to be lovers of Holy Poverty after his own holy heart. And he wants them to be steadfast in maintaining the Tradition that his foster-Son's Apostles have handed down to them under the protection of the Holy Ghost.

Our Lord left His home after the death of Saint Joseph, although His Blessed Mother was never far from Him. She was with Him to the end, as is noted in great detail. He left to be baptized symbolically by his cousin, St. John the Baptist, who had been preparing the way for His Public Ministry. "He must increase, I must decrease," said the Baptist. His work was over. Our Lord's had just begun.

Noah spent forty days and forty nights in the ark. The Chosen People spent forty years in the desert. Our Lord spent forty days in the desert, praying and fasting before He assumed His Public Ministry. The forty days of Lent prepare us to be more willing to cooperate with the graces won for us by Our Lord by the shedding of His Most Precious Blood, for we are able to resist the Devil as Our Lord did when He was tempted in the desert. We are able to walk the rocky road that leads to the narrow gate of Life Himself.

Chapter IV
Our Lord's Public Ministry

Our Lord left the desert to call His Twelve Apostles, one for each of the twelve tribes of Israel. He called them by name. He called each of *us* by name when we were Christened, when we were baptized. He gave them a mission to bring all people into the true Church, a mission that we received in baptism--and reaffirmed when we received the Sacrament of Confirmation. He called the Apostles, knowing full well that they were full of shortcomings, that they would be slow to understand Him, that all but one of them would run away from Him during His Passion and Death. He calls us, knowing that we are crooked lines, men who are in constant need of forgiveness.

Our Lord taught and preached for three years prior to the events of Holy Week. He performed His first miracle at Cana, turning the water into wine at the wedding feast there at the request of His Most Blessed Mother, a foreshadowing of the transubstantiation of wine into His Most Precious Blood at the Last Supper. He cured the lame, restored sight to the blind, healed the leprous, made the deaf hear and the dumb speak. He expelled demons. And He raised the dead. But His physical miracles were always signs of the fact of His Sacred Divinity, that He had the power to forgive sins.

Indeed, one of the enduring themes of His Public Ministry was forgiveness and mercy. He came to give it to us unworthy vessels of clay. He expects each one of us to give it others, freely and unconditionally. "Neither will your sins be forgiven you unless you forgive your brother from your heart." As the late Father John A. Hardon, S.J., said at a conference in Detroit, Michigan, in 1996, " God permits us to sin so that we can show mercy to each other."

However, the compassion of Our Lord for sinners is no expression of mere human sentimentality, as many would have us believe today. Far from it. When He came upon Saint Mary Magdalen as she was caught in adultery, Our Lord asked if anyone ready to cast stones was without sin. As each man dropped the stone he was about to cast at Lazarus's sister, Our Lord told her that no one had condemned her--and that He did not do so. However, He told her to go, and sin no more. True compassion, Our Lord was teaching us, understands the weakness of fallen human nature. But it never reaffirms another person--or us--in that which is sinful. God's grace is sufficient for us to resist temptation.

Forgiveness was the keynote of the Parable of the Prodigal Son. The Father stands ready to forgive us at any moment of our lives if only we have the humility to acknowledge our sins in the hospital of Divine Mercy, the confessional. For it is in the Sacrament of Penance that the merits of the shedding of Our Lord's Most Precious Blood are applied to us through a priest acting in persona Christi. We must never be slow to recognize how our sins wounded Our Lord once in time, how they caused Seven Swords of Sorrow to be thrust through and through the Sorrowful and Immaculate Heart of Mary, how they wound the Church Militant on earth today, and how they make us less capable of shining forth His love in the world. Our Lord's Throne of Forgiveness, the Cross, reminds us of how much we have offended Him--but how limitless His mercy is if only we seek it out.

All of this was hard for the people of His time to hear. Theirs was a merciless age. Their hearts had been hardened. That is why it was difficult for them to endure what He taught in the Sermon on the Mount. Every one of the Beatitudes contradicted the prevailing spirit of the times. Indeed, they contradict the prevailing spirit of our times, do they not?

"Blessed are the poor in spirit, for theirs is the kingdom of Heaven.

"Blessed are the meek, for they shall possess the earth.

"Blessed are they who mourn, for they shall be comforted.
"Blessed are they who hunger and thirst for justice, for they shall be satisfied.

"Blessed are the merciful, for they shall obtain mercy.

"Blessed are the clean of heart, for they shall see God.

"Blessed are the peacemakers, for they shall be called children of God.

"Blessed are they who suffer persecution for justice's sake, for theirs is the kingdom of Heaven.
"Blessed are you when men reproach you, and persecute you, and, speaking falsely, say all manner of evil against you, for My sake.

"Rejoice and exult, because your reward in great in heaven; for so did they persecute the prophets before you" (Mt. 5:3-12).

Our Lord came to tell people that the problems of the world were caused by sin, that they had to undergo a daily conversion of mind, heart, and soul. There is no once and for all solution to our own problems or those of the world. The state of the world depends upon the state of individual souls. Therefore, it is important for us to remember that we are, as Our Lord said in the Sermon on the Mount, the salt of earth and the light of the world. We are called to add His seasoning, His leaven, if you will, in the midst of this fallen, fractured world. We are called to provide His light shining through us into this darkened will. And each of us is called to take up our cross on a daily basis, deny our very selves and follow Him through His Holy Church.

Most of this was pretty difficult for the people of Our Lord's time to understand and accept. Our Lord had not come to be popular, however. He did not come to preach a theology of ecumenical indifferentism. He proclaimed Himself to be the Way, the Truth, and the Life. People either loved Him or they hated Him. There was no middle ground. Some, like the rich young man in the Gospel of St. Mark, walked away because they did not want to give up their possessions. Others did not want to reform their lives.

Perhaps the major turning point in Our Lord's Public Ministry came when He gave the Eucharistic Discourse after the miracles of the loaves and fishes. As recorded in the Gospel of St. John, Our Lord proclaimed Himself to be the True Manna come down from Heaven.

"I am the bread of life. Your fathers ate the manna in the desert, and have died. This is the bread that comes down from heaven, so that if anyone eat of it he will not die. I am the living bread that has come down from heaven. If anyone eat of this bread he shall live forever; and the bread that I will give is my flesh for the life of the world. . . .Amen, amen, I say to you, unless you eat of the flesh of the Son of Man, and drink His Blood, you shall not have life in you. He who eats My Body and drinks My Blood has life everlasting and I will raise him up on the last day. For My Flesh is food indeed, and My Blood is drink indeed. He who eats My Flesh, and drinks My Blood, abides in Me and I in him. As the living Father has sent Me, and as I live because of the Father, so he who eats Me, he also shall live because of Me. This is the bread that has come down from Heaven; not as your fathers ate the manna, and died. He who eats this bread shall live forever" (Jn. 6:48-52, 54-60).

Many of the Jews found what Our Lord said very hard to accept.

"From this time many of his disciples turned back and no longer went about with him" (Jn. 6:67).

Sadly, even some Catholic priests and religious no longer believe in the Real Presence of Our Lord in the Eucharist. St. Peter spoke for those of us who do believe in the Real Presence when the Master asked the Twelve if they wanted to leave him too. "Lord, to whom shall we go? Thou hast the words of everlasting life, and we have come to believe and to know that thou art the Christ, the Son of God" (Jn. 6:69-70).

No, Jesus of Nazareth, known to be the son of Joseph the Carpenter, was not what the world expected the Messias to be. He taught with authority. His miracles proved His Sacred Divinity. The scribes and the Pharisees did not know how to deal with him, especially after a lot of people began to follow Him after He raised his friend Lazarus of Bethany from the dead. He had to be done away with, His message obliterated. Little did the plotters realize, however, that they were helping to fulfill His Co-Equal and Co-Eternal God the Father's plan for their own redemption which He had in mind at the very moment of creation.

Chapter V
Astride a Donkey to Shouts of Hosanna in the Highest, Jeered as a Reviled Criminal

Yes, less than five days after Our Lord was welcomed triumphantly as He entered Jerusalem He was subjected to treatment as a common criminal. Hailed as a King to the shouts of "Hosanna in the highest" on this very day, the first Palm Sunday nearly two millennia ago, only to be reviled and scorned by the same crowd with the words "Crucify Him!" The crowd that laid palm fronds in the path of the beast He rode into Jerusalem mocked Him as He hung on the Holy Cross:

> [36] And they sat and watched him. [37] And they put over his head his cause written: THIS IS JESUS THE KING OF THE JEWS. [38] Then were crucified with him two thieves: one on the right hand, and one on the left. [39] And they that passed by, blasphemed him, wagging their heads, [40] And saying: Vah, thou that destroyest the temple of God, and in three days dost rebuild it: save thy own self: if Thou be the Son of God, come down from the cross. In like manner also the chief priests with the scribes and the ancients, mocking, said: He saved others, Himself He cannot save: if He be the king of Israel, let Him now come down from the cross, and we will believe in Him; He trusted in God, let Him now deliver Him if He will have Him; for He said: I am the Son of God. And the self-same thing the thieves also that were crucified with Him reproached Him with" (Matthew)

The popularity of Our Lord with the fickle crowd was very fleeting.

Each of us plays a multiplicity of characters in the drama that unfolds during Holy Week. But, then, each of us plays a multiplicity of characters in our own lives. Often we are Saint John the Evangelist, faithful to the end. More often than we would like to admit, however, we are vacillating and boastful Peter, exclaiming that we will defend Our Lord with all of our strength but shrinking from that boast o u t of fear, pride, weakness or malice. There are other characters whose names are not mentioned in the accounts of the Passion contained in the Gospels. And it is perhaps these nameless characters who best exemplify our own ambivalence about following Our Lord consistently in every aspect of our daily and social lives without any exception whatsoever.

Enter the Passion

The Last Supper that Our Blessed Lord and Saviour Jesus Christ shared with His Apostles in the Upper Room on the first Holy Thursday marked the beginning of the New and Eternal Testament of the New Moses Who is Himself, Our Blessed Lord and Saviour Jesus Christ.

The first Moses, a prefiguring of Our Lord, had led the Chosen People out of Egypt, where they had been enslaved for over four centuries. The new Moses, Our Lord, used the occasion of this Last Supper, in which He offers us His own Body and Blood, Soul and Divinity, to lead us out of our enslavement to sin and eternal death, to make it possible for us to pass over from the desert journey of life to the eternal Canaan, Heaven.

The priesthood of heredity of the Old Dispensation is superseded by the Priesthood and Victimhood of Our Lord and Saviour Jesus Christ, which He entrusts to mere men until the end of the world to be the instruments through which the graces He won for us on Calvary are channeled into human souls by the working of the Third Person of the Most Blessed Trinity, God the Holy Ghost, and through the most loving hands of Our Lady, the Mediatrix of All Graces. This day truly marks the replacement of the old wineskins by the new wineskin of Faith in the Son of God made Man in Our Lady's Virginal and Immaculate Womb, He Who came to earth precisely to undergo His Passion and Death for our salvation.

The sacerdotal, hierarchical priesthood of the New and Eternal Testament makes it possible for mere men to make Our Lord incarnate under the appearance of the mere elements of this earth, bread and wine. Our Lord calls men to serve Him in the priesthood to re-present or perpetuate His one bloody Sacrifice on the wood of the Holy Cross in an unbloody manner at altars of sacrifice. Conscious of this fact, therefore, men who have been ordained to the priesthood must strive for the holiness of Our Lord Himself. They enter into the holy of holies every day as they walk in with their birettas to transcend time, to make present in time the one Sacrifice of the Cross that was offered by the God-Man Himself to the Father in Spirit and in Truth on Good Friday. The sanctuary in which Holy Mass is offered is symbolic of many things, chief among them the distinction between eternity and time, and the distinction between the sacerdotal, hierarchical priesthood of the ordained priest and the common priesthood of each of us by means of our baptism.

Dom Prosper Gueranger, O.S.B., commented on the institution of the priesthood in *The Liturgical Year*:

> The institution of the holy Eucharist, both as a Sacrament and a Sacrifice, is followed by another: the institution of a new priesthood. How could our Saviour have said: 'Except you eat the Flesh of the Son of man, and drink His Blood, you shall not have life in you,' unless He resolved to establish a ministry upon earth, whereby He would renew, even to the end of time, the great mystery He thus commands us to receive? He begins it to-day, in the cenacle. The twelve apostles are the first to partake of it; but observe what He says to them: 'Do this for a commemoration of Me.' By these words, He gives them power to change bread into His Body, and wine into His Blood; and this sublime power shall be perpetuated in the Church, by holy Ordination, even to the end of the world. Jesus will continue to operate, by the ministry of mortal and sinful men, the mystery of the last Supper. By thus enriching His Church with one and perpetual Sacrifice, He also gives us the means of abiding in Him, for He gives us, as He promised, the Bread of heaven. To-day, then, we keep the anniversary, not only of the institution of the holy Eucharist, but also the equally wonderful institution of the Christian priesthood. (Dom Prosper Gueranger, *The Liturgical Year*.)

Pope Pius XI noted the following in *Ad Catholici Sacerdotii*, December 20, 1935, about the dignity of the priest, the one who channels the graces that the Divine Redeemer won on the wood of the Holy Cross on Good Friday into the souls of the faithful:

> The human race has always felt the need of a priesthood: of men, that is, who have the official charge to be mediators between God and humanity, men who should consecrate themselves entirely to this mediation, as to the very purpose of their lives, men set aside to offer to God public prayers and sacrifices in the name of human society. For human society as such is bound to offer to God public and social worship. It is bound to acknowledge in Him its Supreme Lord and first beginning, and to strive toward Him as to its last end, to give Him

thanks and offer Him propitiation. In fact, priests are to be found among all peoples whose customs are known, except those compelled by violence to act against the most sacred laws of human nature. They may, indeed, be in the service of false divinities; but wherever religion is professed, wherever altars are built, there also is a priesthood surrounded by particular marks of honor and veneration.

Yet in the splendor of Divine Revelation the priest is seen invested with a dignity far greater still. This dignity was foreshadowed of old by the venerable and mysterious figure of Melchisedech, Priest and King, whom St. Paul recalls as prefiguring the Person and Priesthood of Christ Our Lord Himself.

The priest, according to the magnificent definition given by St. Paul, is indeed a man Ex hominibus assumptus, "taken from amongst men," yet pro hominibus constituitur in his quae sunt ad Deum, "ordained for men in the things that appertain to God": his office is not for human things, and things that pass away, however lofty and valuable these may seem; but for things divine and enduring. These eternal things may, perhaps, through ignorance, be scorned and contemned, or even attacked with diabolical fury and malice, as sad experience has often proved, and proves even today; but they always continue to hold the first place in the aspirations, individual and social, of humanity, because the human heart feels irresistibly it is made for God and is restless till it rests in Him.

The Old Law, inspired by God and promulgated by Moses, set up a priesthood, which was, in this manner, of divine institution; and determined for it every detail of its duty, residence and rite. It would seem that God, in His great care for them, wished to impress upon the still primitive mind of the Jewish people one great central idea. This idea throughout the history of the chosen people, was to shed its light over all events, laws, ranks and offices: the idea of sacrifice and priesthood. These were to become, through faith in the future Messias, a source of hope, glory, power and spiritual liberation. The temple of Solomon, astonishing in richness and splendor, was still more wonderful in its rites and ordinances. Erected to the one true God as a tabernacle of the divine Majesty upon earth, it was also a sublime poem sung to that sacrifice and that priesthood, which, though type and symbol, was still so August, that the sacred figure of its High Priest moved the conqueror Alexander the Great, to bow in reverence; and God Himself visited His wrath upon the impious king Balthasar because he made revel with the sacred vessels of the temple. Yet that ancient priesthood derived its greatest majesty and glory from being a foretype of the Christian priesthood; the priesthood of the New and eternal Covenant sealed with the Blood of the Redeemer of the world, Jesus Christ, true God and true Man.

The Apostle of the Gentiles thus perfectly sums up what may be said of the greatness, the dignity and the duty of the Christian priesthood: Sic nos existimet homo Ut ministros Christi et dispensatores mysteriorum Dei -- "Let a man so account of us as of the ministers of Christ and the dispensers of the mysteries of God." The priest is the minister of Christ, an instrument, that is to say, in the hands of the Divine Redeemer. He continues the work of the redemption in all its world-embracing universality and divine efficacy, that work that wrought so marvelous a transformation in the world. Thus the priest, as is said with good reason, is indeed "another Christ"; for, in some way, he is himself a continuation of Christ. "As the

Father hath sent Me, I also send you," is spoken to the priest, and hence the priest, like Christ, continues to give "glory to God in the highest and on earth peace to men of good will."

For, in the first place, as the Council of Trent teaches, Jesus Christ at the Last Supper instituted the sacrifice and the priesthood of the New Covenant: "our Lord and God, although once and for all, by means of His death on the altar of the cross, He was to offer Himself to God the Father, that thereon He might accomplish eternal Redemption; yet because death was not to put an end to his priesthood, at the Last Supper, the same night in which He was betrayed in order to leave to His beloved spouse the Church, a sacrifice which should be visible (as the nature of man requires), which should represent that bloody sacrifice, once and for all to be completed on the cross, which should perpetuate His memory to the end of time, and which should apply its saving power unto the remission of sins we daily commit, showing Himself made a priest forever according to the order of Melchisedech, offered to God the Father, under the appearance of bread and wine, His Body and Blood, giving them to the apostles (whom He was then making priests of the New Covenant) to be consumed under the signs of these same things, and commanded the Apostles and their successors in the priesthood to offer them, by the words 'Do this in commemoration of Me.'"

And thenceforth, the Apostles, and their successors in the priesthood, began to lift to heaven that "clean oblation" foretold by Malachy, through which the name of God is great among the gentiles. And now, that same oblation in every part of the world and at every hour of the day and night, is offered and will continue to be offered without interruption till the end of time: a true sacrificial act, not merely symbolical, which has a real efficacy unto the reconciliation of sinners with the Divine Majesty.

"Appeased by this oblation, the Lord grants grace and the gift of repentance, and forgives iniquities and sins, however great." The reason of this is given by the same Council in these words: "For there is one and the same Victim, there is present the same Christ who once offered Himself upon the Cross, who now offers Himself by the ministry of priests, only the manner of the offering being different." (Pope Pius XI, *Ad Catholici Sacerdotii*, December 20, 1935.)

Our priests make it possible for us to be fed with the true Manna Who came from Heaven to redeem us. The Chosen People ate the manna in the desert to feed their bodies. We, however, have the true Bread came down from Heaven to feed us, Our Blessed Lord and Saviour Jesus Christ. By virtue of the events of the Easter Triduum which we enter into on Maundy Thursday, He left us with all of the supernatural helps necessary to follow Him on a daily basis, to resist temptation, to grow in holiness--and by doing so to provide an example to the world of fidelity to His Holy Cross. The Mass, the perfect prayer, which was consummated on the wood of the Holy Cross on Good Friday, provides us with an opportunity every day of the year except on Good Friday to be present as His one Sacrifice to the Father in Spirit and in Truth is offered in an unbloody manner at the hands of an *alter Christus*. We are truly present at Calvary during each Mass we are privileged to hear.

Our love of the Sacrament of the Eucharist instituted at the Last Supper is not confined to the Mass, however.

Just as Our Lord spent nine months as the prisoner of the tabernacle of Our Lady's Virginal and Immaculate womb, so does He remain the prisoner of each tabernacle in every true Catholic Church until the end of time by His Real Presence in the Most Blessed Sacrament. We have the opportunity immediately after the procession on Maundy Thursday to worship Our Lord in the repository, calling to mind the agony in the Garden of Gethsemane He underwent this night prior to His arrest, trial, imprisonment, scourging at the pillar, and crowning with thorns.

Yes, that opportunity is available to us every day, with the exception of the time after the morning of Good Friday until after the Easter Vigil Mass. Maundy Thursday, however, is the day above all other days to keep company with Our Lord in His Real Presence as He waits for us to adore Him in the Tabernacle (the Repository) on the Altar of Reposition. We keeping company with Our Lord not only with those who happen to be with us in a particular church on Maundy Thursday. We keep Him company with Saints Peter, James and John, each of whom fell asleep in the Garden of Gethsemane, and with Our Lady, Saint Joseph and all of the angels and the saints.

Which one of us would not make the time to keep one of our loved ones company as he or she was about to undergo some terrible ordeal? Haven't we made time in our lives to comfort those we loved who were about to undergo surgery, as well as those in our families who were on the verge of dying? Does it not make sense for us to keep company with Our Lord on the actual date of the first Maundy Thursday, yes, the night in which the very thought of coming into contact with our sins caused Him to sweat droplets of His Most Precious Blood?

Pope Leo XIII explained the necessity of devotion to Our Lord's Real Presence to societies as well as individuals, something that one is not going to read in, say, any "conservative" journal. "For as men and states alike necessarily have their being from God, so they can do nothing good except in God through Jesus Christ, through whom every best and choicest gift has ever proceeded and proceeds."

These passages from Pope Leo's *Mirae Caritatis*, May 28, 1902, indicate the connection between Eucharistic picty and social order:

> Indeed it is greatly to be desired that those men would rightly esteem and would make due provision for life everlasting, whose industry or talents or rank have put it in their power to shape the course of human events. But alas! we see with sorrow that such men too often proudly flatter themselves that they have conferred upon this world as it were a fresh lease of life and prosperity, inasmuch as by their own energetic action they are urging it on to the race for wealth, to a struggle for the possession of commodities which minister to the love of comfort and display. And yet, whithersoever we turn, we see that human society, if it be estranged from God, instead of enjoying that peace in its possessions for which it had sought, is shaken and tossed like one who is in the agony and heat of fever; for while it anxiously strives for prosperity, and trusts to it alone, it is pursuing an object that ever escapes it, clinging to one that ever eludes the grasp. For as men and states alike necessarily have their being from God, so they can do nothing good except in God through Jesus Christ, through whom every best and choicest gift has ever proceeded and proceeds. But the source and chief of all these gifts is the venerable Eucharist, which not only nourishes and sustains that life the desire whereof demands our most strenuous efforts, but also enhances beyond measure that

dignity of man of which in these days we hear so much. For what can be more honourable or a more worthy object of desire than to be made, as far as possible, sharers and partakers in the divine nature? Now this is precisely what Christ does for us in the Eucharist, wherein, after having raised man by the operation of His grace to a supernatural state, he yet more closely associates and unites him with Himself. For there is this difference between the food of the body and that of the soul, that whereas the former is changed into our substance, the latter changes us into its own; so that St. Augustine makes Christ Himself say: "You shall not change Me into yourself as you do the food of your body, but you shall be changed into Me" (confessions 1. vii., c. x.).

Moreover, in this most admirable Sacrament, which is the chief means whereby men are engrafted on the divine nature, men also find the most efficacious help towards progress in every kind of virtue. And first of all in faith. In all ages faith has been attacked; for although it elevates the human mind by bestowing on it the knowledge of the highest truths, yet because, while it makes known the existence of divine mysteries, it yet leaves in obscurity the mode of their being, it is therefore thought to degrade the intellect. But whereas in past times particular articles of faith have been made by turns the object of attack; the seat of war has since been enlarged and extended, until it has come to this, that men deny altogether that there is anything above and beyond nature. Now nothing can be better adapted to promote a renewal of the strength and fervour of faith in the human mind than the mystery of the Eucharist, the "mystery of faith," as it has been most appropriately called. For in this one mystery the entire supernatural order, with all its wealth and variety of wonders, is in a manner summed up and contained: "He hath made a remembrance of His wonderful works, a merciful and gracious Lord; He hath given food to them that fear Him" (Psalm cx, 4-5). For whereas God has subordinated the whole supernatural order to the Incarnation of His Word, in virtue whereof salvation has been restored to the human race, according to those words of the Apostle; "He hath purposed...to re-establish all things in Christ, that are in heaven and on earth, in Him" (Eph. I., 9-10), the Eucharist, according to the testimony of the holy Fathers, should be regarded as in a manner a continuation and extension of the Incarnation. For in and by it the substance of the incarnate Word is united with individual men, and the supreme Sacrifice offered on Calvary is in a wondrous manner renewed, as was signified beforehand by Malachy in the words: "In every place there is sacrifice, and there is offered to My name a pure oblation" (Mal. I., 11). And this miracle, itself the very greatest of its kind, is accompanied by innumerable other miracles; for here all the laws of nature are suspended; the whole substance of the bread and wine are changed into the Body and the Blood; the species of bread and wine are sustained by the divine power without the support of any underlying substance; the Body of Christ is present in many places at the same time, that is to say, wherever the Sacrament is consecrated. And in order that human reason may the more willingly pay its homage to this great mystery, there have not been wanting, as an aid to faith, certain prodigies wrought in His honour, both in ancient times and in our own, of which in more than one place there exist public and notable records and memorials. It is plain that by this Sacrament faith is fed, in it the mind finds its nourishment, the objections of rationalists are brought to naught, and abundant light is thrown on the supernatural order.

But that decay of faith in divine things of which We have spoken is the effect not only of pride, but also of moral corruption. For if it is true that a strict morality improves the quickness of man's intellectual powers, and if on the other hand, as the maxims of pagan philosophy and the admonitions of divine wisdom combine to teach us, the keenness of the mind is blunted by bodily pleasures, how much more, in the region of revealed truths, do these same pleasures obscure the light of faith, or even, by the just judgment of God, entirely extinguish it. For these pleasures at the present day an insatiable appetite rages, infecting all classes as with an infectious disease, even from tender years. Yet even for so terrible an evil there is a remedy close at hand in the divine Eucharist. For in the first place it puts a check on lust by increasing charity, according to the words of St. Augustine, who says, speaking of charity, "As it grows, lust diminishes; when it reaches perfection, lust is no more" (De diversis quaestionibus, Ixxxiii., q. 36). Moreover the most chaste flesh of Jesus keeps down the rebellion of our flesh, as St. Cyril of Alexandria taught, "For Christ abiding in us lulls to sleep the law of the flesh which rages in our members" (Lib. iv., c. ii., in Joan., vi., 57). Then too the special and most pleasant fruit of the Eucharist is that which is signified in the words of the prophet: "What is the good thing of Him," that is, of Christ, "and what is His beautiful thing, but the corn of the elect and the wine that engendereth virgins" (Zach. ix., 17), producing, in other words, that flower and fruitage of a strong and constant purpose of virginity which, even in an age enervated by luxury, is daily multiplied and spread abroad in the Catholic Church, with those advantages to religion and to human society, wherever it is found, which are plain to see. (Pope Leo XIII, *Mirae Caritatis*, May 28, 1902.)

Men, including leaders of their fellow men, need to spend time in prayer before Our Lord's Real Presence in the Most Blessed Sacrament. As will be discussed in a later chapter, many of the rulers of Christendom did spend such time in prayer, receiving many infused graces today. That leaders of men no longer understand this or, worse yet, mock it and reject it entirely, satisfies the adversary to no end as he desires to convince men that they can "save" the world by their own unaided powers.

It should be remembered as well that a hatred of the Holy Priesthood instituted by Our Lord at the Last Supper is a hatred of Him. It is a denial of His very words contained in the Eucharistic discourse as recorded in the Gospel according to Saint John the Evangelist. And it is a fundamental hatred of thc Catholic priesthood that Our Lord instituted to make it possible for us to be fed by His very Body, Blood, Soul and Divinity in the Holy Eucharist. Consider the hatred of the priesthood possessed by a "founding father" of the United States of America:

History, I believe, furnishes no example of a priest-ridden people maintaining a free civil government. **This marks the lowest grade of ignorance of which their civil as well as religious leaders will always avail themselves for their own purposes.** (Thomas Jefferson, Letter to Alexander von Humboldt, December, 1813.)

May it be to the world, what I believe it will be, (to some parts sooner, to others later, but finally to all) the signal of arousing men to burst the chains under which monkish ignorance and superstition had persuaded them to bind themselves, and to assume the blessings and security of self-government. That form which we have substituted, restores the free right to the unbounded exercise of reason and freedom of opinion. All eyes are opened, or opening, to the rights of man. The general spread of the light of science has already laid open to every view the palpable truth, that the mass of mankind has not been born with saddles on their backs, nor a favored few booted and spurred, ready to ride them legitimately, by the grace of God. These are grounds of hope for others. For ourselves, let the annual return of this day forever refresh our recollections of these rights, and an undiminished devotion to them. (Thomas Jefferson, Letter to Roger Weigthman, June 24, 1826, ten days before Jefferson's death.)

No country can know God's true blessings where a majority of its citizens do not understand that Catholicism is the one and only foundation of personal and social order, if they do not understand that the events of Our Lord's Sacred Passion, Death and Resurrection are meant to shape every aspect of our own lives without any exception at all.

How can anyone claim to love Our Lord while ignoring the truths contained in His Sacred Deposit of Faith or, as is the case in our own land today, promote sinful behavior under cover of the civil law?

Those who prefer to ignore Divine Revelation as It has been entrusted to the Catholic Church and/or who promote sinful behavior under cover of the civil law and applaud its spread through what is considered to be "popular culture" need to reflect on how each of our sins caused Him to suffer during His Passion and Death, a suffering that was shared perfectly by His Most Blessed Mother.

Into the Garden of Gethsemane

Only a handful of genuine mystics have understood the depths of the sorrows that our sins, both Mortal and Venial, caused Our Blessed Lord and Saviour Jesus Christ and His Most Blessed Mother to suffer during the events of His Passion, Death and Burial. Oh, we can come to some degree of an intellectual comprehension of the fact that it was indeed the thought of coming into contact with the very antithesis of Our Lord's Sacred Divinity, our own sins(!), our sins in His Sacred Humanity that caused Him to sweat droplets of His Most Precious Blood as He beseeched His Co-Equal Father in Heaven to take the Chalice of suffering away from Him. To even begin to enter into even a tiny, minuscule portion of a true understanding of the horrors to which our sins caused Our Lord and His Most Blessed Mother to suffer during the events of His Passion and Death, therefore, we need the assistance of spiritual masters such as the late Father Frederick Faber of the Brompton Oratory of Saint Philip Neri.

Consider these powerful words of Father Faber's, contained in *The Foot of the Cross* (published originally as The Dolors of Mary in England in 1857):

> The Passion may be said to begin on the Thursday in Holy Week in the house of Lazarus at Bethany. Mary, as might have been expected, opened the long avenue of sorrows, great epochs in substance, though brief in time. Jesus had entered Jerusalem on Palm Sunday in the modesty of His well-known triumph. He had spent that day teaching in the temple, as well as the following Monday and Tuesday, returning however to Bethany at nights, as no one in Jerusalem had the courage to offer Him hospitality, as the rulers were incensed with Him because of the recent resurrection of Lazarus, and none of those who had cried Hosanna on Sunday had the courage to put themselves forward individually and so draw the resentful notice of the chief priests upon them. The Wednesday He is supposed to have spent in prayer on the Mount of Olives, and to have seen the elect of all ages of the world pass before Him in procession, while He prayed severally for each. Judas meanwhile was

arranging his treachery with the rulers. It is supposed also that our Blessed Saviour spent the Wednesday night out of doors praying in the recesses of the hill. On the Thursday morning He went to Bethany to bid His Mother farewell, and to obtain her consent to His Passion, as He had done before His Incarnation. Not that it was necessary in the first case as it was in the last, but it was fitting and convenient to the perfection of His filial obedience. Sister Mary of Agreda in her revelations describes the affecting scene, how Jesus knelt to His Mother, and begged her blessing, how she refused to bless her God, and fell upon her knees and worshiped Him as her Creator, how He persisted, how they both remained upon their knees, and how at last she blessed Him, and He blessed her. Who can doubt but that He also enriched with a special blessing His beloved Magdalen, the first and most favoured of all the daughters of Mary? He then went to Jerusalem, whither His Mother followed Him, together with Magdalen, in order that she might receive the Blessed Sacrament. The last Supper, the First Mass, took place that night, our Lord's first unbloody Sacrifice, to be followed on the morrow by the dreadful one of blood.

By a miraculous grace she assists, in spirit at the Agony in the Garden, sees our Lord's Heart unveiled throughout, and feels in herself, and according to her measure, a corresponding agony. She sees the treachery of Judas consummated, in spite of her intense prayers for that unhappy soul. Then the curtain falls; the vision grows dim; she is left for a while to the anguish of uncertainty. With the brave, gentle Magdalen, she goes forth into the streets. She tries to gain admittance both to the houses of Annas and Caiaphas, but is repulsed, as she was at Bethlehem three-and-thirty years ago. She hears the voice of Jesus; she hears also the blow given to her Beloved. Jesus is put in prison for the night; and St. John comes forth, and leads our Blessed Mother home to the house in which the last Supper had been eaten. At all the horrors of the morning she is present. She hears the sound of the scourging, and sees Him at the pillar, and the people around Him sprinkled with His Blood. She hears the gentle murmurs, the almost inaudible bleatings, of her spotless Lamb; she hears them, and Omnipotence commands her still to live. In spirit--if not in bodily presence--she sees the guards of Herod mock the Everlasting. She has beheld the ruffians in the guard-room celebrate the cruel coronation of the Almighty King. She has seen the eyes of the All-Seing bandaged, and the offscouring of the people daring to bend the knee in derision before Him Who is one day to pronounce their endless doom. She has looked up to the steps of Pilate's hall, and has beheld--beautiful in His disfigurement--Him Who was a worm and no man, so had they trodden Him under foot, and mangled Him, and turned Him almost out of human shape by their atrocities. She heard Pilate say, "Behold the Man;" and verily there was need that some one should testify that He was man, who, if He had been only Man, could never have survived the crushing of the winepress which the threefold pressure--of His Father, of demons, and of men--had inflicted upon Him. Then rose over the crowded piazza that wild yell of blasphemous rejection by His own people, which still rings in our ears, still echoes in history, still dwells even in that calm heaven above, in the Mother's ear who heard it in all the savage frightfulness of its reality. Now the Magdalen leads her home, whither John is to come with news of the sentence when it is passed. (Father Frederick Faber, *The Foot of the Cross*, published originally in England in 1857 under the title of *The Dolors of Mary*, republished by TAN Books and Publishers, pp. 204-206.)

Saints Peter, James and John had been taken up by Our Blessed Lord and Saviour Jesus Christ to the top of Mount Thabor when He was transfigured in glory before their very eyes, showing forth the glory that He possessed from all eternity with the Father and the Holy Ghost. He showed them this glory in the presence of Moses and Elias so as to take away the scandal of the Holy Cross when the appointed time, this very night upon which He entered into His Passion, had arrived. What was their response? They were sound asleep as He agonized in the Garden of Gethsemane, seeing before His Mind's Eye each and every single sin of each and every human being from Adam and Eve until the end of time, including each one of ours. Yes, Saints Peter, James and John slept their way through the first Holy Hour.

Human beings must make acts of thanksgiving for everything they have been given, especially for the crosses that are sent their way each day. Each cross is a gift from God. Each cross is a sign of His Provident Love for His rational creatures. Each cross is a sign of His ineffable Mercy for men, the very means by which they can pay back the temporal punishment due for our sins and to help the Poor Souls in Purgatory and to help convert the most hardened of sinners in this passing, mortal vale of tears, offering each cross to His Most Sacred Heart through the Sorrowful and Immaculate Heart of Mary as her consecrated slaves, freely relinquishing the merits earned by the patient endurance of various crosses so that those merits may be disposed of by Our Lady as she sees fit for the honor and glory of the Most Blessed Trinity and for the good of souls.

Remember, none of us suffers as his sins deserve. No cross we are asked to bear is the equal of what one of our least Venial Sins caused Our Blessed Lord and Saviour Jesus Christ to suffer in His Sacred Humanity on the wood of the Holy Cross on Good Friday, and caused Our Lady's Sorrowful and Immaculate Heart to be thrust through and through with Seven Swords of Sorrow. We must thank God for our crosses. We must love the Cross of the Divine Redeemer, at which stood His Most Blessed Mother with such great valor and dignity as she brought us to birth spiritually as the adopted sons and daughters of the Living God.

And it is the Holy Cross that must be omnipresent in the view of men lest they worship figurative golden calves and make of their bread and circuses the very purpose of human existence as their lives are wasted in worldly pursuits and pleasures and the merit that they could have earned for bearing their share of the hardship which the Gospel entails is lost for all eternity along with their own souls, which have been redeemed at so great a cost.

The Most Solemn Day of the Year

The most powerful sermon ever preached was given by Our Blessed Lord and Savior Jesus Christ as He hung on the gibbet of the Holy Cross for three hours, nailed there by our sins having transcended time. Our Lord spoke very few words as He died a painful death. The power in His preaching was the suffering He endured to pay back in His Sacred Humanity the debt of our own sins to Himself in His Infinity as God. His death on this very day destroyed the power of sin and eternal death forever, making it possible for each of us to join the Good Thief in Heaven if only we persevere to the point of our dying breaths in states of Sanctifying Grace. The Paschal Lamb, Who had instituted the New and Eternal Covenant at the Last Supper, now ratifies the New Covenant in His Most Precious Blood as He, the new Moses, effects the New and Eternal Passover from sin and death to eternal life with Him for all eternity in Heaven.

Our Lord had been betrayed by one of His chosen Apostles, Judas Iscariot, and denied by His Vicar three times. He was tried before the Sanhedrin as lying witnesses testified against Him. He spent the night in jail prior to being taken before the Roman governor, Pontius Pilate, who desperately wanted to find a way to release Him while at the same time appeasing his Jewish collaborators in the Roman occupation of the Holy Land, the Pharisees. He was scourged and crowned with thorns, suffering the loss of massive quantities of His Most Precious Blood. He was tormented by the crowd, which was motivated by our own sins, and condemned to death as an insurrectionist, Barabbas, promising political salvation, was released in His place. He picked up His heavy Cross to carry it on the Via Dolorosa en route to Calvary, where He encountered His Most Blessed Mother, whose suffering in Her Sorrowful and Immaculate Heart was a perfect participation in His own work of Redemption.

Good Friday belongs in a special way to Our Lady. She was present at the foot of the Cross as she gave birth to us as the adopted sons and daughters of the living God. She is present--along with all of the angels and saints--at every offering of the Holy Sacrifice of the Mass, which is the unbloody re-presentation of her Divine Son's one Sacrifice to the Father in Spirit and in Truth. We must keep close to her this day, calling to mind that the perfection of the communion between her own Immaculate Heart and the Sacred Heart of her Divine Son caused her to suffer as no purely human being could ever suffer. She kept a silent vigil by the foot of the Cross. We must mirror her silence this day, placing ourselves totally in her maternal care so that we will grieve-- truly grieve--for each of our sins and that we will resolve to have such a perfect love for God that even the thought of sin may become as repulsive to us as it was for saints such as the Little Flower, Saint Therese of Lisieux.

Saint Alphonsus de Liguori described Our Lady's sorrows on Good Friday in his *Victories of the Martyrs*:

> We have now to witness a new kind of martyrdom--a Mother condemned to see an innocent Son, and one whom she loves with the whole affection of her soul, cruelly tormented and put to death before her own eyes.

> There stood by the cross of Jesus His Mother. St. John believed that in these words he had said enough of Mary's martyrdom. Consider her at the foot of the cross in the presence of her dying Son, and then see if there be a sorrow like unto her sorrow. Let us remain for awhile this day on Calvary, and consider the fifth sword which, in the death of Jesus, transfixed the heart of Mary.

> As soon as our agonized Redeemer had reached the Mount of Calvary, the executioners stripped Him of His clothes, and piercing His hands and feet "not with sharp but with blunt nails," as St. Bernard says, to torment Him more, they fastened Him on the cross. Having crucified Him, they planted the cross, and thus left Him to die. The executioners left Him; but not so Mary. She then drew nearer to the cross, to be present at His death; "I did not leave Him (thus the Blessed Virgin revealed to St. Bridget), "but stood nearer to the cross."

"But what doth it avail thee, O Lady," says St. Bonaventure, "to go to Calvary, and see this Son expire? Shame should have prevented thee; for His disgrace was thine, since thou were His Mother. At least, horror of witnessing such a crime as the crucifixion of a God by His own creatures should have prevented thee from going there." But the same saint answers, "Ah, they heart did not then think of its own sorrows, but of the sufferings and death of thy dear Son: and therefore thou wouldst thyself be present, at least to compassionate Him. "Ah, true Mother," says Abbot William, "most loving Mother, whom not even the fear of death could separate from thy beloved Son!"

But, O God, what a cruel sight was it there to behold this Son in agony on the cross, and at its foot this Mother in agony, suffering all the torments endured by her Son! Listen to the words in which Mary revealed to St. Bridget the sorrowful state in which she saw her dying Son on the Cross: "My dear Jesus was breathless, exhausted, and in his last agony on the cross; His eyes were sunk, half-closed, and lifeless; His lips hanging, and His mouth open; His cheeks hollow and drawn in; His face elongated, His nose sharp, His countenance sad; His head had fallen on His breast, His hair was black with blood, His stomach collapsed, His arms and legs stiff, and His whole body covered with wounds and blood."

All these sufferings of Jesus were also those of Mary; "Every torture inflicted on the body of Jesus," says St. Jerome, "was a wound in the heart of the Mother." "Whoever then was present on the Mount of Calvary," says St. John Chrysostom, "might see two altars, on which two great sacrifices were consummated; the one in the body of Jesus, the other in the heart of Mary." Nay, better still may we say with St. Bonaventure, "there was but one altar--that of the cross of the Son, on which, together with his divine Lamb, the victim, this Mother was also sacrificed;" therefore the saint asks this Mother, "O Lady, where art thou? near the cross? thyself with thy Son." St. Augustine assures us of the same thing: "The Cross and nails of the Son were also those of His Mother; with Christ crucified the Mother was also crucified." Yes; for, as St. Bernard says, "Love inflicted on the heart of Mary the tortures caused by nails in the body of Jesus." So much so, that, as St. Bernardine writes, "At the same time that the Son sacrificed His body, the Mother sacrificed her soul." (Saint Alphonsus de Liguori, *Victories of the Martyrs*.)

Whenever anyone of us believes that we have received a cross that is "too heavy" for us we should review these words from Saint Alphonsus Liguori. All we need to do is to look at the Cross, which is the true book of learning, and to recognize the simple fact that there is nothing--and I mean absolutely nothing--that we can suffer in this mortal life that is the equal of what one of our least Venial Sins caused Our Lord to suffer in His Sacred Humanity on the wood of the Cross. There is nothing that we can suffer that is the equal of what the suffering we imposed upon the God-Man caused His Most Blessed Mother to suffer in her Sorrowful and Immaculate Heart.

Good Friday reminds us to learn this lesson once and for all and to accept each and every cross that comes our way as having been perfectly tailored for us for all eternity to be given back to the Most Blessed Trinity through the Immaculate Heart of Mary with complete resignation and abandonment to the will of God. Yes, crosses hurt. They are meant to hurt.

Alas, nothing we endure compares to what our sins imposed upon the Divine Redeemer's Most Sacred

Heart and His Most Holy Mother's Sorrowful and Immaculate Heart. We must console them on this day of days, the day on which our salvation was wrought for us on the wood of the Holy Cross. True liberation from self-concern comes only when we surrender ourselves as the consecrated slaves of Our Lady's Sorrowful and Immaculate Heart, which was pierced with a Fifth Sword of Sorrow at the moment of her Divine Son's death on the Cross, a death that made it possible for us to live forever in the glory of the Beatific Vision.

Good Friday, the only day in the liturgical year on which the Holy Sacrifice of the Mass is not offered and Our Lord's Real Presence is hidden from the faithful for public adoration after the Mass of the Presanctified, is reserved for calling to mind the horror of sin and the love and mercy Our Lord extended to us, His executioners, through His Most Sacred Heart, which we must seek to console as best as we can as the consecrated slaves of the Sorrowful and Immaculate Heart of Mary.

Every Mass gives us an opportunity to transcend time and to be present on the "right" side of the Cross to make up for the fact that our sins had placed us on the wrong side of the Cross nearly two millennia ago. And the Immemorial Mass of Tradition communicates the solemnity of Calvary in countless ways throughout the liturgical year, preparing us to enter more deeply into the mysteries of redemptive love shown us by God in the flesh as He was nailed to the Holy Cross.

The Immemorial Mass of Tradition in all of its essential elements was taught to the Apostles by Our Lord Himself between the time of His Resurrection on Easter Sunday and His Ascension to the Father's right hand in glory on Ascension Thursday. It is the Immemorial Mass of Tradition that communicates fully and completely the simple fact that every offering of Holy Mass is the extension of Calvary in time, which is why it can never become a carnival or an expression of community self-congratulations replete with jokes and back-slapping.

The Mass must reflect the reverence and solemnity of what happened once in time on Good Friday and is re-presented in an unbloody manner at the hands of an *alter Christus* acting *in persona Christi*. The perfection of the Immemorial Mass of Tradition in communicating this reverence and solemnity has been such over the centuries that it succeeded in producing scores upon scores of saints during epochs when few people could read. These saints learned from the eloquent lessons preached by the very solemnity and reverence communicated in all of the component parts of the Mass of the ages of the Roman Rite, just as Our Lord preached so eloquently as He suffered and died once in time on this very day.

Our Lord forgave His executioners, namely, each one of us as He died on the wood of the Holy Cross. He promised Heaven to the Good Thief. He gave Our Lady to be our Mother through Saint John the Beloved. He thirsted for our souls. We must simply surrender to Him, recognizing that we have the duty to carry the cross with love every day of our lives and to lift it high in the midst of a hostile and unbelieving world. Every moment of our lives has been redeemed by the shedding of Our Lord's Most Precious Blood on the wood of the Holy Cross. The graces He won for us on this very day are sufficient to endure whatever sufferings we are asked to bear, each of which is perfectly suited to be offered to Our Lady's Sorrowful and Immaculate Heart to be used precisely as she sees fit for the honor and glory of the Blessed Trinity and for the sanctification and salvation of human souls.

Consider the words of Saint Louis Marie de Montfort, found in his *Friends of the Cross*:

> Let him take up his cross, the one that is his. Let this man or this woman, rarely found and worth more than the entire world, take up with joy, fervently clasp in his arms and bravely set upon his shoulders this cross that is his own and not that of another; his own cross, the one that My wisdom designed for him in every detail of number, weight and measurement; his own cross whose four dimensions, its length, breadth, thickness and height, I very accurately gauged with My own hands; his own cross which all out of love for him I carved from a section of the very Cross I bore in Calvary; his cross, the grandest of all the gifts I have for My chosen ones on earth; his cross, made up in its thickness of temporal loss, humiliation, disdain, sorrow, illness and spiritual trial which My Providence will not fail to supply him with every day of his life; his cross, made up in its length of a definite period of days or months when he will have to bear with slander or be helplessly stretched out on a bed of pain, or forced to beg, or else a prey to temptation, to dryness, desolation and many another mental anguish; his cross, made up in its breadth of hard and bitter situations stirred up for him by his relatives, friends or servants; his cross, finally, made up in its depth of secret sufferings which I will have him endure nor will I allow him any comfort from created beings, for by My order they will turn from him too and even join Me in making him suffer.
>
> Let him carry it, and not drag it, not shoulder it off, not lighten it, nor hide it. Let him hold it high in hand, without impatience or peevishness, without voluntary complaint or grumbling without dividing or softening, without shame or human respect.
>
> Let him place it on his forehead and say with St. Paul: "God forbid that I should glory save in the Cross of Our Lord Jesus Christ."
>
> Let him carry it on his shoulders, after the example of Jesus Christ, and make it his weapon to victory and the scepter of his empire.
>
> Let him root it in his heart, and there change it into a fiery bush, burning day and night with the pure love of God, without being consumed.
>
> The cross: it is the cross he must carry for there is nothing more necessary, more useful, more agreeable and more glorious than suffering for Jesus Christ.
>
> All of you are sinners and there is not a single one who is not deserving of hell; I myself deserve it the most. These sins of ours must be punished either here or hereafter. If they are punished in this world, they will not be punished in the world to come.
>
> If we agree to God's punishing here below, this punishment will be dictated by love. For mercy, which holds sway in this world, will mete out the punishment, and not strict justice. This punishment will be light and momentary, blended with merit and sweetness and followed up with reward both in time and eternity. . . .
>
> Be resolved then, dear Friends of the Cross, to suffer every kind of cross without excepting or choosing any: all poverty, all injustice, all temporal loss, all illness, all humiliation, all

contradiction, all calumny, all spiritual dryness, all desolation, all interior and exterior trials. Keep saying, "My heart is ready, O God, my heart is ready." Be ready to be forsaken by everyone. Be ready to undergo hunger, thirst, poverty, nakedness, exile, imprisonment, the gallows and all kinds of torture, even though you are innocent of everything with which you may be charged. What if you were cast out of your own home like Job and Saint Elizabeth of Hungary; thrown, like this saint, into the mire; or dragged upon a manure pile like Job, malodorous and covered with ulcers, without anyone to bandage your wounds, without a morsel of bread, never refused to a horse or a dog? Add to these dreadful misfortunes all the temptations with which God allows the devil to prey upon you, without pouring upon your soul the least feeling of consolation. Firmly believe that this is the summit of divine glory and real happiness for a true, perfect Friend of the Cross. (Saint Louis de Montfort, *Friends of the Cross.*)

The first Adam lost our birthright to Heaven when he stretched out his arm to a tree. The second Adam stretched out His arms to a tree and made it possible to enter Heaven by being incorporated as members of His one, true Church and persisting in a state of sanctifying grace until the point of our dying breaths. What was lost for us on the Tree of the Knowledge of Good and Evil in the Garden of Eden was won back for us on the Tree of Life that is the Holy Cross. The One whose newborn Body was placed in a manger, a feeding trough for animals, was affixed by our sins to the wood of the Holy Cross, which has become the true manger from which we are fed His very own Body, Blood, Soul, and Divinity in the Most Blessed Sacrament. Oh, what sublime mysteries of love and mercy, of forgiveness and redemption. Our Lord, the Chief Priest and Victim of every Mass, extends His arms in the gesture of the Eternal High Priest on the horizontal beam of His Most Holy Cross to lift us up on the vertical beam to His Father in Heaven for all eternity:

> Now is the judgment of the world: now shall the prince of this world be cast out. And I, if I be lifted up from the earth, will draw all things to myself. (Now this he said, signifying what death he should die.) The multitude answered him: We have heard out of the law, that Christ abideth for ever; and how sayest thou: The Son of man must be lifted up? Who is this Son of man? Jesus therefore said to them: Yet a little while, the light is among you. Walk whilst you have the light, that the darkness overtake you not. And he that walketh in darkness, knoweth not whither he goeth. (John 12: 31-35.)

We must thank Our Lord for His gift to us of our Redemption, a gift which we did not and do not merit. We must thank Him for the gift of the true Church. And those of us who have embraced, perhaps much later than we should have, the glories of the Church's authentic tradition in the catacombs where shepherds make no concessions to conciliarism or to the nonexistent legitimacy of its false shepherds must thank Him and His Blessed Mother, the Co-Redemptrix and the Mediatrix of all graces, for helping us to see that the sermon preached on Calvary can be heard only if Catholics of the Roman Rite assist exclusively at the Immemorial Mass of Tradition, where everything points to the Cross of the Divine Redeemer--and from there to the glories of an unending Easter Sunday in Paradise if we remain faithful to the point of our dying breaths.

Pope Pius XII, writing in *Summi Pontificatus*, October 10, 1939, explained that there must be darkness over the earth in a world that does not acknowledge the Redemptive Act of the Divine Redeemer and makes sinful man and his naturalistic desires the measure of all things, that it is only the Catholic Faith that can unite men in a bond of true peace, that of the King of Calvary Himself:

The Holy Gospel narrates that when Jesus was crucified "there was darkness over the whole earth" (Matthew xxvii. 45); a terrifying symbol of what happened and what still happens spiritually wherever incredulity, blind and proud of itself, has succeeded in excluding Christ from modern life, especially from public life, and has undermined faith in God as well as faith in Christ. The consequence is that the moral values by which in other times public and private conduct was gauged have fallen into disuse; and the much vaunted civilization of society, which has made ever more rapid progress, withdrawing man, the family and the State from the beneficent and regenerating effects of the idea of God and the teaching of the Church, has caused to reappear, in regions in which for many centuries shone the splendors of Christian civilization, in a manner ever clearer, ever more distinct, ever more distressing, the signs of a corrupt and corrupting paganism: "There was darkness when they crucified Jesus" (Roman Breviary, Good Friday, Response Five).

Many perhaps, while abandoning the teaching of Christ, were not fully conscious of being led astray by a mirage of glittering phrases, which proclaimed such estrangement as an escape from the slavery in which they were before held; nor did they then foresee the bitter consequences of bartering the truth that sets free, for error which enslaves. They did not realize that, in renouncing the infinitely wise and paternal laws of God, and the unifying and elevating doctrines of Christ's love, they were resigning themselves to the whim of a poor, fickle human wisdom; they spoke of progress, when they were going back; of being raised, when they groveled; of arriving at man's estate, when they stooped to servility. They did not perceive the inability of all human effort to replace the law of Christ by anything equal to it; "they became vain in their thoughts" (Romans I. 21).

With the weakening of faith in God and in Jesus Christ, and the darkening in men's minds of the light of moral principles, there disappeared the indispensable foundation of the stability and quiet of that internal and external, private and public order, which alone can support and safeguard the prosperity of States.

It is true that even when Europe had a cohesion of brotherhood through identical ideals gathered from Christian preaching, she was not free from divisions, convulsions and wars which laid her waste; but perhaps they never felt the intense pessimism of today as to the possibility of settling them, for they had then an effective moral sense of the just and of the unjust, of the lawful and of the unlawful, which, by restraining outbreaks of passion, left the way open to an honorable settlement. In Our days, on the contrary, dissensions come not only from the surge of rebellious passion, but also from a deep spiritual crisis which has overthrown the sound principles of private and public morality.

Among the many errors which derive from the poisoned source of religious and moral agnosticism, We would draw your attention, Venerable Brethren, to two in particular, as being those which more than others render almost impossible or at least precarious and uncertain, the peaceful intercourse of peoples.

The first of these pernicious errors, widespread today, is the forgetfulness of that law of human solidarity and charity which is dictated and imposed by our common origin and by the equality of rational nature in all men, to whatever people they belong, and by the redeeming Sacrifice offered by Jesus Christ on the Altar of the Cross to His Heavenly Father on behalf of sinful mankind.

In fact, the first page of the Scripture, with magnificent simplicity, tells us how God, as a culmination to His creative work, made man to His Own image and likeness (cf. Genesis I. 26, 27); and the same Scripture tells us that He enriched man with supernatural gifts and privileges, and destined him to an eternal and ineffable happiness. It shows us besides how other men took their origin from the first couple, and then goes on, in unsurpassed vividness of language, to recount their division into different groups and their dispersion to various parts of the world. Even when they abandoned their Creator, God did not cease to regard them as His children, who, according to His merciful plan, should one day be reunited once more in His friendship (cf. Genesis xii. 3).

The Apostle of the Gentiles later on makes himself the herald of this truth which associates men as brothers in one great family, when he proclaims to the Greek world that God "hath made of one, all mankind, to dwell upon the whole face of the earth, determining appointed times, and the limits of their habitation, that they should seek God" (Acts xvii. 26, 27).

A marvelous vision, which makes us see the human race in the unity of one common origin in God "one God and Father of all, Who is above all, and through all, and in us all" (Ephesians iv. 6); in the unity of nature which in every man is equally composed of material body and spiritual, immortal soul; in the unity of the immediate end and mission in the world; in the unity of dwelling place, the earth, of whose resources all men can by natural right avail themselves, to sustain and develop life; in the unity of the supernatural end, God Himself, to Whom all should tend; in the unity of means to secure that end.

It is the same Apostle who portrays for us mankind in the unity of its relations with the Son of God, image of the invisible God, in Whom all things have been created: "In Him were all things created" (Colossians I. 16); in the unity of its ransom, effected for all by Christ, Who, through His Holy and most bitter passion, restored the original friendship with God which had been broken, making Himself the Mediator between God and men: "For there is one God, and one Mediator of God and men, the man Christ Jesus" (I Timothy ii. 5).

And to render such friendship between God and mankind more intimate, this same Divine and universal Mediator of salvation and of peace, in the sacred silence of the Supper Room, before He consummated the Supreme Sacrifice, let fall from His divine Lips the words which reverberate mightily down the centuries, inspiring heroic charity in a world devoid of love and torn by hate: "This is my commandment that you love one another, as I have loved you" (Saint John xv. 12).

These are supernatural truths which form a solid basis and the strongest possible bond of a union, that is reinforced by the love of God and of our Divine Redeemer, from Whom all receive salvation "for the edifying of the Body of Christ: until we all meet into the unity of faith, and of the knowledge of the Son of God, unto a perfect man, unto the measure of the age of the fullness of Christ" (Ephesians iv. 12, 13).

In the light of this unity of all mankind, which exists in law and in fact, individuals do not feel themselves isolated units, like grains of sand, but united by the very force of their nature and by their internal destiny, into an organic, harmonious mutual relationship which varies with the changing of times.

 And the nations, despite a difference of development due to diverse conditions of life and of culture, are not destined to break the unity of the human race, but rather to enrich and embellish it by the sharing of their own peculiar gifts and by that reciprocal interchange of goods which can be possible and efficacious only when a mutual love and a lively sense of charity unite all the sons of the same Father and all those redeemed by the same Divine Blood. (Pope Pius XII, *Summi Pontificatus*, October 10, 1939.)

The Cross of the Divine Redeemer, at which stood His Most Blessed Mother, is the one and only standard of human liberty. Crucifixes would be displayed very prominently in every community in the United States of America and every other nation in the world if He was recognized as King as He has revealed Himself to men exclusively through His Catholic Church. His Most Blessed Mother would be honored publicly in each community by all citizens with shrines and weekly Rosary processions. The overthrow of the Social Reign of Christ the King wrought by the Protestant Revolt against the Divine Plan that God Himself had instituted to effect man's return to Him through His Catholic Church and thus to order nations rightly along the paths of temporal justice pursued in light of man's own Last End, a revolt against both Christ the King and Mary our Immaculate Queen that was institutionalized by the rise of Judeo-Masonry and its religiously indifferentist civil state, has plunged mankind into barrenness and darkness and barbarism.

Father Benedict Baur wrote the following reflection about Good Friday, the most solemn day of the year:

> This is a day of mourning for the Church and for the faithful. The cross occupies the most prominent place in the liturgy of the day. It was on the cross that the Lord carried out the will of the Father to its last detail by giving up His life for our sins. He "loved me and delivered Himself for me" (Gal. 2: 20)

> "And when they were come to the place which is called Calvary, they crucified Him there; and the robbers, one on the right hand and the other on the left. And Jesus said: Father, forgive them, for they know not what they do. But they, dividing His garments, cast lots. And the people stood beholding, and the rulers with them derided Him saying: He saved others; let Him save Himself if He be the Christ, the elect of God. And the soldiers also mocked Him, coming to Him and offering Him vinegar, and saying: If Thou be the king of the Jews, save thyself. And also there was a superscription written over Him in letters of Greek and Latin and Hebrew: This is the King of the Jews. And one of those robbers who were hanged blasphemed him, saying: If Thou be the Christ save Thyself and us. . . . And it was almost the sixth hour; and there was darkness over all the earth until the ninth hour. And the sun was darkened, and the veil of the temple was rent in the midst. And Jesus, crying with a loud voice, said: Father, into Thy hands I commend My spirit. And saying this, He gave up the ghost" (Luke 23: 33 ff.)

"He humbled Himself, becoming obedient unto death, even to the death of the cross" (Phil. 2: 8). "Oh all ye that pass by the way attend and see if there is any sorrow like to my sorrow." (Lam. 1: 12)

The holy body has been torn by the cruel scourge until it is one mass of burning and bleeding wounds. The terrible crown of thorns has pierced His head, and He is consumed by thirst. To this unspeakable physical pain is added an anguish of soul that is even more terrible. He hears the shocking cry of His blinded people: "His blood be upon us and upon our children" (Matt. 27: 25). He hears the exultant yells of His enemies, and He looks into the future and sees that millions of men will repay suffering and His love with the basest ingratitude and the cruelest indifference. Why do they act thus? They have no time to attend to Christ. The grace which He won for them with such prodigal suffering and which so much love they neglect, abuse, and thus run the risk of losing their immortal souls. The immense inheritance which He purchased by His blood they allow to slip through their fingers. How this ingratitude and blindness tortures Him! With Mary and John we stand under His cross today to share His agony.

Christ died in our stead. "Surely he hath born our infirmities and carried our sorrows; and we have thought of him as it were a leper, and as one struck by God and afflicted. But he was wounded for our iniquities; he was bruised for our sins; the chastisement of our peace was upon him, and by his bruises we are healed. All we like sheep have gone astray, every one hath turned aside into his own way; and the Lord hath laid on him the iniquity of us all" (Isa. 53: 4-6). No mortal man could satisfy for the insult offered to God by sin; not even the highest of the angels could make adequate satisfaction. "Search not for a man to redeem you; Christ the God-man alone can perform works of sufficient value" (St. Basil). He takes our indebtedness upon Himself and lifts it up to His cross. "Knowing that you were not redeemed with corruptible things, as gold or silver, from your vain conversation of the tradition of your fathers; but with the precious blood of Christ as of a lamb unspotted and undefiled (1 Pet. 1: 18 f.). The penalties which Christ suffered should have been our penalty. "Greater love than this no man hath, that a man lay down his life for his friends" (John 15: 13).

Christ has died for each one of us personally. The wages of sin is death. All the penalties of sin press upon us at death. God's justice has not prepared anything so frightening as the prospect of death. Every creature shrinks from the thought of it. Nothing is so surely a punishment for sin as is death. Death cuts the bonds that secure the body and soul to the earth, just as sin first severed the bond which bound men to God. Christ the Lord delivers Himself up freely to death for our sake. His love is "strong as death." His submission to this most terrifying of God's punishments is the highest token of His love. He chooses the most terrible prospect of death that He may give me the surest sign of His love. In giving over His body to death, He destroys the body of sin and death on the cross. Having bathed mankind in His Precious Blood, He has provided humanity with a new and holy body. Men thus reborn are worthy to become the sons of God and merit eternal life and eternal glory.

Christ died for us on the cross. What a mysterious dispensation of God's providence! The unjust man commits the sin, but the Just One satisfies for it. The guilty one escapes the penalty of sin, but the Innocent One pays the penalty. What a contrast between the wickedness of man, and the goodness and justice and mercy of God! God has done all this for us: what we have done for Him? (Father Benedict Baur, *The Light of the World*, Volume I, pp. 424-426.)

A world that n o t does live in the shadow of the Holy Cross, which must, as noted just before, be omnipresent in our mind's eye and in public view, will always be in the grip of the devil, who knows that the Cross is the instrument of his defeat as he seeks mightily to keep men from this knowledge so that they and their nations will refuse to submit to the Divine Redeemer Who hung upon It, Christ the King, as He has revealed Himself us through the true Church that He founded upon the Rock of Peter, the Pope.

When about to ascend into heaven He sends His Apostles in virtue of the same power by which He had been sent from the Father; and he charges them to spread abroad and propagate His teaching. "All power is given to Me in Heaven and in earth. Going therefore teach all nations....teaching them to observe all things whatsoever I have commanded you" (Matt. xxviii., 18-1920). So that those obeying the Apostles might be saved, and those disobeying should perish. "He that believeth and is baptized shall be saved, but he that believed not shall be condemned" (Mark xvi., 16). But since it is obviously most in harmony with God's providence that no one should have confided to him a great and important mission unless he were furnished with the means of properly carrying it out, for this reason Christ promised that He would send the Spirit of Truth to His Disciples to remain with them for ever. "But if I go I will send Him (the Paraclete) to you....But when He, the Spirit of Truth is come, He will teach you all truth" John xvi., 7 13). "And I will ask the Father, and He shall give you another Paraclete, that he may abide with you for ever, the Spirit of Truth" (Ibid. xiv., 16-17). "He shall give testimony of Me, and you shall give testimony" (Ibid. xv., 26-27). Hence He commands that the teaching of the Apostles should be religiously accepted and piously kept as if it were His own - "He who hears you hears Me, he who despises you despises Me" (Luke x., 16). Wherefore the Apostles are ambassadors of Christ as He is the ambassador of the Father. "As the Father sent Me so also I send you" John xx., 21). Hence as the Apostles and Disciples were bound to obey Christ, so also those whom the Apostles taught were, by God's command, bound to obey them. And, therefore, it was no more allowable to repudiate one iota of the Apostles' teaching than it was to reject any point of the doctrine of Christ Himself. (Pope Leo XIII, *Satis Cognitum*, June 29, 1896.)

These words of Pope Leo XIII aptly summarize the meaning of Our Lord's Ascension into Heaven, marking the presence of a corporeal being there. Our Lord, Who had become Man in His Most Blessed Mother's Virginal and Immaculate Womb at the Annunciation by the power of God the Holy Ghost, returned to Heaven with His glorified Body, thus preparing a place for all of the elect who die in a state of Sanctifying Grace and whose bodies will be raised up incorrupt and glorious on the Last Day to take their place with Him and His Most Blessed Mother, who had the singular privilege of being Assumed into Heaven body and soul upon her death.

It was on Ascension Thursday that Our Blessed Lord and Savior Jesus Christ, after having instructed the Eleven for forty days following His Resurrection from the dead on Easter Sunday morning, including teaching them how to offer the Mass of the ages, gave His Apostles the commandment to baptize all men and to teach all nations. There is no time limit on this commandment. It is in force until He comes again in glory with a blare of trumpet blasts and the choirs of angels on the Last Day to judge the living and the dead.

The mission of converting souls to the true Faith founded upon the Rock of Peter, the Pope, however, could not begin until the Third Person of the Blessed Trinity, the Holy Ghost, descended upon them--and our dear Blessed Mother--in tongues of flame ten days later, on Pentecost Sunday. The Apostles, adding Matthias to their number to replace the traitor, Judas Iscariot, spent nine days in prayer to prepare for the coming of the Paraclete upon them, having no idea at all what a marvelous transformation He would make in their lives and how He would enlighten their intellects to understand everything that Our Blessed Lord and Saviour Jesus Christ had taught them and to strengthen their wills to act perfectly in accord with His truths in cooperation with the graces that had been won for them--and for all men--on the wood of the Holy Cross.

The good of the world depends upon the conversion of all men to Catholicism. Our own good as individual Catholics depends upon our daily conversion away from sin and to a greater love of the Blessed Trinity with every beat of our hearts, consecrated as they must be to the Immaculate Heart of Mary and to the Most Sacred Heart of Jesus. The state of the Church and of the world begins with us. Each of us plays our own role in building up or tearing down the Church Militant here on earth. Our human condition is such that we do a little bit of both in our lives, perhaps more of the latter than the former, although we will not see ourselves as we truly are until our lives are reflected in the Mirror of Divine Justice Himself at the moment of our Particular Judgments.

The good of the world depends upon the conversion of all nations to Catholicism, the heresies of conciliarism notwithstanding, as the fruit of the conversion of all men to the true Faith. Pope Leo XIII put it this way in *A Review of His Pontificate*, March 19, 1902:

> So society in its foolhardy effort to escape from God has rejected the Divine order and Revelation; and it is thus withdrawn from the salutary efficacy of Christianity which is manifestly the most solid guarantee of order, the strongest bond of fraternity, and the inexhaustible source of all public and private virtue. This sacrilegious divorce has resulted in bringing about the trouble which now disturbs the world. Hence it is the pale of the Church which this lost society must re-enter, if it wishes to recover its well-being, its repose, and its salvation.

> Just as Christianity cannot penetrate into the soul without making it better, so it cannot enter into public life without establishing order. With the idea of a God Who governs all, Who is infinitely wise, good, and just, the idea of duty seizes upon the consciences of men. It assuages sorrow, it calms hatred, it engenders heroes. If it has transformed pagan society--and that transformation was a veritable resurrection--for barbarism disappeared in proportion as Christianity extended its sway, so, after the terrible shocks which unbelief has given to the world in our days, it will be able to put that world again on the true road, and bring back to order the States and peoples of modern times. But the return of Christianity will not be efficacious and complete if it does not restore the world to a sincere love of the one Holy Catholic and Apostolic Church. In the Catholic Church Christianity is Incarnate. It identifies itself with that perfect, spiritual, and, in its own order, sovereign society, which is the Mystical Body of Jesus Christ and which has for Its visible head the Roman Pontiff, successor of the Prince of the Apostles. It is the continuation of the mission of the Savior, the daughter and the heiress of His Redemption. It has preached the Gospel, and has defended it at the price of Its blood, and strong in the Divine assistance and of that immortality which has been promised It, It makes no terms with error but remains faithful to the commands which It has received, to carry the doctrine of Jesus Christ to the uttermost limits of the world and to the end of time, and to protect It in Its inviolable integrity. Legitimate dispenser of the teachings of the Gospel It does not reveal Itself only as the

consoler and Redeemer of souls, but It is still more the internal source of justice and charity, and the propagator as well as the guardian of true liberty, and of that equality which alone is possible here below. In applying the doctrine of its Divine Founder, It maintains a wise equilibrium and marks the true limits between the rights and privileges of society. The equality which it proclaims does not destroy the distinction between the different social classes It keeps them intact, as nature itself demands, in order to oppose the anarchy of reason emancipated from Faith, and abandoned to its own devices. The liberty which it gives in no wise conflicts with the rights of truth, because those rights are superior to the demands of liberty. Not does it infringe upon the rights of Justice, because those rights are superior to the claims of mere numbers or power. Nor does it assail the rights of God because they are superior to the rights of humanity. (Pope Leo XIII, *A Review of His Pontificate*, March 19, 1902.)

By way of re-emphasis here: "But the return of Christianity will not be efficacious and complete if it does not restore the world to a sincere love of the one Holy Catholic and Apostolic Church. In the Catholic Church Christianity is Incarnate." This is considerably different than what has been taught by the conciliar "popes." Has this eternal teaching, rooted in the very words of Our Lord to the Apostles on this very day, lost its force somehow? Judge for yourselves.

As was the case with the Apostles themselves, however, we have been charged by means of our Baptism with the same mission that was given to them this very day, Ascension Thursday, by Our Lord Himself. We have the mission to do what we can to convert our little corners of the world to Catholicism. The mission given us by God Himself in the baptismal font is to get home to Heaven as Catholics and to help as many other people, starting with our own families, to do so as well. We must keep this uppermost in the eyes of our souls even as we recognize the pitfalls of conciliarism and how it has helped to undermine, if not eclipse, the *sensus Catholicus* in the lives of so many Catholics around the world. We have no chance of planting even a few small seeds for the restoration of the Church and of Christendom in the world if we are not first and foremost seeking to Catholicize every aspect of our lives without any concessions to the spirit of the world, the flesh and the devil.

That is, we are meant to look Heavenward as we do the work that God has assigned to us here in this mortal vale of tears. Our every word and action must help to foster the attainment of our Last End in light of our First Cause. Everything we seek to do with the breath of life that God gives us must be inspired by a love for the true Faith.

We must aspire to ascend to Heaven every day in our thoughts, our deeds and words, starting with mental prayer immediately upon our arising and assisting at the Immemorial Mass of Tradition if we are blessed enough in these spiritually barren times to have access to this great treasure on a daily basis.

We must make our Morning Offering and seek to give all that we do to the Blessed Trinity through the Sorrowful and Immaculate Heart of Mary, recognizing that everything that happens to us, including all pains and difficulties and misunderstandings and humiliations and illnesses and tragedies, are opportunities to be united and thus conformed more closely to the Cross of the Divine Redeemer Himself.

A soul seeking to ascend to Heaven every day must long for some moments in adoration before his Beloved in His Real Presence in the Most Blessed Sacrament. Our ardor for possessing the glory of the Beatific Vision in Heaven for all eternity must prompt us to oblate our souls in fervent prayer before the King of Kings and the Lord of Lords, mindful that such time in prayer will help us to despise the world and all its allurements as we seek only Heavenly riches. A soul seeking to ascend to Heaven every day must meditate upon the mysteries of our salvation contained in Our Lady's Most Holy Rosary.

Jacobus de Voragine explained several of the benefits of Our Blessed Lord and Saviour Jesus Christ's Ascension into Heaven:

> The fifth benefit is our dignity. Very great indeed is our dignity, when our nature is exalted to the right hand of God! The angels, having in mind the dignity of mankind, forbade man to worship them, as we read in Apoc. 19:10: "I fell down at his feet to adore him. And he said to me, you must not do that. I am a fellow servant with you and our brethren." To this the Gloss adds: "[The angel] allowed himself to be adored, but after the Lord's ascension, seeing a man exalted above himself, he was afraid to receive adoration." Pope Leo, in a sermon on the Lord's ascension, says: "On this day the nature of our humanity was raised up beyond the height of every power to be seated with God the Father, in order that God's grace should become more wondrous, since what men had thought to have a just claim to their veneration had been removed from their sight, yet faith did not falter nor hope waver nor charity grow cool."
>
> The sixth fruit of the Lord's ascension is the strengthening of our hope; Heb. 4:14: "Having therefore a great high priest who has passed into the heavens, Jesus the Son of God, let us hold fast to the confession of our hope"; and Heb 6:18-19 (RSV): "That we who fled for refuge might have strong encouragement to seize the hope set before us. We have this as a sure and steadfast anchor of the soul, a hope that enters into the inner shrine behind the curtain, where Jesus has gone as a forerunner in our behalf." On this, Leo again: "Christ's ascension is our elevation, and where the glory of the head has gone before, there the hope of the body tends also."
>
> The seventh benefit is that the way is marked out for us; Mic. 2:13: "He shall go up that shall open the way before them." Augustine: "The Savior himself has become your way: arise and walk, you have the way, don't be sluggish!" The eighth fruit is the opening of the gate of heaven; for as the first Adam opened the gates of hell, so the second the gates of paradise. So the Church sings: "You overcame the pain of death and opened the kingdom of heaven to those who believe." The ninth is the preparation of the place; John 14:2 "I go to prepare a place for you." Augustine: "O Lord, do prepare what you are preparing; for you are preparing us for yourself and you are preparing yourself for us when you prepare a place for yourself in us and for us in yourself." (Jacobus de Voragine, *The Golden Legend*, translated by William Granger Ryan, Volume I, Princeton University Press, 1995, p. 298.)

There are so many pitfalls in the world today. Yes, our own fallen natures drag us down quite enough without any further pitfalls being placed in our way. This is quite true. It is easy for any one of us to slip on a figurative banana peel by making a "little" compromise with the spirit of the world or by thinking that there is some way in which we can help form the souls of our children by being blithe about the company they keep or permitting them to participate in the latest fads so that they will not feel "left out" amongst their peers. A Catholic home must be so oriented to the things of Heaven that the only thing that matters to our children is they will not want to do anything that will make them left out of Heaven at the moment of their deaths, which can occur at any time.

We live in a world today where one slip-up can ruin a young child's innocence forever. To seek to convert our little corners of the world so as to produce defenders and propagators of the Holy Faith we must remove the devil's tools, such as television and contemporary "music" and magazines, from our homes. We must not visit the homes of others who have such tools, recognizing that the children formed in these homes might be able to entice and thus to deform the souls of our children. This is not Jansenism. This is Catholicism.

The parents of Saint Therese of the Child Jesus and the Holy Faith, Louis and Zelie Martin, went to great lengths to protect their children from all pernicious influences. They wanted to foster religious vocations and to get their children home to Heaven. So must we. A happy family reunion in Heaven can only occur if the hard, daily planning for such a reunion is drawn up and then implemented in a Catholic home.

Naturalism pulls us down to the depths of the depravity of the world, which is why we must think and act and speak supernaturally at all times. Father Frederick Faber explained this in *The Precious Blood*:

> It is plain that some millions of sins in a day are hindered by the Precious Blood; and this is not merely a hindering of so many individual sins, but it is an immense check upon the momentum of sin. It is also a weakening of habits of sin, and a diminution of the consequences of sin. If then, the action of the Precious Blood were withdrawn from the world, sins would not only increase incalculably in number, but the tyranny of sin would be fearfully augmented, and it would spread among a greater number of people. It would wax so bold that no one would be secure from the sins of others. It would be a constant warfare, or an intolerable vigilance, to preserve property and rights. Falsehood would become so universal as to dissolve society; and the homes of domestic life would be turned into wards either of a prison or a madhouse. We cannot be in the company of an atrocious criminal without some feeling of uneasiness and fear. We should not like to be left alone with him, even if his chains were not unfastened. But without the Precious Blood, such men would abound in the world. They might even become the majority. We know of ourselves, from glimpses God has once or twice given us in life, what incredible possibilities of wickedness we have in our souls. Civilization increases these possibilities. Education multiplies and magnifies our powers of sinning. Refinement adds a fresh malignity. Men would thus become more diabolically and unmixedly bad, until at last earth would be a hell on this side of the grave. There would also doubtless be new kinds of sins and worse kinds. Education would provide the novelty, and refinement would carry it into the region of the unnatural. All highly-refined and luxurious developments of heathenism have fearfully illustrated this truth. A wicked barbarian is like a beast. His savage passions are violent but intermitting, and his necessities of sin do not appear to grow. Their circle is limited. But a highly-educated sinner, without the restraints of religion, is like a demon. His sins are less confined to himself. They involve others in their

misery. They require others to be offered as it were in sacrifice to them. Moreover, education, considered simply as an intellectual cultivation, propagates sin, and makes it more universal.

The increase of sin, without the prospects which the faith lays open to us, must lead to an increase of despair, and to an increase of it upon a gigantic scale. With despair must come rage, madness, violence, tumult, and bloodshed. Yet from what quarter could we expect relief in this tremendous suffering? We should be imprisoned in our own planet. The blue sky above us would be but a dungeon-roof. The greensward beneath our feet would truly be the slab of our future tomb. Without the Precious Blood there is no intercourse between heaven and earth. Prayer would be useless. Our hapless lot would be irremediable. It has always seemed to me that it will be one of the terrible things in hell, that there are no motives for patience there. We cannot make the best of it. Why should we endure it? Endurance is an effort for a time; but this woe is eternal. Perhaps vicissitudes of agony might be a kind of field for patience. But there are no such vicissitudes. Why should we endure, then? Simply because we must; and yet in eternal things this is not a sort of necessity which supplies a reasonable ground for patience. So in this imaginary world of rampant sin there would be no motives for patience. For death would be our only seeming relief; and that is only seeming, for death is anything but an eternal sleep. Our impatience would become frenzy; and if our constitutions were strong enough to prevent the frenzy from issuing in downright madness, it would grow into hatred of God, which is perhaps already less uncommon than we suppose.

An earth, from off which all sense of justice had perished, would indeed be the most disconsolate of homes. The antediluvian earth exhibits only a tendency that way; and the same is true of the worst forms of heathenism. The Precious Blood was always there. Unnamed, unknown, and unsuspected, the Blood of Jesus has alleviated every manifestation of evil which there has ever been just as it is alleviating at this hour the punishments of hell. What would be our own individual case on such a blighted earth as this? All our struggles to be better would be simply hopeless. There would be no reason why we should not give ourselves up to that kind of enjoyment which our corruption does substantially find in sin. The gratification of our appetites is something; and that lies on one side, while on the other side there is absolutely nothing. But we should have the worm of conscience already, even though the flames of hell might yet be some years distant. To feel that we are fools, and yet lack the strength to be wiser--is not this precisely the maddening thing in madness? Yet it would be our normal state under the reproaches of conscience, in a world where there was no Precious Blood. Whatever relics of moral good we might retain about us would add most sensibly to our wretchedness. Good people, if there were any, would be, as St. Paul speaks, of all men the most miserable; for they would be drawn away from the enjoyment of this world, or have their enjoyment of it abated by a sense of guilt and shame; and there would be no other world to aim at or to work for. To lessen the intensity of our hell without abridging its eternity would hardly be a cogent motive, when the temptations of sin and the allurements of sense are so vivid and strong.

What sort of love could there be, when we could have no respect? Even if flesh and blood made us love each other, what a separation death would be! We should commit our dead to the ground without a hope. Husband and wife would part with the fearfullest certainties of a reunion more terrible than their separation. Mothers would long to look upon their little ones in the arms of death, because their lot would be less woeful than if they lived to offend God with their developed reason and intelligent will. The sweetest feelings of our nature would become unnatural, and the most honorable ties be dishonored. Our best instincts would lead us into our worst dangers. Our hearts would have to learn to beat another way, in order to avoid the dismal consequences which our affections would bring upon ourselves and others. But it is needless to go further into these harrowing details. The world of the heart, without the Precious Blood, and with an intellectual knowledge of God, and his punishments of sin, is too fearful a picture to be drawn with minute fidelity.

But how would it fare with the poor in such a world? They are God's chosen portion upon the earth. He chose poverty himself, when He came to us. He has left the poor in his place, and they are never to fail from the earth, but to be his representatives there until the doom. But, if it were not for the Precious Blood, would any one love them? Would any one have a devotion to them, and dedicate his life to merciful ingenuities to alleviate their lot? If the stream of almsgiving is so insufficient now, what would it be then? There would be no softening of the heart by grace; there would be no admission of the obligation to give away in alms a definite portion of our incomes; there would be no desire to expiate sin by munificence to the needy for the love of God. The gospel makes men's hearts large; and yet even under the gospel the fountain of almsgiving flows scantily and uncertainly. There would be no religious orders devoting themselves with skillful concentration to different acts of spiritual and corporal mercy. Vocation is a blossom to be found only in the gardens of the Precious Blood. But all this is only negative, only an absence of God. Matters would go much further in such a world as we are imagining.

Even in countries professing to be Christian, and at least in possession of the knowledge of the gospel, the poor grow to be an intolerable burden to the rich. They have to be supported by compulsory taxes; and they are in other ways a continual subject of irritated and impatient legislation. Nevertheless, it is due to the Precious Blood that the principle of supporting them is acknowledged. From what we read in heathen history--even the history of nations renowned for political wisdom, for philosophical speculation, and for literary and artistic refinement--it would not be extravagant for us to conclude that, if the circumstances of a country were such as to make the numbers of the poor dangerous to the rich, the rich would not scruple to destroy them, while it was yet in their power to do so. Just as men have had in France and England to war down bears and wolves, so would the rich war down the poor, whose clamorous misery and excited despair should threaten them in the enjoyment of their power and their possessions. The numbers of the poor would be thinned by murder, until it should be safe for their masters to reduce them into slavery. The survivors would lead the lives of convicts or of beasts. History, I repeat, shows us that this is by no means an extravagant supposition.

Such would be the condition of the world without the Precious Blood. As generations succeeded each other, original sin would go on developing those inexhaustible malignant powers which come from the almost infinite character of evil. Sin would work earth into hell. Men would become devils, devils to others and to themselves. Every thing which makes life tolerable, which counteracts any evil, which softens any harshness, which sweetens any bitterness, which causes the machinery of society to work smoothly, or which consoles any sadness--is simply due to the Precious Blood of Jesus, in heathen as well as in Christian lands. It changes the whole position of an offending creation to its Creator. It changes, if we may dare in such a matter to speak of change, the aspect of God's immutable perfections toward his human children. It does not work merely in a spiritual sphere. It is not only prolific in temporal blessings, but it is the veritable cause of all temporal blessings whatsoever. We are all of us every moment sensibly enjoying the benignant influence of the Precious Blood. Yet who thinks of all this? Why is the goodness of God so hidden, so imperceptible, so unsuspected? Perhaps because it is so universal and so excessive, that we should hardly be free agents if it pressed sensibly upon us always. God's goodness is at once the most public of all his attributes, and at the same time the most secret. Has life a sweeter task than to seek it, and to find it out?

Men would be far more happy, if they separated religion less violently from other things. It is both unwise and unloving to put religion into a place by itself, and mark it off with an untrue distinctness from what we call worldly and unspiritual things. Of course there is a distinction, and a most important one, between them; yet it is easy to make this distinction too rigid and to carry it too far. Thus we often attribute to nature what is only due to grace; and we put out of sight the manner and degree in which the blessed majesty of the Incarnation affects all created things. But this mistake is forever robbing us of hundreds of motives for loving Jesus. We know how unspeakably much we owe to him; but we do not see all that it is not much we owe him, but all, simply and absolutely all. We pass through times and places in life, hardly recognizing how the sweetness of Jesus is sweetening the air around us and penetrating natural things with supernatural blessings.

Hence it comes to pass that men make too much of natural goodness. They think too highly of human progress. They exaggerate the moralizing powers of civilization and refinement, which, apart from grace, are simply tyrannies of the few over the many, or of the public over the individual soul. Meanwhile they underrate the corrupting capabilities of sin, and attribute to unassisted nature many excellences which it only catches, as it were by the infection, by the proximity of grace, or by contagion, from the touch of the Church. Even in religious and ecclesiastical matters they incline to measure progress, or test vigor, by other standards rather than that of holiness. These men will consider the foregoing picture of the world without the Precious Blood as overdrawn and too darkly shaded. They do not believe in the intense malignity of man when drifted from God, and still less are they inclined to grant that cultivation and refinement only intensify still further this malignity. They admit the superior excellence of Christian charity; but they also think highly of natural philanthropy. But has this philanthropy ever been found where the indirect influences of the true religion, whether Jewish or Christian, had not penetrated? We may admire the Greeks for their exquisite refinement, and the Romans for the wisdom of their political moderation. Yet look at the position of children, of servants, of slaves, and of the poor, under both these systems, and see if, while extreme refinement only pushed sin to an extremity of foulness, the same exquisite culture did not also lead to a social cruelty and an individual selfishness which made life unbearable to the masses. Philanthropy is but a theft from the gospel, or rather a shadow, not a substance, and as unhelpful as shadows are want to be. . . .

I reckon failure to be the most universal unhappiness on earth. Almost everybody and every thing are failures--failures in their own estimation, even if they are not so in the estimation of others. Those optimists who always think themselves successful are few in number, and they for the most part fail in this at least, namely, that the cannot persuade the rest of the world of their success. Philanthropy can plainly do nothing here, even if it were inclined to try. But philanthropy is a branch of moral philosophy, and would turn away in disdain from unhappiness which it could prove to be unreasonable, even while it acknowledged it to be universal. It is simply true that few men are successful; and of those few it is rare to find any who are satisfied with their own success. The multitude of men live with a vexatious sense that the promise of their lives remains unfulfilled. Either outward circumstances have been against them, or they have been misappreciated, or they have got out of their grooves unknowingly, or they have been the victims of injustice. What must all life be but a feverish   disappointment, if there be no eternity in view? The religious man is the only successful man. Nothing fails with him. Every shaft reaches the mark, if the mark be God. He has wasted no energies. Every hope has been fulfilled beyond his expectations. Every effort has been disproportionately rewarded. Every means has turned out marvelously to be an end, because it had God in it, Who is our single end. In piety, every battle is a victory, simple because it is a battle. The completest defeats have something of triumph in them; for it is a positive triumph to have stood up and fought for God at all. In short, no life is a failure which is lived for God; and all lives are failures which are lived for any other end. If it is part of any man's disposition to be peculiarly and morbidly sensitive to failure, he must regard it as an additional motive to be religious. Piety is the only invariable, satisfactory, genuine success. (Father Frederick Faber, *The Precious Blood*, published originally in England in 1860, republished by TAN Books and Publishers, pp. 53-59; 63.)

The task of ascending to Heaven in our thoughts, words and deeds every day is made difficult not only by the false spirits of the world, including the anti-Incarnational spirit of Americanism that took deep root in the soil of the United States of America.

The task of ascending to Heaven in our thoughts, words and deeds every day has been made more difficult by the fact that the false shepherds of the counterfeit church of conciliarism tell us all of the time that it is not absolutely necessary to urgently seek the conversion of all men to the Catholic Faith, no less to teach them that Faith as it has been handed down to us over the centuries from the Apostles themselves, who received it from Our Lord and were then enlightened by God the Holy Ghost to teach all nations.

The spirit of false ecumenism has robbed almost every conciliar "bishop" in the world of the understanding that he has the responsibility to seek the conversion of all non-Catholics in his diocesan boundaries to the true Church, outside of which there is no salvation and without which there is no true social order. Do the false "bishops" of the counterfeit church of conciliarism today understand that they have the obligation to baptize all men and to teach all nations?

Thus, we must see to it that we fulfill our own responsibilities to teach the Faith and to seek the conversion of all of the non-Catholics who cross our paths so that they can live every day as they ascend in their thoughts and prayers to Heaven. We can do this in a variety of ways. No one approach works with all people, which is why we pass out Miraculous Medals and Green Scapulars, trusting in Our Lady and pledging to her our continued prayers to her Immaculate Heart for the conversion of the people to whom we give (or on whose property we hide) these great sacramentals. And the two greatest ways we can help to bring people to the baptismal font--and/or to be confirmed as members of the true Church--is to have Masses said for them and remember them in our daily Rosaries without fail.

Indeed, Our Lady's Rosary is, after Holy Mass itself, the chief means by which our souls are lifted up to Heaven every day. Our meditation upon the mysteries of our very salvation will prompt us to cling all the more to Our Blessed Mother, who made possible our salvation by her perfect fiat to the will of the Father at the Annunciation. We can never say enough Rosaries in the course of a day. Not enough time? Make it. At least one set of mysteries must be prayed by a family together on their knees every day, all three if at all possible. Busy fathers and mothers can offer a decade here and a decade there as the day goes along. This is not impossible. Not if we want to possess Heaven for all eternity, that is. Not if we want to have our bodies rise up incorrupt and glorious on the Last Day and to ascend into Heaven for all eternity with our souls. No, it is not impossible at all.

Our Lady is, indeed, our life, our sweetness, and our hope. She will see us through all of the troubling times of our own lives. She will see us through all of the troubling times of apostasy and betrayal. She will help us to bear patiently the wrongs that others do us--and to do penance for the wrongs we do to others. She will help us to deal charitably with and to pray fervently for those who calumniate us. She will help us to pray for more sufferings and more humiliations so that we will be more and more configured to the Cross of her Divine Son, at Whose feet she stood so valiantly (and where she stands at every offering of the Holy Sacrifice of the Mass). She will help us to truly despise the world and all of its honors, seeking only the joys of Heaven, into which Our Blessed Lord and Saviour Jesus Christ Ascended on this very day, taking into Heaven that which He did not have from all eternity with His Co-Equal Father: the Sacred Humanity He received from His Most Blessed Mother by the power of God the Holy Ghost at the Annunciation, the Sacred Humanity with which He redeemed us on the wood of the Holy Cross, making it possible for to ascend to Heaven every day in our thoughts and to do so body and soul on the Last Day at the General Judgment of the Living and the Dead. That Last Day will be a time of a happy reconciliation with everyone, friend and foe, who has died in a state of Sanctifying Grace, which is why we must be careful in this mortal vale of tears to bear no other person any malice while always willing his good, which is his eternal salvation. Our Lady will help us, in other words, to raise our entire beings to God through her Immaculate Heart in this life so that we might share the joys she herself is privileged to experience in both body and soul in the unending Easter Sunday of glory that is Heaven.

Chapter VII
The Work of Holy Mother Church Begins

Pentecost Sunday marked the beginning of Holy Mother Church's missionary efforts to convert men and nations to the true Faith, the very birthday of Holy Mother Church. The Paraclete or Advocate promised by Our Blessed Lord and Saviour Jesus Christ proceeds forth from His Co-Eternal Father and Himself on this day, fifty days after His Resurrection from the dead on Easter Sunday and ten days following his glorious Ascension into Heaven on Ascension Thursday:

> But the Paraclete, the Holy Ghost, whom the Father will send in my name, he will teach you all things, and bring all things to your mind, whatsoever I shall have said to you. Peace I leave with you, my peace I give unto you: not as the world giveth, do I give unto you. Let not your heart be troubled, nor let it be afraid. You have heard that I said to you: I go away, and I come unto you. If you loved me, you would indeed be glad, because I go to the Father: for the Father is greater than I. And now I have told you before it comes to pass: that when it shall come to pass, you may believe. I will not now speak many things with you. For the prince of this world cometh, and in me he hath not any thing. (John 14: 26-30)

The first bishops, headed by the Visible Head of the Church on earth, Saint Peter, became bold proclaimers of the Gospel of Our Blessed Lord and Saviour Jesus Christ immediately following the descent of the Third Person of the Blessed Trinity, God the Holy Ghost, upon them and our dear Blessed Mother in tongues of flame in the same Upper Room in Jerusalem where Our Lord had instituted the priesthood and the Eucharist just fifty-three days before.

The Church's great zeal to seek with urgency the conversion of all non-Catholics to the true Church, outside of which there is no salvation and without which there can be no true social order, thus began on Pentecost Sunday and continued unabated until the ethos of the dark clouds of conciliarism, which emanated from spirits that are not so holy, began to hover over the life of Catholics from the 1960s to the present day. There is no way to reconcile the refusal of the false "popes" of the counterfeit church of conciliarism to seek, no less their prohibition on ordinary Catholics to seek the conversion of those steeped in the errors of Protestantism and Orthodoxy and Judaism and other false religions with the fidelity the Church exhibited from Pentecost Sunday to the false pontificate of Angelo Roncalli/John XXIII, which began on October 28, 1958.

The Apostles sought to effect the conversion of Jews and Gentiles alike to Catholicism. The Acts of the Apostles records this zeal for souls, a zeal that stands in stark contrast to the belief, expressed both in words and actions, of the conciliar "pontiffs" that those in false religions have no need to seek to be Catholic to save their souls.

The late Karol Wojtyla/John Paul II urged the followers of "Brother" Roger Schutz in Taize, France, in 1996 to be "faithful" to their denominational traditions, which begs the following question: If heretics and schismatics must be faithful to their false "traditions," why can't Catholics be faithful to theirs?

Joseph Ratzinger/Benedict XVI said Schutz, who never converted to the true Faith, had attained "eternal joy" following the latter's murder by a devoted follower in 2005 (Benedict Mourns Murder of Taizé's Brother Roger).

The Assisi events of 1986 and 2002 and 2011 would have been condemned by the Apostles as an exercise in idol worship.

So would Joseph Ratzinger/Benedict XVI's reception of symbols of false religions at the "Pope" John Paul II Cultural Center in Washington, District of Columbia, on Thursday, April 17, 2008.

So would Ratzinger/Benedict's praise given to mosques and his belief that false religions can be instruments in the building of the "better world."

The Apostles and the many millions of martyrs for the Faith who followed them preferred death rather than to do anything that even appeared to betray the Faith, no less praise the practitioners of false religions.

Most of the first fifteen or so chapters in The Acts of the Apostles deal directly with the efforts of the Apostles to preach the Gospel so as to win converts for the true Faith. Let the Holy Ghost, under Whose inspiration the Bible was written, speak for Himself in the fifth book of the New Testament, which was written by Saint Luke:

> And when the days of the Pentecost were accomplished, they were all together in one place: And suddenly there came a sound from heaven, as of a mighty wind coming, and it filled the whole house where they were sitting. And there appeared to them parted tongues as it were of fire, and it sat upon every one of them: And they were all filled with the Holy Ghost, and they began to speak with divers tongues, according as the Holy Ghost gave them to speak. Now there were dwelling at Jerusalem, Jews, devout men, out of every nation under heaven.

> And when this was noised abroad, the multitude came together, and were confounded in mind, because that every man heard them speak in his own tongue. And they were all amazed, and wondered, saying: Behold, are not all these, that speak, Galileans? And how have we heard, every man our own tongue wherein we were born? Parthians, and Medes, and Elamites, and inhabitants of Mesopotamia, Judea, and Cappadocia, Pontus and Asia, Phrygia, and Pamphylia, Egypt, and the parts of Libya about Cyrene, and strangers of Rome, Jews also, and proselytes, Cretes, and Arabians: we have heard them speak in our own tongues the wonderful works of God. And they were all astonished, and wondered, saying one to another: What meaneth this? But others mocking, said: These men are full of new wine. But Peter standing up with the eleven, lifted up his voice, and spoke to them: Ye men of Judea, and all you that dwell in Jerusalem, be this known to you, and with your ears receive my words. For these are not drunk, as you suppose, seeing it is but the third hour of the day:

> But this is that which was spoken of by the prophet Joel: And it shall come to pass, in the last days, (saith the Lord), I will pour out of my Spirit upon all flesh: and your sons and your daughters shall prophesy, and your young men shall see visions, and your old men shall dream dreams. And upon my servants indeed, and upon my handmaids will I pour out in those days of my spirit, and they shall prophesy. And I will shew wonders in the heaven above, and signs on the earth beneath: blood and fire, and vapour of smoke. The sun shall be turned into

darkness, and the moon into blood, before the great and manifest day of the Lord come.

And it shall come to pass, that whosoever shall call upon the name of the Lord, shall be saved. Ye men of Israel, hear these words: Jesus of Nazareth, a man approved of God among you, by miracles, and wonders, and signs, which God did by him, in the midst of you, as you also know: This same being delivered up, by the determinate counsel and foreknowledge of God, you by the hands of wicked men have crucified and slain. Whom God hath raised up, having loosed the sorrows of hell, as it was impossible that he should be holden by it. For David saith concerning him: I foresaw the Lord before my face: because he is at my right hand, that I may not be moved.

For this my heart hath been glad, and any tongue hath rejoiced: moreover my flesh also shall rest in hope. Because thou wilt not leave my soul in hell, nor suffer thy Holy One to see corruption. Thou hast made known to me the ways of life: thou shalt make me full of joy with thy countenance. Ye men, brethren, let me freely speak to you of the patriarch David; that he died, and was buried; and his sepulchre is with us to this present day. Whereas therefore he was a prophet, and knew that God hath sworn to him with an oath, that of the fruit of his loins one should sit upon his throne.

Foreseeing this, he spoke of the resurrection of Christ. For neither was he left in hell, neither did his flesh see corruption. This Jesus hath God raised again, whereof all we are witnesses. Being exalted therefore by the right hand of God, and having received of the Father the promise of the Holy Ghost, he hath poured forth this which you see and hear. For David ascended not into heaven; but he himself said: The Lord said to my Lord, sit thou on my right hand, Until I make thy enemies thy footstool.

Therefore let all the house of Israel know most certainly, that God hath made both Lord and Christ, this same Jesus, whom you have crucified. Now when they had heard these things, they had compunction in their heart, and said to Peter, and to the rest of the apostles: What shall we do, men and brethren? But Peter said to them: Do penance, and be baptized every one of you in the name of Jesus Christ, for the remission of your sins: and you shall receive the gift of the Holy Ghost. For the promise is to you, and to your children, and to all that are far off, whomsoever the Lord our God shall call. And with very many other words did he testify and exhort them, saying: Save yourselves from this perverse generation.

They therefore that received his word, were baptized; and there were added in that day about three thousand souls. And they were persevering in the doctrine of the apostles, and in the communication of the breaking of bread, and in prayers. And fear came upon every soul: many wonders also and signs were done by the apostles in Jerusalem, and there was great fear in all. And all they that believed, were together, and had all things common. Their possessions and goods they sold, and divided them to all, according as every one had need.

And continuing daily with one accord in the temple, and breaking bread from house to house, they took their meat with gladness and simplicity of heart; Praising God, and having favour with all the people. And the Lord increased daily together such as should be saved. (Acts 2: 1-47)

The first pope, Saint Peter, spoke a little differently than did Karol Wojtyla/John Paul II in 1986 when he visited a synagogue in Rome. He spoke a little differently than did Joseph Ratzinger/Benedict XVI when he spoke in a synagogue in Cologne, Germany, on Friday, August 19, 2005, and as the now retired "pope" did at the Rome Synagogue on January 17, 2010, and as Jorge Mario Bergoglio/Francis has done so throughout the course of his supposed "pontificate."

By saying that the counterfeit church of conciliarism is committed to "tolerance, respect, friendship and peace between all peoples, cultures and religions" the conciliar "popes" have been saying that all active proselytizing of those outside of her ranks must be avoided. And what is this nonsense about a "theological evaluation of the relationship between Judaism and Christianity"? Our Lord has revealed Himself to be the Way, the Truth, and the Life. End of evaluation. People either accept Him as He has revealed Himself through His true Church or they do not. Period.

Saint Peter did not believe that any "evaluation" had to take place before he preached to the Jews to urge them to convert to Catholicism.

Prompted by the immediate indwelling of God the Holy Ghost upon his soul, Saint Peter proclaimed the Gospel out of fidelity to the Divine Master and out of true love for the salvation of the souls of his own Jewish brethren. There was no ambiguous call for "the conversion of Israel." There was simply a call for individual mean to "do penance, and be baptized every one of you in the name of Jesus Christ, for the remission of your sins: and you shall receive the Holy Ghost." There was nothing ambiguous about the Apostles. They were willing to suffer everything, including death itself, to proclaim the Name of Our Lord and Saviour Jesus Christ in the midst of a hostile world.

Chapter 5 of The Acts of the Apostles records the aftermath of Saint Peter's curing of a lame man:

> And by the hands of the apostles were many signs and wonders wrought among the people. And they were all with one accord in Solomon's porch. But of the rest no man durst join himself unto them; but the people magnified them. And the multitude of men and women who believed in the Lord, was more increased: Insomuch that they brought forth the sick into the streets, and laid them on beds and couches, that when Peter came, his shadow at the least, might overshadow any of them, and they might be delivered from their infirmities.
>
> And there came also together to Jerusalem a multitude out of the neighboring cities, bringing sick persons, and such as were troubled with unclean spirits; who were all healed. Then the high priest rising up, and all they that were with him, (which is the heresy of the Sadducees,) were filled with envy. And they laid hands on the apostles, and put them in the common prison. But an angel of the Lord by night opening the doors of the prison, and leading them out, said: Go, and standing speak in the temple to the people all the words of this life.
>
> Who having heard this, early in the morning, entered into the temple, and taught. And the high priest coming, and they that were with him, called together the council, and all the ancients of the children of Israel; and they sent to the prison to have them brought. But when the ministers came, and opening the prison, found them not there, they returned and told, Saying:

The prison indeed we found shut with all diligence, and the keepers standing before the doors; but opening it, we found no man within. Now when the officer of the temple and the chief priests heard these words, they were in doubt concerning them, what would come to pass. But one came and told them: Behold, the men whom you put in prison are in the temple standing, and teaching the people.

Then went the officer with the ministers, and brought them without violence; for they feared the people, lest they should be stoned. And when they had brought them, they set them before the council. And the high priest asked them, Saying: Commanding we commanded you, that you should not teach in this name; and behold, you have filled Jerusalem with your doctrine, and you have a mind to bring the blood of this man upon us. But Peter and the apostles answering, said: We ought to obey God, rather than men. The God of our fathers hath raised up Jesus, whom you put to death, hanging him upon a tree.

Him hath God exalted with his right hand, to be Prince and Saviour, to give repentance to Israel, and remission of sins. And we are witnesses of these things and the Holy Ghost, whom God hath given to all that obey him. When they had heard these things, they were cut to the heart, and they thought to put them to death. But one in the council rising up, a Pharisee, named Gamaliel, a doctor of the law, respected by all the people, commanded the men to be put forth a little while. And he said to them: Ye men of Israel, take heed to yourselves what you intend to do, as touching these men.

For before these days rose up Theodas, affirming himself to be somebody, to whom a number of men, about four hundred, joined themselves: who was slain; and all that believed him were scattered, and brought to nothing. After this man, rose up Judas of Galilee, in the days of the enrolling, and drew away the people after him: he also perished; and all, even as many as consented to him, were dispersed. And now, therefore, I say to you, refrain from these men, and let them alone; for if this council or this work be of men, it will come to nought; But if it be of God, you cannot overthrow it, lest perhaps you be found even to fight against God. And they consented to him. And calling in the apostles, after they had scourged them, they charged them that they should not speak at all in the name of Jesus; and they dismissed them.

And they indeed went from the presence of the council, rejoicing that they were accounted worthy to suffer reproach for the name of Jesus. And every day they ceased not in the temple, and from house to house, to teach and preach Christ Jesus. (Acts 5: 12-42)

Yes, the Apostles rejoiced because there were deemed worthy to "suffer reproach for the name of Jesus."

Which one of the conciliar "bishops" today is willing to suffer reproach for the Holy Name of Our Blessed Lord and Saviour Jesus Christ?

Which one of the conciliar "bishops" bishops today is willing to preach the Gospel to those who deny the Sacred Divinity of Our Blessed Lord and Saviour Jesus Christ and who are in steeped in the darkness of the Talmud? Joseph Ratzinger/Benedict XVI? Jorge Mario Bergoglio/Francis?

Which one of the conciliar "bishops" today exhibits any degree of apostolic zeal for the salvation of the souls of the very people from whom Our Lord took His Sacred Humanity, whose conversion to the Faith Saint Paul tells us in his Epistle to the Romans is an important sign of end times (which means, obviously, that we're not quite there right now)? Which one of the conciliar "popes" or "bishops" has spoken to the children of Abraham and Moses as Saint Stephen, the Church's Protomartyr, spoke just before his martyrdom?

And Stephen, full of grace and fortitude, did great wonders and signs among the people. Now there arose some of that which is called the synagogue of the Libertines, and of the Cyrenians, and of the Alexandrians, and of them that were of Cilicia and Asia, disputing with Stephen. And they were not able to resist the wisdom and the spirit that spoke.

Then they suborned men to say, they had heard him speak words of blasphemy against Moses and against God. And they stirred up the people, and the ancients, and the scribes; and running together, they took him, and brought him to the council. And they set up false witnesses, who said: This man ceaseth not to speak words against the holy place and the law. For we have heard him say, that this Jesus of Nazareth shall destroy this place, and shall change the traditions which Moses delivered unto us. And all that sat in the council, looking on him, saw his face as if it had been the face of an angel.

Then the high priest said: Are these things so? Who said: Ye men, brethren, and fathers, hear. The God of glory appeared to our father Abraham, when he was in Mesopotamia, before he dwelt in Charan. And said to him: Go forth out of thy country, and from thy kindred, and come into the land which I shall shew thee. Then he went out of the land of the Chaldeans, and dwelt in Charan. And from thence, after his father was dead, he removed him into this land, wherein you now dwell. And he gave him no inheritance in it; no, not the pace of a foot: but he promised to give it him in possession, and to his seed after him, when as yet he had no child.

And God said to him: That his seed should sojourn in a strange country, and that they should bring them under bondage, and treat them evil four hundred years. And the nation which they shall serve will I judge, said the Lord; and after these things they shall go out, and shall serve me in this place. And he gave him the covenant of circumcision, and so he begot Isaac, and circumcised him the eighth day; and Isaac begot Jacob; and Jacob the twelve patriarchs. And the patriarchs, through envy, sold Joseph into Egypt; and God was with him, And delivered him out of all his tribulations: and he gave him favour and wisdom in the sight of Pharao, the king of Egypt; and he appointed him governor over Egypt, and over all his house.

Now there came a famine upon all Egypt and Chanaan, and great tribulation; and our fathers found no food. But when Jacob had heard that there was corn in Egypt, he sent our fathers first: And at the second time, Joseph was known by his brethren, and his kindred was made known to Pharao. And Joseph sending, called thither Jacob, his father, and all his kindred, seventy-five souls. So Jacob went down into Egypt; and he died, and our fathers.

And they were translated into Sichem, and were laid in the sepulchre, that Abraham bought for a sum of money of the sons of Hemor, the son of Sichem. And when the time of the promise drew near, which God had promised to Abraham, the people increased, and were multiplied in Egypt, Till another king arose in Egypt, who knew not Joseph. This same dealing craftily with our race, afflicted our fathers, that they should expose their children, to the end they might not be kept alive. At the same time was Moses born, and he was acceptable to God: who was nourished three months in his father's house.

And when he was exposed, Pharao's daughter took him up, and nourished him for her own son. And Moses was instructed in all the wisdom of the Egyptians; and he was mighty in his words and in his deeds. And when he was full forty years old, it came into his heart to visit his brethren, the children of Israel. And when he had seen one of them suffer wrong, he defended him; and striking the Egyptian, he avenged him who suffered the injury. And he thought that his brethren understood that God by his hand would save them; but they understood it not.

And the day following, he shewed himself to them when they were at strife; and would have reconciled them in peace, saying: Men, ye are brethren; why hurt you one another? But he that did the injury to his neighbour thrust him away, saying: Who hath appointed thee prince and judge over us? What, wilt thou kill me, as thou didst yesterday kill the Egyptian? And Moses fled upon this word, and was a stranger in the land of Madian, where he begot two sons. And when forty years were expired, there appeared to him in the desert of mount Sina, an angel in a flame of fire in a bush.

And Moses seeing it, wondered at the sight. And as he drew near to view it, the voice of the Lord came unto him, saying: I am the God of thy fathers; the God of Abraham, the God of Isaac, and the God of Jacob. And Moses being terrified, durst not behold. And the Lord said to him: Loose the shoes from thy feet, for the place wherein thou standest, is holy ground. Seeing I have seen the affliction of my people which is in Egypt, and I have heard their groaning, and am come down to deliver them. And now come, and I will send thee into Egypt. This Moses, whom they refused, saying: Who hath appointed thee prince and judge? him God sent to be prince and redeemer by the hand of the angel who appeared to him in the bush.

He brought them out, doing wonders and signs in the land of Egypt, and in the Red Sea, and in the desert forty years. This is that Moses who said to the children of Israel: A prophet shall God raise up to you of your own brethren, as myself: him shall you hear. This is he that was in the church in the wilderness, with the angel who spoke to him on mount Sina, and with our fathers; who received the words of life to give unto us. Whom our fathers would not obey; but thrust him away, and in their hearts turned back into Egypt, Saying to Aaron: Make us gods to go before us. For as for this Moses, who brought us out of the land of Egypt, we know not what is become of him.

And they made a calf in those days, and offered sacrifices to the idol, and rejoiced in the works of their own hands. And God turned, and gave them up to serve the host of heaven, as it is written in the books of the prophets: Did you offer victims and sacrifices to me for forty years, in the desert, O house of Israel? And you took unto you the tabernacle of Moloch, and the star of your god Rempham, figures which you made to adore them. And I will carry you away beyond Babylon. The tabernacle of the testimony was with our fathers in the desert, as

God ordained for them, speaking to Moses, that he should make it according to the form which he had seen. Which also our fathers receiving, brought in with Jesus, into the possession of the Gentiles, whom God drove out before the face of our fathers, unto the days of David.

Who found grace before God, and desired to find a tabernacle for the God of Jacob. But Solomon built him a house. Yet the most High dwelleth not in houses made by hands, as the prophet saith: Heaven is my throne, and the earth my footstool. What house will you build me? saith the Lord; or what is the place of my resting? Hath not my hand made all these things?

You stiffnecked and uncircumcised in heart and ears, you always resist the Holy Ghost: as your fathers did, so do you also. Which of the prophets have not your fathers persecuted? And they have slain them who foretold of the coming of the Just One; of whom you have been now the betrayers and murderers: Who have received the law by the disposition of angels, and have not kept it. Now hearing these things, they were cut to the heart, and they gnashed with their teeth at him. But he, being full of the Holy Ghost, looking up steadfastly to heaven, saw the glory of God, and Jesus standing on the right hand of God. And he said: Behold, I see the heavens opened, and the Son of man standing on the right hand of God.

And they crying out with a loud voice, stopped their ears, and with one accord ran violently upon him. And casting him forth without the city, they stoned him; and the witnesses laid down their garments at the feet of a young man, whose name was Saul. And they stoned Stephen, invoking, and saying: Lord Jesus, receive my spirit. And falling on his knees, he cried with a loud voice, saying: Lord, lay not this sin to their charge. And when he had said this, he fell asleep in the Lord. And Saul was consenting to his death. (Acts 6: 8-15; 7: 1-59)

We have not only witnessed a refusal of the conciliar "popes" and "bishops" to speak as Saint Stephen spoke. We have witnessed them consorting with pro-abortion rabbis without once condemning their support of baby-killing, no less seeking their conversion to the true Faith (cf. Joseph Ratzinger/Benedict XVI with the "papal knight," Rabbi Arthur Schneier, Friday, April 18, 2008, April 18, 2008.) We have witnessed them bestowing papal honors upon pro-abortion rabbis (see Karol Wojtyla/John Paul II, Joseph Ratzinger/Benedict XVI, "Archbishop" Donald Wuerl, and "Bishop" Tod Brown). Let me put it to you this way: when was the last time you heard a conciliar "pope" or a "cardinal" or a "bishop" refer to the miraculous conversion of Alphonse Ratisbonne from Judaism to Catholicism when Our Lady appeared to him as she appears on the Miraculous Medal that he, Ratisbonne, once mocked?

The story of Alphonse Ratisbonne is remarkable because it was effected by Our Lady herself, who was in the Upper Room in Jerusalem on Pentecost Sunday as the Apostles left to start the missionary work of the infant Church. Ratisbonne, who became a priest, wrote:

> "I had come out of a dark pit, out of a tomb...and I was alive, completely alive. I thought of my brother Theodore with inexpressible joy. But how I wept as I thought of my family, of my fiancee, of my poor sisters. I wept indeed, as I thought of them whom I so loved and for whom I said the first of my prayers. Will you not raise your eyes to the Savior whose blood

blots out original sin? Oh! How hideous is the mark of this taint, and how does it alter beyond recognition the creature made in God's own likeness!"

When priests wanted to delay his Baptism for a time, Alphonse Ratisbonne said:

"The Jews who heard the preaching of the Apostles were baptized immediately, and you want to put me off, after I have 'heard' the preaching of the Queen of the Apostles?"

There you have it. Alphonse Ratisbonne knew on January 20, 1842, in the Church San Andrea delle Fratte in Rome, Italy, that Our Lady wanted him to be converted out of Judaism in imitation of what happened on Pentecost Sunday and thereafter by the working of God the Holy Ghost. What's wrong with the conciliar popes and bishops? The loss of the Catholic Faith. Isn't this obvious? God the Holy Ghost does not change His mind. He is God. He does not contradict Himself. The preaching of Saint Peter on Pentecost Sunday cannot be valid then and not valid now. It is valid for all eternity. Only formal apostates reject the timeless nature of the work of the Apostles to convert souls.

The aftermath of Ratisbonne's conversion to the true Faith is recounted in *Mary's Miraculous Medal*:

> News of this miraculous event spread quickly all over Europe, especially in diplomatic and financial circles, when Ratisbonne, de Bassierers and de La Ferronays were widely known.
> The city of Rome itself was in a stir and a special Church commission was established to study the astonishing conversion. Faced with the overpowering evidence, the court fully recognized the signal miracle wrought by God through the intercession of the Blessed Virgin Mary in the spontaneous conversion of Marie Alphonse Ratisbonne from Judaism to Catholicism. It was a major triumph of the Miraculous Medal.

Alphonse Ratisbonne became a Catholic priest, serving in the Holy Land. "So great was the love he had for his people, that he dedicated the remainder of his life, as did his brother, Father Theodore, to work for the conversion of their immortal souls. Among the converts of these two priest brothers were a total of twenty-eight members of their own family." Is this work being done in the Holy Land at present by Catholic bishops of the West and of the East? Not that you would notice. How is this not apostasy of the highest order?

Pope Pius XII wrote approvingly of the zeal for the conversion of souls that prompted the missionaries of the First Millennium and thereafter to Christianize Europe by bringing all souls into the Barque of Saint Peter. Writing in *Evangeli Praecones*, June 2, 1951, Pope Pius noted:

> Likewise all know that the Gospel followed the great Roman roads and was spread not only by Bishops and priests but also by public officials, soldiers and private citizens. Thousands of Christian neophytes, whose names are today unknown, were fired with zeal to promote the new religion they had embraced and endeavored to prepare the way for the coming of the Gospel. That explains why after about 100 years Christianity had penetrated into all the chief cities of the Roman Empire.

St. Justinus, Minucius Felix, Aristides, the consul Acilius Glaber, the patrician Flavius

Clemens, St. Tarsicius and countless holy martyrs of both sexes, who strengthened and enriched the growth of the Church by their labors and the shedding of their blood, can in a certain sense be called the advance guard and forerunners of Catholic Action. Here We wish to cite the striking observation of the author of the letter to Diognetus, which even today has a message for us: "Christians dwell in their native countries as though aliens; . . . every foreign land is their home and the land of their birth is foreign soil."

During the barbarian invasions of the Middle Ages, we see men and women of royal rank and even workmen and valiant Christian women of the common people using every endeavor to convert their fellow citizens to the religion of Jesus Christ and to fashion their morals according to its pattern, so as to safeguard both religion and the state from approaching danger. Tradition tells us that when our immortal Predecessor, Leo the Great, courageously opposed Attila, when he invaded Italy, two Roman consuls stood by his side. When formidable hordes of Huns were besieging Paris, the holy virgin Genevieve, who was given to a life of continuous prayer and austere penance, cared for the souls and bodies of her fellow citizens with wondrous charity. Theodolinda, Queen of the Lombards, zealously summoned her people to embrace the Christian religion. King Reccaredus of Spain endeavored to rescue his people from the Arian heresy and to lead them back to the true Faith. In France, there were not only bishops, such as Remigius of Rheims, Caesarius of Arles, Gregory of Tours, Eligius of Noyon and many others, who were eminent for virtue and apostolic zeal, but queens also can be found during that period who taught the truths of Christianity to the untutored masses and who gave food and shelter and renewed strength to the sick, the hungry and the victims of every human misfortune. For example, Clotilda so influenced Clovis in favor of the Catholic religion that she had the great joy of bringing him into the true Church. Radegunda and Bathilda cared for the sick with supreme charity and even restored lepers to health. In England, Queen Bertha welcomed St. Augustine when he came to evangelize that nation and earnestly exhorted her husband Ethelbert to accept the teachings of the Gospel. No sooner had the Anglo-Saxons, of both high and low degree, men and women, young and old, embraced the Christian faith, than they were led as though by divine inspiration to unite themselves to this Apostolic See by the closest bonds of piety, fidelity and devotion.

In Germany, we witness the admirable spectacle of St. Boniface and his companions traversing those regions in their apostolic journeys and making them fruitful by their generous labors. The sons and daughters of that valiant and noble land felt inspired to offer their efficient collaboration to monks, priests and Bishops in order that the light of the Gospel might be daily more widely diffused throughout those vast regions and that Christian doctrine and Christian virtue might ever make greater advances and reap a rich harvest of souls.

Thus in every age, thanks to the tireless labors of the clergy and also to the cooperation of the laity, the Catholic Church has not only advanced its spiritual kingdom, but has also led nations to increased social prosperity. Everybody knows the social reforms of St. Elizabeth in Hungary, of St. Ferdinand in Castile and of St. Louis IX in France. By their holy lives and zealous labors they brought about salutary improvement in the different classes of society by instituting reforms, by spreading the true faith everywhere, by valiantly defending the Church and above all by their personal example. Nor are We unaware of the excellent merits of the guilds during the Middle Ages. In these guilds artisans and skilled workers of both sexes were enrolled, who, notwithstanding the fact that they lived in the world, kept their eyes fixed upon the sublime ideal of evangelical perfection. Not only did they eagerly pursue this ideal, but together with the clergy they exerted every effort to bring all others to do the same. (Pope Pius XII, *Evangeli Praecones*, June 2, 1951.)

The work of the Apostles is the work of seeking the conversion of all men and of all nations to the true Faith. All men. Everywhere. At all times. Without exception. Protestants must convert. Jews must convert. Mormons must convert. Seventh Day Adventists must convert. Jehovah's Witnesses must convert. Buddhists must convert. Hindus must convert. Quakers must convert. Mohammedans must convert. Practitioners of Bah'ai must convert. Animists must convert. Atheists must convert. Jainists must convert. All other manner of pagans must convert. And the exponents of conciliarism and its false religion that flies in the face of the missionary work of the Apostles must convert back to the Faith of our fathers, recapturing the zeal of the Apostles for the conversion of souls. Conciliarism seeks to "meet people where they are" to engage them in meaningless "dialogue." True apostolic zeal for souls seeks to challenge people to convert, lest they die in their false religions.

True love of God and for the souls for whom He shed every single drop of His Most Precious Blood on the wood of the Holy Cross impels all Catholics, especially popes and bishops and priests, to seek the conversion of all men everywhere to the true Faith. How many diocesan priests in the past sixty years can say that they have done what the late Father Daniel Johnson did during his twenty-five years as the pastor of Saint Mary's by the Sea in Huntington Beach, California: knock on every door, commercial and residential alike, in his parish's boundaries three times during the course of twenty-five years, converting 554 people along the way? How many diocesan priests can say that they have ever considered *doing* such a thing as part of the pastoral work God Himself expects them to complete while pastor of a particular parish? Oh, no, such zeal for souls is not in the "job description" of conciliarism and not useful to one who seeks to climb the clerical ladder rather than imitate the zeal of the Apostles themselves.

Father Benedict Baur's reflection for the birthday of Holy Mother Church should teach us that only those shepherds who understand that the mission of the Church is to convert all men and all nations to the Faith of Christ the King are truly Catholic:

Seven times seven days, a complete jubilee octave, have passed since Easter. Now the Holy Ghost, the Third Person of the Blessed Trinity, the eternal expression of the mutual love of the Father and the Son, comes to us. He comes with the sound of a mighty wind, appearing to the apostles in the form of tongues of fire which rest upon each of them. Made bold by this baptism of fire, they go forth into the world and proclaim by word and deed, even by the sacrificing of their lives, that Christ the crucified One is truly risen.

The first Pentecost. The historical event of Pentecost is related in the Epistle. The apostles and Mary, the Mother of Jesus, are gathered together in one place. About the third hour (about nine o'clock) they hear a mighty rush of wind as if a storm were approaching. Then tongues of fire appear above the heads of each of them. They are filled with the Holy Ghost and begin to speak in various tongues, according as the Holy Ghost inspired them. Outside the house a great crowd of people has gathered, who cannot imagine what has happened. Then they hear the disciples and the apostles speaking in various languages, and each one, in the language in which he was born, hears of the wonderful things which God has done. A new Pentecost! In ancient times God confirmed His covenant with Israel to the accompaniment of thunder and lightning. But the law He gave was the law of fear, the law of severity, the law of servitude. This is a new Pentecost, a Pentecost that fills the hearts of men with love, freedom, and holy joy. The Holy Ghost appears with a mighty wind, penetrating and filling the hearts of the disciples. They are freed from their former timidity and hesitancy. The Holy Ghost enlightens men, guides their thoughts, provides for their needs, controls their desires, inspires their affections, adjusts their motives, and elevates them to the kingdom of the spirit. He teaches them a new manner of life. He gives them courage, strength of character, stability, inexhaustible patience, a readiness for sacrifice, a will to suffer for the sake of Christ. They are indeed a new creation.

Our Pentecost. In the mind of the liturgy, Pentecost is not merely the commemoration of a past event; the wonders related in the Epistle are repeated today in us. We also gather in one place in the celebration of the Holy Sacrifice of the Mass and unite in prayer, awaiting the coming of the Holy Ghost. For this reason we pray at the end of the Epistle: "Come, Holy Ghost, fill the hearts of Thy faithful, and kindle in them the fire of Thy love." When the glorified Savior appears in our midst at the Consecration of the Mass, He will bring the Holy Ghost with Him. In our reception of Holy Communion the events of Pentecost will take visible form. The Holy Ghost comes to each of us and fills us with His fire and His power. He does not come to us in the form of fiery tongues, but in the form of a fragile host which is the glorified body of Christ and contains also the Spirit of Christ, the Holy Ghost. When we receive Holy Communion, we receive again the baptism of the Spirit. Having been filled with the Holy Ghost, having become bearers of the Spirit and apostles of the Lord, we announce the marvelous works of the Lord. During the distribution of Holy Communion, the Church sings: "Suddenly there came a sound from heaven as of a mighty wind coming. . . . and they were all filled with the Holy Ghost, speaking the wonderful works of God, alleluia, alleluia." Pentecost has been repeated in the present.

"If any one love Me, he will keep My word, and My Father will love him, an We will come to him and will make Our abode with him" (Gospel). Thus our Lord describes the love of the Father, and of the Son, and of the Holy Ghost, the love which binds us all together. God is never very far from us; He is actually within us. This is the joyful message of Pentecost: God is within us! The Father loves us, not only for today or for tomorrow, but for all eternity. God is within us and we are filled with light and warmth. We must let His rays shine into our hearts: we must let Him come and make His abode within us. We are filled with His power and fire, which will consume all evil and all sin within us. This fire is our holy zeal to serve God our Savior.

Pentecost is the seal and perfection of the mystery of Easter. If Easter is baptism, Pentecost is confirmation. Easter gives us a new birth; Pentecost brings us to maturity. At Pentecost we reach our full stature, we are brought to maturity. At Pentecost we reach our full stature, we are brought to man's estate, to perfection by the power of the Holy Ghost. The baptism of the Spirit prepares us for heroic deeds, sanctifies our thoughts, purifies our motives. It makes us perfect Christians. (Father Benedict Baur, O.S.B., *The Light of the World*, Volume 1, pp. 574-576.)

The missionary work of Holy Mother Church began on Pentecost Sunday. Most of the Jews, however, did not convert even though Our Lord gave them thirty-seven years after His Passion, Death, Resurrection and Ascension to have His Holy Gospel preached to them.

As he had prophesied, therefore, Jerusalem was destroyed by the Romans in 70 A.D., thus signifying the end of Temple worship once and for all as God made known publicly for all to see that the curtain in the Temple that had been torn in two from top to bottom when the earth quaked at the moment that Our Blessed Lord and Saviour Jesus Christ died marked the end of the Old Covenant, which was superseded by the New and Eternal Covenant that He instituted at the Last Supper and ratified by the shedding of every single drop of His Most Precious Blood on the wood of the Holy Cross on Good Friday.

The leaders of the Jewish Sanhedrin had persecuted the first Catholics with great ferocity in the thirty-seven years between Our Lord's Sacred Passion and the destruction of the Temple in Jerusalem in the year 70 A.D. Holy Mother Church survived. Most of the Jews were dispersed by the Romans, who, pagans though they were, had been used by God to serve as the means of His Divine chastisement upon them for their treatment of the Divine Redeemer and His followers.

As we live in a world of empty sentimentality replete with one historical falsehood after another, most Catholics do not understand these facts. Many reject them because it is not what they have been taught. Indeed, they are taught quite the contrary by the lords of conciliarism. The dispersal of the Jews as an expression of Divine retribution, however, is simply a truth of the Faith that is denied by the conciliar officials:

> As one recalls, the Temple was destroyed as part of the punishment for the crime of Deicide perpetrated by the Jews - the high priests, scribes and Pharisees together with the people, who asked that the Blood of Jesus Christ, Son of God, fall over them and their offspring - as reported in the Gospels.
>
> After the destruction of the Temple by Titus in the year 70 A.C., one attempt was made by Emperor Julian the Apostate to rebuild that edifice. He meant to destroy the belief that the chastisement was due to the Death of Our Lord. His initiative was prevented by earthquakes and balls of fire falling from the sky that destroyed what had been made and frightened the workers. Julian died in June of 363 during that attempt to rebuild the Temple. Confessing his failure in his struggle against Jesus Christ, he cried out while dying: "Thou hast won, O Galilean!"
>
> After that, no one ever tried to rebuild that cursed edifice.
>
> Benedict XVI, like John Paul II before him, defied the wrath of God when he went to "pray" in that place - purposely ignoring the punishment of God it represents.
>
> In the prayer he wrote, the Pope depicts himself neither as a representative of Jesus Christ, whose Name he did not mention, nor as the Sovereign Pontiff of the Catholic Church, but

rather as a self-appointed ambassador of "all who call upon God's name." Ignoring the Passion of Our Lord which He suffered in that very City of Jerusalem, Benedict XVI addressed the "God of Abraham, Isaac and Jacob," supposedly the same God of Catholics, Jews and Muslims. (Tradition in Action website)

Having rejected Our Lord and served as the means by which our own sins, having transcended time, caused Him to be Crucified, the Jews were thus dispersed, their religion having been abolished. What is today called "Judaism" is not the Judaism of the superseded Old Covenant. The false religion of contemporary Judaism is based on the blasphemous Talmud, its "rabbinical" system an invention to perpetuate the "traditions" of a dead, superseded religion that is, as all false religions are, hated by God. There is one thing that Talmudic Judaism has in common with the Judaism of the Old Covenant at the time of Our Lord's life here on earth and in the thirty-seven years after His Ascension to the Father's right hand: a hatred of Him, His Holy Name, His Holy Church, and the instrument upon which He redeemed us, the Holy Cross.

Although there have been few organized efforts to convert the Jews since their dispersal from Palestine in 70 A.D., there were some Catholic missionaries who made efforts, including Father Maria-Alphonse Ratisbonne and his brother, Father Theodore Ratisbonne, both of whom were mentioned earlier.

One of the most famous to have sought the conversion of the Jews of the Talmud was Saint Vincent Ferrer, O.P., who preached in southern France and the kingdoms of Spain at the end of the Fourteenth and the beginning of the Fifteenth Centuries during the time of the Great Western Schism. Harkening back to the spirit of the Apostles on Pentecost Sunday, Saint Vincent Ferrer preached convincingly to the Jews, converting them by the thousands, succeeding also in his mission to convert thousands of Mohammedans to the true Faith:

> St. Vincent's mission was not less fruitful among the Jews than among heretics. He converted an incalculable number of them. God seemed to have accorded him a special grace for the conversion of people who are proverbially hostile to the Christian name. There was at that period, a population of Jews both numerous and powerful in Spain. The process of his canonization shows that in the space of thirteen months he converted twenty thousand in Castile alone; that in the year 1415, within six months, more than fifteen thousand were led to embrace the true faith in Aragon and Catalonia, and that on another occasion in the same country over thirty thousand were baptized at the close of his preaching. This historians of the sect do not hesitate to confirm these facts by their own testimony. In a work entitled *Juehasin,* it is related that in the year 142, a Friar named Brother Vincent, having preached to the Jews, the latter renounced their law to a number of more than two hundred thousand.
>
> The Saint had an ardent zeal and tender love for these unhappy wanderers. In the cities where he found them, he took care that a place should always be reserved for them, and after his exhortations he treated them with much consideration. These acts full of sweetness gained their hearts. The learning of the great preacher completed their conviction, and they presented themselves in a body to receive Holy Baptism. Thus, at Perpignan seventy families embraced the Christian faith. In other places whole synagogues abjured their errors. Their place of meeting was changed into a church. In Castile, they were so unanimously converted that none

remained, and the Bishop of Palencia saw himself deprived of a large revenue, produced by a special impost on them. Among the Jews whom St. Vincent brought to the Divine Messias, many of them in their turn became the apostles of their co-religionists. Thus, one of them, who was afterward raised to the Episcopate, had the satisfaction of making forty thousand proselytes among his fellow countrymen. (Father Andrew Pradel, O.P., *St. Vincent Ferrer: The Angel of Judgment*, Published in England 1875 and reprinted by TAN Books and Publishers in 2000, pp. 80-81.)

The missionary work of the Church began among the Jews on Pentecost Sunday. Saint Vincent Ferrer was not content to leave souls redeemed by the shedding of the Most Precious Blood of the Divine Redeemer in a false religion until the point of their deaths. He had the same missionary spirit of the Apostles themselves, a missionary spirit that Holy Mother Church, starting with the Apostles, took to the Gentiles in the known quarters of the world in the decades after Pentecost Sunday, and it would be in Europe. It was in Europe where this missionary spirit was to take deep root over the course of the First Millennium, resulting in the Age of Christendom that has been rejected by the "wisdom" of Modernity and the "accommodations" made by Modernists in the conciliar church to it.

As will be seen in subsequent chapters, what happened in the former English colonies that became the first thirteen states of the United States of America was unique in Holy Mother Church's history. Catholics were content simply to have the "freedom" to practice their Faith in what they believed to be, despite all of the bigotry and violence directed at them, an environment that was perfectly compatible with Catholicism. Instead, however, most of them and their descendants were converted by the prevailing ethos of the "American way" that led them to accept political and cultural developments that were in direct opposition to the Holy Faith and thus to the determent of their own souls and of all social order as a result.

What happened in the United States of America, as events unfolded over the course of time was, despite the winning of converts to the Faith, the gradual conversion of Catholics to American mores rather than of the country to the Social Reign of Christ the King and of Mary our Immaculate Queen.

Chapter VIII
Holy Mother Church in Her Infancy

Holy Mother Church must pass through each of the phases of the Incarnation, Nativity, Hidden Years, Public Ministry, Passion, Death and Resurrection of her Divine Founder and Invisible Head, Our Blessed Lord and Saviour Jesus Christ.

Holy Mother Church was in her Infancy during the time between Pentecost Sunday and the destruction of the Temple in Jerusalem by the Romans in 70 A.D. This period of Infancy continued as Saint Paul the Apostle spread the Faith to the Gentiles through the Hellenic world and as both he and Saint Peter, our first pope, planted the seeds of the Faith in Rome, the capital of the world that was to become the capital of the Catholic Faith.

Catholics were viewed with suspicion from the time of Caesar Tiberius to that of Caesar Nero. They were tolerated, viewed as an eccentric sect that professed belief in a God Who had become Incarnate, was Crucified under Pontius Pilate and then rose from the dead. These baby Catholics, if you will, tread cautiously, going underground to hear Holy Mass as offered by Saints Peter and Paul. While they never denied the Faith before men, they did not go out of their way to identify themselves as followers of Our Blessed Lord and Saviour Jesus Christ if they did not have to do so, trusting that the power of their example would draw others to the Faith, leaving it to Saints Peter and Paul to proclaim the Faith in their Masses and meetings.

Catholics were good citizens of Rome. They obeyed just laws. They paid their taxes. Some even served in the military. There was one thing that they would not do: break the First and Second Commandments. They would not offer false worship, whether it be to the emperor or other false gods and their symbols. They would not participate in false religious exercises to save their lives. Their fidelity to the truths of the Holy Faith won them the suspicion and hatred of many among both the "educated" classes and masses of ordinary citizens.

Typical of this suspicion was the view expressed by Caecilius Natalis:

> "The Christians are a men of a desperate, lawless, reckless faction, who collect together out of the rabble the thoughtless portion, and credulous women seduced by the weakness of their sex, and form a mob of impure conspirators, whose bond of union is nocturnal assemblies and solemn fastings and unnatural food. A tribe lurking and light-hating, dumb for the public, talkative in corners, they despise our temples as if graves, spit at our gods, deride our religious forms; pitiable themselves, they pity, forsooth, our priests; half-naked themselves, they despise our honor and purple; monstrous folly and incredible imprudence! Day after day their abandoned morals wind their serpentine course; over the whole world are those most hideous rites of an impious association growing into shape. They recognize each other by marks and signs, and love each other almost before they recognize each other; promiscuous lust is their   religion. Thus does their vain and mad superstition glory in crimes; Why their mighty effort to hide and shroud whatever it is they worship, since things honest ever like the open day, and crimes are secret? Why have they no altars, no temples, no images known to us, never speak in public, never assemble freely, were it not that what they worship and suppress is subject either of punishment or of shame." (Translation of text

by John Henry Cardinal Newman, as found in Father John Laux, *Church History*, Benziger Brothers, 1939, pp. 45-46.)

Holy Mother Church was in her infancy yet she was hated. It is the same today as she, having gone through her Mystical Passion, Death and Burial, is in the tomb mystically awaiting the day of her resurrection. It is the same.

A constellation of forces, each of which has been inspired by the devil, has formed to attack and persecute her, succeeding in creating a rump church that claims to be Catholic while promoting the exact concept of religious liberty that could have saved the lives of the early Catholics if only they had been willing to engage in showing signs of esteem and respect for false religions and their symbols. We are witnessing, therefore not only the same pagan and barbarian forces of the world working against Holy Mother Church today, but the forces of Modernism in the counterfeit church of conciliarism that embraces the very type of religious "liberty" and "respect" for false religions that our first martyrs knew were so hideous to true God of Divine Revelation that they preferred death rather than evidencing any sign of acceptance of such sacrilege and blasphemy.

Things came to a head, however, as the venal, vain, corrupt and narcissistic megalomaniac named Nero, who was the Roman emperor between 54 A.D. and 68 A.D., began to persecute Catholics in 64 A.D., beginning two hundred forty-nine years of on-gain/off-again persecutions designed to wipe out the infant Church just as King Herod the Great sought to kill the Infant Jesus shortly after his birth by ordering the killing of all male children under the age of two. Saint Peter, our first pope, was crucified upside down on Vatican Hill on the site of the Basilica of Saint Peter. Saint Paul the Apostle was beheaded on the site of what is now the Basilica of Saint Paul Outside the Walls in Rome. Over thirteen million Catholics were killed during the two hundred forty-nine years between 64 A.D. and the issuance of the Edict of Milan by Emperor Constantine in the year 313 A.D.

There were ten major periods of persecution during these two hundred forty-nine years, not including localized persecutions that arose in various places from time to time. Although just a small fraction of the population of the Roman Empire, Catholics were hated and persecuted. Believing Catholics are hated and persecuted today while those who get along well with the world and its false currents do all right for themselves insofar as material success and popularity are concerned. The Catholics who suffered and died in the first three centuries of the Church were concerned only about pleasing the true God of Divine Revelation, the Most Holy Trinity: God the Father, God the Son, and God the Holy Ghost.

The ten major periods of persecution were categorized by Father John Laux in his college textbook, *Church History*, as follows:

1) The persecution of Nero (64-68)
2) The persecution of Domitian (95-96)
3) The persecution of Trajan (106-107)
4) The persecution of Marcus Aurelius (161-180)
5) The persecution of Septimius Severus (202-211)
6) The persecution of Maximin the Thracian (235-238)
7) The persecution of Decius (249-251)

8) The persecution of Valerian (257-260)

9) The persecution of Aurelian (274-275)

10)The persecution of Diocletian and Galerius (303-311) (cf. Father John Laux, *Church History*, p. 45.)

The most violent of these persecutions were those of Nero, Trajan, Septimius Severus, Decius and, of course, that of Diocletian and Galerius. The blood of martyrs was indeed the seed of the Church in her infancy.

Among these martyrs were Holy Mother Church's first thirty-three popes, Saint Ignatius of Antioch, Saint Polycarp, Saint Agnes, Saint Agatha, Saint Lucy, Saint Lawrence the Deacon, Saints Perpetua and Felicity, Saint Cecilia, Saint George, Saint Prisca, Saint Eustace and his Companions, and Saint Chrysogonus.

Father Basil Meramo, who had been the district superior of the Society of Saint Pius X in a region of Mexico before being dismissed in 2009, explained that the demands made upon Catholics by the Roman emperors on their minions to worship false gods and engage in sacrilegious liturgical rites is precisely what the Rome of Modernism today demands of Catholics in the name of false ecumenism:

> Where does Benedict XVI go? He goes to the Synagogue, he goes to the United Nations, and now he goes to the Society (SSPX) – another concubine in the pantheon of false religions.
>
> This is not admissible. This is a tactic of Rome. I want you to know, dear brethren, that Rome of the Roman Empire was able to dominate the world by means of religious compromises. This is why Rome had a pantheon with all the principal gods of the important peoples who were subjugated by it. Since religious alliances were established and Rome had the same gods of the enemies, then there were no mutual attacks. Rome accepted the same gods of the Greeks in order to dominate the Greeks; Rome adopted the same gods of this or that people in order to dominate them. This was its tactic to govern.
>
> **This same tactic continues today in that Rome, which St. Peter - the first Pope of the Church - called Babylon. He was not in the Middle East; he was in Rome and he called it Babylon because it was the Babylon of the religions. He didn't spare words, because it had an altar to every god. All known religions had their representatives there. (…) A Pope quoted in the Breviary – whose name I don't remember at this moment – said that at the end [of history] Rome will again have, as in the beginning, all the religions. It will return to its ancient paganism, rejoicing in hosting all religions. It will return to its old religious prostitution. (Father Basil Meramo, A Bold Show of Dissatisfaction in the SSPX Ranks, Tradition in Action website)**

Our Catholic ancestors preferred death rather than give the slightest trace of respect to false religions even though Joseph Ratzinger/Benedict XVI indicated in his Christmas address to the members of the Roman curia on December 22, 2005, that the first Christian martyrs had died for "religious liberty," a remark that is blasphemous on its very face.

Pope Pius XII noted that the deportment of the Catholic Church had never changed regarding her view of false religions and their symbols and their ceremonies, speaking in the following terms of the fidelity exhibited by our brave martyrs of the first centuries of the Church:

> **Her deportment has not changed in the course of history, nor can it change whenever or wherever, under the most diversified forms, she is confronted with the choice: either incense for idols or blood for Christ. The place where you are now present, Eternal Rome, with the remains of a greatness that was and with the glorious memories of its martyrs, is the most eloquent witness to the answer of the Church. Incense was not burned before the idols, and Christian blood flowed and consecrated the ground. But the temples of the gods lie in the cold devastation of ruins howsoever majestic; while at the tombs of the martyrs the faithful of all nations and all tongues fervently repeat the ancient Creed of the Apostles.** (Pope Pius XII, *Ci Rask*, December 6, 1953.)

The pagan state of Roman antiquity that persecuted Catholics so fiercely during those ten outbreaks of unspeakable bloodshed about which few historians care to write or bother to reference in the slightest is very similar to the contemporary civil state of Modernity. The pagan state of Roman antiquity invented gods to justify its own abuse of temporal power. The contemporary civil state of Modernity has no need of inventing such gods as its leaders have simply made a god of the state, to which we must bend our wills at all times regardless of the evils promoted under cover of civil law and within popular culture in the name of the "human rights" and "toleration." What was common to both, however, is the expectation that everyone, including Catholics, must lay aside their own "private" beliefs to "obey" the edicts of civil potentates. In other words, the pagan state of Roman antiquity and that of Modernity today have been veritable "churches" whose "doctrinal" assertions must be accepted lest one be suspected of disloyalty and treason.

Writing in *The Framework of A Christian State*, Father Edward Cahill, S.J., emphasized this point:

> "The Pagan State. In the ancient Pagan State, the element of religion in public life, albeit the religion was a false one, and the dependence of the State upon the Deity were recognised. Indeed, the fundamental laws of the old Roman Republic were regarded as gifts or deposits from the gods. Hence they were divine, and no human authority could change them. Later on under the Roman Empire, while the same principle still remained in theory, it was in practice disregarded; for the Emperor's authority was absolute and not limited even by the fundamental laws of the old Roman Constitution. Since it was clear, however, even to the ancient pagans that a human authority which recognises no limitations to its competence, not even those set by a natural or a divine law, cannot logically be reconciled with the recognition of a Supreme Being distinct from that authority, the ancient Romans met the difficulty by the crude expedient of deifying the Emperor who was regarded as the sole source of all law, and who, therefore, was honoured as a god. Another consequence of the supposed all-competence of the governing power was that the essential dignity and rights of human personality were totally disregarded. Again, in the Pagan State, the privileges and rights of citizenship were a monopoly of a small ruling caste, the rest of the people being regarded almost as chattels." (Father Edward Cahill, S.J., *The Framework of A Christian State*.)

We can see rather clearly that there are elements of the pagan state to be found in what I call the Modern State, especially here in the United States. Positivists view the United States Constitution, for example, as a source of law unto itself, rendering the plain meaning of the words contained therein so much child's play for their endless deconstructionist exercises. The government, therefore, becomes equivalent to the State, and all its pronouncements must be obeyed without dissent as more and more of legitimate human liberty, as that term is defined properly according the patrimony of the Church (which is the explicator of the natural law), is eliminated by the brute force of the coercive power of the government. The citizen has thus become the slave of the unjust exercise of government power, which is used almost exclusively to keep the ruling class of professional politicians in power. Pronouncements of non-elected judges and bureaucrats must be obeyed as though they had been delivered by Delphic Oracles. Thus, there are many similarities between the pagan state and the modern state.

Father Cahill put the matter as follows:

> "The Pagan State gradually disappeared under the influence of Christianity. Most of its objectionable characteristics, however, have reappeared in modern times under the influence of materialistic, pantheistic and rationalistic philosophy. Thus the teachings of Hegel, according to which man is identified with the Deity, and civil society, the highest and most perfect manifestation of the divinity, leads to the deification of the State and the denial of essential personal rights, as well as the rights and authority of a divinely constituted Church independent of the State. **Again, the principle that the 'King can do no wrong' implying, as it does that the existing civil law is the norm of morality and is always essentially valid and binding, even when it clashes with divine law or essential personal rights is founded on the same pagan ideal of the deification of the ruler.**" (Father Edward Cahill, S.J., *The Framework of A Christian State*.

The civil state of Roman antiquity demanded of our first Catholics a form of obedience that they could not give. Actions have consequences, however. False ideas lead to bad consequences. Always. Inevitably. And those who dare to seek to impose upon the children of Holy Mother Church commands that they violate any of the binding precepts of the Divine Positive Law and the Natural Law while they promote one grave sin after another under cover of the civil law will reap the violent fruit of the rotten seeds that they sow sooner or later.

The Rome of antiquity whose caesars and their minions persecuted Catholics so fiercely and suspected them so regularly was a place of moral debauchery characterized also by cruel mistreatment of slaves and the subjection of the lower classes. Mercy was unknown to the heart of the Roman pagan, something that Father Edward Leen noted in *In The Likeness of Christ*:

> Under the reign of Satan men were hard and unfeeling, without pity or tenderness. The one thing they looked up to was the physical power to dominate, and the one thing they feared was the helplessness of poverty. Their life was divided between pleasure and cruelty. Pride and haughtiness instead of being regarded as defects were regarded as manly virtues. Weakness was almost synonymous with vice, and all this tended to fashion hearts impervious to the grace of God and to every human feeling. Conversion of heart was for them extremely difficult. What God required on the part of man as a necessary condition of their friendship with Him was to them abhorrent, for the practice of the Christian virtues of submission, humility, and patience would be regarded by them as degrading. They had to learn that

what was not degrading to God--since nothing could degrade Him in reality--could not be degrading to them. Turning to God postulated on their part not only a change of heart, but also a change of mentality. Their human values were almost all wrong. In the terse words of St. Ignatius describing the pagan world: "They smite, they slay and they go down to Hell". (Father Edward Leen, *In The Likeness of Christ*, Sheed and Ward, 1936, pp, 17-18.)

All along, however, God had a plan for Rome, which would be transformed from a seat of cruelty and statism and persecution of Catholics to the seat of the King of Mercy Himself, a mercy that overfloweth from the boundless love within the deepest recesses of His Most Sacred Heart. The Roman emperors and their minions brought themselves to ruin by engaging in the same type of excesses and imperial military adventures as we have seen characterize presidential administrations of both major political parties of naturalism in the United States of America, the Republican Party and the Democratic Party.

Dr. Russell Kirk, writing in *The Roots of American Order*, summarized some of the political and cultural reasons for the collapse of Rome that will be responsible one day within the Providence of God for the collapse of the modern civil state of the West that is so exalted even by many Catholics, including, ironically, the late Dr. Kirk himself. One will see here an almost perfect description of our own times, including Diocletian's own version of an economic "stimulus" project to keep the people dependent upon the largesse of the civil state as he robbed them of their own money and freedom:

> Rome was a thousand years old when Diocletian rose to power. Near the railway station in Modern Rome, the colossal remains of the public baths that Diocletian gave to the city still strike the eye; those halls are churches and museums now. Roman art, in Diocletian's time, tottered on the edge of a collapse of style, but the engineering and sculpture of these baths still have the marks of the Golden Age. Diocletian built this bewildering complex for a degraded population which was kept alive by doles and kept quiet by shows in the Colosseum and the Circus Maximus and the other circuses and theaters. Diocletian paid the soldiers, held the frontiers, and ruled as if he were a god, and still built as if Rome would endure forever. By that time, nothing else mattered.
>
> How was it that Rome, though she gave law to the world, could not maintain her own civilization? The answers to that inquiry are too complicated for detailed analysis here; but one may suggest that the causes are to be found both in certain failings in the order of the commonwealth and in certain deficiencies in the inner order of the soul. For the barbarians, conquest of the Roman Empire was like air bursting into a vacuum: the Goths and Vandals and other invaders, at the end, penetrated a kind of hollow shell, within which they encountered little resistance. (Russell Kirk, *The Roots of American Order*, Washington, D.C., Regnery Gateway, 1991, p. 126.)

Divorce, perversity, adultery, pornography, contraception and abortion were all rampant in the latter stages of the Roman Empire in the West as statism and moral decadence weakened it from within, making it susceptible to attacks by foreign invaders. This is a pattern that might sound somewhat familiar. It took the shedding of the blood of the martyrs to plant the seeds for collapse of the Rome of the caesars so that the Rome of Christ the King and His Vicar on earth, the Successor of Saint Peter, could arise and take its place.

Although Catholics lived amongst their fellow citizens of Rome during the periods between outbreaks of persecutions, they did not adopt their worldliness. They were not content to live in a culture of pluralism and statism and moral relativism. The Catholics who lived and suffered and died in the first three centuries of the Church prayed for the conversion of their fellow men and of the empire itself to the true Faith. This desire to effect the conversion of men and of an empire to the Catholic Faith stands in contrast with how Catholics in the infant United States of America became content over time with access to the sacraments and the devotional life while they became immersed in a culture that was hostile to the Faith and hence destructive of personal and social order over the course of the long term.

The Catholics of the first three centuries knew that suffering was the path to Heaven. While they were good citizens of Rome, they were not blind to its faults, nor did they seek to justify its crimes by invoking pleas of "patriotism." Their loyalty was always to the Holy Faith first before any civil potentate. They also recognized that they would have to suffer along with those committed to the promotion of unbridled evil within their midst as they, being sinners themselves, knew that sin had to be punished and that the Holy Faith gave them an opportunity to accept suffering gladly in reparation for their own sins and for those of their neighbors and of the regime.

Saint Augustine wrote as follows in *The City of God* to explain why Christians (Catholics were, of course, the only Christians and are today the only true Christians) had to suffer with the pagans at the time of the barbaric invasions of Rome at the beginning of the Fifth Century:

> What, then, have the Christians suffered in that calamitous period, which would not profit every one who duly and faithfully considered the following circumstances? First of all, they must humbly consider those very sins which have provoked God to fill the world with such terrible disasters; for although they be far from the excesses of wicked, immoral, and ungodly men, yet they do not judge themselves so clean removed from all faults as to be too good to suffer for these even temporal ills. For every man, however laudably he lives, yet yields in some points to the lust of the flesh. Though he does not fall into gross enormity of wickedness, and abandoned viciousness, and abominable profanity, yet he slips into some sins, either rarely or so much the more frequently as the sins seem of less account. But not to mention this, where can we readily find a man who holds in fit and just estimation those persons on account of whose revolting pride, luxury, and avarice, and cursed iniquities and impiety, God now smites the earth as His predictions threatened? Where is the man who lives with them in the style in which it becomes us to live with them? For often we wickedly blind ourselves to the occasions of teaching and admonishing them, sometimes even of reprimanding and chiding them, either because we shrink from the labor or are ashamed to offend them, or because we fear to lose good friendships, lest this should stand in the way of our advancement, or injure us in some worldly matter, which either our covetous disposition desires to obtain, or our weakness shrinks from losing. So that, although the conduct of wicked men is distasteful to the good, and therefore they do not fall with them into that damnation which in the next life awaits such persons, yet, because they spare their damnable sins through fear, therefore, even though

their own sins be slight and venial, they are justly scourged with the wicked in this world, though in eternity they quite escape punishment. Justly, when God afflicts them in common with the wicked, do they find this life bitter, through love of whose sweetness they declined to be bitter to these sinners.

If any one forbears to reprove and find fault with those who are doing wrong, because he seeks a more seasonable opportunity, or because he fears they may be made worse by his rebuke, or that other weak persons may be disheartened from endeavoring to lead a good and pious life, and may be driven from the faith; this man's omission seems to be occasioned not by covetousness, but by a charitable consideration. But what is blame-worthy is, that they who themselves revolt from the conduct of the wicked, and live in quite another fashion, yet spare those faults in other men which they ought to reprehend and wean them from; and spare them because they fear to give offence, lest they should injure their interests in those things which good men may innocently and legitimately use,—though they use them more greedily than becomes persons who are strangers in this world, and profess the hope of a heavenly country. For not only the weaker brethren who enjoy married life, and have children (or desire to have them), and own houses and establishments, whom the apostle addresses in the churches, warning and instructing them how they should live, both the wives with their husbands, and the husbands with their wives, the children with their parents, and parents with their children, and servants with their masters, and masters with their servants,—not only do these weaker brethren gladly obtain and grudgingly lose many earthly and temporal things on account of which they dare not offend men whose polluted and wicked life greatly displeases them; but those also who live at a higher level, who are not entangled in the meshes of married life, but use meagre food and raiment, do often take thought of their own safety and good name, and abstain from finding fault with the wicked, because they fear their wiles and violence. And although they do not fear them to such an extent as to be drawn to the commission of like iniquities, nay, not by any threats or violence soever; yet those very deeds which they refuse to share in the commission of they often decline to find fault with, when possibly they might by finding fault prevent their commission. They abstain from interference, because they fear that, if it fail of good effect, their own safety or reputation may be damaged or destroyed; not because they see that their preservation and good name are needful, that they may be able to influence those who need their instruction, but rather because they weakly relish the flattery and respect of men, and fear the judgments of the people, and the pain or death of the body; that is to say, their non-intervention is the result of selfishness, and not of love.

Accordingly this seems to me to be one principal reason why the good are chastised along with the wicked, when God is pleased to visit with temporal punishments the profligate manners of a community. They are punished together, not because they have spent an equally corrupt life, but because the good as well as the wicked, though not equally with them, love this present life; while they ought to hold it cheap, that the wicked, being admonished and reformed by their example, might lay hold of life eternal. And if they will not be the companions of the good in seeking life everlasting, they should be loved as enemies, and be dealt with patiently. For so long as they live, it remains uncertain whether they may not come to a better mind. These selfish persons have more cause to fear than those to whom it was said through the prophet, "He is taken away in his iniquity, but his blood will I require at the watchman's hand." For watchmen or overseers of the people are appointed in churches, that they may unsparingly rebuke sin. Nor is that man guiltless of the sin we speak of, who, though he be not a watchman, yet sees in the conduct of those with whom the relationships of this life bring him into contact, many things that should be blamed, and yet overlooks them, fearing to give offence, and lose such worldly blessings as may legitimately be desired, but which he too eagerly grasps. Then, lastly, there is another reason why the good are afflicted with temporal calamities—the reason which Job's case exemplifies: that the human spirit may be proved, and that it may be manifested with what fortitude of pious trust, and with how unmercenary a love, it cleaves to God. (Saint Augustine, *The City of God*, Chapter 9.)

Saint Augustine explained the degree of madness that had gripped the Rome of the caesars as ordinary people sought nonstop entertainment, frequently at the expense of their own bodily health as well as their spiritual health. There are great parallels between Saint Augustine's description of the alleged delights of Rome with the way in which so many Catholics today immerse themselves in the popular culture:

> Know then, ye who are ignorant of this, and ye who feign ignorance be reminded, while you murmur against Him who has freed you from such rulers, that the scenic games, exhibitions of shameless folly and license, were established at Rome, not by men's vicious cravings, but by the appointment of your gods. Much more pardonably might you have rendered divine honors to Scipio than to such gods as these. The gods were not so moral as their pontiff. But give me now your attention, if your mind, inebriated by its deep potations of error, can take in any sober truth. The gods enjoined that games be exhibited in their honor to stay a physical pestilence; their pontiff prohibited the theatre from being constructed, to prevent a moral pestilence. If, then, there remains in you sufficient mental enlightenment to prefer the soul to the body, choose whom you will worship. Besides, though the pestilence was stayed, this was not because the voluptuous madness of stage-plays had taken possession of a warlike people hitherto accustomed only to the games of the circus; but these astute and wicked spirits, foreseeing that in due course the pestilence would shortly cease, took occasion to infect, not the bodies, but the morals of their worshippers, with a far more serious disease. And in this pestilence these gods find great enjoyment, because it benighted the minds of men with so gross a darkness and dishonored them with so foul a deformity, that even quite recently (will posterity be able to credit it?) some of those who fled from the sack of Rome and found refuge in Carthage, were so infected with this disease, that day after day they seemed to contend with one another who should most madly run after the actors in the theatres. (Saint Augustine, *City of God*, Chapter 32.)

Saint Augustine noted that what happened at the end of the Roman Empire in the West was just a more perfect manifestation of the evils that were present before the Incarnation and Nativity of Our Blessed Lord and Saviour Jesus Christ:

> Cicero, a weighty man, and a philosopher in his way, when about to be made edile, wished the citizens to that, among the other duties of his magistracy, he must propitiate Flora by the celebration of games. And these games are reckoned devout in proportion to their lewdness. In another and when he was now consul, and the state in great peril, he says that games had

been celebrated for ten days together, and that nothing had been omitted which could pacify the gods: as if it had not been more satisfactory to irritate the gods by temperance, than to pacify them by debauchery; and to provoke their hate by honest living, than soothe it by such unseemly grossness. For no matter how cruel was the ferocity of those men who were threatening the state, and on whose account the gods were being propitiated, it could not have been more hurtful than the alliance of gods who were won with the foulest vices. To avert the danger which threatened men's bodies, the gods were conciliated in a fashion that drove virtue from their spirits; and the gods did not enroll themselves as defenders of the battlements against the besiegers, until they had first stormed and sacked the morality of the citizens. This propitiation of such divinities,—a propitiation so wanton, so impure, so immodest, so wicked, so filthy, whose actors the innate and praiseworthy virtue of the Romans disabled from civic honors, erased from their tribe, recognized as polluted and made infamous;—this propitiation, I say, so foul, so detestable, and alien from every religious feeling, these fabulous and ensnaring accounts of the criminal actions of the gods, these scandalous actions which they either shamefully and wickedly committed, or more shamefully and wickedly feigned, all this the whole city learned in public both by the words and gestures of the actors. They saw that the gods delighted in the commission of these things, and therefore believed that they wished them not only to be exhibited to them, but to be imitated by themselves. But as for that good and honest instruction which they speak of, it was given in such secrecy, and to so few (if indeed given at all), that they seemed rather to fear it might be divulged, than that it might not be practised. (Chapter 27)

Refuting the false charge that Christianity was responsible for the sack and destruction of Rome, Saint Augustine went to great lengths to explain that Rome suffered from many calamities long before the coming of Our Lord and the Apostolic work of Saints Peter and Paul shortly before their own respective martyrdoms:

Let those who have no gratitude to Christ for His great benefits, blame their own gods for these heavy disasters. For certainly when these occurred the altars of the gods were kept blazing, and there rose the mingled fragrance of "Cebuan incense and fresh garlands;" Virgil, Æneid, I. 417. The priests were clothed with honor, the shrines were maintained in splendor; sacrifices, games, sacred ecstasies, were common in the temples; while the blood of the citizens was being so freely shed, not only in remote places, but among the very altars of the gods. Cicero did not choose to seek sanctuary in a temple, because Mucius had sought it there in vain. But they who most unpardonably calumniate this Christian era, are the very men who either themselves fled for asylum to the places specially dedicated to Christ, or were led there by the barbarians that they might be safe. In short, not to recapitulate the many instances I have cited, and not to add to their number others which it were tedious to enumerate, this one thing I am persuaded of, and this every impartial judgment will readily acknowledge, that if the human race had received Christianity before the Punic wars, and if the same desolating calamities which these wars brought upon Europe and Africa had followed the introduction of Christianity, there is no one of those who now accuse us who would not have attributed them to our religion. How intolerable would their accusations have been, at least so far as the Romans are concerned, if the Christian religion had been received and diffused prior to the invasion of the Gauls, or to the ruinous floods and fires which desolated Rome, or to those most calamitous of all events, the civil wars! And those other disasters, which were of so strange a nature that they were reckoned prodigies, had they happened since the Christian era, to whom but to the Christians would they have imputed these as crimes? I do not speak of those things which were rather surprising than hurtful,—oxen speaking, unborn infants articulating some words in their mothers' wombs, serpents flying, hens and women being changed into the other sex; and other similar prodigies which, whether true or false, are recorded not in their imaginative, but in their historical works, and which do not injure, but only astonish men. But when it rained earth, when it rained chalk, when it rained stones—not hailstones, but real stones—this certainly was calculated to do serious damage. We have read in their books that the fires of Etna, pouring down from the top of the mountain to the neighboring shore, caused the sea to boil, so that rocks were burnt up, and the pitch of ships began to run,—a phenomenon incredibly surprising, but at the same time no less hurtful. By the same violent heat, they relate that on another occasion Sicily was filled with cinders, so that the houses of the city Catina were destroyed and buried under them,—a calamity which moved the Romans to pity them, and remit their tribute for that year. One may also read that Africa, which had by that time become a province of Rome, was visited by a prodigious multitude of locusts, which, after consuming the fruit and foliage of the trees, were driven into the sea in one vast and measureless cloud; so that when they were drowned and cast upon the shore the air was polluted, and so serious a pestilence produced that in the kingdom of Masinissa alone they 63 say there perished 800,000 persons, besides a much greater number in the neighboring districts. At Utica they assure us that, of 30,000 soldiers then garrisoning it, there survived only ten. Yet which of these disasters, suppose they happened now, would not be attributed to the Christian religion by those who thus thoughtlessly accuse us, and whom we are compelled to answer? And yet to their own gods they attribute none of these things, though they worship them for the sake of escaping lesser calamities of the same kind, and do not reflect that they who formerly worshiped them were not preserved from these serious disasters. (City God, Book II, Chapter 31).

It is the same now as then. Exactly the same. Why are we so frightful in the midst of chastisements? Do we not realize that sins, including our own, need to be punished?

As noted before, the Catholics who lived in the Roman Empire did not go out of their way to make trouble for themselves. Trouble found them solel because they were Catholic. They never denied the Faith. They resisted the evils of the popular culture. They refused to be converted by the pagan immorality around which they lived. Although it can be argued that Catholics in the United States of America have lived in a cultural environment similar to that of the Roman Empire in the first three centuries of the Church, most Catholics in this country have been willing to deny the Faith by looking favorably upon the "worship" offered to the devil by Protestant sects and other false religions. The Catholics of Rome were not co-opted by Roman spirit. Catholics in this country, however, have been co-opted by the Americanist spirit.

The Rome of the caesars did indeed fall. The Rome of Christ the King arose from its ashes. Holy Mother Church passed from her Infancy and Hidden Years into her Public Life as the missionary work, which had been undergoing even during the times of the persecutions, begun on Pentecost Sunday began to spread and take root amongst the various pagan and barbaric peoples of Europe and elsewhere, resulting in the establishment of the Christ-centered world we refer to as the Christendom of the Middle Ages, which is, approximately speaking, that time in history from the collapse of Rome in the West to the rise of the secular, relativistic Renaissance and the Protestant Revolution, a period of around one thousand years. It is Christendom that is the model for how men must organize themselves around the Divine Plan that God Himself instituted to effect man's return to Him through the Catholic Church, not the American model of pluralism and relativism that are incarnations of the same pathologies as brought down the wrath of God upon the Roman Empire.

Chapter IX
The Rise and the Prospering of Christendom

The spread of the Faith into various parts of Europe took over a millennium to accomplish. This work began during the era of persecution in the first three centuries, accelerating from the time of Emperor Constantine's Edict of Milan in the year 312 A.D. before receiving the approval of Emperor Theodosius, who declared Christianity to be the state religion of Rome in the year 380 A.D. Catholicism was the sole bulwark of retarding the advances of the barbarians after the collapse of the Roman Empire in the West as popes sent missionaries to convert the pagan and barbaric peoples of Europe to the true Faith.

This missionary work took place even in the midst of the turmoil that rocked Holy Mother Church as Arianism, denounced at the Council of Nicea in the year 325 A.D., divided her and led many bishops and priests and the faithful into heresy. This heresy persisted throughout most of the Fourth Century, being fought by such great Catholic heroes as Saint Nicholas of Myra and Saint Basil the Great and Saint Jerome and Saint Athanasius and, of course, Saint Augustine. Other heresies would arise throughout the course of the First Millennium and into the beginning of the Second Millennium. As each heresy arose, Our Lady sent us great saints to combat as her Mystical Spouse, God the Holy Ghost, guided Holy Mother Church's true councils that were convened to refute and combat them.

Despite the presence of these heresies, however, Holy Mother Church continued the long process of converting barbaric peoples to her maternal bosom, outside of which there is no salvation and without which there can be no true social order.

Father Edward Cahill, S.J., provided a very helpful description of the events of the founding of Christendom in the First Millennium:

> **The Teutonic Invasions**.–The period of the Early Middle Ages may be said to extend from about the middle of the 5th century to the Pontificate of Pope Gregory VII (d. 1085). The reign of Emperor Honorius (395-423) had witnessed the beginning of the last struggles of the Roman Empire in Western Europe. From across the Danube the Goths over-ran Italy, Gaul and Spain. The Saxons, Jutes and Angles crossing from the North Sea from the regions south of Denmark, swarmed in Britain. The Alemanni, Franks, Burgundians, and later on the Lombards, advanced from beyond the Rhine; while from the plains of Vistula, the fierce Vandals and the savage race of the Huns poured over Western and Southern Europe. Before the end of the 5th century, the Western Empire was finally dissolved. The Goths were ruling in Spain and the Vandals in Africa. The Franks had obtained mastery in Gaul and along the basin on the Rhine. Soon after, the Lombards definitely established their power in Northern Italy, and the Anglo-Saxons in Britain.
>
> Many of these nations, including the Franks, Burgundians and Anglo-Saxons, were pagan. The Vandals, Lombards, Alemanni and Goths were Christians only in name. They professed Arianism, a debased form of Christianity, in which the mysteries of the Holy Trinity and the Incarnation of the Son of God were rejected.

Ireland and the Barbarians.–Meanwhile, during the second half of the 5th century, the Irish people, who had remained outside the Roman Empire, and were not touched by the barbarian invasions, had been converted to Christianity; and in a short time the Christian spirit had permeated the laws and the social customs of the nation. During the three centuries that ensued, while confusion and turmoil reigned on the continent, Ireland became the principal depository in Europe of the Christian tradition. From Ireland most of the missionaries came that laboured during the 6th and 7th centuries for the conversion of the barbarian conquerors of Western Europe, both pagan and Arian, to Christianity.

Conversion of the Barbarians.–By the end of the 8th century, the nations west of the Danube and Rhine, including Britain, and two hundred years later, practically all Europe with the exception of the Moors in the southern half of Spain, had accepted the Christian faith. But the work of bringing the laws and social life of the converted nations into harmony with Christian principles was a more tedious and difficult task; and much of the pagan spirit and outlook continued to live on among them for centuries after they had nominally embraced Christianity.

Eighth and two following Centuries.–The work of the Church was rendered more difficult by the disturbed state of Europe, and especially by the rise of the Mohammedan power and the invasions of the Norsemen, Hungarians and Slavs. In the early half of the 8th century, the Mohammedan Moors established their power in Spain and continued to push their way into France till the wave of invasion was finally broken by Charles Martel, on the field of Tours (A.D. 732).

Soon after, the pagan Norsemen and Danes began their wars of conquest in the North. These wars continued for more than two centuries and extended even to Italy and Sicily. The Norsemen broke up the civil and ecclesiastical organisation in Northern France, Belgium, Ireland and England, before they were themselves won over to Christianity in the 11th century.

Meanwhile from the East the Slavs, still half pagan, carried on a fierce war against the Christian states on their borders; while the fierce rage of the Magyars or Hungarians began in the 8th century their terrible incursions into central Germany and Northern Italy. All these wars impeded the civilising influence of Christianity and delayed for more than two centuries the formation of Christendom.

Influence of Ecclesiastics.–During the whole of this period the Catholic Church was the one power in Europe that stood for human right and liberty. As the nations became Christian, the Pope gradually gained recognition as the delegate of God who is the source of all legitimate authority. Hence he became the official adviser and ad-monitor of Christian rulers, the mediator between the rulers and the people and the arbiter in international affairs. The local bishops and abbots, and even individual priests, exercised, each in his own limited sphere, an influence similar to that which the Popes possessed in Christendom as a whole. For in those days intellectual training at least outside of the Greek Empire and Ireland was practically confined to the clergy and the monks. Thus it was from the Church's representatives–the

Pope, the Bishops and the clergy–that the serf, the poor and the weak sought and obtained protection against wrong.

And of Christian Teaching.–Historians generally recognize that it was as a result of Christian teaching and the Church's influence that the barbarian nations were gradually moulded to that sense of justice, charity and true liberty, which formed the basis of mediaeval civilization. Leo XIII strongly emphasises this fact:

> Christian Europe has subdued barbarous nations, and changed them from a savage to a civilized condition, from superstition to true worship. It victoriously rolled back the tide of Mohammedan conquest; retained the headship of civilization; stood forth in the front rank as the leader and teacher of all, in every branch of national culture; bestowed on the world the gift of true and many-sided liberty; and most wisely founded very numerous institutions for the solace of human suffering. And if we inquire how it was able to bring about so altered a condition of things, the answer is-beyond all question, in large measure, through religion, under whose auspices so many great undertakings were set on foot, through whose aid they were brought to completion. . . . And, in truth, whatever in the State is of chief avail for the common welfare; whatever has been usefully established to curb the license of rulers who are opposed to the true interests of the people, or to keep in check the leading authorities from unwarrantably interfering in municipal or family affairs; whatever tends to uphold the honour, manhood, and equal rights of individual citizens-of all these things, as the monuments of past ages bear witness, the Catholic Church has always been the originator, the promoter, or the guardian. (Pope Leo XIII, *Immortale Dei*, November 1, 1885.)

It was the Church that checked the tyranny and absolutism of the ruler while teaching the subjects the duty of submission and obedience to lawful authority, thus pointing out to all the path leading to social happiness and peace. It was from the Church's teaching and admonitions that the wealthy and powerful baron learned his duties of justice and charity towards his vassals and serfs, while the latter from the same teaching became conscious of their dignity as children of God and realised the indefeasible rights they had, no less than the price or the feudal baron, to a fair share even of temporal well-being. (Father Edward Cahill, S.J., *The Framework of a Christian State*, published in 1932 and reprinted by Roman Catholic Books, pp. 14-17.)

As Father Cahill noted, the work of converting the pagan and barbaric peoples of Europe was slow and fraught with difficulties and setbacks. Over the course of time and by means of the graces sent by Our Blessed Lord and Saviour Jesus Christ through the loving hands of His Blessed Mother, who is the Mediatrix of all Graces, the seeds planted in the soil of Europe took deep root. This is why the devil would have to attack the Faith with great violence there, never more so than at the outset of the Protestant Revolution in 1517, although he had tried many times before and had been successful in planting his own evil seed for the success of Father Martin Luther's rebellion against the Divine Plan that God Himself instituted to effect man's return to Him through the Catholic Church.

Although there were many conflicts between civil and ecclesiastical officials during the period of Christendom, Pope Gelasius I spelled out very clearly the nature of the Social Kingship of Our Lord Jesus Christ when he wrote the following in the year 494 A.D.:

> There are two powers, August Emperor, by which this world is chiefly ruled, namely, the sacred authority of the priests and the royal power. Of these that of the priests is the more weighty, since they have to render an account for even the kings of men in the divine judgment. You are also aware, dear son, that while you are permitted honorably to rule over human kind, yet in things divine you bow your head humbly before the leaders of the clergy and await from their hands the means of your salvation. In the reception and proper disposition of the heavenly   mysteries you recognize that you should be subordinate rather than superior to the religious order, and that in these matters you depend on their judgment rather than wish to force them to follow your will.
>
> If the ministers of religion, recognizing the supremacy granted you from heaven in matters affecting the public order, obey your laws, lest otherwise they might obstruct the course of secular affairs by irrelevant considerations, with what readiness should you not yield them obedience to whom is assigned the dispensing of the sacred mysteries of religion. **Accordingly, just as there is no slight danger in the case of the priests if they refrain from speaking when the service of the divinity requires, so there is no little risk for those who disdain - which God forbid -when they should obey. And if it is fitting that the hearts of the faithful should submit to all priests in general who properly administer divine affairs, how much the more is obedience due to the bishop of that see which the Most High ordained to be above all others, and which is consequently dutifully honored by the devotion of the whole Church**. (Letter to Emperor Anastasius)

In other words, Holy Mother Church has been given the right from God Himself to remonstrate with civil officials if the good of souls demands her motherly intervention. She is a patient mother, using her offices of teaching and preaching and exhortation before resorting to her penal powers to prevent actions deleterious to the good of souls from being implemented and/or to impose sanctions upon those who have proceeded with such actions after all efforts of persuasion had failed.

The great missionaries of Europe–Saint Martin of Tours in France, Saint Patrick in Ireland, Saint Augustine of Canterbury in England, Saint Boniface in Germany and Saint Hyacinth in northern Europe at the beginning of the Second Millennium–made possible the flowering of the Social Reign of Christ King in Christendom, an era in which people were born and lived and died within the shadow of the Holy Cross, taught to do all things well for the love of God as befitted their dignity as redeemed creatures. Although human nature remained wounded by the vestigial after-effects of Original Sin and by the Actual Sins of men, producing periods of great moral dissolution that God saw fit to punish with wars and pestilences of one sort or another, human beings understood that the purpose of human life was to know, to love and to serve God as He had revealed Himself to men exclusively through His Catholic Church, being ready at all times to face the terrible moment of the Particular Judgment. They accepted suffering as the price of their redemption, understanding that men must suffer on account of their own sins and those of the whole world. It was a time in history unlike our own, a time when men recognized that they were contingent beings and that no one, whether he was a king or other civil official or a lowly peasant who tilled the soil, had any authority from God to violate the binding precepts of the Divine Positive Law and the Natural Law.

A Few Saints Who Helped Catholicize Europe

Saint Patrick and Ireland: Among the saints who Catholicized Europe was the great Saint Patrick, the Apostle of Ireland, who knew this very well, which is why the Catholic Faith took deep such deep root in the Emerald Isle that it was known for centuries as the Land of Saints and Scholars.

Saint Patrick sought to serve only the New and Eternal Covenant instituted by Our Lord on Holy Thursday and ratified by the shedding of every single drop of His Most Precious Blood on the wood of the Holy Cross. He did not have to "search for truth" in inter-religious "dialogue" with the Druids or anyone else in Ireland. He told them that they had to convert to the Catholic Faith, being willing to lay down his life for their conversion if it was necessary for him to do so. He confronted the chieftains on Easter Sunday, 433 A.D., winning the day for Christ the King and thus beginning his work for the conversion of the entirety of Ireland, a work that continued in the years ahead of him as he traveled throughout the Land of Erin, eventually establishing his own primatial see in Armagh.

Although Saint Patrick encountered challenges and difficulties now and again, he never flagged in his efforts to save souls by seeking their conversion to the Catholic Faith. Seeking the conversion of souls never goes out of date. It never has an "expiration date." It is incapable of being consigned to the Orwellian memory hole by the Modernist revolutionaries who exercised great influence at the "Second" Vatican Council and who have held the levers of power and influence in chancery offices and universities and seminaries and colleges and schools and parishes under conciliar captivity from that time forward. Saint Patrick knew that there was only one path to salvation: to preach the true Faith as it had been deposited by the Second Person of the Blessed Trinity made Man in Our Lady's Virginal and Immaculate Womb in the one, true Church He created upon the Rock of Peter, the Pope.

Unlike the late Karol Wojtyla/John Paul II, who praised witch doctors and other shamans for the great "services" they provided to their tribes, and unlike many diocesan "bishops," who merrily participate in pagan rituals in the context of the offering of alleged Masses so as to fulfill the principles of the "inculturation of the Gospel," Saint Patrick wanted to put an end once and for all to the diabolical practices of Druidism. The fact that Druidism has risen again in Ireland in recent decades is partly the result of the counterfeit church of conciliarism's diabolical "reconciliation" with the principles of that "new era inaugurated in 1789," thereby putting an apparent "Catholic" gloss on the Protestant and Judeo-Masonic overthrow of the Social Reign of Christ the King. Saint Patrick sought to establish Catholicism as the one and only foundation of personal and social order on the Emerald Isle. Saint Patrick sought to work for the conversion of the masses by converting the chieftains, thereby establishing the framework for Catholic monarchism throughout Europe. The people, Saint Patrick understood, would likely follow the example of their leaders.

Taking advantage of the structure of hierarchical tribal life, Saint Patrick quickly sought to establish dioceses throughout Ireland so as to accustom the Irish people to the hierarchical nature of the true Church, the Catholic Church. He consecrated no less than 350 bishops during his apostolic work in Ireland. Among those he consecrated as bishops were several who later went on to be raised to the

Church's altars with himself, including his own nephew, Saint Mel, Saint Guasach, Saint MacCarthem, and Saint Loman. His work brought about the conversion of Saint Brigid of Kildare, through Saint Mel, and produced a nation so steeped in Catholicism that it boasts of scores upon scores of canonized saints. Saint Aidan, Saint Brendan, Saint Kevin, Saint Colman of Armagh (as well as several other saints by the name of Colman), Saint Columba, Saint Columban, Saint Kieran, Saint Malachy, and Saint Ita, among many others, learned to love and to live the Catholic Faith as a result of the seeds planted by the glorious Saint Patrick.

Unlike most of the "bishops" of the counterfeit church of conciliarism, most of whom are not exactly noted for austere lives of penance, Saint Patrick combined his great pastoral zeal to convert souls with severe penances, including spending time frequently in what became known as Saint Patrick's Purgatory, Lough Dearg. Saint Patrick spent long hours in prayers and subjected his body to many mortifications. He thought only to teach people to love God as He had revealed Himself solely through His true Church, giving no quarter at all to any false belief or false religious practice. He would NOT accept "gifts" from false religions, as Joseph Ratzinger/Benedict XVI did last year while visiting the United States of America.

Saint Patrick wanted to eradicate false beliefs and false practices and all other types of sin from the lives of the Irish people and from every aspect of the Irish nation, which is why those who seek to march in Saint Patrick's Day Parades by identifying themselves as participants in perversity are dishonoring the great Apostle to the Irish. Saint Patrick despised sin. He knew that sin is what caused Our Lord to suffer unspeakable horror in His Sacred Humanity during His fearful Passion and Death and is what caused His Most Blessed Mother to have Seven Swords of Sorrow pierced through her Sorrowful and Immaculate Heart.

Although the Catholic legacy of Saint Patrick was attacked fiercely by the British following the English Protestant Revolt and has been undermined by cultural forces imported principally from the United States of America, which itself was shaped by the Protestantism and Freemasonry that undermined the Faith of many of the Irish immigrants to this country, Ireland stood out among the nations of Christendom for its sanctity and scholarship for centuries. Saint Patrick would have blanched at the mention of an oxymoronic conciliarist phrase such as a "healthy secularity." He lived and worked and died so that Catholicism would permeate every aspect of the lives of the Irish people. His intercession must be invoked daily for the people of Ireland who still practice the Faith to hold onto the fullness of Tradition without compromise--and for those who have fallen by the wayside to return to the true Sheepfold of Christ. As the Patron Saint of all of the Irish people no matter where they have situated themselves, Saint Patrick's intercession must be invoked in a special way to help those of Irish ancestry outside of Ireland to honor him by their fidelity to the Catholic Tradition he brought to Ireland in the midst of cultural circumstances very similar to the ones we face in the United States today.

Saint Patrick worked for the Catholicization of Ireland. He wants the Catholicization of every land. How it must sadden him in Heaven to see so many sons and daughters of Erin in public life in this country who support all manner of sins under cover of civil law. How it must sadden him further to see so many conciliar "bishops" of Irish descent reaffirm those pro-abortion politicians as they themselves undermine the Deposit of Faith and make war in their own dioceses upon the Immemorial Mass of the ages that he brought to Ireland in the Fifth Century. How much we should pray to him to help us remain steadfast in the Faith on a daily basis so that our prayers, offered to God through Our Lady's Sorrowful and Immaculate Heart, might be more efficacious in bringing about the re-conversion of Irish Catholics, both in Ireland and elsewhere.

Saint Benedict of Nursia and Western Monasticism: Saint Benedict of Nursia is the founder of Western monasticism upon the basis of prayer and work (ora et labora). Monasteries became the focal points of Catholic life in the Middle Ages as a result of the seeds planted by Saint Benedict. Villagers and people from surrounding areas went there to hear Holy Mass and they learned useful trades. It was in monasteries that learning was kept alive in the second half of the First Millennium during the tide of the barbaric invasions that had been described by Father Cahill in the passages above.

Saint Benedict, unlike his namesake, Benedict XVI, was adamantly opposed to paying any kind of respect to false religions or their temples and symbols. Two popes, Pope Saint Gregory the Great and Pope Pius XII, explained this in some detail:

> The castle called Cassino is situated upon the side of a high mountain which riseth in the air about three miles so that it seemed to touch the very heavens. On Monte Cassino stood an old temple where Apollo was worshiped by the foolish country people, according to the custom of the ancient heathen. Round about it, likewise grew groves, in which even until that time, the mad multitude of infidels offered their idolatrous sacrifices. The man of God, coming to that place, broke down the idol, overthrew the altar, burnt the groves and of the temple made a chapel of St. Martin; and where the profane altar had stood, he built a chapel of St. John and, by continual preaching converted many of the people thereabout.

> But the old enemy, not bearing this silently, did present himself in the sight of the Father and with great cries complained of the violence he suffered, in so much that the brethren heard him, though they could see nothing. For, as the venerable Father told his disciples, the wicked fiend represented himself to his sight all on fire and, with flaming mouth and flashing eyes, seemed to rage against him. And they all heard what he said, for first he called him by name, and when the man of God would make no answer, he fell to reviling him. And whereas before he cried, "Benedict, Benedict," and saw he could get no answer, then he cried, "Maledict, not Benedict, what hast thou to do with me, and why dost thou persecute me?" (Pope Saint Gregory the Great, *The Life of Saint Benedict*, republished by TAN Books and Publishers in 1995, pp. 24-25.)

> Then it was that this holy man saw that the time, ordained by God's providence, had come for him to found a family of religious men and to mold them to the perfection of the Gospels. He began under most favorable auspices. "For in those parts he had gathered together a great many in the service of God, so that by the assistance of Our Lord Jesus Christ he built there 12 monasteries, in each of which he put 12 monks with their Superiors, and retained a few with himself whom he thought to instruct further".

> But while things started very favorably, as We said, and yielded rich and salutary results, promising still greater in the future, Our saint with the greatest grief of soul, saw a storm breaking over the growing harvest, which an envious spirit had provoked and desires of earthly gain had stirred up. Since Benedict was prompted by divine and not human

counsel, and feared lest the envy which had been aroused mainly against himself should wrongfully recoil on his followers, "he let envy take its course, and after he had disposed of the oratories and other buildings -- leaving in them a competent number of brethren with superiors -- he took with him a few monks and went to another place". Trusting in God and relying on His ever present help, he went south and arrived at a fort "called Cassino situated on the side of a high mountain . . .; on this stood an old temple where Apollo was worshiped by the foolish country people, according to the custom of the ancient heathens. Around it likewise grew groves, in which even till that time the mad multitude of infidels used to offer their idolatrous sacrifices. The man of God coming to that place broke the idol, overthrew the altar, burned the groves, and of the temple of Apollo made a chapel of St. Martin. Where the profane altar had stood he built a chapel of St. John; and by continual preaching he converted many of the people thereabout".

Cassino, as all know, was the chief dwelling place and the main theater of the Holy Patriarch's virtue and sanctity. From the summit of this mountain, while practically on all sides ignorance and the darkness of vice kept trying to overshadow and envelop everything, a new light shone, kindled by the teaching and civilization of old and further enriched by the precepts of Christianity; it illumined the wandering peoples and nations, recalled them to truth and directed them along the right path. Thus indeed it may be rightly asserted that the holy monastery built there was a haven and shelter of highest learning and of all the virtues, and in those very troubled times was, "as it were, a pillar of the Church and a bulwark of the faith". (Pope Pius XII, *Fulgens Radiatur*, March 21, 1947.)

Saint Augustine of Canterbury: The great Apostle of England, sent there by Pope Saint Gregory the Great to convert King Ethelbert of Kent in the year 595 A.D., planted the seeds of the Faith so deep in the soil of the English that the adversary had to root It out violently when King Henry VIII broke from the Catholic Church in the year 1534 when he had himself declared "supreme head of the Church in England" by the Parliament and began his bloody rage against those who remained faithful to the true Church. *The Liturgical Year*, which was written by a Benedictine, Dom Prosper Gueranger, O.S.B., contains the following account of the Benedictine named Augustine who would re-establish the Catholic Faith in England and thus finally the convert the whole of it for the glory of God and the good of souls:

What a beautiful sight is brought before us to-day, of the first Archbishop of Canterbury, who, after honouring on this day the saintly memory of the holy Pontiff from whom England first received the Gospel [Pope Saint Eleutherius] the eternity of heaven's joy! Who would not acknowledge in this, a pledge of the predilection wherewith heaven has favoured this country, which, after centuries of fidelity to the truth, has now for more than three hundred years been an enemy to her own truest glory?

The work begun by Eleutherius had been almost entirely destroyed by the invasion of the Saxons and Angles; so that a new mission, a new preaching of the Gospel, had become a necessity. It was Rome that again supplied the want. St. Gregory the Great was the originator of the great design. Had it been permitted him, he would have taken upon himself the fatigues of this apostolate to our country. He was deeply impressed with the idea that he was to be the spiritual Father of these poor islanders, some of whom he had seen exposed in the market- place of Rome, that they might be sold as slaves. Not being allowed to undertake the work himself, he looked around him for men whom he might send to as Apostles to our island. He found them in the Benedictine monastery where he himself had spent several years of his life. There started from Rome forty monks, with Augustine at their head, and they entered England under the standard of the Cross.

Thus the new race that then people of the island received the faith, as the Britons had previously done, from the hands of a Pope; and monks were their teachers in the science of salvation. The word of Augustine and his companions fructified in this privileged soil. It was some time of course before he could provide the whole nation with instruction; but neither Rome nor the Benedictines abandoned the work thus begun. The few remnants that were still left of the ancient British Christianity joined the new converts; and England merited to be called, for long ages, the 'Island of Saints.'

The history of St. Augustine's apostolate in England is of thrilling interest. The landing of the Roman missioners, and their marching through the country, to the chant of the Litany; the willing and almost kind welcome given them by king Ethelbert; the influence exercised by his queen Bertha, who was a French-woman and a Catholic, in the establishment of the faith among the Saxons; the baptism of ten thousand neophytes on Christmas day, and in the bed of a river; the foundation of the metropolitan see of Canterbury, one of the most illustrious Churches of Christendom on account of the holiness and noble doings of its Archbishops; all these admirable episodes of England's conversion are eloquent proofs of God's predilection of our dear land. Augustine's peaceful and gentle character, arduous missionary labours, gives an additional charm to this magnificent page of the Church's history. But who can help feeling sad at the thought that a country, favoured as ours has been with such graces, should have apostatized from the faith; have repaid with hatred that Rome which made her Christian; and have persecuted with unheard-of cruelties the Benedictine Order to which she owed so much of her glory? (Dom Prosper Gueranger, O.S.B., *The Liturgical Year*: Paschal Time, Volume II, pp. 604-606.)

This is of particular importance for the study of the Americanist heresy as the English colonies that were founded in the Seventeenth Century in what is now the United States of America would have been expressions of English Catholicism, replete with its distinct characteristics of pious customs that differ from those found in Spain or France.

However, colonists from a Catholic England would have been staunch defenders of the Social Reign of Christ the King as loyal subjects of the Crown. Henry Tudor's revolution against the Church in England and his violent assault upon Catholics who remained faithful to Holy Mother Church set in motion the forces that would bring all manner of Protestant heresies and errors to the colonies up and down the Atlantic seaboard of what is now the United States of America. And, as will be pointed out later, the Catholics who come here as early as 1634 were content just to practice the Faith without having to suffer the persecutions that they and their ancestors had done in the preceding one hundred years in England and Ireland. This made it possible for them to fall prey over the course of time to the errors of Protestantism and to the naturalist errors of Judeo-Masonry that multiplied rapidly in the Seventeenth and Eighteenth Centuries.

England produced one of the greatest exemplars of the Social Reign of Christ the King, **Saint Edward the Confessor**, whose humble service to the poor stands in stark contrast to the haughtiness of civil rulers today, men and women who take money from the citizens and their children and children's children in order to pay for programs designed to keep the populace ever dependent upon the "largesse" of the civil government.

Saint Edward spent thirty years of his life, from age ten to age forty, in exile in Normandy, growing in sanctity, especially by his devotion to the Holy Sacrifice of the Mass, at which he was once privileged to actually see the Chief Priest and Victim of every Mass, Our Blessed Lord and Saviour Jesus Christ, smiling at him. He was solicitous of the poor and the underprivileged.

Saint Edward the Confessor acceded to the throne at the age of thirty-nine, in 1042, receiving a warm welcome from the Danes who had invaded England and gained political mastery there. Edward was respected by all precisely because of his sanctity, which exhibited itself in his gentleness and in his ability to avert conflicts. Although he did repel an invasion from the Welsh and sought to aid King Malcolm III in Scotland as Macbeth plotted to secure the Scottish throne for himself, his twenty-four year reign was one of peace with other kingdoms and justice for the poor in his own kingdom. Saint Edward, the last Anglo-Saxon King of England, was ever conscious of his obligation to rule according to the Mind of Christ the King as He has discharged It exclusively in His Catholic Church. Thus mindful of the rights of private property and the limits of just government, Saint Edward the Confessor reduced taxes during his reign in England.

Saint Edward the Confessor was particularly devoted to Saint John the Evangelist. He refused no request made in the name of the Beloved Apostle. Saint John appeared to Saint Edward as a beggar, who asked him for alms. Having no money to give him, the king took off his ring and gave it away. Saint John returned the ring with a note telling him on what day, January 5, he would die in the year of 1066, just nine months before the Battle of Hastings. Saint Edward immediately ordered that prayers be said for him in preparation for his death. The man who was chosen to be a king in this world was ever mindful of his duties to be submissive to the King of Kings, to Whom he would have to make an account of his life and of the secular authority that had been given to him at the moment of his Particular Judgment.

Saint Edward is thus quite a contrast indeed to the egomaniacal, delusional civil potentates of our own day, some of whom believe that God actually speaks to them ("George, go into Iraq and get Hussein") and "orders" them to rain down bombs on others in order to spread, say, the American concept of civil liberty as the means of a just social order within nations and peace among nations, while others, perhaps one currently in power, suffer from delusions of being a secular saviour ("We are the ones we've been waiting for.")

Saint Edward knew that the basis of peace among men is the peace of Christ in the souls of men that is the fruit of being in a state of sanctifying grace. Saint Edward knew that no man is free who has not been liberated from sin in Christ by means of being baptized as a member of the Catholic Church. Saint Edward knew that no country will be just if it attempts to make idols of his own national myths and ideologies, dismissing as so much "impractical nonsense" the necessity of formal membership in the true Church as the means of the salvation of men and the necessity of kingdoms being subordinated to the King of Kings and the authority of His true Church.

The United States of America would be Catholic today if it had a king such as Edward the Confessor on the throne when the Protestant Revolution was breaking out on the continent of Europe. Such, however, was not to be within the Providence of God.

It was, after all, in England that the Catholic Church did exercise the Social Reign of Christ the King to curb the excesses of kings who sought to subjugate Holy Mother Church to a subordinate position to that of the civil state.

Saint Thomas a Becket, the Archbishop of Canterbury from 1162 until his murder in his own cathedral in 1170, had to fight for the liberties of the Church against King Henry II, who was very intent on making the Church serve his own purposes, a foreshadowing of the evils of another King Henry some 460 years later.

Saint Thomas a Becket, although a friend of King Henry Plantagenet, would not let human respect stand in the way of defending the absolute right of the Catholic Church to be free in matters of her internal governance from any interference by temporal officials. The king of a country had to be subordinate to the King of Kings Who was born for us in poverty and in anonymity in Bethlehem so as to be crucified as Our King of Love on Calvary. No amount of blandishments from even a close friend, whom he had served for a time as the Chancellor of the Realm, and no amount of punishments imposed on his own relatives could persuade Saint Thomas a Becket to disown the King of Kings in order to curry favor with a mere mortal whose own kingship was transitory and circumscribed in the exercise of its legitimate powers by the Deposit of Faith entrusted to the Catholic Church.

Saint Thomas a Becket was a humble man. He prayed day and night. He served the poor with selfless abandon. He preached the Gospel fearlessly in the midst of all of the threats that were being made against him and his relatives. He wore a hair-shirt to mortify his flesh. Nevertheless, he did not hesitate as Archbishop of Canterbury to resist his friend, King Henry II, in order to reclaim lands that belonged rightly to the Church and to oppose with great courage the imposition of unjust taxes upon her by the civil state. Moreover, Saint Thomas asserted the right of the Church to try clerics charged with civil crimes in ecclesiastical courts as opposed to their being tried in civil courts.

Unlike the "bishops" of the counterfeit church of conciliarism in the United States of America and elsewhere who have sought to shield priests guilty of perverted behavior from all real punishments, whether ecclesiastical or civil, Saint Thomas a Becket meant to deal severely with clerics adjudged guilty of having committed crimes. He was simply asserting the right of the Church and not the civil state to do so, recognizing that the civil state might abuse its prosecutorial power to trump up totally bogus charges against priests so as to extort silence from them in the pulpit about matters of civil governance contrary to the demands of objective justice and thus the good of souls. It was in no way the intention of Saint Thomas a Becket to do what Bernard "Cardinal" Law and Roger "Cardinal" Mahony and countless other conciliar "bishops" have done, that is, to protect perverted priests by transferring them to other assignments without either punishing them for their perversity or seeking their spiritual reform for having the predilection to engage in unnatural acts indicative of grave mental disorders. Saint Thomas a Becket was willing to be charged with a bogus charge of "contempt of court" rather than yield for one instant to King Henry II's demands to bring the Church in England to heel under his power.

For the good of the Church, however, and for the sake of civil peace, Saint Thomas was willing to absent himself from Canterbury for a time in order to calm King Henry's anger and to foster the Church's liberties. It was the prayerful hope of Saint Thomas while he was in exile in France, chiefly under the protection of King Louis VII of France, that the rights of the Church be free from any and all threats imposed by the civil state, would be respected anew. Alas, he had to pay with his life for his defense of the liberties of Holy Mother Church against the unjust exercise of civil authority by a fellow Catholic, falling under the blows imposed upon his body during vespers on December 29, 1170, becoming a new kind of martyr: one killed by fellow Catholics who viewed an archbishop's loyalty to Christ the King as disloyalty to the civil state. Coming as it did during the Octave of Christmas 836 years ago, the martyrdom of Saint Thomas a Becket reminds us that there will be those from the household of the Faith itself--and not just from the world-at-large--who will tempt us even during the solemnities of the Church's liturgical year to surrender to the exigencies of the moment rather than to remain steadfast at all times and in all places to the fullness of the Catholic Faith without one moment's hesitation.

Saint Thomas a Becket's witness to the rights of God and His Holy Church against the unjust exercise of civil authority by a Catholic potentate was one of the first instances of Catholic Cains shedding the blood of Catholic Abels, following by ninety-one years the murder of Saint Stanislaus by King Boleslaus in Poland in the year 1079 A.D., and following within that same ninety years or so the plots of Emperor Henry IV against the rights of the Church during the reign of Pope Saint Gregory VII. Catholics were doing the bidding of the adversary by spilling the blood of their brother Catholics to advance the goals of the civil state over moral reform and the rights of God and His Holy Church.

The adversary, who prowls about the world seeking the ruin of souls and to do as much damage to the Church Militant on earth as possible before Our Lord's Second Coming in glory at the end of time on the Last Day, had done likewise with many of the Prophets of the Old Testament, men who had dared to challenge the kings of Israel and Judah to reform their own lives and to govern according to God's laws rather than the dictates of their own disordered wills. It was to be expected, therefore, that some Catholic kings would lose sight of Whose Kingship they were meant to imitate. If King David, of whose royal house Our Lord was born, could arrange the murder of Urias, the husband of his paramour, then it should not be too terribly surprising that men such as Saint Stanislaus and Saint Thomas a Becket would suffer at the hands of their own co-religionists, friends, and relatives for the sake of remaining steadfast to the Gospel of Our Blessed Lord and Saviour Jesus Christ and the rights of Holy Mother Church.

King Henry II was forced to do public penance for the role he played in uttering the words that led to the murder of his friend-turned-adversary, the Archbishop of Canterbury, Saint Thomas a Becket. Although prompted in large part by the overwhelming public outrage over the murder of the beloved Archbishop, a friend to the poor and the downtrodden in the kingdom, King Henry did submit in 1174 to the Papal decree that he be scourged at the tomb of Saint Thomas to make reparation for his stubborn insistence on his own rights rather than those of God and His Church. King Henry II walked barefoot from London to Canterbury in order to be scourged! Largely as a result of the outcry engendered by the murder of Saint Thomas a Becket, King Henry's son, John I, was forced forty-one years later, in the year 1215, to recognize that there are indeed limits that exist in the nature of things upon the exercise of civil power. The Church's own rights were guaranteed at the very beginning and at the end of the Magna Carta:.

> In the first place we have conceded to God, and by this our present charter confirmed for us and our heirs for ever that the English church shall be free, and shall have her rights entire, and her liberties inviolate; and we wish that it be thus observed. This is apparent from the fact that we, of our pure and unconstrained will, did grant the freedom of elections, which is reckoned most important and very essential to the English church, and did by our charter confirm and did obtain the ratification of the same from our lord, Pope Innocent III., before the quarrel arose between us and our barons. This freedom we will observe, and our will is that it be observed in good faith by our heirs for ever. . . .

> Thus, we wish and we firmly ordain that the English church shall be free, and that men in our kingdom shall have and keep all these previously determined liberties, rights, and concessions, well and in peace, freely and quietly, in their fullness and integrity, for themselves and their heirs, from us and our heirs, in all things and all places for ever, as is previously described here.

As Dom Prosper Gueranger, O.S.B., noted in *The Liturgical Year:*

> But in what does this sacred liberty consist? It consists in the Church's absolute independence of every secular power in the ministry of the Word of God, which she is bound to preach in season and out of season, as St. Paul says, to all mankind, without distinction of nation or race or age or sex: in the administration of the Sacraments, to which she must invite all men without exception, in order to advance per the world's salvation: in the practice, free from all human control, of the Counsels, as well as the Precepts, of the Gospel: in the unobstructed intercommunication of the several degrees of her sacred hierarchy: in the publication and application of her decrees and ordinances in matters of discipline: in the maintenance and development of the Institutions she has founded: in holding and governing her temporal patrimony: and lastly in the defence of those privileges which have been adjudged to her by the civil authority itself, in order that her ministry of peace and charity might be unembarrassed and respected.

> Such is the Liberty of the Church. It is the bulwark of the Sanctuary. Every breach there imperils the Hierarchy, and even the very Faith. A Bishop may not flee, as the hireling, nor hold his peace, like those dumb dogs of which the Prophet Isaias speaks, and which are not able to bark. He is the Watchman of Israel: he is a traitor if he first lets the enemy enter the citadel, and then, but only then, gives the alarm and risks his person and his life. The obligation of laying down his life for his flock begins to be in force at the enemy's first attack upon the very outmost of the City, which is only safe when they are strongly guarded.

These stirring words of Dom Gueranger, reminiscent of Pope Saint Gregory the Great's *Pastoral Guide*, have not lost their bite since they were written in the Nineteenth Century. Indeed, they are even more relevant today, especially in light of the fact that most of the conciliar "bishops" today refuse to confront the evils done by civil rulers today, partly out of fear of losing some "privilege" bestowed upon them by the State, such as the counterfeit church of conciliarism's tax-exempt status, and partly because they do not see the promotion of baby-killing under cover of law and the promotion of the agenda of perversity in every aspect of our culture as requiring them to raise their voices in protest whatsoever.

Quite to the contrary, these dumb dogs who have abandoned the role of Watchman of Christ's true flock prefer to get the fleas of their civil masters, showing up at their inaugurations, administering what purports to be Holy Communion to them, never once seeking to discipline them with the plenipotentiary powers at their disposal, always choosing to stress their slavish adherence to whatever fashionable trends that are said to be part of the Left's agenda for "social justice." The failure of the conciliar "bishops" to condemn the powerful of this world who consign the innocent unborn to death and to denounce those who are "tolerant" of perversity stands in very sharp contrast to the heroic witness given to Our Lord and His Holy Church by today's saint and martyr, Saint Thomas a Becket.

Indeed, the conciliar "bishops" today are carrying on the very sad legacy of accommodationism that was evident among some of the hierarchy even in the days of Saint Thomas a Becket. There have been in the past 900 years or so bishops all too willing to play the role of slobbering courtiers at the feet of civil potentates. All but one of the English bishops knuckled under to the threatenings of King Henry VIII when he took England out of the Catholic Church in 1534. Only Saint John Fisher remained steadfast in his loyalty to the true Church, being one of nearly 72,000 Catholics who remained faithful to Rome who were executed on orders from one of the worst monsters of the Second Millennium, Henry Tudor, between 1534 and the time of his death in 1547. Another thirty or so bishops remained faithful to the Catholic Church when Elizabeth I took England out of the Church for good thirty years later, meaning that most of the bishops were as willing under Elizabeth to abandon Christ's true Church as they were under her relentlessly cruel father. And a bevy of bishops served as the sycophants to King Louis XIV, indemnifying him as he refused to consecrate the whole of France to the Most Sacred Heart of Jesus as Sister Margaret Mary Alacoque had said that Our Lord had specifically requested. Oh, yes, what we are experiencing at present has become an all-too-familiar pattern of betrayal on the part of those who have the responsibility to stand up for Our Lord and the rights of His Church at all times, not curry favor with the powerful and with public opinion.

Although it is certainly true that the "opening up to the world" ushered in by Angelo Roncalli/John XXIII and the "Second" Vatican Council has helped to institutionalize treachery and accommodationism to the State on the part of the false bishops, there were plenty of examples of such treachery and accommodationism to the exigencies of the modern State in the years leading up to the council. Then Senator John Fitzgerald Kennedy's embrace in 1960 of the Judeo-Masonic notion of the "separation of Church and State" was heralded by most of the American bishops. The support of the American bishops for John Kennedy's support of a proposition condemned quite specifically by Pope Saint Pius X as one of the chief goals of Modernism came thirty-two years after the first Catholic nominated by a major political party for the American Presidency, then New York Governor Alfred E. Smith, rejected the binding nature of Pope Pius XI's *Quas Primas*. It is said that the Rhine flowed into the Tiber to helped produce the problems at the "Second" Vatican Council. Yes, this is true. No doubt. It is also true that the Potomac flowed into the Tiber. The ethos of Americanism--and the accommodationism of many of the American bishops over the years to the anti-Incarnational errors of the American founding--played a very large role in such documents as *Gaudium et Spes* and *Dignitatis Humanae*.

Saint Boniface: Unlike Joseph Ratzinger/Benedict XVI, who made signs of respect to false religions constantly, including during pilgrimages to his native country, Germany, Saint Boniface (Winifred), sought to eradicate pagan worship in Germany, to which he had been sent as a missionary from England. Father John Laux explained how Saint Boniface, quite unlike Ratzinger/Benedict, mocked the tree worship as a "god" by the German heathens:

> A bold deed which he [Saint Boniface] performed at this time greatly increased his prestige and led to numerous conversions. At Geismar, near Fritzlar, there was a gigantic oak, called the "Tree of Thor," which the pagans of the whole country regarded with the deepest veneration. Mighty as the God of the Christians was, over the oak of Geismar, so they boasted, He had no power, and none of His followers would ever destroy it. This tree the Christians advised Boniface to cut down, assuring him that its fall would shake the faith of the pagans in the power of their gods. Boniface consented, and on the appointed day undertook to lay the ax to the tree with his own hands. A vast crowd of pagans stood around, intently watching to see some dire misfortune overwhelm the desecrator of their shrine. But when the mighty tree fell to the ground under the strokes of the Bishop's ax, they with one accord praised the God of the Christians and asked to be received among the number of His followers. Boniface baptized them, and out of the wood of the tree built a little oratory, which he dedicated to St. Peter. (Father John Laux, *Church History*, published originally by Benziger Brothers, in 1930, republished by TAN Books and Publishers, 1980, p. 149.)

Pope Pius XII explained that Saint Boniface sought with urgency the unconditional conversion of the German pagans to the true Faith. He was not interested in any kind of "dialogue." He was interested only in speaking to the infidels about the true Faith. Saint Boniface had zeal for the destruction of the symbols of false worship:

> When by the grace and favor of God this very important task was done, Boniface did not allow himself his well-earned rest. In spite of the fact that he was already burdened by so many cares, and was feeling now his advanced age and realizing that his health was almost broken by so many labors, he prepared himself eagerly for a new and no less difficult enterprise. He turned his attention again to Friesland, that Friesland which had been the first goal of his apostolic travels, where he had later on labored so much. **Especially in the northern regions this land was still enveloped in the darkness of pagan error. Zeal that was still youthful led him there to bring forth new sons to Jesus Christ and to bring Christian civilization to new peoples. For he earnestly desired "that in leaving this world he might receive his reward there where he had first begun his preaching and entered upon his meritorious career." Feeling that his mortal life was drawing to a close, he confided his presentiment to his dear disciple, Bishop Lullus, and asserted that he did not want to await death in idleness. "I yearn to finish the road before me; I cannot call myself back from the path I have chosen. Now the day and hour of my death is at hand. For now I leave the prison of the body and go to my eternal reward. My dear son, . . . insist in turning the people from the paths of error, finish the construction of the basilica already begun at Fulda and there bring my body which has aged with the passage of many years."**

When he and his little band had taken departure from the others, "he traveled through all Friesland, ceaselessly preaching the word of God, **banishing pagan rites and extirpating immoral heathen customs. With tremendous energy he built churches and overthrew the idols of the temples**. He baptized thousands of men, women and children." After he had arrived in the northern regions of Friesland and was about to administer the Sacrament of Confirmation to a large number of newly baptized converts, a furious mob of pagans suddenly attacked and threatened to kill them with deadly spears and swords. **Then the holy prelate serenely advanced and "forbade his followers to resist, saying, 'Cease fighting, my children, for we are truly taught by Scripture not to return evil for evil, but rather good. The day we have long desired is now at hand; the hour of our death has come of its own accord. Take strength in the Lord, . . . be courageous and do not be afraid of those who kill the body, for they cannot slay an immortal soul. Rejoice in the Lord, fix the anchor of hope in God, Who will immediately give you an eternal reward and a place in the heavenly court with the angelic choirs'." All were encouraged by these words to embrace martyrdom. They prayed and turned their eyes and hearts to heaven where they hoped to receive soon an eternal reward, and then fell beneath the onslaught of their enemies, who stained with blood the bodies of those who fell in the happy combat of the saints." At the moment of this martyrdom, Boniface, who was to be beheaded by the sword, "placed the sacred book of the Gospels upon his head as the sword threatened, that he might receive the deadly stroke under it and claim its protection in death, whose reading he loved in life**. (Pope Pius XII, *Ecclesiae Fastos*, June 5, 1954.)

It was as a result of the work undertaken by Saint Boniface that Germany would produce scores upon scores of saints, including Saint Albert the Great, the teacher of Saint Thomas Aquinas, and Saint Gertrude the Great, whom Our Lord favored with the intimate secrets of His Most Sacred Heart, and her own sister, Saint Mechtilde, Saint Fidelis of Sigmaringen, Saint Florian, Saint Meinrad, Saint John of Cologne, Saint Norbert, and that marvelous exemplar of the Social Reign of Christ the King, **Saint Henry of Bavaria**, whose reign as Holy Roman Emperor saw him support the spread of the Faith into Hungary.

Saint Henry understood that he had the responsibility to help to foster those conditions within the jurisdictional boundaries of his civil rule (first Bavaria, then Germany, then the entirety of the Holy Roman Empire) that would make it more possible for his subjects to save their souls as Catholics. He knew that the best safeguard, although far from an infallible guarantor, of the common good domestically and of peace internationally was the right ordering of souls in cooperation with Sanctifying Grace. He supported the ongoing missionary work of the Church in Central and Eastern Europe at the end of the First Millennium and the beginning of the Second Millennium, and he was personally responsible for the conversion of Saint Stephen of Hungary.

Dom Prosper Gueranger provided us with a wonderful narrative of my own Confirmation patron saint's life and work in behalf of Christ the King:

> Henry of Germany, the second king, but the first emperor of that name, was the last crowned representative of that branch of the house of Saxony descended from Henry the Fowler, to

which God, in the tenth century, entrusted the mission of restoring the work of Chandelling and Leo III. This noble stock was rendered more glorious in the fowlers of sanctity adorning its branches than in the deep and powerful roots it struck in the German soil by great and long-enduring institutions.

The Holy Spirit, who gave Charlemagne His gifts according as He will, was then calling to the loftiest destinies that land which, more than any other, had witnessed the energy of His divine action in the transformation of nations. Won to Christ by St. Boniface and the continuators of his work, the vast country which extends beyond the Rhine and the Danube had become the bulwark of the West, and for many years had been the scene of devastation and ruin. Far from attempting to subjugate her own rule to the formidable tribes that inhabited it, pagan Rome, at the very zenith of her power, had had no higher ambition than to raise a wall of separation between them and the Empire: Christian Rome, more truly mistress of the world, set up in their very midst the seat of the Holy Roman Empire re-established by her Pontiffs. The new Empire was to defend the rights of the common Mother, to protect Christendom from new inroads of barbarians, to win over to the Gospel or else to crush the successive hordes that would come down her frontiers--Hungarians, Slavs, Mongols, Tartars, and Ottomans. Happy had it been for Germany if she had always understood her true glory, if the fidelity of her princes to the Vicar of the Man-God had been equal to her people's faith.

God, on His part, had not closed His hand. To-day's feast shows us the crowning-point of the period of fruitful labour, when the Holy Ghost, having created Germany anew in the waters of the sacred font, would lead her up to the full development of a people's perfect age. The historian, who would know what Providence requires of nations, must study them at such a period of truly creative formation. Indeed, when God creates, whether in the order of nature or of the supernatural vocation of men and societies, He first deposits in His work the principle of that grade of life for which it is destined: it is a precious germ, the development of which, unless thwarted, must lead that being to attain its end; and the knowledge of which, could we observe it before any alteration has taken place, would clearly indicate the divine intention with regard to that being. Now, many times already, since the coming of the Holy Ghost the Sanctifier, we have shown that the principle of life for Christian nations is the holiness of their beginnings: a holiness as manifold as is the Wisdom of God, whose instrument these nations are to be, and as peculiar to each as are their several destinies. This holiness, beginning as it does for the most part from the throne, possesses a social character. The crimes also of princes will but too often bear this same mark, from the very fact of the princes being the representatives of their people before God. Then, too, we have seen how in the name of Mary, who through her divine Maternity is the channel of life to the whole world, a mission has been entrusted to women: the mission of bringing forth to God the families of nations (familiae gentium), which are to the objects of His tenderest love. Whereas the princes, the apparent founders of empires, stand with their mighty deeds in the foreground of history, it is she that, by her secret tears and prayers, give fruitfulness, a loftier aim, and stability to their undertakings.

The Holy Ghost leads many souls to imitate the Mother of God; like Clotilde, Radegond, and Bathildis, who gave the Franks to the Church in troublous times--three chosen souls—Matilda,

Adelaide, and Cunigund--and added the aureole of sanctity to the imperial diadem of Germany. Over the chaos of the tenth century, whence Germany was to spring, they shone out like three bright stars, shedding their peaceful light over the Church and the world in that dark night and thus doing more to suppress anarchy than could even the swords of Otho. The eleventh century opened: Hildebrand had not yet arisen, and the angels of the sanctuary were weeping over many a desecrated altar, when the royal succession was brought to a beautiful close by a virginal union, as though, weary of producing heroes for the world, it would now bear fruit for heaven alone. Was such a step against the interests of Germany? No; it drew down the mercy of God upon the country, which, in the midst of universal corruption, could offer Him the perfume of such a holocaust.

Let earth and heaven this day unite in celebrating the man who carried out to the full the designs of Eternal Wisdom at this period of history. In his single person he discovered all the heroism and sanctity of the illustrious race, whose chief glory it is to have been for a century a worthy preparation for so great a man. Great before men, who knew not whether to admire more this bravery or energetic activity which made him seem to be everywhere at once throughout his vast empire, he was ever successful, putting down internal revolts, chastising the insolence of the Greeks in southern Italy, assisting Hungary to rise from barbarism to Christianity, concluding with Robert the Pious a lasting peace between the Empire and the eldest daughter of the Church [France]. But the virgin spouse of the virgin Cunigund was greater still before God who never had a more faithful lieutenant upon earth. God in His Christ was in Henry's eyes the only King; the interest of Christ and the Church, the only principle of his administration; the most perfect service of the Man-God, his highest ambition. He understood how the truest nobility was hidden in the cloister, where chosen souls, fleeing from the universal degradation, were averting the ruin and obtaining the salvation of the world. It was this thought that led him on the morrow of his imperial coronation, to confide to the famous Abbey of Cluny the golden globe representing the world, which he, as a soldier of the vicar of Christ, was commissioned to defend. It was with this desire of imitating those noble souls that he threw himself at the feet of the Abbot of St. Vannes at Verdun, begging admission into his community, and then, constrained by obedience, returned with a heavy heart to resume the burden of government. (Dom Prosper Gueranger, *The Liturgical Year*, Volume XIII, Time After Pentecost: Book IV, pp. 103-106.)

Dom Prosper Gueranger, O.S.B.'s *The Liturgical Year* provided the account of Saint Henry's life as found in the Roman Breviary:

Henry, surnamed the Pious, Duke of Bavaria, became successively King of Germany and Emperor of the Romans: but not satisfied with a mere temporal principality, he strove to gain an immortal crown, by paying zealous service to the eternal King. As emperor, he devoted himself earnestly to spreading religion, and rebuilt with great magnificence the churches which had been destroyed by the infidels, endowing them generously both with money and lands. He built monasteries and other pious establishments, and increased the income of others; the bishopric of Bamberg, which he had founded out of his family possessions, he made tributary to St. Peter and the Roman Pontiff. When Benedict VIII, who had crowned him emperor, was obliged to seek safety in flight, Henry received him and restored him to his see.

Once when he was suffering from a severe illness in the monastery of Monte Cassino, St. Benedict cured him by a wonderful miracle. He endowed the Roman Church with a most copious grant, undertook in her defence a war against the Greeks, and gained possession of Apulia, which they had held for some time. It was his custom to undertake nothing without prayer, and at times he saw the angel of the Lord, or the holy martyrs, his patrons, fighting for him at the head of his army. Aided thus by the divine protection, he overcame barbarous nations more by prayer than by arms. Hungary was still pagan; but Henry having given his sister in marriage to its King Stephen, the latter was baptized, and thus the whole nation was brought to the faith of Christ. He set the rare example of preserving virginity in the married state, and at his death restored his wife, St. Cunigund, a virgin to her family.

He arranged everything relating to the glory or advantage of the empire with the greatest prudence, and left scattered throughout Gaul, Italy, and Germany, traces of his munificence towards religion. The sweet odour of his heroic virtue spread far and wide, till he was more celebrated for his holiness than for his imperial dignity. At length, his life's work was accomplished, and he was called by our Lord to the rewards of the heavenly kingdom, in the year of salvation 1024. His body was buried in the church of the blessed apostles Peter and Paul at Bamberg. God wished to glorify His servant, and many miracles were worked at his tomb. These being afterwards proved and certified, Eugenius III inscribed his name upon the catalogue of the saints. (The Roman Breviary as quoted in Dom Prosper Gueranger, The Liturgical Year, Volume XIII, Time After Pentecost: Book IV, pp. 106-108.)

Dom Prosper's prayer for Saint Henry's feast day, July 15, speaks to us as clearly in the Twenty-first Century as it did when written in the Nineteenth Century:

From thy throne in heaven, cast down a look of pity on the extensive domain of the Holy Empire, which owed so much to thee, and which heresy has for ever dismembered. Put to confusion those principles, unknown to Germany in happier days, which would reconstruct, for the benefit of earthly prosperity, the grandeurs of the past without the cement of the ancient faith. Return, O emperor of glorious days! return and fight for the Church; gather together the remains of Christendom upon the traditional ground of the interests common to all Catholic nations: then will the alliance, which thy able policy concluded, give to the world a security, a peace, a prosperity, which it can never enjoy so long as it remains on such a slippery footing, and exposed to the violence of every hostile agency. (Dom Prosper Gueranger, *The Liturgical Year*, Volume XIII, Time After Pentecost: Book IV, p. 109.)

Saint Henry has much to teach Catholics who participate in civil governance today about their responsibilities, particularly about their obligation to pursue personal holiness and thus to be ready to suffer everything, including electoral defeat, in order to plant seeds for the restoration of the Social Reign of Christ the King. Saint Henry's exemplary conduct in the service of Christ the King is not something meant only for the history books. His saintly and prudent conduct as a Catholic and as a civil leader is meant to inspire us today. For the graces made available to him in the sacraments during his life a thousand years ago are no less powerful today than they were then. Why do we consider it "unrealistic," therefore, to act and to speak as Catholics without regard to the exigencies of short-term goals in the realm of civil governance and public policy?

Saint Stephen of Hungary, who was married to Saint Henry's sister, Ghisella, excelled in piety and virtue in his own right, completing the work in his native land that had been begun by his brother-in- law, namely, its Catholicization:

> Stephen introduced into Hungary both the faith of Christ and the regal dignity. He obtained the royal crown from the Roman Pontiff; and, having been, by his command, anointed king, offered his kingdom to the apostolic See. He built several houses of charity at Rome, Jerusalem, and Constantinople; and with a wonderful magnificent spirit of religion, he founded the archiepiscopal See of Gran and ten other bishoprics. His love for the poor was equalled only by his generosity towards them; for, seeing in them Christ himself, he never sent anyone away sad or empty-handed. So great indeed was his charity, that, to relieve their necessities, after expending large sums of money, he often bestowed upon them his household goods. It was his custom to wash the feet of the poor with his own hands, and to visit the hospitals at night, alone and unknown, serving the sick and showing them every charity. As a reward for these good deeds his right hand remained incorrupt after death, when the rest of his body had returned to dust.
>
> He was much given to prayer; and would spend almost entire nights without sleep, rapt in heavenly contemplation; at times he seemed ravished out of his senses, and raised in the air. By the help of prayer, he more than once escaped in a wonderful manner from the attacks of powerful enemies. Having married Ghisella of Bavaria, sister of the emperor St. Henry, he had by her a son Emeric, whom he brought up in such regularity and piety as to form him into a saint. He summoned wise and holy men from all parts to aid him in the government of his kingdom and undertook nothing without their advice. In sackcloth and ashes, he besought God with most humble prayer, that he might not depart this life without seeing the whole kingdom of Hungary Catholic. So great indeed was his zeal for the propagation of the faith, that he was called the apostle of the nation, and he received from the Roman Pontiff, both for himself and for his successors, the privilege of having the cross borne before them.
>
> He had the most ardent devotion towards the Mother of God, in whose honour he built a magnificent church, solemnly declaring her patroness of Hungary. In return the blessed Virgin received him into heaven on the very day of her Assumption, which the Hungarians, by the appointment of their holy king, call "the day of the great Lady.' His sacred body, exhaling a most fragrant odour and distilling a heavenly liquor, was, by order of the Roman Pontiff, translated, amidst many and divers miracles, to a more worthy resting-place, and buried with greater honor. Pope Innocent XI. commanded his feast to be celebrated on the fourth of the Nones of September; on which day, Leopold I. emperor elect of the Romans and king of Hungary, had by the divine assistance, gained a remarkable victory over the Turks at the siege of Buda. (Dom Prosper Gueranger, *The Liturgical Year*.)

Other Lands Won for Christ the King: The missionary work of the Church in Europe continued throughout the latter part of the First Millennium and into early part of the Second even as conflicts had raged between some of the Holy Roman Emperors that were not settled until Pope John XII asked Prince Otto of Germany to rescue the papacy from its virtual enslavement to the Carolingian (the line of Charlemagne, Charles I) emperors in the year 962 A.D., thus marking the transfer of power in the empire from the Carolingian Franks to the eastern Franks.

Although the Faith was never accepted in Its entirety by many of the nations of Scandinavia, **Saint Ansgar** convinced Saint Harold of the Danes and his wife to accept the Faith in the year 826 A.D. Saint Ansgar worked tirelessly for the Faith among the Danes and the Swedes. The Faith began its spread to places such as Norway, Iceland and Greenland at this same time, noting that the Vikings remained a problem until the beginning of the Twelfth Century, converting gradually as the kings embraced the true Faith, thus effecting the same kind of top-down conversion amongst them that Saint Patrick effected with the Druids in Ireland by converting their tribal chieftains, whose clansmen followed their lead. One of the great and most holy exemplars of the Social Reign of Christ the King was **Saint Canute IV**, King of Denmark, a ruler noted for his piety and austere manner of living, dying as a martyr for the Faith on July 10, 1086. Saint Canute was also instrumental in bringing the Faith to Scandinavian lands that had not yet fully embraced It.

Bohemia was converted near the end of the Ninth Century, principally because of the missionary work of Saint Methodius, who had worked with his brother, Saint Cyril, for many years to effect the   conversions of much of East Central Europe, including Bohemia and Moravia. These Apostles to the Slavs, who developed an alphabet to transliterate the local dialects into written form (the Cyrillic Alphabet), planted the seeds that would result in the rise of such great saints as Saint Adalbert, the second bishop of Prague (now the capital of the Czech Republic) and Saint Ludmilla, the grandmother of **Saint Wenceslaus**, whose holiness as a ruler according to the mind of Christ the King contrasted greatly with that of his evil brother, Boleslaus, who murdered him on September 28, 935 A.D.

Good King Wenceslaus, who was born in 903 A.D., was willing to forgo all human respect to serve the King of Kings in every aspect of his life. Saint Wenceslaus learned to love God as He has revealed Himself exclusively through His true Church at a young age, having been raised by his saintly grandmother, Saint Ludmilla, following the death of his Catholic father. Wenceslaus learned to love God from Saint Ludmilla, never fearing to offend his pagan mother, Drahomira, or his equally wicked brother, Boleslaus, as he kept himself true to the King, before Whom he would prostrate himself in most fervent prayer in His Real Presence in the Most Blessed Sacrament. He begged the heavenly intercession of Saint Ludmilla after she was murdered by Drahomira to help him rule in the manner of Christ the King following his accession to the throne upon which his father, Wratislaus, had sat as the King of Bohemia.

Drahomira did not have a good end after she had murdered her mother-in-law, Saint Ludmilla. The earth swallowed her up. God sees to it that those who are not contrite for their sins receive their due punishment, which is sometimes in this life and most assuredly at the moment of their Particular Judgments if they have not sought Absolution in the Sacred Tribunal of Penance or even uttered a   perfect Act of Contrition. Drahomira, being a fierce pagan and a promoter of all manner of evil ways, was taken by God to demonstrate to all of the people of Bohemia, which had been so recently brought to the Faith by the missionary work of Saints Cyril and Methodius, that He will have no rivals as kings over his people. Those who rule in this life must rule for Him, the King of Kings, and help to foster those conditions in civil society in which their subjects (or fellow citizens) will be better able to sanctify and thus to save their souls as members of the Catholic Church.

Saint Wenceslaus understood that the only way to serve as a just ruler of others was to let the King of Kings rule over his own immortal soul in every aspect of his life. The good king of Bohemia, therefore, was intent on living a life of holiness so as to serve as a salutary example to his subjects. He did this in so many ways, starting with his own love of the Holy Sacrifice of the Mass and his service to the poor and the imprisoned. He saw in each person the Divine impress, treating them as he would treat Our Blessed Lord and Saviour Jesus Christ Himself. He performed in manhood the lessons he learned in childhood from Saint Ludmilla, which should teach each of us who is a parent the importance of training our children well to love the Catholic Faith and to live the Faith in every aspect of our lives without any exception whatsoever, to prefer even bodily death to all of the blandishments offered by the world, to prefer friendlessness, as the world considers it, rather than to all of the friends in the world who never speak of Our Lord and who believe that t is either inopportune, unrealistic or simply archaic to speak of His Social Kingship over men and their nations or that each nation must give public honor to Mary, Our Immaculate Queen. We can prepare our own children, starting with the enthronement of our homes to the Most Sacred Heart of Jesus and the Immaculate Heart of Mary, to defend the Faith and to live it out as well as Saint Wenceslaus.

Saint Wenceslaus's love for the Holy Sacrifice of the Mass, which was mentioned in my article No Rush Hour at Calvary at around this time in 2007, should serve as the model by which all rulers in all places and at all times without any exception whatsoever should fashion their daily lives. This great king's love of the Holy Sacrifice of the Mass, which is the unbloody re-presentation of the one Sacrifice of the Son to the Father in Spirit and in Truth that was effected on the wood of the Holy Cross atop the heights of the dung heap known as Mount Calvary, should inspire each of us to put First Things first so that we will be ready at all times to live in light of the Last Things (Death, Judgment, Heaven, Hell). Saint Leonard of Port Maurice's recounting of Saint Wenceslaus's love of Holy Mass is worth considering once again, therefore:

> Let us conclude this division with the example of St. Wenceslaus, King of Bohemia, which should at least in part be imitated by all of you. This holy king did not content himself with assisting every day at several Masses, with his knees bent on the bare pavement, nor with serving in person the celebrating priests, and this with greater humility than any cleric that has only received the lowest of minor orders; but besides this, he contributed to the sacred altars the richest jewels of his treasury, and webs of texture and embroidery the most precious in the royal wardrobes. He was, further, in the habit of making with his own hands the altar-bread which was to be used for the holy sacrifice; and with this view, without any regard to the royal dignity, he applied those hands, born to wield the sceptre, in cultivating a field, in directing the plough, in sowing the seed, and in reaping the harvest. Then he ground the grain, separated the finer flour for the oven, and made the breads which should afterward be consecrated; and these he presented, with the lowliest reverence, to the priests, to be converted into the most divine body of the Saviour. O hands worthy to have held the sceptre of this globe! And did other kings despise him for this? Far from it. Almighty God led the Emperor Otho I. to conceive for this holy king an unparalleled regard, so far as to grant him the right to quarter in his arms the imperial device (an eagle sable in an argent field), a favor not extended to any other prince. Thus God, by means of the emperor, rewarded with temporal honors the great devotion of Wenceslaus toward the divine sacrifice. But much more was he rewarded by the

King of heaven when, by means of a most glorious martyrdom, there was granted to him a crown of eternal glory: and we behold him, through his passionate tenderness for holy Mass, doubly crowned, in this and in the other world. Reflect and resolve. (Saint Leonard of Port Maurice, *The Hidden Treasure: Holy Mass*, pp. 65-66; 75-76.)

As noted above, Saint Wenceslaus spent much time in fervent prayer before the Blessed Sacrament in addition to his assisting at Holy Mass on a daily basis. He knew that adorers of Our Lord in His Real Presence receive infused graces that enlighten their intellects and strengthen their wills to more perfectly die to self so that He, the King of Kings, could live in them, thus enabling them to better radiate the refulgent warmth of His ineffable love for the temporal and eternal good of all men. Indeed, Pope Leo XIII, writing in his last encyclical letter, *Mirae Caritatis*, May 28, 1902, explained how those in positions of leadership, whether in the public and private sector, had to make time for the practice of Eucharistic piety that characterized the life and the kingly work of Saint Wenceslaus:

> Indeed it is greatly to be desired that those men would rightly esteem and would make due provision for life everlasting, whose industry or talents or rank have put it in their power to shape the course of human events. (Pope Leo XIII, *Mirae Caritatis*, May 28, 1902.)

Although it was not without difficulty as many civil potentates vied for hegemony over the Vicar of Christ on earth, the principle of the Social Reign of Christ the King became such a part of life in Catholic Europe that Holy Mother Church saw fit to raise to her altars exemplars of the Divine Redeemer's Social Kingship over men and their nations to serve as a salutary lesson to the self-seekers and to give encouragement to ordinary Catholics who were suffering under the yoke of injustice thereby perpetrated.

The Holy Faith spread into Poland by 966 A.D., and it took deep root there, although it had to be revived by the tireless apostolic work of Saint Hyacinth, one of the first followers of Saint Dominic de Guzman, which will be explored in the next section of this chapter. Even Russia had been converted to true Faith by the end of the Tenth Century, although the Faith had been brought there previously, prior to her becoming a seed bed of the errors of Orthodoxy, becoming a progenitor of the errors of Protestantism and of Modernity by subordinating religion to the exigencies of the civil state. Saint Hyacinth tried valiantly, as did others, to effect Russia's return to the true Faith, which is, as Our Lady told Jacinta and Francisco Marto and Lucia dos Santos in the Cova da Iria near Fatima, Portugal in 1917, a desire of the Sorrowful and Immaculate Heart of Mary upon which nothing other than peace in the world and order within Holy Mother Church herself are premised. The errors of Russia are far more than the errors of Marxism-Leninism. The errors of Russia are the errors of Modernity in the world and of Modernism in the conciliar church.

The First Millennium Turns into the Second: Such was the valor of the missionaries of the First Millennium, a period that was filled with many problems, including the Church's fight against multiple heresies, starting with Arianism, that ravaged her children and made the work of converting Europe more difficult.

There were also, however, periods of great moral corruption and abuse of power by the clergy, a problem was that was especially widespread at the end of the First Millennium and the beginning of the Second Millennium as Saint Peter Damian fought the influence of perversity amongst the clergy. Saint Bernard of Clairvaux fought against the laxity and lukewarmness of the clergy, helping the faithful to foster a deep and tender personal devotion to the Blessed Virgin Mary as he fought heresies at the same time. Holy Mother Church had to endure the Greek Schism (1054) and the spread of Mohammedanism into the Balkans and the dangers facing Christian pilgrims to the Holy Land, then in Mohammedan control, prompted Pope Blessed Urban II to call for the First Crusade. As authors of a history of the Church's twenty legitimate councils aptly noted, these were tumultuous times quite indeed.

Saint Stanislaus, the Archbishop of Stanislaus, stood fast against the evil designs of King Boleslaus IV in Poland by condemning his moral profligacy and many injustices. Saint Stanislaus was killed on May 8, 1079, at the best of Boleslaus, just ninety-one years before the murder of Saint Thomas a Becket by barons who thought that they were fulfilling the expressed desire of King Henry II. Such martyrdoms of Catholic bishops by civil potentates and/or their minions who did not want to submit the authority of Christ the King would play an important role in planting seeds for the restoration of the Church Militant on earth in the Thirteenth Century.

Saint Francis of Assisi's austere life of Eucharistic piety, personal penance and mortification and his embrace of Lady Poverty helped to plant the seeds for the rebuilding of the Church Militant on earth after a long period of moral dissolution amongst the clergy.

Through it all, however, missionaries in Europe continued the work of spreading the Faith. Two of these were early spiritual sons of Saint Dominic de Guzman, the founder of the Order of Preachers who had been given the Rosary by Our Lady in 1208 to fight against the Albigensian heresy, from Poland, Saint Hyancinth and his brother, Blessed Ceslaus, who traveled from Rome after meeting with Saint Dominic in 1220. Saint Hyacinth, much like Saint Boniface before him, did battle with false idols, engaging in a fierce struggle with a demon in the Dnieper River in Russia during a missionary trip there:

For a moment all was silence as Hyacinth fixed his eyes in careful scrutiny upon the island. Then suddenly his hands clenched. Drawn up at one side of the island were several small boats. And toward the center, from amidst the thick trees, rose a slender column of smoke!

"The pagans!" he whispered. "They're offering sacrifice!"

Yes, the hour of sunrise was a favorite time for idol worship and gratefully Hyacinth realized that his plans were working out well. More than a hundred men and women must be on the island, kneeling in a secret grove before the ugly statue they believed to be a god. Already there must have been prayers and hymns, then the burning of a lamb or calf before the idol. Soon the service would be over and the pagans would stream down to their boats to return to their homes in Kiev.

"I've no time to lose," he said firmly. "Kneel down, Brother Martin, and pray that I do something really worthwhile to help these poor people!"

Before the young religious could realize what was happening, Hyacinth had turned and started down the grassy slope to the river's edge. His black cloak floated before him like a sail, and for a moment Martin knelt as one in a dream--forgetful of the command to pray. With what speed his beloved superior moved! Why, he was all but flying down the hill! Then the young friar grew really weak, for suddenly he understood that he was witnessing a genuine wonder. By now Father Hyacinth had reached the Dnieper and was starting to cross over to the island. But not in a boat. Ah, no! Father Hyacinth was walking on the river as thought it were dry land!

"Mother of God! cried Martin. "I heard that he did such a thing at Vishogrod . . . on the Vistula! But here? Before me? Oh, no! It's too much!"

Presently Hyacinth landed safely on the island, then disappeared into the thick woods. And, though Martin strained his eyes for several minutes, he could see him no longer. Nor was any sound to be heard save the harsh cries of water birds as they circled over the river in search of food.

As he looked and listened in an agony of suspense, the young religious tried to clasp his trembling hands in prayer. Oh, what was going to happen? Would Father Hyacinth really seek out the pagans? Would he put a stop to their heathen sacrifice?

"It can mean death," he [Martin] thought. "Even I know that the Russian pagans are little more than crude barbarians."

Suddenly there was a clamor in the distance, muted at first, then growing louder, and with a sinking heart, the young man realized that the pagans were aroused. They were pouring out of the woods with screams and shouts. But soon he could see that they were not attacking Father Hyacinth. They were not even making for their boats. Rather, they were throwing themselves on their knees in a very frenzy of terror. And why? Because a black-and-white-clad friar was striding out of the woods and driving before him a horrible creature--half man, half beast--- with flames shooting from its mouth and eyes!

Martin's blood ran cold as he looked at the terrible sight. Could it be that this was the Devil? That Father Hyacinth's prayers had forced him to leave the idol and appear before the pagans in one of his hellish shapes?

"Oh, if only some of the Russian priests could be here!" whispered the young friar, his teeth clattering. "Maybe this would teach them not to speak ill of a true servant of God!"

Martin was wrong. When word of the miracle was noised about in Kiev, the jealousy of the heretical priests reached alarming proportions. So Father Hyacinth had gone to the island and found the pagans worshiping before an old oak tree? With one blow he had sent the great tree crumbling into dust? As the Evil One emerged from the tree, he had fought with him hand to hand, then thrown him into the Dnieper? (Mary Fabean Wyndeatt, Saint Hyacinth: Apostle to the Northland, republished by TAN Books and Publishers, pp.)

This is quite a contrast with the false ecumenism of conciliarism. And it is just one example of the many prodigies worked by Saint Hyacinth, who was on fire for the love of God in the service of His Most Blessed Mother for the good of souls.

As Saint Hyacinth was working in the Northland for the re-evangelization of his homeland, Poland, and the evangelization of Lithuania and Russia, the Thirteenth Century during which so many saints had worked so assiduously to restore the Church Militant from the clerical corruption of the preceding two centuries and as the exercise of the Social Reign of Christ the King reached its apogee.

Saint Francis of Assisi and Saint Dominic each received approval for their new religious communities.

Pope Innocent III orally approved the founding of the Order of Friars Minor in 1209. Pope Honorius III on November 29, 1223, just a little under three years prior to his death on October 3, 1226, formally approved the Order of Friars Minor. The Poor Clares, organized in 1212, received final ecclesiastical approbation on August 9, 1253, by Pope Innocent IV. The final rule of the Third Order of Saint Francis of Assisi was approved by Pope Nicholas IV on August 18, 1289. It was within a short period of time that this order of mendicant friars gave Holy Mother Church the likes of Saint Anthony of Padua and Saint Bonaventure, both of whom still teach us much as they intercede for us from Heaven.

Saint Dominic de Guzman was favored by the Mother of God with Our Lady's Psalter, her Most Holy Rosary, in 1208, founding a religious community to fight the Albigensian heresy and to spread the Faith in 1214, receiving the approval from Pope Honorius III for his Order of Preachers on December 22, 1216. The Dominicans were stalwart in defense of the truths of the Holy Faith, giving us such illustrious scholars as Saint Albert the Great and his prized student, Saint Thomas Aquinas, whose Scholasticism remains the official philosophy of the Catholic Church, praised by Pope Leo XIII in *Aeterni Patris*, August 4, 1879, by citing the testimonials given by his predecessors in the Throne of Saint Peter to the work of the Angelic Doctor, who was a true and devoted spiritual son of Saint Dominic de Guzman:

>Innocent VI: "The teaching of this Doctor above all others, with the exception of Canon Law, has precision in terminology, propriety of expression, truth of judgment: so that never is one who has held it been found to have deviated from the path of truth."

>Pius V: "It was wrought by the providence of Almighty God that by the force and truth of the Angelic Doctor's teaching, by which he illumined the Apostolic Church with the refutation of innumerable errors, that the many heresies which have arisen after his canonization have been confounded, overthrown and dispersed. This has been made evident both earlier and recently in the sacred decrees of the Council of Trent."

>Clement VIII to the Neapolitans: "Devoutly and wisely are you thinking of adopting a new patron of your city, your fellow citizen, the Angelic interpreter of the Divine Will, splendid in the sanctity of his life and by his miracles, Thomas Aquinas, since indeed is this honor owed with the greatest justification to his virtues joined to his admirable doctrine. Indeed, witness to his doctrine is the great number of books which he composed, in a very brief time, in almost every class of learning, with a matchless arrangement and wondrous clearness, without any error whatsoever."

Paul V: "We greatly rejoice in the Lord that honor and veneration are increasing daily for the most splendid champion of the Catholic Faith, blessed Thomas Aquinas, by the shield of whose writings the Church Militant successfully parries the spears of the heretics."

And Leo XIII, at once embracing and surpassing all of the praises of his predecessors, says of him: "Distinguishing reason from Faith, as is proper, but nevertheless combining the two in a friendly alliance, he both preserved the rights of each and had regard for the dignity of both, in such a way too that reason, carried on the wings of Thomas to the highest human limit, now almost cannot rise any higher, and faith almost cannot expect more or stronger helps from reason than it has already obtained through Thomas."

--And again, presenting St. Thomas to Catholics as a model and patron in various sciences, he says: "In him are all the illustrious ornaments of mind and character by which he rightly calls others to the imitation of himself: the richest doctrine, incorrupt, fittingly arranged; obedience to the Faith, and a marvelous consonance with the truths divinely handed down; integrity of life with the splendor of the greatest virtues." (Readings from the Dominican Breviary (II Nocturn) for the feast of the Patronage of Saint Thomas Aquinas, November 13.)

But, furthermore, Our predecessors in the Roman pontificate have celebrated the wisdom of Thomas Aquinas by exceptional tributes of praise and the most ample testimonials. Clement VI in the bull "In Ordine;" Nicholas V in his brief to the friars of the Order of Preachers, 1451; Benedict XIII in the bull "Pretiosus," and others bear witness that the universal Church borrows luster from his admirable teaching; while St. Pius V declares in the bull "Mirabilis" that heresies, confounded and convicted by the same teaching, were dissipated, and the whole world daily freed from fatal errors; others, such as Clement XII in the bull "Verbo Dei," affirm that most fruitful blessings have spread abroad from his writings over the whole Church, and that he is worthy of the honor which is bestowed on the greatest Doctors of the Church, on Gregory and Ambrose, Augustine and Jerome; while others have not hesitated to propose St. Thomas for the exemplar and master of the universities and great centers of learning whom they may follow with unfaltering feet. On which point the words of Blessed Urban V to the University of Toulouse are worthy of recall: "It is our will, which We hereby enjoin upon you, that ye follow the teaching of Blessed Thomas as the true and Catholic doctrine and that ye labor with all your force to profit by the same." Innocent XII, followed the example of Urban in the case of the University of Louvain, in the letter in the form of a brief addressed to that university on February 6, 1694, and Benedict XIV in the letter in the form of a brief addressed on August 26, 1752, to the Dionysian College in Granada; while to these judgments of great Pontiffs on Thomas Aquinas comes the crowning testimony of Innocent VI: "His teaching above that of others, the canonical writings alone excepted, enjoys such a precision of language, an order of matters, a truth of conclusions, that those who hold to it are never found swerving from the path of truth, and he who dare assail it will always be suspected of error."

The ecumenical councils, also, where blossoms the flower of all earthly wisdom, have always been careful to hold Thomas Aquinas in singular honor. In the Councils of Lyons, Vienna, Florence, and the Vatican one might almost say that Thomas took part and presided over the deliberations and decrees of the Fathers, contending against the errors of the Greeks, of heretics and rationalists, with invincible force and with the happiest results. But the chief and special glory of Thomas, one which he has shared with none of the Catholic Doctors, is that the Fathers of Trent made it part of the order of conclave to lay upon the altar, together with   sacred Scripture and the decrees of the supreme Pontiffs, the "Summa" of Thomas Aquinas, whence to seek counsel, reason, and inspiration.

A last triumph was reserved for this incomparable man -- namely, to compel the homage, praise, and admiration of even the very enemies of the Catholic name. For it has come to light that there were not lacking among the leaders of heretical sects some who openly declared that, if the teaching of Thomas Aquinas were only taken away, they could easily battle with all Catholic teachers, gain the victory, and abolish the Church. A vain hope, indeed, but no vain testimony. (Pope Leo XIII, *Aeterni Patris*, August 4, 1879.)

It is no accident that the Scholasticism of the Angelic Doctor, Saint Thomas Aquinas, is rejected by the Modernist adherent of the "new theology," Joseph Ratzinger/Benedict XVI, who has had a hatred for the work of Saint Thomas since his seminary days:

The cultural interests pursued at the seminary of Freising were joined to the study of a theology infected by existentialism, beginning with the writings of Romano Guardini. Among the authors preferred by Ratzinger was the Jewish philosopher Martin Buber. Ratzinger loved St. Augustine, but never St. Thomas Aquinas: "By contrast, I had difficulties in penetrating the thought of Thomas Aquinas, whose crystal-clear logic seemed to be too closed in on itself, too impersonal and ready-made" (op. cit., p.44). This aversion was mainly due to the professor   of philosophy at the seminary, who "presented us with a rigid, neo-scholastic Thomism that was simply too far afield from my own questions" (ibid.). According to Cardinal Ratzinger, whose current opinions appear unchanged from those he held as a seminarian, the thought of Aquinas was "too closed in on itself, too impersonal and ready-made," and was unable to respond to the personal questions of the faithful. This opinion is enunciated by a prince of the Church whose function it is to safeguard the purity of the doctrine of the Faith! Why, then, should anyone be surprised at the current disastrous crisis of Catholicism, or seek to attribute it to the world, when those who should be the defenders of the Faith, and hence of genuine Catholic thought, are like sewers drinking in the filth, or like gardeners who cut down a tree they are supposed to be nurturing? What can it mean to stigmatize St. Thomas as having a "too impersonal and ready-made" logic? Is logic "personal"? These assertions reveal, in the person who makes them, a typically Protestant, pietist attitude, like that found in those who seek the rule of faith in personal interior sentiment.

In the two years Ratzinger spent at the diocesan seminary of Freising, he studied literature, music, modern philosophy, and he felt drawn towards the new existentialist and modernist theologies. He did not like St. Thomas Aquinas. The formation described does not correspond to the exclusively Catholic formation that is necessary to one called to be a priest, even taking into account the extenuating circumstances of the time, that is, anti-Christian Nazism, the war and defeat, and the secularization of studies within seminaries. It seems that His Eminence, with all due respect, gave too much place to profane culture, with its "openness" to everything, and its critical attitude...Joseph Ratzinger loved the professors who asked many questions, but disliked those who defended dogma with the crystal-clear logic of St. Thomas. This attitude would seem to us to match his manner of understanding Catholic liturgy. He tells us that from childhood he was always attracted to the liturgical movement and was sympathetic towards it. One can see that for him, the liturgy was a matter of feeling, a lived experience, an aesthetically pleasing "Erlebnis," but fundamentally irrational (op. cit. passim.). ("The Memories of a Destructive Mind: Joseph Cardinal Ratzinger's *Milestones*," *Si, Si, No, No*, March 1999.)

Scholasticism flowered at the time of the apogee of Christendom in the Middle Ages. Its rejection by the conciliar "pontiffs," who scoff at the Social Reign of Christ the King in favor of the falsehood known as "healthy secularity" or "healthy laicism," is one of the reasons that the Church Militant on earth now is in the tomb while she awaits her resurrection when the Triumph of the Immaculate Heart of Mary occurs.

It was in the Thirteenth Century that Our Lady gave us the Brown Scapular of Mount Carmel in addition to her Most Holy Rosary. Saint Simon Stock, a member of the Order of Carmel, was given the Brown Scapular on July 16, 1251. Pope John XXII approved the Brown Scapular of Our Lady of Mount Carmel and the Sabbatine Privilege associated with it:

In the night between the 15th and 16th of July of the year 1251, the gracious Queen of Carmel confirmed to her sons [the Carmelites] by a mysterious sign the right of citizenship she had obtained for them in their newly adopted countries [of the West]; as mistress and mother of the entire religious state she conferred upon them with her queenly hands the scapular, hitherto the distinctive garb of the greatest and most ancient family of the West. On giving St. Simon Stock this badge, ennobled by contact with her sacred fingers, the Mother of God said to him: 'Whosoever shall die in this habit shall not suffer eternal flames.' But not against hell fire alone was the all-powerful intercession of the Blessed Mother to be felt by those who should wear the scapular. In 1316, when every holy soul was imploring heaven to put a period to that long and disastrous widowhood of the Church, which followed in the death of Clement V, the Queen of Saints appeared to James d'Euse, whom the world was soon to hail as John XXII; she foretold to him his approaching elevation to the Sovereign Pontificate, and at the same time recommended him to publish the privilege she had obtained from her Divine Son for her children of Carmel--viz., a speedily deliverance from purgatory. 'I, their Mother, will graciously go down to them on the Saturday after their death, and all whom I find in purgatory I will deliver and will bring to the mountain of life eternal.' These are the words of our Lord herself, quoted by John XII in the Bull which he published for the purpose of making known the privilege and which was called the Sabbatine Bull on account of the day chosen by the glorious benefactress for the exercise of her mercy.

We are aware of the attempts made to nullify the authenticity of these heavenly concessions; but our extremely limited time will not allow us to follow up these worthless struggles in all their endless details. The attack of the chief assailant, the too famous Lounoy, was condemned by the Apostolic See, and after, as well as before, these contradictions, the Roman Pontiffs confirmed, as much as need be, by their supreme authority, the substance and even the letter of the precious promises. The reader may find in special works the enumeration of the many indulgences with which the Popes have, time after time, enriched the Carmelite family, as if earth would vie with heaven in favouring it. The munificence of Mary, the pious gratitude of her sons for the hospitality given them by the West, and lastly, the authority of St. Peter's successors, soon made these spiritual riches accessible to all Christians, by the instruction of the Confraternity of the holy Scapular, the members whereof participate in the merits and   privileges of the whole Carmelite Order. Who shall tell the graces, often miraculous, obtained through this humble garb? Who could count the faithful now enrolled in the holy militia? When Benedict XIII, in the eighteenth century, extended the feast of July 16 to the whole Church, he did but give an official sanction to the universality already gained by the cultus of the Queen of Carmel. (Dom Prosper Gueranger, *The Liturgical Year*.)

Our Lady told Saint Dominic the following before he died:

One day, through the Rosary and the Scapular, I will save the world.

Our Lady gave us her shield, the Brown Scapular, and her weapon, her Most Holy Rosary, to help fortify us to cooperate with Sanctifying Graces to save our souls by fighting the forces of the world, the flesh and the devil, and there was no greater foe of these three combined forces than the singularly most exemplary monarch of the Middle Ages, Saint Louis IX, King of France.

The Elder Daughter of the Church Gives Us Christ the King's True Servant: Tradition teaches us that the Catholic Faith was brought to what is now southern France by Saint Mary Magdalene, and her siblings, Saint Lazarus, whom Our Lord had raised from the dead, and Saint Martha, following their exile from the Holy Land by the Jews who were persecuting the first Catholics. Saint Lazarus is considered to be the first bishop of Marseille, planting the seeds of the Faith there, which is why the cathedral of the city of Autun, France, is named Saint Lazaire.

Although the conversion of the first King of the Franks, Clovis, who was baptized by Saint Remigius in Rheims, France, in the year 496 A.D. after the king's wife, Saint Clotilde, had urged him to convert, made France a firm defender of the Faith and of the Vicar of Christ, the Faith had been spreading in France for over four centuries prior to that time.

Saint Denis (Dionysius), who was Bishop of Paris during the time of the Decian persecutions in the middle of the Third Century, was beheaded with a sword in the year 258 A.D. He did not die immediately. Tradition teaches us that he carried his head for six miles as he gave a sermon along the way. All things are, of course, quite possible with God.

Saint Hilary was the Bishop of Poitiers between 363 A.D. and 368 A.D. He was proclaimed a doctor of the universal church by Pope Pius IX in 1851. He was an illustrious foe of Arianism and helped to groom one of France's adopted sons, Saint Martin of Tours, who had been born to pagan parents before he converted to the Faith at the age of eighteen after having experienced a miracle concerning the restoration of a cloak he had torn to give to a beggar, who appeared as Our Lord to him in a dream before awakening to find that the cloak had been made whole again.

France had seen a plethora of saints, including, among many others, Saint Germanus of Auxerre and Saint Gregory of Tours by the time that King Charles I, better known as Charlemagne, the first Holy

Roman Emperor, was crowned at the end of the Eighth Century, that is in the year 800 A.D.

Charlemagne had been born in 742 A.D., the son of Pepin the Short, who was anointed King of the Franks by Pope Stephen III in the year 754 A.D. Charlemagne was anointed as his father's successor at the same time, distinguishing himself in his young adulthood as a tactical military genius and a very good administrator who based his decisions on that which was just and pleasing to God and thus for all parties involved. He became king in 768 A.D., serving as a firm defender of the temporal rights of the Holy See. Charlemagne's military campaigns to defend the papacy won him the esteem of one pope after another, resulting ultimately in his crowning by Pope Leo III as the first Holy Roman Emperor on October 25, 800 A.D., after he had defended the honor of His Holiness against unjust accusers. Thus it was that the Vicar of Christ, the Successor of Saint Peter, chose an emperor for Christendom, firmly establishing the Social Kingship of Jesus Christ as the unifying principle of Christendom.

Charlemagne was not bashful about inserting himself into ecclesiastical matters, doing so not for personal gain or to seek the approval of bishops for nefarious schemes, something that would characterize some of the French kings following the weakening of the Church in France as a result of the Protestant Revolt, but to seek to insure that corrupt, self-seeking bishops were reprimanded in order that they served their flock with greater zeal and as they performed penance for their misdeeds. He provided a summary of the entire doctrine of the Social Reign of Christ the King when he gave the following speech to his nobles in March of 802:

> "Hear me, my beloved brothers! We were sent here for your salvation, to exhort you to faithfully follow the Law of God and to convert you, in justice and mercy, to obey the laws of this world.

> "First, I exhort you to believe in the One Almighty God, Father, Son and Holy Spirit: the only true God, perfect Trinity, true Unity, Creator of all things visible and invisible, Who is our salvation and the Author of all good things. Believe in the Son of God made man for the salvation of the world, born of the Virgin Mary by the work of the Holy Ghost. Believe that for our salvation He suffered death; and that on the third day He rose from the dead and ascended into Heaven where He is seated at the right hand of God. Believe that He will return to judge the living and dead, and that He will give to each one according to his works.

> "Believe in one single Church, the society of the blessed through the entire universe, and know that only they can be saved, and that the Reign of God belongs only to those who persevere to the end in this [Catholic] Faith. Those who are excluded from the Church because of their sins and do not return to her through penance, can never make any action accepted by God. Be convinced that with Baptism you received absolution of your sins. Trust in the mercy of God, Who daily forgives our sins through confession and penance. Believe in the resurrection of the dead, in eternal life and in the never-ending torment of the impious.

> "This is the Faith that will save you if you keep it faithfully, and add to it the practice of good works, because Faith without works is a dead faith; and works without Faith, even when they are good, cannot please God. Therefore, love Almighty God above all things with all your heart and strength. With the help with His grace, do everything, always and as much as

possible, that you believe will please Him. But avoid everything that displeases Him, for the man who pretends to love God and does not observe His Commandments lies.

"Love your neighbor as yourself, and give as many alms to the poor as you can, according to your means. Receive travelers in your houses, visit the poor, and show charity to the prisoners as much as you can. Do evil to no one, and make no compromise with those who do bad things, because it is bad to not only harm your neighbor, but also to be familiar with those who harm him. "Mutually forgive offenses if you want God to forgive your sins. Rescue captives, help those who are unjustly oppressed, defend widows and orphans. Make judgments fairly; never favor any injustice, do not harbor long hatreds; avoid drunkenness and taking part in frivolous feasts.

"Be humble and good to one another; be faithful to your lords. Commit no robberies or perjuries, and avoid any acquaintance with those who commit them. Hatred, jealousy and violence separate us from the Kingdom of God. Reconcile with one another as soon as possible, for while it is human for men to sin, it is angelic to repent and diabolic to persevere in sin.

"Defend the Church of God and help her so that the priests of God can pray for us. Remember your promise in Baptism to renounce the Devil and his works. Do not return to him in anything; nor should you return to the works you have renounced, but rather follow the will of God as you have promised, and love the One who created you and gave you all the gifts and goods you possess.

"Each one should serve God faithfully in the place he finds himself. Wives should submit to their husbands in all goodness and modesty. They should avoid any dishonest action, and not poison others or be jealous, because those who do such actions are in revolt against God. They should raise their children in the fear of God, and give alms with a glad and joyous heart according to their means.

"Husbands should love their wives and speak no rude word to them; they should direct their homes with goodness and frequently gather in church. They should return to others what they owe them without murmuring, and with good will return to God what belongs to Him.

"Children should love and honor their parents; obey them in everything, and remain far from stealing, murdering and debaucheries.

"Clerics and canons should diligently obey the commands of their Bishops; they should live in their residences and not wander here and there among the people. Nor should they enter into secular questions. They should preserve their chastity: the reading of Holy Scriptures should remind them of their service to God and the Church.

"Monks should be faithful to the promises they made to God. They should not do anything against the will of their Abbots or seek any shameful personal benefit. They should know their rule by heart and follow it regularly, reminding themselves that it would be better not to have made any vow than to have made them and not be faithful to them.

"Dukes, counts and judges should be just with the people and merciful to the poor. They should never sell justice for money, and never allow a personal hatred to lead them to condemn an innocent man. They should always have these words of the Apostle in their hearts: 'For we must all appear before the judgment seat of Christ; that every one may receive the things done in his body, according to that which he has done, whether it be good or bad.' (2 Cor. 5:10) The Lord expressed this by the following words: 'For with what judgment you judge, you shall be judged' (Matt 7:2); 'For there is nothing covered, that shall not be revealed; neither hidden, that shall not be known.' (Luke 12:2) 'That every idle word that men shall speak, they shall give account thereof in the day of judgment' (Matt 12:36).

"We must make an effort, therefore, with the help of God, to please Him in all our actions so that after this present life, we will merit eternal happiness in the company of the Saints of the Lord. This life is short, and the hour of death is uncertain. What matters except to be ready? Let us not forget how terrible it is to fall into the hands of the Lord. By means of confession, penance and alms, we make the Lord become merciful and clement. If He sees us turn to Him with a sincere heart, He will show us pity and will have mercy on us.

"May God grant us prosperity in this life and an eternity with His Saints in the future life.

"God keep you, my beloved brothers!" (As translated by Hugh O'Reilly for the Tradition in Action website. Text found in Charles d'Hericault, *Histoire Anecdotique de la France*, Paris: Bloud & Barral, vol. 1, pp 301-304.)

Although temporal rulers challenged the temporal powers of the Successor of Saint Peter on a fairly regular basis in the Middle Ages, resulting in period triumphs of various popes, including that of Pope Saint Gregory VII, who asserted control of the Holy Roman Empire in 1077 after the Investiture Controversy (concerning the control of bishops by civil potentates) that had been wrought by Emperor Henry IV, Charlemagne had enunciated principles of right and just civil governance according to the Mind of the Divine Redeemer, Christ the King, and it was those right principles that animated the thoroughly Catholic mind and heart of **Saint Louis IX, King of France**, from the time he learned the Holy Faith at his mother's knee at the beginning of the Thirteenth Century. While individual rulers may or may not have accepted the principles outlined by Charlemagne, the principles of Catholic truth remain valid regardless as to whether they are observed in fact. It is never impossible to keep the commands and precepts given us by Christ the King.

Saint Louis IX, King of France, learned from his mother's knee to love God and to hate sin. His saintly mother, Blanche of Castile, knew that her son would have to learn to love God as He revealed Himself to men exclusively through the Catholic Church and that he would have to strive to grow in sanctity in order to win Heaven by ruling according to the mind of Christ the King, ever reliant upon Mary our Immaculate Queen. Blanche's ambition for her son was not that he should rule many lands or win many battles for naturalistic reasons. Her ambitions for her son revolved around his winning souls for the Catholic Church and that he would win his own battle against the world, the flesh, and the devil in order to have the crown of eternal glory placed on his head after his earthly crown signifying his kingly rule was removed following his death.

Saint Louis IX was born in 1214 and anointed King of France at Rheims in 1226. Dom Prosper Gueranger describes this accession of Saint Louis to the throne as follows in *The Liturgical Year*:

> He was only twelve years old; but our Lord had given him the surest safeguard of his youth, in the person of his mother, that noble daughter of Spain, whose coming to France, says William de Nangis, was the arrival of all good things. The premature death of her husband Louis VIII left Blanche of Castile to cope with a most formidable conspiracy. The great vassals, whose power had been reduced during the preceding reigns, promised themselves that they would profit of the minority of the new prince in order to regain the rights they had enjoyed under the ancient feudal system to the detriment of the government. In order to remove this mother, who stood up single-handedly between the weakness of the heir to the throne and their ambition, the barons, everywhere in revolt, joined hands with the son of John Lackland, Henry II, who was endeavoring to recover the possessions in France lost by his father in punishment for the murder of prince Arthur. Strong in her son's right and in the protection of Pope Gregory IX, Blanche held out; and she, whom the traitors to their country called the foreigner in order to palliate their crime, saved France by her prudence and her brave firmness. After nine years of regency, she handed over the nation to its king, more united and more powerful than ever since the days of Charlemagne. . . . Yet who was greater than this humble king, making more account of his Baptism at Poissy than of his anointing at Rheims; saying his Hours, fasting, scourging himself like his friends the Friars Preachers and Minors; ever treating with respect those whom he regarded as God's privileged ones, priests, religious, the suffering and the poor? The great men of our days may smile at him for being more grieved at losing his breviary than at being taken captive by the Saracens. But how have they behaved in the like extremity? (Dom Prosper Gueranger, *The Liturgical Year*.)

Saint Louis IX understood that though he had to use the authority as a civil ruler that had been given him by God to rule justly according to His laws, that he would pay a high price at the moment of his Particular Judgment if he did anything contrary to the binding precepts of the Divine positive law and the natural law and/or did anything that put into jeopardy the public honor and glory due the Blessed Trinity and thus damaged the sanctification and salvation of the souls of his subjects. Saint Louis IX knew that there were limits that existed in the nature of things which he had no authority to transgress. And he recognized that the Church herself had the right to interpose herself as a last resort following the exhausting of her Indirect Power of teaching and preaching and exhortation if he proposed to do things–or had in fact done things–contrary to the laws of God and thus deleterious to the salvation of souls. Saint Louis understood that being a good Catholic was an absolute precondition to being a good ruler or a good citizen.

Mirroring the Catholic teaching found in Charlemagne's speech to his nobles in 802 A.D., Saint Louis IX's letter to his son, the future King Philip III, contains principles of right governance and conduct that should serve as the model for all civil rulers at all times, principles that will be used again once the new French monarch arises to fight Antichrist as the Triumph of the Immaculate Heart of Mary is made manifest. Yes, you read this correctly. France, the elder daughter of the Catholic Church, will play a vital role in the resurrection of the Church Militant on earth just as surely as nefarious forces within her played a role in the Church's Passion and Death in the years leading up to and then following the French Revolution, which began on July 14, 1789.

Here are some excerpts from Saint Louis IX's letter to his son Philip:

1.   To his dear first-born son, Philip, greeting, and his father's love.

2.   Dear son, since I desire with all my heart that you be well instructed in all things, it is in my thought to give you some advice in this writing. For I have heard you say, several times, that you remember my words better than those of any one else.

3.   Therefore, dear son, the first thing I advise is that you fix your whole heart upon God, and love Him with all your strength, for without this no one can be saved or be of any worth.

4.   You should, with all your strength, shun everything which you believe to be displeasing to Him. And you ought especially to be resolved not to commit mortal sin, no matter what may happen, and should permit all your limbs to be hewn off, and suffer every manner of torment, rather than fall knowingly into mortal sin. (Letter to His Son Philip)

That is, one entrusted with the rule over others has an obligation to be especially vigilant about the state of his own immortal soul. Mortal sin kills the life of Sanctifying Grace in the soul, thereby darkening the intellect (which is thus more ready to deny the truth or be slower to accept it) and weakening the will, inclining the sinner more and more to a disordered love of self and to an indulgence in his uncontrolled appetites. A soul in a state of Mortal Sin is more apt to act contrary to truth and to do so arbitrarily, leading a life of contradiction and confusion that is ultimately   reflected in his relations with others. As even Plato himself understood from natural reasoning alone, disorder in the soul leads to disorder in society. Well, disorder in the soul is caused principally by unrepentant Mortal Sin. If one wants to know one of the chief reasons why the modern State has been corrupted, one should start by looking at the glorification of Mortal Sin in every aspect of our culture (which is found among those libertarians who believe that the State has no role to play in such issues as contraception or abortion or perversity, that these are all matters of "personal liberty").

Saint Louis went on to explain to his son, the future King Philip III, that he must bear his crosses with patience and be ever grateful for the blessings he receives from God, making sure to avoid becoming   conceited because of the privilege he would be given to serve as a ruler over his subjects:

5. If our Lord send you any adversity, whether illness or other in good patience, and thank Him for it, thing, you should receive it in good patience and be thankful for it, for you ought to believe that He will cause everything to turn out for your good; and likewise you should think that you have well merited it, and more also, should He will it, because you have loved Him but little, and served Him but little, and have done many things contrary to His will.

6. If our Lord send you any prosperity, either health of body or other thing you ought to thank Him humbly for it, and you ought to be careful that you are not the worse for it, either through pride or anything else, for it is a very great sin to fight against our Lord with His gifts.

> 7. Dear son, I advise you that you accustom yourself to frequent confession, and that you
> choose always, as your confessors, men who are upright and sufficiently learned, and who
> can teach you what you should do and what you should avoid. You should so carry yourself
> that your confessors and other friends may dare confidently to reprove you and show you
> your faults. (Letter to His Son Philip)

That is, Saint Louis IX, who suffered much during his lifetime, including imprisonment by the Saracens and failure in his last crusade, was explaining to his son that we must bear our crosses with manly courage, understanding that our sins deserve far worse than we suffer in this life and that there is no suffering we encounter that is the equal of what one of our least venial sins did to Our Lord in His Sacred Humanity on the wood of the Holy Cross. Any prosperity that God sees fit to bestow upon us is His gratuitous gift that can be taken away at any moment. We should be thankful for His gifts but detached from them in order to place our heart where it rightly belongs–to the things of Heaven, thus building up treasure there.

Saint Louis went on to explain to his son that he must be a man of prayer in order to rule justly and thus to be counted among the just when he died:

> 8. Dear son, I advise you that you listen willingly and devoutly to the services of Holy Church,
> and, when you are in church, avoid frivolity and trifling, and do not look here and there;
> but pray to God with lips and heart alike, while entertaining sweet thoughts about Him, and
> especially at the mass, when the body and blood of our Lord Jesus Christ are consecrated, and
> for a little time before. (Letter to His Son Philip)

Saint Louis IX, a Third Order Franciscan--and the Patron Saint of the Third Order of Saint Francis--who assisted at two Masses a day and spent many hours before the Blessed Sacrament in fervent prayer, anticipated by over six hundred fifty Pope Leo XIII's exhortation, contained in *Mirae Caritatis*, May 28, 1902, concerning the necessity of Eucharistic piety as an absolute precondition to the discharge of one's duties in civil office. Saint Louis IX was the personification of all of the virtues that flow from a life steeped in the pursuit of personal sanctity, a life that sought to seek the shelter of Our Lord in His Real Presence and was tenderly devoted to the Mother God, a life that set aside earthly pleasures and honors in order to seek the choicest riches of all: eternal life in the glory of the Beatific Vision in Heaven. Saint Louis IX knew that no one could exercise the powers of civil rule properly unless his mind was enlightened by the Deposit of Faith and his will strengthened by Sanctifying Grace in order to seek God's will first and to help advance the cause of the common good of all society in light of the common end of all men: to be citizens of Heaven for all eternity. Christ must reign first as the King of the hearts of individual men and then as the King of all nations.

Saint Louis IX was a just judge who would spend time under a tree hearing the cases of his subjects, knowing that he would be judged by the Judge of his immortal soul if he, in his own words, "swayed either to the right or the left," if he showed any favoritism in any way that would be a violation of the precepts of justice, both natural and Divine. Having learned from his mother's knee to love God and to grow in holiness, Louis IX is the model for all rulers at all times in all places. He outlined these principles in his letter to his son Philip:

9. Dear son, have a tender pitiful heart for the poor, and for all those whom you believe to be in misery of heart or body, and, according to your ability, comfort and aid them with some alms.

10. Maintain the good customs of your realm, and put down the bad ones. Do not oppress your people and do not burden them with tolls or tailles, except under very great necessity.

11. If you have any unrest of heart, of such a nature that it may be told, tell it to your confessor, or to some upright man who can keep your secret; you will be able to carry more easily the thought of your heart.

12. See to it that those of your household are upright and loyal, and remember the Scripture, which says: "Elige viros timentes Deum in quibus sit justicia et qui oderint avariciam"; that is to say, "Love those who serve God and who render strict justice and hate covetousness"; and you will profit, and will govern your kingdom well.

13. Dear son, see to it that all your associates are upright, whether clerics or laymen, and have frequent good converse with them; and flee the society of the bad. And listen willingly to the word of God, both in open and in secret; and purchase freely prayers and pardons.

14. Love all good, and hate all evil, in whomsoever it may be.

15. Let no one be so bold as to say, in your presence, words which attract and lead to sin, and do not permit words of detraction to be spoken of another behind his back.

16. Suffer it not that any ill be spoken of God or His saints in your presence, without taking prompt vengeance. But if the offender be a clerk or so great a person that you ought not to try him, report the matter to him who is entitled to judge it.

17. Dear son, give thanks to God often for all the good things He has done for you, so that you may be worthy to receive more, in such a manner that if it please the Lord that you come to the burden and honor of governing the kingdom, you may be worthy to receive the sacred unction wherewith the kings of France are consecrated.

18. Dear son, if you come to the throne, strive to have that which befits a king, that is to say, that in justice and rectitude you hold yourself steadfast and loyal toward your subjects and your vassals, without turning either to the right or to the left, but always straight, whatever may happen. And if a poor man have a quarrel with a rich man, sustain the poor rather than the rich, until the truth is made clear, and when you know the truth, do justice to them.

19. If any one have entered into a suit against you (for any injury or wrong which he may believe that you have done to him), be always for him and against yourself in the presence of your council, without showing that you think much of your case (until the truth be made known concerning it); for those of your council might be backward in speaking against you, and this you should not wish; and command your judges that you be not in any way upheld more than any others, for thus will your councillors judge more boldly according to right and truth.

20. If you have anything belonging to another, either of yourself or through your predecessors, if the matter is certain, give it up without delay, however great it may be, either in land or money or otherwise. If the matter is doubtful, have it inquired into by wise men, promptly and diligently. And if the affair is so obscure that you cannot know the truth, make such a settlement, by the counsels of of upright men, that your soul, and the souls of your predecessors, may be wholly freed from the affair. And even if you hear some one say that your predecessors made restitution, make diligent inquiry to learn if anything remains to be restored; and if you find that such is the case, cause it to be delivered over at once, for the liberation of your soul and the souls of your predecessors.

21. You should seek earnestly how your vassals and your subjects may live in peace and rectitude beneath your sway; likewise, the good towns and the good cities of your kingdom. And preserve them in the estate and the liberty in which your predecessors kept them, redress it, and if there be anything to amend, amend and preserve their favor and their love. For it is by the strength and the riches of your good cities and your good towns that the native and the foreigner, especially your peers and your barons, are deterred from doing ill to you. I will remember that Paris and the good towns of my kingdom aided me against the barons, when I was newly crowned.

22. Honor and love all the people of Holy Church, and be careful that no violence be done to them, and that their gifts and alms, which your predecessors have bestowed upon them, be not taken away or diminished. And I wish here to tell you what is related concerning King Philip, my ancestor, as one of his council, who said he heard it, told it to me. The king, one day, was with his privy council, and he was there who told me these words. And one of the king's councillors said to him how much wrong and loss he suffered from those of Holy Church, in that they took away his rights and lessened the jurisdiction of his court; and they marveled greatly how he endured it. And the good king answered: "I am quite certain that they do me much wrong, but when I consider the goodnesses and kindnesses which God has done me, I had rather that my rights should go, than have a contention or awaken a quarrel with Holy Church." And this I tell to you that you may not lightly believe anything against the people of Holy Church; so love them and honor them and watch over them that they may in peace do the service of our Lord.

23. Moreover, I advise you to love dearly the clergy, and, so far as you are able, do good to them in their necessities, and likewise love those by whom God is most honored and served, and by whom the Faith is preached and exalted.

24. Dear son, I advise that you love and reverence your father and your mother, willingly remember and keep their commandments, and be inclined to believe their good counsels.

25. Love your brothers, and always wish their well-being and their good advancement, and also be to them in the place of a father, to instruct them in all good. But be watchful lest, for the love which you bear to one, you turn aside from right doing, and do to the others that which is not meet.

26. Dear son, I advise you to bestow the benefices of Holy Church which you have to give, upon good persons, of good and clean life, and that you bestow them with the high counsel of upright men. And I am of the opinion that it is preferable to give them to those who hold nothing of Holy Church, rather than to others. For, if you inquire diligently, you will find enough of those who have nothing who will use wisely that entrusted to them.

Saint Louis IX, quite unlike the war-happy leaders of the past century who have considered war to be a first resort to the resolution of international conflicts and disputes rather than a regrettable last resort after all peaceful means to avoid armed military conflict have been exhausted, adhered to the principles of the Just War Theory, outlined below, that would be defended by Saint Thomas Aquinas in his *Summa Theologica*:

27. Dear son, I advise you that you try with all your strength to avoid warring against any Christian man, unless he have done you too much ill. And if wrong be done you, try several ways to see if you can find how you can secure your rights, before you make war; and act thus in order to avoid the sins which are committed in warfare.

28. And if it fall out that it is needful that you should make war (either because some one of your vassals has failed to plead his case in your court, or because he has done wrong to some church or to some poor person, or to any other person whatsoever, and is unwilling to make amends out of regard for you, or for any other reasonable cause), whatever the reason for which it is necessary for you to make war, give diligent command that the poor folk who have done no wrong or crime be protected from damage to their vines, either through fire or otherwise, for it were more fitting that you should constrain the wrongdoer by taking his own property (either towns or castles, by force of siege), than that you should devastate the property of poor people. And be careful not to start the war before you have good counsel that the cause is most reasonable, and before you have summoned the offender to make amends, and have waited as long as you should. And if he ask mercy, you ought to pardon him, and accept his amends, so that God may be pleased with you.

29. Dear son, I advise you to appease wars and contentions, whether they be yours or those of your subjects, just as quickly as may be, for it is a thing most pleasing to our Lord. And Monsignore Martin gave us a very great example of this. For, one time, when our Lord made it known to him that he was about to die, he set out to make peace between certain clerks of his archbishopric, and he was of the opinion that in so doing he was giving a good end to life.

One can see that Saint Louis IX's advice to his son was a cogent summary of the following principles of the Just War Theory that must, of course, be applied in the concrete circumstances by leaders, meaning that errors in judgment are bound to be made now and again given the nature of fallen creatures. It is nevertheless true that there must be a real consideration of these factors, something that Saint Louis IX, just man that he was, understood entirely.

1) There must be a wound to justice that poses a real and imminent threat to the good order of nations and/or to the territorial integrity or well-being of innocents by an aggressor. The threat must be real, not imaginary, not concocted for political purposes.

2) All peaceful means to avoid armed hostilities must be exhausted. Diplomatic efforts to avert war must be genuine. It was the Holy Father himself who attempted to broker disputes in order to avoid war during the Middle Ages and at various times thereafter.

3) A duly constituted authority must make the determinations concerning the waging of war. This means that a legitimate governing authority, one that has not usurped power or which seeks war unjustly to prosecute plans of territorial expansion and/or nationalistic or ideological ends, guided by right intentions and right principles must be in charge of the decision-making process.

4) The goals of a war must be well-defined and have a reasonable chance of being realized. In other words, there must be a reasonable chance for success in the pursuit of narrowly defined goals. Goals are to be defined narrowly so as to limit the harm caused by a needlessly protracted war, yes, even when a nation is prosecuting a just cause.

5) The good end being sought must not be outweighed by the foreseen evil to be done. This is known as the Catholic principle of proportionality, which states that a good end can be rendered unjust to pursue if a judgment is made that the amount of the foreseen evil to be done in the prosecution of a just war will cause greater evils than the one the war is being waged to eradicate. This is different than the heresy of proportionalism (heretics use Catholic sounding phrases so as to connect themselves in the minds of Catholics as understanding Catholic principles), which asserts that a preponderance of "good intentions" and of the "relative exigencies of the moment" can make a moral act that is naturally evil capable of being pursued justly on the part of one who believes the weight of the evidence in his case justifies a subjective violation of an objective moral law to do good. Thus, proportionalism, which has been propounded by the late Father Richard McCormick, S.J. (not to be confused with the priest from the Archdiocese of Hartford, Connecticut, who foments dissent at the University of Notre Dame and in his nationally syndicated columns, Father Richard McBrien), can be used by a woman to justify the killing of her preborn child. After all, more good will be done in her life by killing the child than if she permitted him to interfere unduly with her life's goals.

6) As far as is possible, noncombatants must never be deliberately targeted in warfare. The United States has a mixed record when it comes to the realization of this part of the Just War Theory. Our military forces have tried to use remarkable restraint in many instances. Other times, however, they have not. William Tecumseh Sherman used raw terrorism against civilian population centers as he cut a swath of fiery destruction from the Atlantic Ocean to Atlanta during the War between the States. As noted earlier, we aided bloodthirsty revolutionaries in Mexico. Dresden, Hiroshima, and Nagasaki (the latter two of which were known to contain the highest concentrations of Catholics in Japan) were bombed during World War II. Something less than laser precision caused thousands of civilian casualties during the Gulf War and during our continued bombing in Afghanistan, which commenced on October 7, 2001, and during and after the American invasion and occupation of Iraq on March 20, 2003.

7) A just cessation to hostilities must be realized as soon as possible. Once again, the record

of the United States in this regard is very mixed. The dropping of the atomic bombs on Hiroshima and Nagasaki was done so as to force an unconditional surrender from Japan, something that the Soviets insisted on in the Potsdam Conference as their condition for entering the war against Japan (so that they could recover claims lost in the Russo-Japanese War of 1904-05.) Japan was willing to surrender conditionally. Those who are convinced of their absolute moral and racial superiority over others, though, cannot consider ending hostilities even if it is possible to conclude a peace that is just without having humiliated one's enemies.

The final part of Saint Louis IX's letter to his son Philip deals with the care that a civil ruler must take to see to the good administration of his own government and that he is a good son of the Vicar of Christ:

32. Dear son, freely give power to persons of good character, who know how to use it well, and strive to have wickednesses expelled from your land, that is to say, nasty oaths, and everything said or done against God or our Lady or the saints. In a wise and proper manner put a stop, in your land, to bodily sins, dicing, taverns, and other sins. Put down heresy so far as you can, and hold in especial abhorrence Jews, and all sorts of people who are hostile to the Faith, so that your land may be well purged of them, in such manner as, by the sage counsel of good people, may appear to you advisable. Further the right with all your strength. Moreover I admonish you that you strive most earnestly to show your gratitude for the benefits which our Lord has bestowed upon you, and that you may know how to give Him thanks therefore

33. Dear son, take care that the expenses of your household are reasonable and moderate, and that its moneys are justly obtained. And there is one opinion that I deeply wish you to entertain, that is to say, that you keep yourself free from foolish expenses and evil exactions, and that your money should be well expended and well acquired. And this opinion, together with other opinions which are suitable and profitable, I pray that our Lord may teach you.

34. Finally, most sweet son, I conjure and require you that, if it please our Lord that I should die before you, you have my soul succored with masses and orisons, and that you send through the congregations of the kingdom of France, and demand their prayers for my soul, and that you grant me a special and full part in all the good deeds which you perform.

35. In conclusion, dear son, I give you all the blessings which a good and tender father can give to a son, and I pray our Lord Jesus Christ, by His mercy, by the prayers and merits of His blessed Mother, the Virgin Mary, and of angels and archangels and of all the saints, to guard and protect you from doing anything contrary to His will, and to give you grace to do it always, so that He may be honored and served by you. And this may He do to me as to you, by His great bounty, so that after this mortal life we may be able to be together with Him in the eternal life, and see Him, love Him, and praise Him without end. Amen. And glory, honor, and praise be to Him who is one God with the Father and the Holy Spirit; without beginning and without end. Amen. (From Saint Louis' Advice to His Son, in Medieval Civilization, trans. and eds. Dana Munro and George Clarke Sellerym New York: The Century Company, 1910, pp. 366-375.)

No, a confessional Catholic State is not a guarantor of social order, only the necessary precondition for it. Individual men must choose to cooperate with God's grace to build up the Kingship of Christ in their own souls and hence in every aspect of their nation's life. This is never an easy task given the frailties of fallen human nature, which is why the Church's shepherds must exhort the faithful to lives of holiness unspotted by the world and proclaim the immutable doctrine, contained in the Ordinary Magisterium of the Catholic Church, of the Social Reign of Christ the King that was exemplified so well by Saint Louis IX in the Thirteenth Century.

It is good to consider just the following passage, noting the great leader of France during most of the Thirteenth Century, Saint Louis IX, summarized the whole of the doctrine of the Social Kingship of Jesus Christ when he wrote:

> 31. Dear son, I advise you always to be devoted to the Church of Rome, and to the sovereign pontiff, our father, and to bear him the reverence and honor which you owe to your spiritual father. (Letter to His Son Philip)

There is no more cogent summary of the Social Kingship of Jesus Christ. Saint Louis was telling his son that he, although destined to be a king, was subordinate to the Church founded by Our Lord upon the Rock of Peter, the Pope. All States, no matter the construct of their civil governments, must be so subordinate. Remember this and remember well: Catholics do not care about "states' rights." They care about God's laws, which bind all men at all times, whether they are acting individually in their own lives or in the institutions of civil governance.

Importantly, as noted just above, Saint Louis admonished his son as follows:

> Dear son, freely give power to persons of good character, who know how to use it well, and strive to have wickednesses expelled from your land, that is to say, nasty oaths, and everything said or done against God or our Lady or the saints. In a wise and proper manner put a stop, in your land, to bodily sins, dicing, taverns, and other sins. Put down heresy so far as you can, and hold in especial abhorrence Jews, and all sorts of people who are hostile to the Faith, so that your land may be well purged of them, in such manner as, by the sage counsel of good people, may appear to you advisable.

The State has the obligation to work to remove those conditions that breed sin in the midst of its cultural life. Yes, sin there will always be. True. However, the State, which the Church teaches has the obligation to help foster those conditions in civil society in which citizens can better save their souls, must not tolerate grave evils (such as blasphemy or willful murder) under cover of law. Saint Thomas Aquinas understood that some evils may have to be tolerated in society. Graver evils, however, undermine the common good and put into jeopardy the pursuit of man's last end. Pope Saint Pius X made this point in *Vehementer Nos*, February 11, 1906, as he condemned the law of separation of Church and State that had been passed in Saint Louis IX's beloved country of France by the successors of the French revolutionaries.

That the State must be separated from the Church is a thesis absolutely false, a most pernicious error. Based, as it is, on the principle that the State must not recognize any religious cult, it is in the first place guilty of a great injustice to God; for the Creator of man is also the Founder of human societies, and preserves their existence as He preserves our own. We owe Him, therefore, not only a private cult, but a public and social worship to honor Him. Besides, this thesis is an obvious negation of the supernatural order. It limits the action of the State to the pursuit of public prosperity during this life only, which is but the proximate object of political societies; and it occupies itself in no fashion (on the plea that this is foreign to it) with their ultimate object which is man's eternal happiness after this short life shall have run its course. **But as the present order of things is temporary and subordinated to the conquest of man's supreme and absolute welfare, it follows that the civil power must not only place no obstacle in the way of this conquest, but must aid us in effecting it.** (Pope Saint Pius X, *Vehementer Nos*, February 11, 1906.)

The Catholic spirit of the Middle Ages, that era in which men worked long and hard to build the great cathedrals and churches and shrines and in which men took great pains to provide us with beautiful works of art and composed music that lifted the human soul to Heaven, is far from the anti-Incarnational, naturalistic and semi-Pelagian spirit of Modernity that has been embraced by the lords of the counterfeit church of conciliarism. For far from upholding the immutable teaching of the Catholic Church that has condemned the separation of the Church and State, Joseph Ratzinger/Benedict XVI has endorsed this thesis, which was termed absolutely false by Pope Saint Pius X. So has Jorge Mario Bergoglio/Francis. Something that is absolutely false and a most pernicious error in 1906 does not become true and good a century later. Truth is immutable because God Himself is immutable.

Social classes lived in harmony with each other. Men were unafraid to defend the cause of Christ the King and His true Church to fight in the Crusades to reclaim the Holy Land and to do battle with the Mohammedans. Chivalry was the hallmark of the Catholic gentleman. And perhaps most importantly, human beings saw in each other the Divine impress, attempting to treat each other as they would Our Lord in the very Flesh.

Father Edward Cahill summarized the political spirit of Christendom very succinctly in *The Framework of a Christian State*:

> **Social Life Permeated by the Christian Spirit**.—The whole structure of mediaeval society was founded upon Christianity. All the people were Catholic; and ecclesiastical influence was very powerful. Christian principles were inculcated in the current literature, the pulpit, the schools, and the tribunal of Penance; and were taken for granted, even when not faithfully followed, by all classes of society. The laws and their administration, the economic policy of the State, the recognised relations between the different classes, even international politics, were judged by Christian standards. So strong and deep-rooted was public opinion in the mater that it was difficult for individuals to disregard these standards openly.
>
> Kenelm Digby mentions many interesting particulars illustrating the Catholic tone of public life. Thus: "A painting of the Crucifixion was usually to be seen in the great chambers of the parliaments... and over the seats of justice. The great, solemn thirteenth century paintings of sacred subjects on the walls of the great hall of Sienna, in which the grand council of the Republic assembled, are an evidence of the tone of the government."

In the choice of public functionaries, fidelity and probity were the great qualities insisted on. The injunction contained in one of the Capitularies of Charlemagne gives an idea of the spirit which continued during mediaeval times to dominate public administration.

> "Let no count hold his plaids [viz. placita generalia–a kind of local council] unless he be fasting and fed with sense."

Again, Digby quotes the following term from a mediaeval collection of municipal laws:

> "The town sheriff has to visit the round of the walls at night to see that the watch has sufficient clothing. He has to inspect the provisions destined for the poor."

Political Principles.–The fundamental principle of all mediaeval teaching upon public authority and civic rights was that authority comes from God and is given to the ruler solely for the people's good; and that the people whose good was to be promoted included all classes equally, rich and poor, high and low, serf, burgher and feudal lord. Further, owing to the ingrained spirit of Christianity in favour of the poor and the weak, the principle was commonly admitted that the humbler classes had the first claim upon the consideration and solicitude of the ruling powers. Thus John of Salisbury (d. 1180), a typical 12th century political philosopher, writes:

"Then and only then will the health of the commonwealth be sound and flourishing when the higher members devote themselves to the lower; and when similarly the lower members cooperate with the higher so that each and all are as it were members of one another, and each believes his own interest best served by what he knows to be most usefully provided for others."

Again, the same author writes:

> "All things are to be referred to the public good; and whatever is useful to the humbler classes, that is, the multitude should be pursued in all things. . . . Christ will hear the poor when they cry out, and it will be in vain to multiply vows, and to endeavour, as it were, to bribe God by gifts."

Hence, Henry II of England describes himself (and was described) as the "Defender of the Poor and the Defenceless."

Vincent Beauvais of the Order of Saint Dominic (d. 1264), who was tutor to the children of St. Louis, writes in much the same strain as John of Salisbury on the duty of government:

> "There must be mutual safety for the king and the people; he errs who thinks that the king is safe when nothing is safe from the king."

Tyrannical Rule Reprobated.–Another fundamental principle strongly insisted upon in the political teaching of that age is that the absolute power is regulated by fundamental laws against which whatever is done is of its own nature null and void. This principle, at variance alike with the pagan principles of absolutism and the modern Liberalist view of the omnipotence of a majority, is frequently emphasized by St. Thomas (d. 1274). Thus he writes:

> "One is bound to obey civil rulers, in as far as the order of justice demands. Hence if the power is not held justly, but is rather a usurpation, or if the laws are unjust, the subjects are not bound to obey, unless perchance in order to avoid scandal or danger."

Again the same writer has:

> "Those who defend the common good are not to be called seditious in resisting those who oppose it. . . . The tyrant himself it is that is seditious, who encourages disunion and sedition in the people he rules, in order that hey may more easily retain his control over them. For this is tyranny to aim, namely, at the personal advantage of the ruler to the detriment of the people."

We find in Dante (d. 1321), whose work contains so faithful a picture of the mediaeval spirit, many echoes of this attitude towards unjust rule. For instance a certain group in the infernal regions are thus referred to:

> "Those are the souls of tyrants, who were given To blood and rapine. Here they wail aloud Their merciless wrongs."

Mediaeval Christian Democracy.–Such doctrines commonly acknowledged, and the structure of a society fashioned under their influence, effectually secured a high degree of genuine democratic rule. Despotism, understood in the sense of irresponsible rule exercised mainly in the interest of the rulers and practically regardless of the people's rights–the system of government which obtained all over Europe before the rise of Christianity and was reintroduced as a result of the Protestant Revolt–did not generally prevail under the Christian regime of the Middle Ages. This fact, which is strongly asserted by the Catholic apologists, is acknowledged even by historians hostile to the Church. Thus Lecky writes: "The balance of power produced by the numerous corporations which she [viz., the Church] created or sanctioned, the reverence for tradition resulting from her teaching which created a network of unwritten customs with the force of public laws, by the dependence of the civil upon the ecclesiastical power, and the rights of excommunication and deposition [exercised by the ecclesiastical authorities] all combined to lighten the pressure of despotism". . . .

Hallam, while acknowledging the prevailing spirit of justice of justice and democratic independence in the mediaeval system, does not state that this was due to the influence of Christianity.

Decentralisation of Political Power.–Another very important safeguard against tyranny was the decentralisation of political power. In this the mediaeval state contrasts strongly with the ancient pagan state as well as with the royal absolutism of the 17th and 18th centuries and the centralising tendencies of the modern bureaucracies. The extensive power conferred by royal charter on the city municipalities, which were organised on a democratic basis, and the fundamental laws and privileges of the provinces were all strong safeguards against centralised despotism. So was the guild organisation of the towns, to which Pius XI refers as:

> "The highly-developed social life which once flourished in a variety of institutions organically linked with each other."

On the other hand the very real power of the king, which depended largely upon popular support, acted as a check against the abuses of local barons.

Conclusion.–Hence, although wicked and unprincipled rulers are to be met with even in the period of which we write, their power to injure and oppress was much more limited than that of a modern bureaucracy. Widespread injustice and continued tyranny were scarcely possible; and the oppression and tyranny which did exist here and there were partially counteracted by the resources which religion supplied. (Father Edward Cahill, S.J., *The Framework of a Christian State*, pp. 30-34.)

Multiple volumes of books would be necessary to treat of each of the glories of Christendom in the Middle Ages as music, art, literature and architecture flourished. Economic systems were in place that assured justice and the practice of usury, so common today, was unthinkable as immoral. There was also an adherence to the just price, distinguishing the era of Christendom from that which exists in our own Protestant-Judeo-Masonic world of unbridled capitalistic individualism and profiteering;

> Application in Mediaeval Times.–The mediaeval law of Just Price is another example of the altruistic spirit which permeated the social and economic life of the middle ages. Individuals were not permitted to use freely the property they controlled in ways that might be detrimental to the common good. They were compelled, when the needs of others required it, to place the goods they had to dispose of at the service of the public *under equitable conditions.* Thus poor and weak were protected against unfair competition, so that all might be secured a fair access to the material goods of the community.
>
> The laws of Just Price had to be observed in wages, buying and selling and every contract of exchange; otherwise the contracted was accounted unjust and invalid in conscience, and the aggrieved party had a claim to restitution. "Whoever," writes Trithemius, a well-known fifteenth century author, "buys up corn, meat and wine in order to drive up their prices, and amass money at the cost of others, is, according to the laws of the Church, no better than a common criminal. In a well-government community all arbitrary raising of prices in the case of articles of food and clothing is peremptorily stopped. In times of scarcity merchants who have supplies of such commodities can be compelled to sell them at fair prices; for in every community care should be taken that all the members should be provided for, lest a small number be allowed to grow rich, and revel in luxury to the hurt and prejudice of the many."

Contract between Christian and Non-Christian Standpoint. In the old Roman law, just as in   modern Liberal states, selfishness was assumed to be the dominating motive in every contract; and the fullest liberty was allowed to both parties to decide the price and even to over-reach each other, provided nothing was done that the law regarded as fraud. According to mediaeval teaching on the other hand, the price of a commodity was supposed to be determined by objective value alone; and could not be justly influenced by the special need or ignorance of buyer or seller.

Doctrine of the Just Price.–This doctrine, which was universally accepted in mediaeval times, is thus summarised by St. Thomas:

"It the price exceeds the value of the thing, or if the thing is worth more than the price paid, the equality which justice requires is done away with."

The seller cannot justly extract a higher price merely on account of the special need the buyer may have of the thing, or the accidental advantage that may accrue to him from it; for in such cases he would be selling what is not his. Hence the criterion of exchange value was something intrinsic to the commodity itself, not merely competition or the higgling of the market. Hence, too, the modern distinction between value in use and value in exchange was recognized to a very limited extent. (Father Edward Cahill, *The Framework of a Christian State*, pp. 42-44.)

Also practiced during the Middle Ages was the principle of the living wage, that is, an amount that is paid to a worker that would permit him to meet the obligations of his state of life without forcing his wife to leave the home and the care of the children to support the family. While those paid a wage, even though they might have been few in number during Middle Ages as the contemporary "salaried" position became commonplace during the rise of the Industrial Revolution in the Eighteenth and Nineteenth Centuries, had a responsibility to live within their means and to, if possible, acquire a bit of savings from their earnings, employers were nevertheless expected to deal justly with their workers   so that those who had the greater need (more children, poor health, critical circumstances) received   the higher amount. This was such a universally respected principle during the Middle Ages that even Saint Thomas Aquinas and his own teacher, Saint Albert the Great, did not believe that it was necessary to elaborate upon it as it was simply part of the fabric of Christendom.

Similarly, the practice of usury, that is, of lending money by the charging of interest, no less of exorbitant interest rates, was condemned by the Church and rejected universally by the Catholics of Christendom as offends justice, practiced more often than not by Talmudic money-lenders. Pope Leo XIII made advertence to the Church's condemnation of all forms of rapacious usury in *Rerum Novarum*, May 15, 1891. The 1917 Code of Canon Law, recognized that money itself had become a form of capital and that lenders could charge a rate of interest permitted by the civil law unless that rate is "clearly excessive." There has been no change of Catholic teaching, only a change in what is considered to be capital.

This is what Pope Leo XIII wrote in *Rerurm Novarum*, May 15, 1891:

In any case we clearly see, and on this there is general agreement, that some opportune remedy must be found quickly for the misery and wretchedness pressing so unjustly on the majority of the working class: for the ancient workingmen's guilds were abolished in the last century, and no other protective organization took their place. **Public institutions and the laws set aside the ancient religion. Hence, by degrees it has come to pass that working men have been surrendered, isolated and helpless, to the hardheartedness of employers and the greed of unchecked competition. The mischief has been increased by rapacious usury, which, although more than once condemned by the Church, is nevertheless, under a different guise, but with like injustice, still practiced by covetous and grasping men.** To this must be added that the hiring of labor and the conduct of trade are concentrated in the hands of comparatively few; so that a small number of very rich men have been able to lay upon the teeming masses of the laboring poor a yoke little better than that of slavery itself. (Pope Leo XIII, *Rerum Novarum*, May 15, 1891.)

This analysis is even more relevant to our times as it was in 1891.

Holy Mother Church recognizes the changes that take place in economic systems even though she may not approve of those changes or believe that they are optimal for the realization of man's Last End. And thus it is that money, as opposed to land or some other tangible good, has become capital, meaning that there can be a just interest charged on those who lend it. There is thus no contradiction between the Catholic Church's consistent condemnation of usury and Canon 1543 of the 1917 Code of Canon Law:

> "If a commodity which is consumed by its first use (such as money, bread, etc.), be lent on the stipulation that it becomes the property of the borrower, who is bound to return to the lender not the thing itself but its equivalent only, the lender may not receive any payment by reason of the loan itself. In the giving or lending of such a commodity, however, it is not in itself unlawful to make an arrangement for the recovery of interest at the rate allowed by the civil law (*de luco legali pacisi*) unless that rate is clearly excessive: One may even arrange for a still higher rate of interest, if there be a just title for doing so, in proportion to the amount of the excess." (Canon 1543, 1917 Code of Canon Law.)

What has changed is the nature of the commercial transaction itself, not the Church's condemnation of usury, which has been made many times, including the Tenth Session of the Fifth Lateran Council, May 4, 1515, which was presided over by Pope Leo X.

Father Cahill explained the effects of the Church's prohibition of usury in the Middle Ages, a practice that has been widespread in our own day as our world is governed by principles that are based upon rank profiteering and the exploitation of the weak and impoverished:

> The Church's legislation [on usury] did not, it is true, succeed in completely preventing the practice of usury, especially on the part of the Jews. These laws and principles were, however, an immense check upon the unjust activities of money-lenders and speculators, so that anything approaching the systematised extortion and stock-gambling of modern times was impossible.

Conclusion.–It is commonly admitted that the undue concentration of wealth under the control of the few is one of the radical causes of the social misery and unrest that prevail at the present day. Individuals controlling great wealth have excessive power in almost every phase of social activity, and following the tendency of human nature, they too often use their power unjustly and tyrannically. Those huge fortunes are usually amassed by unjust profiteering, artificially created monopolies, usury, unjust reduction of wages, the sudden fluctuations of the markets which play into the hands of greedy speculators. The mediaeval economic doctrines and legislation and the public opinion they produced and fostered made impossible, or at least kept in check, such methods of accumulating wealth, and so were a potent safeguard against one of the worst types of social injustice. (Father Edward Cahill, S.J., *The Framework of a Christian State*, p. 51.)

The economics of the Middle Ages were also characterized in the Twelfth Century by the rise that made possible the training of masters in various fields of commerce (merchants and crafts) after first serving years of apprenticeships and then working as journeymen. The object of these guilds was to produce a cooperative spirit so that individual guild members could pursue their own interests without endangering the common interests of their mutual trades. It was the true spirit of Catholic charity that bound the guild members together to such an extent that they provided for each other what would be called "welfare" today, administering this assistance according to the Natural Law principle of subsidiarity that requires human problems to be remedied at the lowest levels of life, staring with the family. The guilds made it possible for those with needs that could not be meet by their families to receive assistance without the "strings" attached by the monster civil state of Modernity and without bankrupting the entire body politic:

> The greatest spirit of solidarity and mutual help animated the whole guild organisation. Thus money was advanced on easy terms to members who needed it. Those suffering from sickness, old age, accidents, etc., were liberally provided for. Even a guildman who might get into trouble with the municipal or state authorities had a right to the protection of the guild. If, after investigation by the council, his case was considered a deserving one he was defended in the courts at the common expense. Sick members were visited; and wine and food were sent from the public banquets to those whom illness or weakness prevent from attending. The dead, if the family was poor, was buried at the expense of their guild with all the honours befitting their position, and their daughters dowered for marriage or the convent.

The Religious Character of the Guilds.–Another peculiarly Christian characteristic of these guilds was their practical recognition of the intimate connection of religion with commercial relations and with all the activities of life. Although the primary object of the associations was economic, the guilds made every effort to secure good conduct and fidelity to religious duties on the part of the members. Individuals were punished or sometimes expelled from the guilds for immoral or irreligious conduct.

Every guild was under the protection of a patron saint or was specially dedicated to the Holy Trinity or to the Blessed Mother of God under one of her titles. The portrait of the guild patron was painted on the banner of the guild which was borne in the public processions. Thus the guild of wood-workers was under the protection of St. Joseph. The shoemakers usually had on their banner paintings of SS. Crispin and Crispinian. Bakers were often under the patronage of St. Honorius, and so on. The association of the heavenly patron with the grade that belonged to the guild intensified the craftsmen's pride in their work and the men's esteem for the nobility of manual labour. The Church Feast of the patron was always the occasion of the great annual banquet of the guild.

Many guilds had their own special chapels; and we commonly find provision made in the guild statutes for the support of a chaplain and sometimes of several chaplains. Some of the most beautiful mediaeval churches belonged to or were built by the guilds. Provision was also regularly made for the celebration of Masses for the intentions of the guild, and for the offering of candles at holy shrines. On the death of a member care was taken to have Masses offered and alms given for his eternal rest. Almsgiving, which was practiced even towards the poor outside the gild, was an important item of the ordinary guild expenditure. Oftentimes a guild gave feasts in its buildings to the poor of the whole town. (Father Edward Cahill, *The Framework of a Christian State*, pp. 79-80.)

Christendom would continue beyond the Thirteenth Century. It was, however, at its height in the Thirteenth Century, which is why the devil used the weakness of men to embrace the world just a "little bit at a time" in the two centuries between its end and the beginning of the revolutions of Modernity that began with Father Martin Luther's posting of his ninety-five theses on the door of Castle Church in Wittenberg, Germany, on October 31, 1517. And one of Martin Luther's principal goals was to separate Church and State, a separation that has been nothing other than disastrous for the right ordering of men and their nations.

Although the era of Christendom was far from perfect as man's fallen estate will always cause difficulty for himself and others and his society, it was, of course the apogee, the high point, of man's social organization.

As noted in the previous chapter, men were born and died in an environment that was permeated by the truths of the Holy Faith, surrounded by churches and shrines, enveloped in glorious music and magnificent works of art. They made time to make pilgrimages in honor of the Mother of God and took seriously the salvation of their immortal souls. Those who were bold enough to give public scandal were rebuked or shunned. The members of the various classes cooperated with each other without envy, something that characterized the best of the feudal system as Christendom was being constructed following the barbaric invasions of the second half of the First Millennium. Those who worked the land were assured of food to eat and of a place to live. What mattered to all was to die in a state of Sanctifying Grace as a member of the Catholic Church.

Statecraft and economics were all governed by the binding precepts of the Divine Positive Law, noting, of course, that clever self-seekers sought to rule as automatons and even made war upon Holy Mother Church when they believed that it was expedient to so, something that King Philip IV of France did with Pope Boniface VIII, who, despite whatever vainglory earned him a sentence of eternal damnation in Dante's *Inferno*, asserted in the papal bull *Unam Sanctam*, November 18, 1303, the primacy of the papacy over every man on earth as necessary for salvation. King Philip IV of France, seeking to assert his own authority over the French bishops and relentless in his desire to tax the clergy of France to finance his wars, accused Pope Boniface VIII of various moral crimes, to which the pope replied by excommunicating him. Thus began the slide downward from the glories of the beneficent Saint Louis IX, who accepted correction from the hand of the Holy Father, Pope Clement IV, in a direct exercise of the Social Reign of Christ the King, to the time that Father Martin Luther of the Order of Saint Augustine posted his ninety-five theses on the door of Castle Church in Wittenberg, Germany, on October 31, 1517.

Consider the parallelism here:

Saint Louis IX, King of France from 1226 to 1270, was one of the greatest exemplars of the Social Reign of Christ the King. He was prayerful, devout and pious as pertains to First and Last Things and he was just in all of his temporal affairs, starting within his own household.

King Philip IV, also known as Philip the Fair, was the antithesis of his grandfather, Saint Louis, starting military hostilities with England in 1294 that lasted off and on until 1303, but which proved to be the origins of the disastrous Hundred Years' War in 1337 during which Saint Joan of Arc was burned at the stake at the hands of English bishops on May 30, 1431, twenty-two years before the end of that war. Far from respecting and fostering the temporal power of the Vicar of Christ on earth as had his saintly grandfather, Philip IV wanted to reduce that temporal power and to make the papacy a prisoner of himself and future French king. Father John Laux describes the conflict as follows in *Church History*:

If the King refused to submit [to Unam Sanctam], he was excommunicated and deposed. But before the Bull of excommunication was published, two of Boniface's most vindictive enemies, William of Nogaret, one of Philip's chief advisers, and Sciarra Colonna, with a band of hired ruffians surprised the aged Pontiff in his palace at Anagni and brutally mistreated him; it is said that Colonna struck him with his iron glove. The Pope remained in their power for three days; the third day he was rescued by the citizens of Anagni and borne in triumph to Rome. A few weeks later (October 11, 1303) he died of the pain and humiliation and the savage ill-treatment to which he had been subjected.

> "This outrage at Anagni," says the French publicist Carriere in his book The Pope, "is without excuse because it is beyond all reason and devoid of any dignity. Otto, Henry II, Henry IV, Barbarossa, Frederick II treated the Popes as enemies, but at least as kings. Philip behaved, not as one of the powerful of the earth at war with another power, but like a vindictive boor preparing an ambush and hiring with gold the cut-throats charged to carry out his vengeance. . . . Whatever may have been the errors of this Pope, he was, none the less, the Vicar of Christ, recognized by all Christendom; he borne upon his forehead and upon his shoulders the insignia of his office, and he was an old man. . . ." We can understand the anger of Dante, even though he was an enemy of Boniface VIII. He has branded forever the perpetrators of this cowardly assault in the immortal verses:
>
> > Lo! the fleurs-de-lys
> > Enters Anagni; in His Vicar Christ
> > Himself a captive, and His mockery
> > Acted again, Lo! to His holy lip
> > The vinegar and gall once more applied;
> > And He 'twixt living robbers doomed to bleed. (Dante, *Purgatorio*, XX, 86- 90.) (As found in Father John Laux, *Church History*, Benziger Brothers, 1930, pp, 394-395.)

Pope Boniface VIII's successor, Pope Benedict XI, "was found dead four weeks after he had excommunicated Nogaret and some of his accomplices" and there were rumors that he had been poisoned (cf. Father Laux, *Church History*, p. 396.) It was within six years that the dominance of the French kings became so great that the seat of the papacy was moved from Rome to Avignon, France, where each of the popes between then and 1377 were French, including Pope John XXII, Jacques d'Euse, provoking a battle in 1316 with Emperor Louis of Bavaria over the temporal power of the papacy. Emperor Louis, aided by the English theologian William of Ockham, contended that the emperor had the right to depose a pope who fell into heresy, admitting that a pope could exercise some temporal power if a civil ruler had failed to do his duty. "Although a settlement was reached with Louis's successor, Charles IV, the "temporal supremacy of the Papacy seemed assured; but it was a delusion; the temporal supremacy of the Popes was a thing of the past" (Father Laux, *Church History*, p. 399):

> The principles proclaimed by Gregory VII and upheld by his successors, after accomplishing their providential mission, had become unsuited to control the destinies of

Europe. "The Papal power of judgment in political affairs (as Pius IX declared later) had been granted by the public consent of Christendom; it was not by that same public consent being refused."

The long-drawn-out conflict with Louis of Bavaria could not but diminish the prestige of the Holy See and shake the allegiance of thousands to its authority. The celebrated Mystic, St. Bridget of Sweden, who spent the last thirty years of her life in Rome, wrote to the Popes at Avignon and expressed the fear that, unless they soon returned to Italy, they would forget not only their temporal, but also their spiritual authority. When Urban IV, who had taken up his residence in Rome for two years (1368-1370), went back to Avignon, she prophesied his speedy death; which actually took place a few months later.

St. Bridget did not live to see the conclusion of the unnatural exile in France. It was another heroic woman, St. Catherine of Siena, "one of the most marvelous figures in the history of the world," who broke the spell which Philip the Fair had bound the Papacy. (Father Laux, *Church History*, p. 399.)

Yes, it was to a daughter of Saint Dominic, Saint Catherine of Siena, that the papacy, subordinate to the whims of the French kings for sixty-eight years, that the mission of bring the pope back to Rome–and thus to a measure of independence form earthly rulers–had been entrusted.

Saint Catherine of Siena's Mission: Saint Catherine of Siena suffered much within her wealthy family as she sought the things of Heaven and eschewed the pleasures and riches of this passing, mortal vale of tears. She was very misunderstood and very harshly treated at times by her own mother, who reduced her to the status of a family servant when she, Catherine Bennicasa, announced at the age of twelve that she would not marry and that she desired a life of solitude in prayer. Saint Catherine of Siena preferred God to creatures, accepting all manner of calumnies and sufferings as the price she had to pay for her mystical espousal to Christ the King at the age of twelve.

Yes, it is difficult to "kick against the goad" in the world. It is hard, humanly speaking, for many to realize that we must be confessional Catholic at all times and in all places and to all people no matter the consequences that might befall us in this passing, mortal vale of tears. However, we must indeed come to accept the simple truth that all will be confusion and chaos and disorder and rot in the lives of individuals and their nations unless each person has a due subordination to the Deposit of Faith   and a due reliance upon the supernatural helps available only in and from the Catholic Church, now found in the catacombs. Saint Catherine of Siena wanted only to please God. Her heart was on fire for love of Him as He has revealed Himself to us exclusively through the Church that He Himself founded upon the Rock of Peter, the Pope. And she was quite willing to "kick against the goad" to be faithful to her Beloved.

We must, therefore, persevere in defense of the Faith in the spirit with which Saint Catherine of Siena persevered in the face of that fierce opposition, sometimes bordering on mockery, within her own family that she accepted with such serenity and joy. We must accept suffering and misunderstanding and rejection and ridicule with that same sort of serenity and joy as our sins imposed suffering, misunderstanding, rejection and ridicule upon Our Divine Redeemer, Our Blessed Lord and Saviour Jesus Christ, during His Passion and Death. Who are we to be exempted from the same kind of suffering and rejection and ridicule and mockery? We deserve far, far worse than anything we are privileged to suffer in this life as we make reparation for our sins to the Most Sacred Heart of Jesus through the Sorrowful and Immaculate Heart of Mary. Suffering is the path to salvation. There is none other.

Saint Catherine of Siena understood this. She was given infused knowledge by Our Lord Himself, which made her so suspect in the eyes of some that she was called before a general chapter of the Order of Preachers to defend herself. Her examiners were astounded at the clarity and theological precision of her answers. It was from that point forward in her brief thirty-three years of life that she became, in effect, a spiritual director to priests and learned theologians, reconciling enemies to each   other and serving the plague-stricken, including several of her priest-followers, when Siena was in the grip of a severe outbreak of the plague. Saint Catherine's holy name even suffered after her death as she, whose body was incorrupt, was blamed for precipitating the Great Western Schism in 1379 by having convinced Pope Gregory XI to return to the seat of the Holy Faith, Rome, from exile in Avignon, France, a move that made her hated among many within the papal curial, most of them being French themselves, who did not want to leave the creature comforts of Avignon for the grime and filth of Rome at the end of the Fourteenth Century. It is most likely the case that Saint Catherine knew that she would be excoriated many years after her death as she had been in life. This did not matter at all. Right was right; no amount of "strategic considerations" could ever cause her to veer from the course that she knew to be correct.

Although formally unschooled and for a time completely illiterate, unable to read or write until she asked for the gift to do so (asking later that the same gift be taken away from her), she wrote her famous Dialogue, which many masters of the interior life consider to be one of the most brilliant expositions of the deepest secrets of Divine Intimacy. She also composed this eloquent letter to Pope Gregory XI to urge him to return to the seat of the legitimate successors of Saint Peter, Rome:

In the name of Jesus Christ crucified and of sweet Mary: Most holy and most reverend my father in Christ Jesus: I Catherine your poor unworthy daughter, servant and slave of the servants of Christ, write to you in His precious blood; with desire to see you a good shepherd. For I reflect, sweet my father, that the wolf is carrying away your sheep, and there is no one found to succor them. So I hasten to you, our father and our shepherd, begging you on behalf of Christ crucified to learn from Him, who with such fire of love gave Himself to the shameful death of the most holy cross, how to rescue that lost sheep, the human race, from the hands of the demons; because through man's rebellion against God they were holding him for their own possession.

Then comes the Infinite Goodness of God, and sees the evil state and the loss and the ruin of these sheep, and sees that they cannot be won back to Him by wrath or war. So, notwithstanding they have wronged Him-for man deserves an infinite penalty for his disobedient rebellion against God-the Highest and Eternal Wisdom will not do this, but finds an attractive way, the gentlest and most loving possible to find. For it sees that the heart of man is in no way so drawn as by love, because he was created by love. This seems to be the reason why he loves so much: he was created by nothing but love, both his soul and his body. For by love God created him in His Image and Likeness, and by love his father and mother gave him substance, conceiving and bearing a son.

God, therefore, seeing that man is so ready to love, throws the book of love straight at him, giving him the Word, His Only-Begotten Son, who takes our humanity to make a great peace. But justice wills that vengeance should be wrought for the wrong that has been done to God: so comes Divine Mercy and unspeakable Charity, and to satisfy justice and mercy condemns His Son to death, having clothed him in our humanity, that is, in the clay of Adam who sinned. So by His death the wrath of the Father is pacified, having wrought justice on the person of His son: so He has satisfied justice and has satisfied mercy, releasing the human race from the hands of demons. This sweet Word jousted with His arms upon the wood of the most holy Cross, death fighting a tournament with life and life with death: so that by His death He destroyed our death, and to give us life He sacrificed the life of His body. So then with love He has drawn us to Him, and has overcome our malice with His benignity, in so much that every heart should be drawn to Him: since greater love one cannot show-and this He himself said-than to give one's life for one's friend. And if He commended the love which gives one's life for one's friend, what then shall we say of that most burning and perfect love which gave its life for its foe? For we through sin had become foes of God. Oh, sweet and loving Word, who with love hast found Thy flock once more, and with love hast given Thy life for them, and hast brought them back to Thy fold, restoring to them the Grace which they had lost!

Holiest sweet father of mine, I see no other way for us and no other aid to winning back your sheep, which have left the fold of Holy Church in rebellion, not obedient nor submissive to you, their father. I pray you therefore, in the name of Christ crucified, and I will that you do me this grace, to overcome their malice with your benignity. Yours we are, father! I know and realize that they all feel that they have done wrong; but although they have no excuse for their crimes, nevertheless it seemed to them that they could not do differently, because of the many sufferings and injustices and iniquitous things they have endured from bad shepherds and governors. For they have breathed the stench of the lives of many rulers whom you know yourself to be incarnate demons, and fallen into terrible fears, so that they did like Pilate, who not to lose his authority killed Christ; so did they, for not to lose their state, they maltreated you. I ask you then, father, to show them mercy. Do not regard the ignorance and pride of your sons, but with the food of love and your benignity inflict such mild discipline and benign reproof as shall satisfy your Holiness and restore peace to us miserable children who have done wrong.

I tell you, sweet Christ on earth, on behalf of Christ in Heaven, that if you do this, without strife or tempest, they will all come grieving for the wrong they have done, and lay their heads on your bosom. Then you will rejoice, and we shall rejoice, because by love you have restored the sheep to the fold of Holy Church. And then, sweet my father, you will fulfill your holy desire and the will of God by starting the holy Crusade, which I summon you in His name to do swiftly and without negligence. They will turn to it with great eagerness; they are ready to give their lives for Christ. Ah me, God, sweet Love! Raise swiftly, father, the banner of the most holy Cross and you will see the wolves become lambs. Peace, peace, peace, that war may not delay that happy time!

But if you will wreak vengeance and justice, inflict them on me, poor wretch, and assign me any pain and torment that may please you, even death. I believe that through the foulness of my iniquities many evils have occurred, and many misfortunes and discords. On me then, your poor daughter, take any vengeance that you will. Ah me, father, I die of grief and cannot die! Come, come, and resist no more the will of God that calls you; the hungry sheep await your coming to hold and possess the place of your predecessor and Champion, Apostle Peter. For you, as the Vicar of Christ, should abide in your own place. Come, then, come, and delay no more; and comfort you, and fear not anything that might happen, since God will be with you. I ask humbly your benediction for me and all my sons; and I beg you to pardon my presumption. I say no more. Remain in the holy and sweet grace of God-Sweet Jesus, Jesus Love. (As found in an article about Saint Catherine of Siena's life: http://www.ewtn.com/library/MARY/CATSIENA.htm.)

Even with this great accomplishment of bringing the Bishop of Rome back to the Eternal City, however, Saint Catherine of Siena was blamed by many and held in bitter contempt for her having done so, especially as the Great Western Schism broke out in 1378 after the death of Pope Gregory XI in 1378 and the election of Pope Urban VI, who was determined to resist the entreaties of French cardinals to return the papacy to Avignon. The French cardinals, fearing that Pope Urban VI was going to curb the luxury to which they had grown accustomed in the south of their country at Avignon, elected an antipope on September 30, 1378, who took the name "Clement VII." Saint Catherine of Siena's name suffered in death as it had in life, at least for a time, until her prodigies and her incorrupt body convinced one and all that she had been a saint her entire life.

The Great Western Schism tore apart the entirety of Christendom. Tracts filled with bitter accusations were printed and circulated, inflaming the populace of Europe. England and supported Urban VI while France, of course, supported antipope Clement VII. There were two colleges of cardinals and as many as two or three supposed superiors of the religious communities. Saint Vincent Ferrer, who worked assiduously, for the conversion of Jews and Mohammedans in the south of France and in the Iberian Peninsula at the end of the Fourteenth and the beginning of the Fifteenth Centuries, followed an antipope "successor" of Clement VII, "Benedict XIII," with as much ardor as Saint Catherine of Siena had supported Pope Urban VI.

The Black Death had decimated Europe between 1348 and 1350, although there were outbreaks of the plague throughout the remainder of the Fourteenth Century and well into the Fifteenth Century. The loss of between thirty and sixty percent of the population of Europe occurred at a time when the Hundred Years' War, which had begun in 1337, was taking place. The Great Western Schism occurred after the Black Death had decimated the population of Europe.

Although the Council of Constance ended the Great Western Schism in 1417, various popes in the Fifteenth Century become so immersed in the worldliness of the pagan elements of the Renaissance that they and their cardinals came to be seen as more concerned with material extravagance and vanity rather than as shepherds of souls. The adversary was planting the cockle that would produce conditions favorable for the widespread acceptance of Martin Luther's revolution against the true Faith as Catholics failed to make a distinction between the moral flaws of their shepherds and the integrity of the Faith, which had not once come into question even during the excesses of the Renaissance.

A Rebirth of Sophistry and a Prelude to Vatican II: Different historians provide different dates to define the period known as the Renaissance. Broadly speaking the era can be said to begin in the latter part of the Fourteenth Century, reaching its height in the Fifteenth and early Sixteenth Centuries prior to the beginning of the Protestant Revolution in 1517.

The Renaissance touched upon every branch of learning and arts and science. Some considered it to be the flowering of the Middle Ages while others considered it be a rejection. There is merit to both views, although this writer believes that the Renaissance, when viewed as a whole without denigrating in the slightest the great works of art and literature produced during some of its phases, was indeed a transition from the Middle Ages to Modernity.

At the root of the Renaissance, however, was an inordinate preoccupation with man rather than with God. What was "old" was considered, at least in the minds of some Renaissance "thinkers," had to be "rethought" anew. This was particularly true as pertains to the interpretation of Sacred Scripture, which some believed had been put into a "box" by the Scholasticism of Saint Thomas Aquinas. In other words, elements of the Renaissance and its humanism, of which there were Christian elements, are directly related to the whole spirit of the "Second" Vatican Council and the "magisterium" of the conciliar "popes."

Although the focus here will be on the rebirth of moral and philosophical relativism during the Renaissance, it is useful to note that even those who have different perspectives about this era of history admit that there were problems that did indeed contribute to the acceptance of the devil's deceits in the various Protestant sects after they formed in the Sixteenth Century and thereafter. Indeed, there is still much visceral talk amongst ill-read and ill-informed Catholics about this era that results in their believing that the corruption of the clergy signifies the corruption of what they teach.

Father John Laux, who treated of the Renaissance in a generally favorable manner, admitted the worldliness of the popes and the cardinals in the Fifteenth Century did scandalize the faithful, whose kingdoms were taxed heavily to finance their patronage of the arts and their building program:

> The Popes from Eugene IV to Leo X are known as the Renaissance Popes. Following the trend of the times, these Popes collected manuscripts of the classical authors, pictures, statues, precious stones, and all kinds of works of art and learning, and gathered about them a host of artists and men of letters. They erected magnificent buildings and adorned them with masterpieces of sculpture and painting. As lords of the Papal States their court was brilliant, and most of them lived in magnificent splendor. Statesmen and diplomats, poets and artists, scientists and philosophers, were always sure of a cordial welcome and costly entertainment. But many of those who found their way into the Roman court sought only wealth and luxurious living; and it was these voluptuaries who brought the Curia into ill-repute throughout Christendom. The maintenance of the princely court of the Popes required vast sums of money; to collect these the Papal revenues had to be increased from year to year. The whole of Europe was put under contribution by levying taxes of various kinds and under different names. That the highest ecclesiastics in the government of the Church only too often succumbed to the temptations which surrounded them on all sides; that they became "intoxicated with the wine of the Renaissance to the point of totally forgetting the Catholic spirit, forgetting that they were priests, bishops, cardinals, Popes, remembering only that they were "humanists"–this is one of the reasons why the Protestant

revolt was promptly popular and so largely successor.

The Renaissance Popes have also been styled the "political Popes." The circumstances of the time forced them to be political Popes. The Papal States had become an Italian national power from the moment that the Christian commonwealth of Europe was disrupted. The popes were drawn into the political struggles of Italy, and much of their time, energy, and resources was consumed in the task of maintaining and increasing their territories and power. They had to keep a standing army, like their neighbors, and were often engaged in warlike enterprises. Owing to the great influence exercised by the Curia on European politics, the various States sought to win over as many cardinals as possible to their side, and those who succumbed to the temptation served their foreign patrons more faithfully that their own master, the Pope. In self- defense, the Popes surrounded themselves with members of their own families, nephews, as a rule, whom they raised to the highest offices and provided with incomes from the possessions of the Church. This system, known as Nepotism, did much to lower the prestige of the Holy See. Many of them were young and inexperienced and, being in most cases devoid of any sense of the responsibility that rested on them, gave themselves up to a life of self-indulgence and political ambition. They also exercised a baneful influence on the Papal elections, several of them by their intrigues attaining to the height of their ambition, the Papal Throne. Of the thirteen Popes who reigned from 1431 to 1534 only three–Nicholas V, Innocent VIII, and Adrian VI–were not related to one of their predecessors or successors (Father John Laux, *Church History*, pp. 412-413.)

The tendency of members of the Catholic hierarchy to fall prey to attractions of the world and the blandishments of the powerful, although far from unknown prior to this time, became even more pronounced after the Renaissance and after the Protestant Revolution broke. All but one of the English bishops defected when King Henry VIII took England out of the Faith in 1534 as they wanted to please their king while saving their own heads and continuing the privileges and perquisites of their offices. Bishops in France frequently curried favor with their king, taking his stand against popes, who were fearful of losing France to the Protestant Revolution and thus, although condemning Gallicanism (the belief that bishops can "sift" through the words and commands of a true pope), were powerless to curb the excesses of Kings Louis XIV and XV or of Joseph I in the Austro-Hungarian Empire.

Many have been the cardinals and bishops in the United States of America who were more than willing to do the bidding of various civil potentates, dating all the way back to the anti-Catholic founders and continuing on to develop alliances with naturalists of one or both political parties, something that more than once pitted bishop against bishop publicly, something that will be discussed later in this book.

Dr. Aleksandr I. Solzhenitsyn, the famed Soviet dissident and Nobel Prize laureate in literature who had been exiled from his beloved Russia for over twenty years (1974 to 1996), had a very jaundiced view of the Middle Ages, considering it to have been a "repression" of the natural in favor of the supernatural, an assessment that is simply wrong on its face. He did, however, recognize the Renaissance for what it was, a turning away from the supernatural in favor of all that was merely natural:

How has this unfavorable relation of forces come about? How did the West decline from its triumphal march to its present debility? Have there been fatal turns and losses of direction in   its development? It does not seem so. The West kept advancing steadily in accordance with its proclaimed social intentions, hand in hand with a dazzling progress in technology. And all of a sudden it found itself in its present state of weakness.

This means that the mistake must be at the root, at the very foundation of thought in modern times. I refer to the prevailing Western view of the world in modern times. I refer to the prevailing Western view of the world which was born in the Renaissance and has found political expression since the Age of Enlightenment. It became the basis for political and social doctrine and could be called rationalistic humanism or humanistic autonomy: the proclaimed and practiced autonomy of man from any higher force above him. It could also be called anthropocentricity, with man seen as the center of all.

The turn introduced by the Renaissance was probably inevitable historically: the Middle Ages had come to a natural end by exhaustion, having become an intolerable despotic repression of man's physical nature in favor of the spiritual one. But then we recoiled from the spirit and embraced all that is material, excessively and incommensurately. The humanistic way of thinking, which had proclaimed itself our guide, did not admit the existence of intrinsic evil in man, nor did it see any task higher than the attainment of happiness on earth. It started modern Western civilization on the dangerous trend of worshiping man and his material needs.

Everything beyond physical well-being and the accumulation of material goods, all other human requirements and characteristics of a subtle and higher nature, were left outside the area of attention of state and social systems, as if human life did not have any higher meaning. Thus gaps were left open for evil, and its drafts blow freely today. Mere freedom per se does not in the least solve all the problems of human life and even adds a number of new ones. (Aleksandr I. Solzhenitsyn, "A World Split Apart," Harvard University commencement address, June 8, 1978.)

Although Solzhenitsyn, a fervent partisan of the heretical and schismatic Russian Orthodox Church and virulent foe of Catholicism, did the Middle Ages a grave injustice, he did recognize that the Renaissance and subsequent events paved the way for the triumph of the ideologies of Modernity, including those of Americanism and Communism.

Perhaps more to the point, however, are the insights of a Catholic writer named Lyle Arnold, who assessed the spirit of the Renaissance and then compared it to that of the "Second" Vatican Council, something that this writer believes is very apt:

Medici also pushed their revolution into the realm of art, through the profane works of artists such as Sandro Botticelli, whose style would dominate the last quarter of the 15th century in Florence. His message was that "a harmonious relationship between human beings and the world can only be achieved through the triumph of reason, intelligence and beauty over brute force and arms" (7). Sensuous in the extreme, his works represent well the new mentality of the Renaissance that sprang from the disastrous victory of the desire to enjoy life's pleasures over Catholic militancy and the austerity of the Cross. (8)

By its intrinsic nature, culture has a profound influence on the human soul, and this first Renaissance changed culture. Culture is, indeed, the very "life-blood of a people, the flow of moral energy that holds society intact." (9) To change culture for the worse is to release poisonous fumes into the moral oxygen of a people, and a grave sin. This is what happened in the first Renaissance. But it was only the beginning. The second Renaissance came about in the middle of the 20th century.

The 'second' Renaissance and the 'second' John XXIII

Angelo Giuseppe Roncalli, the second John XXIII could not have picked a more appropriate name for the mission he was to accomplish. The fact that there were a number of Popes named John during the first 1400 years of the Church and then no more for over 500 years is probably due to the controversial figure that Antipope represented. After he was deposed, no Pope wanted to take that name again. It was a surprise and shock to many when the good-natured Roncalli picked the name John XXIII, given the first John's bad end. (Lyle Arnold, Tradition in Action website, July 17, 2008.)

Although not entirely hostile to Protestantism, from which he converted to Catholicism, and a positive admirer of the American constitutional framework, the late Dr. Russell Kirk did nevertheless provide a thoughtful critique of the whole spirit of the Renaissance that will illustrate that it was indeed a turning point away from Christendom to the chaos of Modernity. Kirk started his analysis of the Renaissance with a critique of Dante's *The Divine Comedy*, followed by a penchant discussion of some of the major philosophical problems with the Renaissance and its "humanism":

> In the fifteenth century commenced those sweeping intellectual and social changes which we call Renaissance and Reformation. The medieval order crumbled, and gradually its place was taken by a new order of things, which in part persists down to our time.

> Medieval civilization attained its highest expression in Dante Alighieri, at the beginning of the fourteenth century; for the rest of that century, especially in the south of Europe, the Age of Faith would dissolve. Dante, the most nobly imaginative of poets since his exemplar Virgil, was an exile from Florence for the last two decades of his life, seeing all about him the flood of disorder rising in Italy. Yet knowing that divine love had created the earth and all the stars, he trusted in the City of God. Hell itself is necessary to the human condition, he saw in his "high dream"; most of us limp through Purgatory, here and hereafter; though unworthy, the redeemed will wind through to the blinding light of Paradise. Beyond sin and time, divine order endures forever.

> In *The Divine Comedy* lie two meanings, Dante wrote to Can Grande de Scala, master of Verona, his protector: literally, its meaning is the state of souls after death; allegorically, the subject of that poem is man's free choice of good or evil. Scholastic philosophy and medieval imagery are joined in Dante. His great poem was a synthesis of knowledge, in that

he drew his ideas and his images from the Hebrew prophets, the classical philosophers, the Roman jurists,   the Schoolmen, and even the Arab scholars. Half a century earlier, Saint Thomas Aquinas had given system to Christian and medieval thought: theology, metaphysics, morals, and politics all were summed up in Aquinas' powerful work. In Dante, that same synthesis–that ordering and harmonizing of knowledge and belief–is expressed through poetic insights and symbols. Truth was knowable; order was real. Truth was obscured by man's appetites and desire for power. Yet right reason might disclose truth to men's eyes again, and order might be regained by courageous acts of will. Such was the vision of *The Divine Comedy*.

For the most part, the order of the soul is the subject of Dante's tremendous poem. But Dante was a political thinker as well. How might the order of the commonwealth be regained in the tormented Europe of the late Middle Ages? In his political treatise, *De Monarchia*, Dante sought for the restoration of social unity. The imperial power, the papacy, and the universities must join wholeheartedly in a common conservative undertaking to reaffirm law, truth, and grace. In the new Emperor Henry VII, Dante thought he saw the monarch who might bring about this synthesis in the world of men. But it did not come to pass. After initial successes in   his progress through Italy, the German Emperor lost the support of the Pope, Clement V, and failed to pacify the Italian states; he died suddenly at Siena, in 1313. After that, the medieval order gave at the seams.

Social decadence beset fourteenth-century Europe. Nearly every country was ravaged by war, while the Black Death, the plague, depopulated towns and countryside. Public and private morality sank steadily. The feudal structure, that elaborate balance of loyalties, began to collapse between pressures from national monarchs and rising commercial interests, and in the old free cities of the South despots were arising upon the ruins of civic liberty. These things   are described in the stanzas after Dante's death. The Age of Faith approached its close, and with   it the sense of unity and spiritual community under the medieval ideal of Christendom. No longer would Europe be held together by a common Church, by the international character of its universities, and by a pattern of social ties that grew out of village communities and town guilds. Renaissance and Reformation would rush in to fill this moral and social vacuum left by the withering of medieval civilization.

As the ideal of the Holy Roman Empire, with its German sovereigns, faded in the West, the   last vestige of the Byzantine Empire vanished in the East. In the year 1453, Constantinople fell   to the Turks. At the end of the Crusades, Greek emperors had regained possession of the scraps of the Byzantine territories. But the stump of the Roman Empire of the East was hacked by the ambitions of the Italian merchants from one side and by the ambitions of the Turkish sultans on the other; Constantine's capital fell at last. The wonder was that it had endured so long–the bastion of classical and Christian civilization for eleven imperial centuries.

As this disaster approached, Byzantine scholars and nobles fled into Italy. There, especially in Florence, they waked the West to a fuller interest in Plato and in the whole heritage of the vanished classical civilization. Philosophy, theology, the arts, and presently politics were   deeply affected by this new "humanism" of the Renaissance. This

Renaissance–this conscious rebirth of ancient culture– had commenced earlier, but was now accelerated by catastrophic events in the East. Courts, universities, and the papacy itself began to cast aside the medieval synthesis and medieval institutions, that they might enjoy the things of this world.

For although this word "humanism" originally signified an earnest devotion to the Greek classics, as the revelation of ancient forgotten insights, presently the word came to imply a concern for the present and dawning Europe, by contrast the other worldliness of medieval philosophy and religion. The Renaissance became many things, but to the medieval order it was death. (Russell Kirk, *The Roots of American Order*, third edition, Regnery Gateway, 1991, pp. 221-224.)

Dr. Kirk did not believe that the Renaissance had a direct influence on the American founding. He was mistaken in this view as one of the Renaissance philosophers he alternately praises and criticizes, Pico della Mirandola, had a view of "human dignity" that was closely related to that possessed by some of the "Enlightenment" "philosophers" who had a direct influence on the American founding. Count Mirandola also was favorably disposed to the Pelagian view of grace and nature, which is of the very essence of the American founding and of so-called American "exceptionalism", namely, that men more or less stir up graces within themselves, making them, in essence, self-redemptive.

Kirk provided the evidence for this without realizing that he had done so:

But Pico was no pillar of orthodoxy. He declared that crosses and images ought not to be venerated; on the doctrine of sin, he tendered more toward Saint Augustine's adversary Pelagius than toward the approved teaching of the Church, saying that sin is a force shaping human nature; he doubted whether Christ had descended literally into Hell; and though he argued that astrology was a false science, he believed in an arcane magical knowledge. (Russell Kirk, *The Roots of American Order*, third edition, Regnery Gateway, 1991, p. 227.)

Unfortunately for the late Dr. Kirk, you see, the spirit of Pelagianism is indeed the spirit of Modernity, especially in the United States of America, a land where most people are convinced that Americans "can do anything they want to do as long as they put their minds to doing so," which is not other than a belief in human self-redemption that is at the heart of all naturalistic political philosophies and ideologies. Father Frederick Faber explained this in *The Precious Blood*, which was published in 1860:

All devotions have their characteristics; all of them have their own theological meanings. We must say something, therefore, upon the characteristics of the devotion to the Precious Blood. In reality the whole Treatise has more or less illustrated this matter. But something still remains to be said, and something will bear to be repeated. We will take the last first. Devotion to the Precious Blood is the devotional expression of the prominent and characteristic teaching of St. Paul. St. Paul is the apostle of redeeming grace. A devout study of his epistles would be our deliverance from most of the errors of the day. He is truly the apostle of all ages. To each age doubtless he seems to have a special mission. Certainly his mission to ours is very special. **The very air we breathe is Pelagian. Our heresies are**

only novel shapes of an old Pelagianism. The spirit of the world is eminently Pelagian. Hence it comes to pass that wrong theories among us are always constructed round a nuclear of Pelagianism; and Pelagianism is just the heresy which is least able to breathe in the atmosphere of St. Paul. It is the age of the natural as opposed to the supernatural, of the acquired as opposed to the infused, of the active as opposed to the passive. This is what I said in an earlier chapter, and here repeat. Now, this exclusive fondness for the natural is on the whole very captivating. It takes with the young, because it saves thought. It does not explain difficulties; but it lessens the number of difficulties to be explained. It takes with the idle; it dispenses from slowness and research. It takes with the unimaginative, because it withdraws just the very element in religion which teases them. It takes with the worldly, because it subtracts the enthusiasm from piety and the sacrifice from spirituality. It takes with the controversial, because it is a short road and a shallow ford. It forms a school of thought which, while it admits that we have an abundance of grace, intimates that we are not much better for it. It merges privileges in responsibilities, and makes the sovereignty of God odious by representing it as insidious. All this whole spirit, with all its ramifications, perishes in the sweet fires of devotion to the Precious Blood.

The time is also one of libertinage; and a time of libertinage is always, with a kind of practical logic, one of infidelity. Whatever brings out God's side in creation, and magnifies His incessant supernatural operation in it, is the controversy which infidelity can least withstand. Now, the devotion to the Precious Blood does this in a very remarkable way. It shows that the true significance in every thing is to be found in the scheme of redemption, apart from which it is useless to discuss the problems of creation. (Father Frederick Faber, *The Precious Blood*, written in 1860, republished by TAN Books and Publishers, pp. 258-259.)

The spirit of Modernity was indeed born in the Renaissance as the "rights of man" have been asserted to the exclusion and hatred of the Divine Rights of Christ the King and His Holy Church, which tried, despite the imperfections of man and the personal faults of various popes and civil rulers, to provide men with the eternal truths and efficacious graces that they needed to order their own lives and thus to organize themselves together to seek the common temporal good in light of their Last End, the possession of the glory of the Beatific Vision for all eternity in Heaven.

There is another aspect to Kirk's rather mild criticism of Pico della Mirandola that bears a bit of commentary at this point.

Pico della Mirandola was a Judaizer, that is, a person who believed that there was some utility to providing "insights" and/or using the "methods" of Talmudists to prove various points about the Faith or to advance "progress" in the midst of the world. Talmudists would make full use of the overthrow of the Social Reign of Christ the King wrought by the Protestant Revolution and thus of the separation of millions of souls from the bosom of Holy Mother Church to plant evil seeds that would flower in the anti-Incarnational civil state of Modernity. This is not a minor point whatsoever.

Far from the spirit of service to Christ the King was the mind of Niccolo Machiavelli, who is the principal philosophical bridge between Christendom and Modernity. Machiavelli wrote many works, the two most influential being *The Prince* and *Discourses on Livy*, each of which was meant to give rebirth to the moral relativism of the Sophists of ancient Athens in the Fifth Century before the coming of Our Blessed Lord and Saviour Jesus Christ.

Instead of adhering to Catholic principles of statecraft and diplomacy that, although honored in the breach more often than not during parts of the Middle Ages, characterized the life's work of those civil rulers that Holy Mother Church has raised to her altars as saints, some of whom were mentioned in the previous chapter of this book, Niccolo Machiavelli believed that the "ends justified the means," that civil rulers could lie, cheat, steal or even kill to acquire and then to retain power and that they could pursue whatever means necessary to win military battles and entire wars without regard for moral truths. This is called "amorality," the belief that actions may be undertaken without regard to their inherent morality or immorality, that the only thing that matters is the realization of a given end no matter the methods employed to realize it.

Here is an excerpt from Machiavelli's *Discourses on Livy*:

> Although to use deceit in every action is detestable, none the less in the managing of a war it **is a laudable and glorious thing; and that man is equally lauded who overcomes the enemy by deceit, as is he who overcomes them by force**. And this is seen by the judgment which those men make who write biographies of great men, and who praise Hannibal and others who have been very notable in such ways of proceeding. Of which so many examples have been cited that I will not repeat any. I mention only this, that I do intend that that deceit is glorious which makes you break your trust and treaties that you made; for although it sometimes acquires a State and a Kingdom for you, as has been discussed above, will never acquire them for you gloriously. But I speak of that deceit which is employed against that enemy who distrusts you, and in which properly consists the managing of a war; as was that of Hannibal when he feigned flight on the lake of Perugia in order to close in the Consul and the Roman army; and when to escape from the hands of Fabius Maximus he fired (the fagots on) the horns of his cattle. A similar deceit was also employed by Pontius, the Captain of the Samnites, in order to close in the Roman army within the Caudine forks, who, having placed his army behind a mountain, sent some of his soldiers under the dress of shepherds with a large herd upon the plain; who, being taken by the Romans and asked where the army of the Samnites was, all agreed according to the orders given by Pontius to say that it was at the siege of Nocera. Which was believed by the Consuls, and caused them to be enclosed within the defiles (of Claudium), where (having entered) they were quickly besieged by the Samnites. And this victory obtained by deceit would have been most glorious to Pontius, if he had followed the counsels of his father, who wanted the Romans either to be liberally set free, or all put to death, and would not take the middle way: Never make a friend or remove an enemy. Which way was always pernicious in the affairs of a State, as has been discussed above in another place. (Niccolo Machiavelli, *Discourses on Livy*, Book Three, Chapter XL.)

Machiavelli's models of civil rule are the pagans of Roman antiquity, each filled with boundless reserves of cruelty and cunning, or barbarians such as Hannibal. Saint Edward the Confessor? Saint Margaret of Scotland? Saint Henry the Emperor? Saint Stephen of Hungary? Saint

Wenceslaus? Saint Casimir? Saint Canute? Saint Louis the IX, King of France? Saint Elizabeth of Hungary or her husband, Blessed Louis of Thuringia? No, Machiavelli's models of statecraft and military strategy were from paganism and barbarism. Niccolo Machiavelli did not care for the Just War Theory that had been advanced by Saint Augustine and Saint Thomas Aquinas.

The following excerpts, taking from Machiavelli's *The Prince*, provides an excellent summary of the "realpolitik" (real politics devoid of considerations of inherent moral truth) that is at the very foundation of modern politics, policy-making and the planning and conduct of war:

> WHENEVER those states which have been acquired as stated have been accustomed to live under their own laws and in freedom, there are three courses for those who wish to hold them: the first is to ruin them, the next is to reside there in person, the third is to permit them to live under their own laws, drawing a tribute, and establishing within it an oligarchy which will keep it friendly to you. Because such a government, being created by the prince, knows that it cannot stand without his friendship and interest, and does its utmost to support him; and therefore he who would keep a city accustomed to freedom will hold it more easily by the means of its own citizens than in any other way.

> There are, for example, the Spartans and the Romans. The Spartans held Athens and Thebes, establishing there an oligarchy, nevertheless they lost them. The Romans, in order to hold Capua, Carthage, and Numantia, dismantled them, and did not lose them. They wished to hold Greece as the Spartans held it, making it free and permitting its laws, and did not succeed. So to hold it they were compelled to dismantle many cities in the country, for in truth there is no safe way to retain them otherwise than by ruining them. And he who becomes master of a city accustomed to freedom and does not destroy it, may expect to be destroyed by it, for in rebellion it has always the watch-word of liberty and its ancient privileges as a rallying point, which neither time nor benefits will ever cause it to forget. And what ever you may do or provide against, they never forget that name or their privileges unless they are disunited or dispersed but at every chance they immediately rally to them, as Pisa after the hundred years she had been held in bondage by the Florentines.

> But when cities or countries are accustomed to live under a prince, and his family is exterminated, they, being on the one hand accustomed to obey and on the other hand not having the old prince, cannot agree in making one from amongst themselves, and they do not know how to govern themselves. For this reason they are very slow to take up arms, and a prince can gain them to himself and secure them much more easily. But in republics there is more vitality, greater hatred, and more desire for vengeance, which will never permit them to allow the memory of their former liberty to rest; so that the safest way is to destroy them or to reside there. (Niccolo Machiavelli, *The Prince*, Chapter V.)

> Hence it is to be remarked that, in seizing a state, the usurper ought to examine closely into all those injuries which it is necessary for him to inflict, and to do them all at one stroke so as not to have to repeat them daily; and thus by not unsettling men he will be able to reassure them, and win them to himself by benefits. He who does otherwise, either from timidity or evil advice, is always compelled to keep the knife in his hand; neither can he rely on his subjects, nor can they attach themselves to him, owing to their continued and repeated

wrongs. For injuries ought to be done all at one time, so that, being tasted less, they offend less; benefits ought to be given little by little, so that the flavour of them may last longer.

And above all things, a prince ought to live amongst his people in such a way that no unexpected circumstances, whether of good or evil, shall make him change; because if the necessity for this comes in troubled times, you are too late for harsh measures; and mild ones will not help you, for they will be considered as forced from you, and no one will be under any obligation to you for them. (Niccolo Machiavelli, *The Prince*, Chapter VIII.)

Machiavelli's writing was very influential. Saint Thomas More's successor as Chancellor of the Realm, Thomas Cromwell, kept a copy of *The Prince* by his bedside so that he could better advance the schemes of the king he served, Henry VIII. As influential as Machiavelli was in his time, however, his amorality could not have been as triumphant as it was had it not been for the Protestant Revolution that made it possible for civil potentates to rule without regard to any "interference" from any local bishop or the Vicar of Christ and with even less regard for the salvation of their immortal souls or the actual good of their commonwealths. And it is that Protestant Revolution that paved the way for the triumph once again of monarchical despotism and the despotism of modern political parties and the mobs who support them in the so called "democratic republics" of Modernity.

Chapter XI
Revolting Against God Himself and Thus Against All Social Order

Human beings, suffering from the vestigial after-effects of Original Sin and the ravages of their own Actual Sins, have the propensity to rebel against their First Cause and Last End, God.

We are made by God to know, to love and to serve Him in this life so as to be happy with Him for all eternity in Heaven. Anything and everything that impedes our path to Heaven is of the devil and must be discarded from our lives. Our Blessed Lord and Saviour Jesus Christ taught us this when He said the following:

> [8] And if thy hand, or thy foot scandalize thee, cut it off, and cast it from thee. It is better for thee to go into life maimed or lame, than having two hands or two feet, to be cast into everlasting fire. [9] And if thy eye scandalize thee, pluck it out, and cast it from thee. It is better for thee having one eye to enter into life, than having two eyes to be cast into hell fire. [10] See that you despise not one of these little ones: for I say to you, that their angels in heaven always see the face of my Father who is in heaven. (Matthew 18: 1-10.)

The devil hates us because our immortal souls, the very animating principle of our bodies, are made in the image and the likeness of the Most Blessed Trinity. Having failed in his war to overthrow God, the devil prowls about the world looking for souls to devour because he hates God and thus wants to lead us, God's rational creatures, away from our Final End, the glory of the Beatific Vision in Heaven, to be in the misery and torments of Hell for all eternity where the damned souls are deprived of the vision of God and the companionship of the Blessed Mother, Saint Joseph and all of the angels and saints, including each of our family members who died in a state of Sanctifying Grace as members of His true Church.

One of the many ways that the devil uses to lead souls astray is the bad example given by those who are known to practice the true Faith, the Catholic Faith. People who are known to be daily communicants and for spending time in prayer before Our Lord's Real Presence in the Most Blessed Sacrament are examined by unbelievers and/or by lukewarm Catholics with great scrutiny in an effort to detect the slightest fault that could them a pretext to continue their own infidel or tepid ways, if not to mock the Faith in Its entirety. Those who hold ecclesiastical offices are examined with even greater scrutiny as they are called to make greater efforts to demonstrate an inward and outward integrity of life. There are few things the devil loves more than causing a pope or a cardinal or a bishop or a priest or a consecrated religious to cause public scandal or to be so obstreperous in his dealings with others that even a single soul is given a pretext to falsely ascribe such scandal to the Faith rather than to the frailties of fallen human nature.

Each of us is, of course, to avoid giving scandal to others as we are to avoid even the near occasion of sins. It is a horrific offense to God and to souls to be the cause of scandal to others. It is also a horrific offense to be a near occasion of sin to others, no less than to lead others into even one sin as one fall could lead to a persistence in sin over the course of a lifetime or to the constant struggling against that sin as a person stays in the Purgative Stage of the interior life until death. This is why Our Lord, as recorded in the two verses of Chapter Eighteen of the Gospel according to Saint Matthew that precede the ones quoted just above, admonishes us to avoid giving even the

183

slightest bit of scandal:

> [6] But he that shall scandalize one of these little ones that believe in me, it were better for
> him that a millstone should be hanged about his neck, and that he should be drowned in the
> depth of the sea. [7] Woe to the world because of scandals. For it must needs be that scandals
> come: but nevertheless woe to that man by whom the scandal cometh. (Matthew 18: 6-7.)

Scandals will indeed come. We, however, must avoid giving them.

All of this having been noted, however, we are also to recognize that none of us is without sin. It is one thing to be sorry and to seek out the mercy of the Divine Redeemer in the Sacred Tribunal of Penance. It is quite another to persist in sin unrepentantly and/or to seek justify one's sins before men, no less to promote sinful behavior as a "civil right" under cover of the law and as part of what passes for popular culture. Each of us is a sinner in need of being absolved of our sins by a true priest in the confessional. We should understand at all times, therefore, that the weaknesses and scandals of others give us no reason to defect from the Faith, which has been revealed by God, Who canst neither deceive or be deceived. It is never licit to project unto the Faith and Holy Mother Church the faults of her children. This is infantile as children are always looking for excuses to use the faults of their parents as justification for refusing to obey their just commands.

The scandalous, extravagant and even immoral lives led by many ecclesiastics in the Fifteenth Century, although certainly serious and in need of public correction and condemnation, provided no legitimate pretext to Father Martin Luther of the Order of Saint Augustine or to anyone else to blame the Faith for such bad example. Those who sin scandalously are answerable to God as their souls are examined with exacting scrutiny at the moment of the Particular Judgment. Such people must be the object of prayers and sacrifices offered to the Most Sacred Heart of Jesus through the Sorrowful and Immaculate Heart of Mary while they are called to correction according to these words of Saint Thomas Aquinas:

> "It must be observed, however, that if the faith were endangered, a subject ought to rebuke
> his prelate even publicly.

> "Article 2: Fraternal correction is a matter of obligation (precept) out of charity for the
> sinner. And if the order of fraternal correction has been observed (beginning with private
> admonitions until there is no other recourse for the sake of the faith than to publicly
> proclaim the prelate), to do so for the sake of the faith can be meritorious."

The ecclesiastical scandals caused by some of the some Renaissance popes and cardinals and bishops and priests, which involved the selling of indulgences to pay for the construction of various buildings, including the rebuilding of the Basilica of Saint Peter in Rome, were used by a very tortured, twisted Augustinian monk, Father Martin Luther, steeped in sins of lust and intemperance, to start a revolution against God Himself that is the proximate cause of all of the social problems of Modernity just as Adam's Fall is the remote cause of all personal and social problems.

The entire Protestant Revolution against the Divine Plan that Our Blessed Lord and Saviour Jesus Christ Himself personally instituted to effect man's return to Him through His Catholic Church was born as a result of the unwillingness of Martin Luther to refrain from breaking the Sixth and Ninth Commandments and wound up propagating one lie after another as being compatible with the Gospel of Our Lord Jesus Christ. Luther invented an entire system of theological relativism to reaffirm himself in his sins by claiming that all a "believer" had to do was to "say" that he was "sorry" for his sins and he would know "forgiveness" from God without any priestly intermediary. This system   of theological relativism has wreaked havoc in the world in the past nearly five hundred years.

Monsignor Patrick F. O'Hare, writing in *The Facts About Luther*, provided a good thumbnail description of the twists and turns that existed in the tortured mind of the German priest responsible for paving the way for the social revolutions of Modernity and of the doctrinal and liturgical revolutions of conciliarism:

> "Anointed," as Luther was, "to preach the Gospel of peace," and commissioned to communicate to all the knowledge which uplifts, sanctifies and saves, it is certainly pertinent to ask what was his attitude towards the ministry of the divine word, and in what manner did he show by speech and behavior the heavenly sanctions of law: divine, international and social?

> As we draw near this man and carefully examine his career, we find that in an evil moment he abandoned the spirit of discipline, became a pursuer of novelty, and put on the ways and manners of the "wolf in sheep's clothing" whose teeth and claws rent asunder the seamless garment of divine knowledge which should have been kept whole for the instruction and the comfort of all who were to seek the law at his lips. His words lost their savor and influence for good, and only foulness and mocking blasphemy filled his mouth, to deceive the ignorant and lead them into error, license and rebellion against both Church and state. Out of the abundance of a corrupt heart this fallen priest, who had departed from the divine source of that knowledge, which is unto peace, shamelessly advanced theories and principles which cut at the root of all   order, authority and obedience, and inaugurated an antagonism and a disregard for the sanctity of law such as the world had not seen since pagan times. His Gospel was not that of the Apostles, who issued from the upper room of Jerusalem in the power of those "parted tongues, as it were of fire." His doctrine, stripped of its cunning and deceit, was nothing else, to use the words of St. James describing false teaching, but "earthly, sensual, devilish"; so much so, that men of good sense could no longer safely "seek the law at his mouth" and honestly recognize him as "the angel of the Lord of Hosts" sent with instructions for the good of the flock and the peace of the nations. Opposed to all law, order and restraint, he could not but disgrace his ministry, proclaim his own shame, and prove to every wise and discerning follower of the true Gospel of peace, the groundlessness of his boastful claims to be in any proper sense a benefactor of society, an upholder of constituted authority and a promoter of the best interests   of humanity.

> Luther, like many another framer of religious and political heresy, may have begun his course blindly and with little serious reflection. He may never have stopped to estimate the lamentable and disastrous results to which his heretofore unheard-of-propaganda would inevitably lead. He may not have directly intended the ruin, desolation and misery

which his seditious preaching effected in all directions. "But," as Verres aptly says, "if a man standing on one of the snowcapped giants of the Alps were to roll down a little stone, knowing what consequences would follow, he would be answerable for the desolation caused by the avalanche in the valley below. **Luther put into motion not one little stone, but rock after rock, and he must have been shortsighted indeed--or his blind hatred made him so--if he was unable to estimate beforehand what effect his inflammatory appeals to the masses of the people and his wild denunciations of law and order would have."** He should, as a matter of course, have weighed well and thoroughly the merits or demerits of his "new gospel" before he announced it to an undiscriminating public, and wittingly or unwittingly unbarred the floodgates of confusion and unrest. Deliberation, however, was a process little known to this man of many moods and violent temper. To secure victory in his quarrel with the Church absorbed his attention to the exclusion of all else, and, although he may not have reflected in time on the effects of his revolutionary teachings, he is nonetheless largely responsible for the religious, political and social upheaval of his day which his wild and passionate harangues fomented and precipitated. Nothing short of a miracle could have prevented his reckless, persistent and unsparing denunciations of authority and its representatives from undermining the supports by which order and discipline in Church and state were upheld. As events proved, his wild words, flung about in reckless profusion, fell into souls full of the fermenting passions of time and turned Germany into a land of misery, darkness and disorder. (Monsignor Patrick F. O'Hare. *The Facts About Luther*, published originally in Cincinnati, Ohio, by Frederick Pustet Company in 1916, reprinted in 1987 by TAN Books and Publishers, pp. 215-217.)

Luther's revolution began when he posted ninety-five theses on the door of Castle Church in Wittenberg, Germany on October 31, 1517. He excited the passions of people and incited the ambitions of the German princes who gave him protection so that they could be freed once and for all from "Roman interference" in their affairs of state. The effects of Luther's revolution, condemned by Pope Leo X in the Papal Bull *Exsurge Domine*, June 15, 1520, were widespread and they were disastrous.

Fathers Denis Fahey and Edward Cahill provided descriptions of the nature of Protestantism and a description of the chaos let loose by Luther's revolution against the Divine Plan that Our Lord Himself instituted to effect man's return to Him through the Catholic Church and thus to order his affairs in this life according to binding precepts contained in the Sacred Deposit of Faith that He had entrusted exclusively to that true Church for Its infallible explication and eternal safekeeping:

The organization of the Europe of the thirteenth century furnishes us with one concrete realization of the Divine Plan. It is hardly necessary to add that there were then to be seen defects in the working of the Divine Plan., due to the character of fallen man, as well as to an imperfect mastery of physical nature. Yet, withal, the formal principle of ordered social organization in the world, the supremacy of the Mystical Body, was grasped and, in the main, accepted. **The Lutheran revolt, prepared by the cult of pagan antiquity at the Renaissance, and by the favour enjoyed by the Nominalist philosophical theories, led to the rupture of that order.**

"The great cardinal principle of Protestantism is that every man attains salvation by entering into an immediate relation with Christ, with the aid of that interior faith by which he believes that, though his sins persist, they are no longer imputed to him, thanks to the merits of our Lord Jesus Christ. All men are thus priests for themselves and carry out the work of their justification by treating directly and individually with God. The Life of Grace, being nothing else than the external favour of God, remains outside of us and we continue, in fact, in spite of Lutheran faith in Christ, corrupt and sinful. Each human being enters into an isolated relation with our Lord, and there is no transforming life all are called to share. Luther never understood the meaning of faith informed by sanctifying grace and charity. Accordingly, the one visible Church and the Mystical Body is done away with, as well as the priesthood and the sacrifice of the Mystical Body, the Holy Sacrifice of the Mass. The only purpose of preaching and such ceremonies were retained by Protestants was to stir up the individual's faith."

Hence the True Church of Christ, according to the Protestant view, is noting else than the assembly of those who, on account of the confidence interiorly conceived of the remission of their sins, have the justice of God imputed to them by God and are accordingly predestined to eternal life. And this Church, known to God alone, is the unique Church of the promises of indefectibility, to which our Lord Jesus Christ promised His assistance to the consummation of the world. Since, however, true believers, instructed by the Holy Ghost, can manifest their faith exteriorly, can communicate their impressions and feelings to other and may employ the symbols of the Sacraments to stir up their faith, they give rise to a visible church which, nevertheless, is not the Church instituted by Christ. Membership of this Church is not necessary for salvation, and it may assume different forms according to different circumstances. The true invisible Church of Christ is always hidden, unseen in the multitude.

"Protestantism, therefore, substituted for the corporate organization of society, imbued with the spirit of the Mystical Body and reconciling the claims of personality and individuality in man, a merely isolated relation with our Divine Lord. This revolt of human individual against order on the supernatural level, this uprise of individualism, with its inevitable chaotic self-seeking, had dire consequences both in regard to ecclesiastical organization and in the realms of politics and economics. Let us take these in turn."

The tide of revolt which broke away from the Catholic Church had the immediate effect of increasing the power of princes and rulers in Protestant countries. The Anabaptists and the peasants in Germany protested in the name of 'evangelical liberty,' but they were crushed. We behold the uprise of national churches, each of which organizes its own particular form of religion, mixture of supernatural and natural elements, as a department of State. The orthodox Church in Russia was also a department of State and as such exposed to the same evils. National life was thus withdrawn from ordered subjection to the Divine Plan and the distinction laid down by our Divine Lord Himself, between the things that are God's and the things that are Caesar's, utterly abolished. Given the principle of private judgment or of individual relation with Christ, it was inevitable that the right of every individual to arrange his own form of religion should cause the pendulum to swing from a Caesarinism supreme in Church and State to other concrete expressions of 'evangelical liberty.' One current leads to the direction of indefinite multiplication of sects. Pushed to its ultimate conclusion, this would give rise to as many churches as there are individuals, that is, there would not be any church at all. As this is too opposed to man's social nature, small groups tend to coalesce. The second current tends to the creation of what may be termed broad or multitudinist churches. The exigencies of the national churches are attenuated until they are no longer a burden to anybody. The Church of England is an example of this. As decay in the belief of the Divinity of Jesus continues to increase, the tendency will be to model church organization according to the political theories in favour at the moment. The democratic form of society will   be extolled and a 'Reunion of Christendom,' for example, will be aimed at, along the a lines of the League of Nations. An increasing number of poor bewildered units will, of course, cease to bother about any ecclesiastical organization at all.

The first [political] result was an enormous increase in the power of the Temporal Rulers, in fact a rebirth of the pagan regime of Imperial Rome. The Spiritual Kingship of Christ, participated in by the Pope and the Bishops of the Catholic Church being no longer acknowledged, authority over spiritual affairs passed to Temporal Rulers. They were thus, in Protestant countries, supposed to share not only in His Temporal Kingship of Christ the King, but also in His spiritual Kingship. As there was no Infallible Guardian of order above the Temporal Rulers, the way was paved for the abuses of State Absolutism. The Protestant oligarchy who ruled England with undisputed sway, from Charles the Second's time on, and who treated Ireland to the Penal Laws, may be cited, along with that cynical scoundrel, Frederick of Prussia, as typical examples of such rulers. Catholic monarchs, like Louis XIV of France and Joseph II of Austria, by their absolutist tendencies and pretensions to govern the Catholic Church show the influence of the neighboring Protestant countries. Gallicanism and Josephism are merely a revival of Roman paganism.

A few words about the erroneous doctrine of the Divine Right of Kings, so strongly held by the two Protestant Stuart Kings of England, James I and Charles I, and which the legists had taught long before the seventeenth century, may not be here out of place. This idea is, at has been said, an error and not Catholic doctrine. Political Power, as an imperfect and created participation, in the Temporal Ruler, of the Infinite Power, by which God directs all things towards their supreme destinies, is this sense divine. This is the meaning of St. Paul's teaching: "Let every soul be subject to higher powers: for there is no power but from God: and those that are, are ordained of God. Therefore he that resisteth the power, resisteth the ordinance of God. And they that resist, purchase to themselves damnation" (Romans xiii. 1, 2). Of course, the mode of accession to power may be legitimate or the reverse; in the former case, it is in accordance with the Divine Law, in the latter, opposed to it. Again, the use of power may be in conformity with the Divine Law or opposed to it. Political Power then, comes from God, but it is false that any particular form of power is necessary and willed of God to the exclusion of others. The error, which has been held by the French Sillon in recent times on behalf of Democracy, as by the Stuart Kings above alluded to on behalf of Monarchy, aims at confiscating the prerogatives, conferred by God on political power in general, to the profit of one form of government in particular. At the bottom of it, is the tendency to put political power, the particular form of which has been abandoned to men, on the same level as the religious power of the Catholic Church, of which the monarchical form has been determined by our Lord Jesus Christ.

The first political consequence of the Protestant rebellion against order was, accordingly, the extreme error of State Absolutism. The principle of private judgment prepared the way for the opposite error of "holy rebellion" and the "right" of the people to overthrow authority whenever it displeases them. The doctrine, that all men are equal in the Mystical Body and are their own priests, sowed the seeds of that spirit, which was given a body in the naturalistic Masonic society, when the advance of time had brought about the decay of belief in the supernatural life.

Economic Consequences of Protestant Revolt–When men lived the life of the Mystical Body, looking upon themselves as Christ's members, they evolved economic organizations in accordance with their inner convictions. The guilds of the Middle Ages were the economic expression of accepted solidarity in Christ. They are not to be looked upon as primarily economic organizations to which religious practices were superadded. No, by them men gave expression in their arrangements for the production and distribution of the Divine Plan for ordered life. The rending of the Mystical Body by the so-called Reformation movement has resulted in the pendulum swinging from the extreme error of Judaeo-Protestant Capitalism to the opposite error of the Judaeo-Masonic Communism of Karl Marx.

The uprise of individualism rapidly led to unbridled self-seeking. Law-makers who were arbiters of morality, as heads of the Churches, did not hesitate to favour their own enterprising spirit. The nobles and rich merchants in England, for example, who got possession of the monastery lands, which had maintained the poor, voted for the poor laws in order to make the poor a charge on the nation at large. The enclosure of common lands in England and the development of the industrial system are a proof of what private judgment can do when transplanted into the realm of production and distribution. The Lutheran separation of Church from the Ruler and the Citizen shows the decay in the true idea of membership of our Lord's Mystical Body.

> "Assuredly," said Luther, "a prince can be a Christian, but it is not as a Christian that he ought to govern. As a ruler, he is not called a Christian, but a prince. The man is Christian, but his function does not concern his religion." (Father Denis Fahey, The Mystical Body of Christ in the Modern World, pp. 10-15.)

The false doctrine of the separation of Church and State is at the heart of the interrelated errors of Modernity and of Modernism in the counterfeit church of conciliarism, as was noted in the first chapter of this book:

> **The rejection by Luther of the visible Catholic Church opened the door, not only to the abuses of absolute rulers, supreme in Church and State, but soon led to an indifference to all ecclesiastical organizations. As faith in the supernatural life of grace and the supernatural order grew dim and waned, the way was made smooth for the acceptance of Freemasonry**. The widespread loss of faith in the existence of the supernatural life and the growing ignorance of the meaning of the Redemption permitted the apostles of Illuminism and Masonry to propagate the idea that the true religion of Jesus Christ had never been understood or been corrupted by His disciples, especially by the Church of Rome, the fact being that only a few sages in secret societies down the centuries

had kept alive the true teaching of Jesus Christ. According to this 'authentic' teaching our Saviour had not established a new religion, but had simply restored the religion of the state of nature, the religion of the goodness of human nature when left to itself, freed from the bonds and shackles of society. Jesus Christ died a martyr for liberty, put to death by the rulers and priests. Masons and revolutionary secret societies alone are working for the true salvation of the world. By them shall original sin be done away with and the Garden of Eden restored. But the present organization of society must disappear, by the elimination of the tyranny of priests, the despotism of princes and the slavery resulting from national distinctions, from family life and from private property. (Father Denis Fahey, *The Mystical Body of Christ in the Modern World*, pp. 10-14.)

Father Edward Cahill, S.J., writing in *The Framework of a Christian State*, wrote the following about Luther and his revolution against the Church that Our Blessed Lord and Saviour Jesus Christ founded upon the Rock of Peter, the Pope:

The assertion that Protestantism has introduced into Europe, or promoted, democratic freedom or real liberty of conscience is still more patently untrue. It is a fact, indeed, that at the beginning of the revolt Luther's professions were radically democratic. He promised to benefit the people at large by curtailing the power of both Church and State. But he and his followers ended up by supporting an irresponsible despotism such as Europe had not known since the days of the pagan Emperors of Rome.

Inspired by Luther's democratic professions and his denunciations of the "tyranny and oppression" of the rulers, the knights and the lesser nobility of many of the German States, and later on, the peasants rose in open revolt against the princes. When the revolution was crushed in blood (1525) the victorious princes, now without a rival and no longer kept in check by the moderating influence of the Catholic Church, used their augmented power to establish a despotism which they exceeded for their own personal advantage, in opposition to the interests of the people; while Luther, with unscrupulous inconsistency, now proclaimed the doctrine of the unlimited power of rulers.

Soon even the Church in the Protestant States fell completely under the control of the ruling princes, who were thus established as the absolute masters of both Church and State. The wealth of the Church, which hitherto had been the patrimony of the poor; its authority; all the ecclesiastical institutions, including hospitals, schools, homes of refuge, etc., passed into the hands of the kings, princes, and the town magistrates. At the Peace of Augsburg (1555), which ended the first phase of the revolution in Germany, the principle was formally adopted that the prince of each state was free to dictate the religion of each and all of his subjects." (Father Edward Cahill, S.J., *The Framework of a Christian State*, published in 1932 in Ireland and republished by Roman Catholic Books, pp. 93-94.)

Three principal strands of Protestantism emerged between 1517 and 1536. Those forms are what we call today Lutheranism, Calvinism and Anglicanism, although the latter emerged before Calvinism but did not represent at first a coherent set of beliefs as it was an attempt on the part of the murderous Henry Tutor, as he understood things, simply to establish an "English Catholic Church" that was not under the control of the pope. It is from the Lutheran and Calvinist strains of

Protestantism that each of the subsequent thousands upon thousands of Protestants sects evolved with this or that variation or set of variations, and it is from these two strains that Anglicanism devolved from maintaining what appeared to be a semblance of Catholic tradition to what it is today, a withering assembly of rationalists, many of whom do not even believe in the Sacred Divinity of Our Blessed Lord and Saviour Jesus Christ.

Here is a brief review of the Lutheran strain of Protestantism, which influences the entire ethos of the modern world in a never-ending variety of ways:

First, Luther believed that man was totally corrupted by Original Sin. In other words, man is evil. This is contrary to Catholic teaching as man is flawed by Original Sin and thus inclined to evil by its vestigial after-effects in the soul (the darkened intellect, the weakened will, the overthrow of the balance between man's higher rational faculties with his power sensual passions in favor of the latter), not evil. God is not the author of evil, which is, of course, the privation of Him. Luther believed that man is but a "dung heap" covered by a few snowflakes of grace.

Luther based this belief upon his own refusal to reform his life in cooperation with Sanctifying Grace, projecting upon the Faith Itself his own unwillingness to quit his sins as he came up with the ultimate rationalization: it is unnecessary to attempt to reform one's life of sin at it is not necessary to do so. God, Luther believed, forgives us immediately as long we have established a "personal relationship" with Him by means of professing Our Lord Jesus Christ as his "personal saviour" on their lips and in their hearts.

Martin Luther's own lecherous life, which he refused to reform in cooperation with the Sanctifying Graces sent to him, prompted him to devise an entire theology based on the erroneous proposition that the human being has been totally corrupted by Original Sin. The human being, according to Luther, is nothing more than a "dung heap covered by a few snowflakes of grace." This means that we will sin no matter our best efforts to resist temptations. The best that we can do is to make a "profession of faith" in our hearts and our lips in the "Name of the Lord Jesus" are we are, more or less, assured of our salvation. There is almost no sin that one can commit that "revokes" this "profession of faith," which makes one "justified" in the sight of God and is the path to salvation.

Luther himself put the matter this way:

> Be a sinner and sin boldly, but believe and rejoice in Christ even more boldly.... as long as we are here [in this world] we have to sin.... No sin will separate us from the Lamb, even though we commit fornication and murder a thousand times a day." (Let Your Sins Be Strong: A Letter from Martin Luther to Philip Melancthon. number 99, August 1, 1521)

Such a heretical view of sin and its effects on the soul--and on the entire Church Militant here on the face of this earth--is nothing other than an open invitation to sin, heedless of the ways in which each Actual Sin, whether Mortal or Venial, darkens the intellect, weakens the will and disorders our already disorderly passions more and more. Such a heretical view of sin and its effects on the soul--and on the entire Church Militant here on the face of this earth--denies the simple truth that Mortal Sin does indeed deprive one of the state of Justification, that is, of Sanctifying Grace, making one a mortal enemy of God until he has been reconciled to Him in the Sacred Tribunal of Penance, which was instituted by Our Lord Himself when He spoke these words to the Apostles on Easter Sunday after His Resurrection from the dead:

> He said therefore to them again: Peace be to you. As the Father hath sent me, I also send you. When he had said this, he breathed on them; and he said to them: Receive ye the Holy Ghost. Whose sins you shall forgive, they are forgiven them: and whose sins you shall retain, they are retained. (John 20: 21-23.)

Second, Luther rejected the fact that Our Lord created a visible, hierarchical Church to sanctify or to govern men, either individually or socially. The denial of the visible, hierarchical church meant that individuals no longer had the sure guidance of the Catholic Church as to how to live their lives and that civil rulers no longer had to answer to a pope or a local bishop if they did things contrary to the good of souls. This opened up the way to unbridled monarchical despotism in European kingdoms and principalities where potentates sided with Luther, giving rise to our own modern totalitarianism. Individual licentiousness and civil despotism are the logical results of a world where the Catholic Church is no longer recognized and obeyed as the true, infallible teacher and sole sanctifier of man.

Third, Luther believed that the Bible was the sole source of Divine Revelation, rejecting the 1,500 years of belief in Apostolic or Sacred Tradition as the other source of Divine Revelation.

Fourth, Luther believed that each individual was his own "interpreter" of the Bible. He thus planted the seeds of contemporary deconstructionism, which reduces all written documents to the illogical and frequently mutually contradictory private judgments of individual readers, by rejecting the Catholic Church as the repository and explicator of the Deposit of Faith, making the "private judgment" of individuals with regard to the Bible supreme. If mutually contradictory and inconsistent interpretations of the Bible can stand without correction from a supreme authority instituted by God, then it is an easy thing for all written documents, including a Constitution that makes no reference at all to the God-Man or His Holy Church, to become the plaything of whoever happens to have power over its interpretation.

Fifth, Luther taught that each believer was part of the "universal priesthood" and thus the minister was merely a "presider" at the "Mass" or "Lord's Supper" where the substance, not the accidents, of the bread and wine coexist with the Body, Blood, Soul and Divinity of Our Lord. This is called "consubstantiation." The Catholic Church teaches solemnly that the accidents of the bread and wine remain after the consecration at Holy Mass but that every particle of their substance become the Body, Blood, Soul and Divinity of the Divine Redeemer Himself.

Sixth, there is salvation by "faith alone" and it is not necessary to perform good works in demonstration of that faith because everyone "sins" whenever he performs any kind of work. The "profession of faith" alone is sufficient to forgive sins and thus to release from all penalties incurred by their commission.

Such a conglomeration of falsehoods led to consequences, some of which will be summarized below, from which the world is suffering to this very day.

Luther's falsehoods played a very large role in shaping the theological views of Thomas Cranmer, who became the Archbishop of Canterbury in 1532, in the years leading up to King Henry VIII's break with Rome in 1534. Cranmer would be influenced by Lutheran ideas, which he was able use to influence the mind of the young Edward VI, using him as the means to introduce false liturgical rites and a heretical "Book of Common Prayer" that has been accepted by Joseph Ratzinger/Benedict as valid for use by Anglican "converts" to the conciliar church even though Pope Saint Pius V had declared them heretical in the Papal Bull excommunicating Queen Elizabeth I, *Regens in Excelsis*, March 5, 1570.

Following closely upon the events of Luther's revolution and that begun by Henry VIII in 1534 that will be discussed shortly was the heretical work of John Calvin, whose "theology," such as it is, has played a definitive role in shaping the nature of contemporary economics and politics in the modern world, especially in the United States of America. It is impossible to understand the ethos of the heresy of Americanism without understanding Calvinism, which is really a strange mixture of a heretical view of Christianity and Talmudism, and its false precepts.

1) Along with Martin Luther, John Calvin rejected the truth that Our Blessed Lord and Saviour Jesus Christ founded a visible, hierarchical Church upon the Rock of Peter, the Pope.

2) The absence of a visible, hierarchical Church meant that each individual believer was "equal" to other believers. Those who "presided" at liturgies were merely the representatives of the rest of the "community," in whose name and by whose selection they served in their "leading" capacities.

3) Calvin's warfare against a belief in the visible, hierarchical Church and his belief in the strict equality of all believers resulted in a vicious spirit of anticlericalism that unleashed a violent wave of assaults against Catholic priests in Switzerland and The Netherlands and France (See the appendices about the life and the martyrdom of Saint Fidelis of Sigmaringen and the Martyrs of Gorkum, victims each of the bloody band of men known as Calvinists, men who are actually disciples of the devil). The Calvinist spirit of anticlericalism is widespread in the world today, reflected most especially in the text of the Texas Declaration of Independence, March 1, 1836:

> When the Federal Republican Constitution of their country [Mexico], which they have sworn to support, no longer has a substantial existence, and the whole nature of their government has been forcibly changed, without their consent, from a restricted federative republic, composed of sovereign states, to a consolidated central military despotism, in which every interest is disregarded but that of the army and the priesthood, both the eternal enemies of civil liberty, the ever-ready minions of power, and the usual instruments of tyrants. (Texas Declaration of Independence, March 2, 1836.)

4) As was the case with Luther, John Calvin believed that man is evil. That is, Calvin believed that man is totally corrupted by Original Sin. The Catholic Church teaches us that man is wounded by Original Sin, not totally corrupted. Those who are regenerated in the

Baptismal font by having Original Sin flooded out of their souls and the very inner life of the Most Blessed Trinity flooded into their souls by means of Sanctifying Grace suffer from the vestigial after-effects of Original Sin, the darkened intellect and the weakened will and the overthrowing of the delicate balance between our higher, rational faculties and our lower, sensual passions in favor of the lower passions. Those so regenerated are not totally corrupted by Original Sin. Man is a good being who has a flawed nature that is inclined to commit evil. This is quite an important distinction that was rejected by John Calvin.

5) John Calvin believed that men were predestined by an arbitrary "God" to Heaven or Hell. Nothing that any man did on the face of this earth could change the face of his predestination to Heaven or Hell. In other words, the human being did not have a free will by which to choose to cooperate with the graces won for him on Calvary by the shedding of every single drop of Our Blessed Lord and Saviour Jesus Christ's Most Precious Blood that flow into our hearts and soul through the loving hands of Our Lady, she who is the Mediatrix of All Graces.

6) John Calvin believed that the purpose of civil government was to separate the "saved" from the "damned." That is, the civil government had the obligation to weed out the "undesirables," those who the arbitrary God had destined for Hell from all eternity. Obviously, the Catholic Church teaches us that God alone is the final judge of the subjective state of souls and that, barring private revelations given to genuine mystics or a declaration by the authority of the Catholic Church as she declares solemnly and infallible that a certain person is in Heaven, we do not know what happens to a given soul at the time of death. We do not know whether a particular person who was known as a notorious sinner or as an arch-heretic was given the grace to make a perfect Act of Contrition.

7) The basis upon which John Calvin believed that those in the civil government could separate the "saved" from the "damned" was the degree of their material success here on earth. John Calvin believed that material success was a sign of "divine election." Thus it is that we have the Calvinist "work ethic" as those who subscribe to Calvin's warped, heretical views of God and man work hard not to give honor and glory to the Most Holy Trinity through the Immaculate Heart of Mary but to show to others that they are "saved" by virtue of their material "success" in this passing, mortal vale of tears.

It is this seventh point, prescinding from all of the rest, that has provided the foundation for the modern economic system that has forced man off of the land and dehumanized him as he has been made a slave of "material success" by the captains of industry and banking. Calvinism, which is little more than Talmudic Judaism with a slight Christian gloss, has engendered all manner of economic abuses, not the least of which is the contemporary practice of usury, discussed earlier in this book, founded in the belief that men may ignore the binding precepts of the Divine Positive Law and the Natural Law in order to be "successful" in this world.

The injustices engendered by this amoral, naturalistic view of the world helped to encourage open atheists and anti-Theists, such as Karl Marx and Vladimir Lenin, to postulate an utopian system of naturalism based upon a materialistic view of man that denied his supernatural essence. The diabolical lie of Marxism-Leninism is but the logical consequence of John Calvin's materialistic view of man that denied that there could be an Omnipotent and Omniscient God Who created rational beings with free wills to choose for or against Him as He has revealed Himself to us through His true Church.

Father Fahey elaborated on the effects of Protestantism, especially the warmed over version of Talmudic Judaism that is Calvinism, in *The Mystical Body of Christ in the Modern World*:

> It was, however, the Calvinistic doctrine on predestination and the signs by which a man's divine election could be recognized, which specially favored the advent of the unlimited competition, unscrupulous underselling and feverish advertising of the present day. In his able work, from which a passage has already been quoted, Professor O'Brien shows that it was in the peculiarly British variety of Calvinism, known as Puritanism, that all the Calvinist doctrines of succession life as a sign of man's predestination, of the respect and veneration due to wealth, had their fullest development.
>
> > "When all is said and done, Calvinism remains the real nursing-father of the civic industrial capitalism of the middle classes. . . . Since the aggressively active ethic inspired by the doctrine of predestination urges the elect to the full development of his God-given powers, and offers him this sign by which he may assure himself of his election, work becomes rational and systematic. In breaking down the motive of ease and enjoyment, asceticism lays the foundation of the tyranny of work over men . . . production for production's sake is declared to be a commandment of religion." (Father Denis Fahey, *The Mystical Body of Christ in the Modern World*.)

This has great application in every aspect of contemporary life. Most people work not for the honor and glory of God, thus giving him the fruit of their labors as the consecrated slaves of His Most Blessed Mother's Sorrowful and Immaculate Heart, but for the sake of "success," to gain what is considered to be financial "wealth" and earthly "success" as ends that justify each and every method used to achieve such success. This has been the Calvinist "contribution" to the world, so enshrined in   the ethos of the "American dream," which eschews the Holy Poverty of the Holy Family of Nazareth   and of such great saints as Saint Francis of Assisi and his helper and fellow adorer of the Most Blessed Sacrament, Saint Clare of Assisi. Father Fahey quoted Gilbert Keith Chesterton's observation about the insidious influence of that wretched people known as the Puritans (or Pilgrims) in a footnote on page sixteen of *The Mystical Body of Christ in the Modern World*:

> "The Americans have established a Thanksgiving Day to celebrate the fact that the Pilgrim Fathers reached America. The English might very well establish another Thanksgiving Day to celebrate the happy fact that the Pilgrim Fathers left England."

The Protestants, however, were not alone in helping to usher in the world of amorality in commerce and politics and statecraft and popular culture, including what has become known as competitive sports. Father Fahey explained the "Talmudic connection," if you will, from which the Calvinist world-view is derived:

The learned writer, Werner Sombart, in his great work, Die Juden and das Wirtschafsleben

("The Jews in Economic Life"), attributes the great, if not the deciding, role in the formation of the modern economic outlook or mentality to the Jewish race, for to them he attributes the introduction of the ideas of "free commerce" and "unchecked competition" into a society with quite different ideas. He points out the contrast between this Jewish mentality and the ordered outlook of the Middle Ages in phrases that are worthy of citation:--

> "When we examine matters more closely . . . we shall immediately see that the struggle between Jewish and Christian merchants is a struggle between two views of the world, or, at least, between two economic mentalities imbued with principles that are different or even opposed. In order to understand this statement we must represent to ourselves the spirit which inspired that economic life into which, since the sixteenth century, Jewish elements have forced their way in ever increasing volume. To this spirit they openly showed themselves so rudely opposed that they were everywhere felt to be interfering with the livelihood and subsistence of the people. During the whole time which I have designated as the period of incipient capitalism . . . the same fundamental outlook on economic relations prevailed as had been accepted during the Middle Ages. . . The unrestrained, unbridled striving after gain was considered by most people during this whole period as unlawful, as unchristian, because the spirit of the old Thomistic economic philosophy as yet swayed men's minds, at least officially." The Jewish mentality was opposed to the outlook on life impressed on society by the Catholic Church, for (:)

> "the Jew stands out as the business man pure and simple, as the man who, in business, takes account only of business, and who in conformity with the spirit of true capitalist economy, proclaims, in the presence of all natural ends, the supremacy of gain and profit." (Father Denis Fahey, *The Mystical Body of Christ in the Modern World.*)

Has not the "supremacy of gain and profit" come to define almost every aspect of contemporary life, taking into account not at all the eternal good of our immortal souls? This "supremacy of gain and profit" results in the corruption of daily living, contributing to the naturalistic belief, which itself is founded in pantheism, as Father Fahey notes, that is, that man is "divine" and is above all. The achievement of our earthly goals is what defines us as human beings, and no "external" authority, such as the Catholic Church, had better get in our way of this achievement.

A final passage from Father Fahey will underscore this point:

> The Jew it was, according to Sombart, who broke down the mentality of the Middle Ages and commercialized the relations of men.

> Professor O'Brien dissents from Werner Sombart's thesis that the growth of the capitalistic spirit, the spirit of subordination of all other considerations to that of profit, was due to the Jews. He admits, however, that Sombart's contention would be quite correct, if for the "Jews" we substituted "Judaism," and he points out the importance of Calvin's justification of usury in preparing the way for modern developments. The Puritans adopted Old Testament ideas: the Old Testament idea of the reward of virtue in this world fitted in

with the Puritan teaching about the fulfillment of one's vocation.

It is unnecessary for the purpose of this work to apportion responsibility for the triumph of what we may call the does it pay? mentality in the world, between Jews and Puritans. At any rate, if the Puritans subordinated men to production, the Jews completed the process, by subordinating production itself to money. The right order, of money as a means for production and production subservient to man, is now, as we know, reversed. (Father Denis Fahey, *The Mystical Body of Christ in the Modern World*.)

Professor George O'Brien, cited in Father Fahey's The Mystical Body of Christ in the Modern World, summarized his judgment about the effects of Protestantism upon the contemporary world in *An Essay on the Economic Effects of the Reformation* (IHS Press, Norfolk, Virginia, 2003):

The thesis we have endeavoured to present in this essay is, that the two great dominating schools of modern economic thought have a common origin. The capitalist school, which, basing its position on the unfettered right of the individual to do what he will with his own, demands the restriction of government interference in economic and social affairs within the narrowest possible limits, and the socialist school, which, basing its position on the complete subordination of the individual to society, demands the socialization of all the means of production, if not all of wealth, face each other today as the only two solutions of the social question; they are bitterly hostile towards each other, and mutually intolerant and each is at the same weakened and provoked by the other. In one respect, and in one respect only, are they identical--they can both be shown to be the result of the Protestant Reformation.

We have seen the direct connection which exists between these modern schools of economic thought and their common ancestor. Capitalism found its roots in the intensely individualistic spirit of Protestantism, in the spread of anti-authoritative ideas from the realm of religion into the realm of political and social thought, and, above all, in the distinctive Calvinist doctrine of a successful and prosperous career being the outward and visible sign by which the regenerated might be known. Socialism, on the other hand, derived encouragement from the violations of established and prescriptive rights of which the Reformation afforded so many examples, from the growth of heretical sects tainted with Communism, and from the overthrow of the orthodox doctrine on original sin, which opened the way to the idea of the perfectibility of man through institutions. But, apart from these direct influences, there were others, indirect, but equally important. Both these great schools of economic thought are characterized by exaggerations and excesses; the one lays too great stress on the importance of the individual, and other on the importance of the community; they are both departures, in opposite directions, from the correct mean of reconciliation and of individual liberty with social solidarity. These excesses and exaggerations are the result of the free play of private judgment unguided by authority, and could not have occurred if Europe had continued to recognize an infallible central authority in ethical affairs.

The science of economics is the science of men's relations with one another in the domain of acquiring and disposing of wealth, and is, therefore, like political science in another sphere, a branch of the science of ethics. In the Middle Ages, man's ethical conduct, like his religious conduct, was under the supervision and guidance of a single authority, which claimed at the same time the right to define and to enforce its teaching. The machinery for enforcing the observance of medieval ethical teaching was of a singularly effective kind; pressure was brought to bear upon the conscience of the individual through the medium of compulsory periodical consultations with a trained moral adviser, who was empowered to enforce obedience to his advice by the most potent spiritual sanctions. In this way, the whole conduct of man in relation to his neighbours was placed under the immediate guidance of the universally received ethical preceptor, and a common standard of action was ensured throughout the Christian world in the all the affairs of life. All economic transactions in particular were subject to the jealous scrutiny of the individual's spiritual director; and such matters as sales, loans, and so on, were considered reprehensible and punishable if not conducted in accordance with the Christian standards of commutative justice.

The whole of this elaborate system for the preservation of justice in the affairs of everyday life was shattered by the Reformation. The right of private judgment, which had first been asserted in matters of faith, rapidly spread into moral matters, and the attack on the dogmatic infallibility of the Church left Europe without an authority to which it could appeal on moral questions. The new Protestant churches were utterly unable to supply this want. The principle of private judgment on which they rested deprived them of any right to be listened to whenever they attempted to dictate moral precepts to their members, and henceforth the moral behaviour of the individual became a matter to be regulated by the promptings of his own conscience, or by such philosophical systems of ethics as he happened to approve. The secular state endeavoured to ensure that dishonesty amounting to actual theft or fraud should be kept in check, but this was a poor and ineffective substitute for the powerful weapon of the confessional. Authority having once broken down, it was but a single step from Protestantism to rationalism; and the way was opened to the development of all sorts of erroneous systems of morality. Dr. George O'Brien, *An Essay   on the Economic Effects of the Reformation*, IHS Press, Norfolk, Virginia, 2003.)

As Father Fahey pointed out, there is no real conflict between Werner Sombart and George O'Brien. There are a multiplicity of proximate causes that have produced the world in which we live, noting, as always, that fallen human nature is the remote cause of all human problems. That having been noted, however, it is important to examine the proximate causes as they help to explain the simple fact that so many billions of people over the past five centuries have lived their entire lives without knowing the true purpose of human existence, which is to know, to love and to serve God as He has revealed Himself exclusively through the Catholic Church so that they can be happy with Him for all eternity in the glory of His Beatific Vision in Heaven. Billions upon billions of people have sought their "happiness" in the things of this passing world, living relativistic and naturalistic lives while either giving no thought to the things of Heaven or believing, falsely, that their salvation was absolutely assured, if not "proved' by their material success and worldly honors and esteem.

Father Edward Cahill, S.J., writing in The Framework of a Christian State, wrote the following about Luther and his revolution against the Church that Our Blessed Lord and Saviour Jesus Christ founded upon the Rock of Peter, the Pope:

The assertion that Protestantism has introduced into Europe, or promoted, democratic freedom or real liberty of conscience is still more patently untrue. It is a fact, indeed, that at the beginning of the revolt Luther's professions were radically democratic. He promised to benefit the people at large by curtailing the power of both Church and State. But he and his followers ended up by supporting an irresponsible despotism such as Europe had not known since the days of the pagan Emperors of Rome.

Inspired by Luther's democratic professions and his denunciations of the "tyranny and oppression" of the rulers, the knights and the lesser nobility of many of the German States, and later on, the peasants rose in open revolt against the princes. When the revolution was crushed in blood (1525) the victorious princes, now without a rival and no longer kept in check by the moderating influence of the Catholic Church, used their augmented power to establish a despotism which they exceeded for their own personal advantage, in opposition to the interests of the people; while Luther, with unscrupulous inconsistency, now proclaimed the doctrine of the unlimited power of rulers.

Soon even the Church in the Protestant States fell completely under the control of the ruling princes, who were thus established as the absolute masters of both Church and State. The wealth of the Church, which hitherto had been the patrimony of the poor; its authority; all the ecclesiastical institutions, including hospitals, schools, homes of refuge, etc., passed into the hands of the kings, princes, and the town magistrates. At the Peace of Augsburg (1555), which ended the first phase of the revolution in Germany, the principle was formally adopted that the prince of each state was free to dictate the religion of each and all of his subjects." (Father Edward Cahill, S.J., *The Framework of a Christian State*, published in 1932 in Ireland and republished by Roman Catholic books, pp. 93-94.)

Thus began the rise of the statism that is upon us at this time. There is no way to regard the growth of statism by making advertence to some kind of "generic" Christianity and/or by relying upon the Judeo-Masonic principles of naturalism and its religious indifferentism. Catholicism is but the one and only foundation of personal and social order, which is why the devil worked very hard to plant the seeds of corruption in the two centuries leading up to Martin Luther' revolution against God and His true Church. And far from being "peaceful," Luther's revolution was born in blood as Catholic churches and convents were plundered and ransacked.

The Protestant Revolution in England was caused principally by the lust of King Henry VIII, who had acceded to the English throne in 1509 at the age of eighteen following the death of his father, King Henry VII. Henry VIII became Prince of Wales when his older brother, Prince Arthur, died in 1501 at the age of fifteen. Arthur had been married for a period of twenty weeks to Princess Catherine of Aragon, the daughter of King Ferdinand and Queen Isabella of Spain. Henry VII arranged for the future Henry VIII to marry his brother's widow when he was of the age to do so. Queen Isabella herself interceded with Pope Julius II to grant a papal dispensation for her daughter to be betrothed to her deceased son-in-law's brother. Although Henry VIII may have resented his arranged marriage, which was quite common (Saint Elizabeth of Hungary accepted her arranged marriage with Louis of Thuringia as being the will of God for her and never complained), Catherine dearly loved her husband and forgave him all that she had to suffer on account of his infidelities and riotous behavior.

Queen Catherine wrote the following letter to her husband, who had entered into a bigamous and adulterous "marriage" with Anne Boleyn, with whom he had become infatuated, shortly before she died a natural death on January 7, 1536:

My most dear lord, King and husband,

The hour of my death now drawing on, the tender love I owe you forceth me, my case being such, to commend myself to you, and to put you in remembrance with a few words of the health and safeguard of your soul which you ought to prefer before all worldly matters, and before the care and pampering of your body, for the which you have cast me into many calamities and yourself into many troubles. For my part, I pardon you everything, and I wish to devoutly pray God that He will pardon you also. For the rest, I commend unto you our daughter Mary, beseeching you to be a good father unto her, as I have heretofore desired. I entreat you also, on behalf of my maids, to give them marriage portions, which is not much, they being but three. For all my other servants I solicit the wages due them, and a year more, lest they be unprovided for. Lastly, I make this vow, that mine eyes desire you above all things.

Katharine the Queen (Letter of Katharine of Aragon to her husband.)

We are *still* suffering the consequences of Henry Tudor's infidelity to his long-suffering true wife, Queen Catherine of Aragon, as the English colonies that were settled up and down the Atlantic seaboard of what is now the United States of America would have been founded by Catholics, not Protestants and out-and-out naturalists.

While there were differences and distinctive cultural "accents," if you will, between and among Catholics in Europe, it is certainly the case that the settlement of the English colonies by English Catholics who were loyal to a king who was himself loyal to Christ the King might (emphasis on might) have made a rebellion against the English Crown entirely unnecessary. National independence would have occurred gradually as Catholics in the freed colonies sought to organize their civil state on the principles of Catholic Social Teaching.

Yes, indeed, we are still suffering the consequences of King Henry VIII's infidelity to Queen Catherine of Aragon by the attention he gave to the plotting Anne Boleyn, who was all too willing to cater to the crypto-Protestants, such as Thomas Cranmer, eager to be free of "Rome" once and for all.

In like manner, of course, the Protestant Revolt in England engendered murder and violence, much of which was state-sponsored as Henry Tudor, who had been seeking an annulment of his marriage with   Queen Catherine from 1525 to the time of his bigamous "marriage" to Anne Boleyn in 1533, was responsible between November of 1534, when Parliament declared Henry VIII and his legitimate successors to be the "the only supreme head on earth of the Church in England," and his death on January 28, 1547, for ordering the executions of over 72,000 Catholics who remained faithful to the Catholic Church.

Among those martyred were Saint Thomas More, who was beheaded on July 6, 1535, and Saint John Fisher, martyred on June 22, 1535, was the only bishop in England out of one hundred to remain faithful to the Vicar of Christ at the time of Henry Tudor's break with Rome. As was the case in the German states as princes gave Luther protection so that they, the princes, could govern in a Machiavellian manner free of any interference from Rome or their local bishops, so was it the case in England that the Protestant Revolution provided the receipt for the unchecked tyranny of English monarchs.

Indeed, the kind of state-sponsored social engineering that has created the culture of entitlement in England and elsewhere in Europe has its antecedent roots in Henry's revolt against the Social Reign of Christ the King and His Catholic Church in the Sixteenth Century.

Henry had Parliament enact various laws to force the poor who had lived for a nominal annual fee on the monastery and convent lands (as they produced the food to sustain themselves, giving some to the monastery or convent) off of those lands, where their families had lived for generations, in order to redistribute the Church properties he had stolen to those who supported his break from Rome. Henry quite cleverly created a class of people who were dependent upon him for the property upon which they lived and the wealth they were able to derive therefrom, making them utterly supportive of his decision to declare himself Supreme Head of the Church in England. Those of the poorer classes who had been thrown off of the monastery and convent lands were either thrown into prison (for being poor, mind you) or forced to migrate to the cities, where many of them lost the true Faith and sold themselves into various vices just to survive.

A pamphlet, *Breaking With The Past*, contains four sermons that were given on the Sundays in Advent in 1913 at the Cathedral of Saint Patrick in the City of New York, New York, by Abbot Francis Aidan Gasquet, O.S.B., the Abbot-President of the English Benedictines, and provides a superb summary of the revolutionary nature of these events:

> Suddenly and almost as a bolt from the blue, difficulties between the King of England and the Pope began to show themselves. Grave events often spring from slight causes, and, whatever may be said by professional controversialists, there can be no doubt that it was a mere love affair of Henry VIII, which initiated the royal policy and finally dragged England into schism and heresy. To some people, indeed, in these days the action of the Pope in refusing to allow Henry to have his own willful way in putting aside his wedded wife, Katherine, and to marry another woman, with whom he had had illicit relations, may appear to have been the height of unwisdom. Certainly as a result it has had the most disastrous consequences to the English Church. But this at least all must confess: that the Pope's courageous action is a manifest proof of the impossibility of ecclesiastical authority interfering without right reason with the indissoluble sanctity of a true Christian marriage.

> To obtain the support of Parliament the King suggested that the nation had incurred the extreme penalties of *praemunire* by admitting the legatine powers of Cardinal Wolsey, even though this had been done with his royal knowledge and authority. His lay subjects were at once pardoned for a mere technical offence against the statute laws, but the clergy were excluded in order to hold the penalties *in terrorem* over them. With his royal hand on the throats of his ecclesiastical subjects he demanded a recognition of his Headship over the

Church in England, and finally Convocation, after a debate which extended over two and thirty sessions, gave an unwilling assent to a clause admitting the King as "the Protector and Supreme Head: of the English Church." This was the thin edge of the wedge by which the cleavage from Rome and the Pope was subsequently effected. At the time, there can be no doubt that the inward meaning of the acknowledgment was not understood. Dean Hook says that the statement was not "regarded as inconsistent with the legitimate claims of the papacy," and as Froude admits, it is certain that "the title was not intended to imply what it implied when, four years later, it was conferred by Act of Parliament, and when England virtually was severed by it from the Roman communion."

In 1532 by an Act entitled "The Submission of the Clergy" the king received their pledge not to legislate in ecclesiastical matters in convocation without his royal leave. By this "Submission" the English Church deprived itself of all corporate action and in the same year the aged Archbishop Warham died. "We cannot doubt," writes the late Dr. James Gardiner, the most competent judge of the events of this reign and himself not a Catholic, "We cannot doubt that the event (i.e. the death of the Archbishop of Canterbury) at once suggested to the King a new method of achieving his end" and divorcing Queen Katherine. He obtained from the Pope the appointment of Thomas Cranmer, a priest who in defiance of the canons had secretly married in Germany the niece of Osiander, the German Reformer, as a second wife.

Having secured this appointment from the Holy See, the King directed Cranmer to consider the divorce question, and the decree having been pronounced by the subservient archbishop, Henry made Anne Boleyn his Queen on June 1, 1533. Six months later the Convocations of Canterbury and York, under strong royal pressure formally accepted the declaration "the bishop of Rome has not in Scripture and greater jurisdiction in the Kingdom of England than any foreign bishop." Finally in March, 1534, the severance of England from Rome ecclesiastically was effected by the *Supreme Head* act which styled the King the only "Supreme head in earth of the Church of England" and granted him the most ample powers of ecclesiastical Visitation. Then the final touch was given to the work by the *Act of Verbal Treasons*, by which it was declared to be high treason to "imagine" any bodily harm to either the King or Queen or "to deprive them of their dignity, title, style," etc.

There were various other religious changes initiated during the remainder of this reign, like the destruction of shrines and the prohibition of devotion to the saints, but it is one of the perplexing problems of this time why there was not a more radical reconstruction of religion in England upon the lines of the Lutheran principles of the Reformation. The fact is that, though for his own purposes Henry was willing enough to get rid of the Pope, he was never a Lutheran at heart. He had defended Catholic principles against the German Reformed doctrines in his work on the Seven Sacraments. He never wholly lost his Catholic instinct, and to the last he maintained with a strong hand the ancient Catholic Sacramental teaching, and in particular in regard to the most Holy Eucharist and the doctrine of Transubstantiation. In this regard the re-forming party, as long as he lived, was kept in check and had to wait for the King's death to further changes.

To us Catholics, by the act of cutting England from Rome, the principle of Christian Unity was rejected and sacrificed. The branch cut from the tree no longer feeds upon the sap of the parent stock, and disintegration is merely a matter of time. We who look back over the centuries, which have passed since the severance of the English church from Union with Rome was effected, can see how the disintegration as to doctrine, has gone on ever since. Few can deny that it is still proceeding at a rate which is rightly alarming those who still cling even to the shreds of the religious formularies evolved in the Reformation settlement. Hundreds of religious bodies, all claiming to be Christian and all differing on vital and essential matters of belief, can be seen round about us to-day. The process of division is still going on and it must continue where there is no authority to speak with a divine commission. We Catholics, as we review this chaos, may we thank God that our English and Irish forefathers have fought and suffered to maintain for us the Christian principle of a Supreme authority in religion. (Abbot Francis Aidan Gasquet, O.S.B., *Breaking With The Past*, pp. 11-19.)

The effects of this exercise of state-sponsored social engineering are reverberating in the world today, both politically and economically. Indeed, many of the conditions bred by the disparity in wealth created by Henry's land grab in the Sixteenth Century would fester and help to create the world of unbridled capitalism and slave wage that so impressed a German emigre in London by the name of Karl Marx. Unable to recognize the historical antecedents of the real injustices he saw during the Victorian Era, Marx set about devising his own manifestly unjust system, premised on atheism and anti-Theism, to rectify social injustice once and for all. In a very real way, Henry of Tudor led the way to Lenin of Russia.

Although England was restored to the Faith during the reign of Queen Mary I, the daughter of King Henry VIII and Queen Catherine of Aragon, from July 17, 1553, to November 17, 1553, Queen Elizabeth I, Henry VIII's daughter by Anne Boleyn, took England out of the Faith permanently by means of the various laws, including another "act of supremacy," which were passed by the English Parliament to restore England to Protestantism, this time once and for all and, of course, with devastating social and economic consequences. A bloody persecution of Catholics began, featuring unspeakable acts of brutal torture, taking the lives of between five hundred and one thousand Catholics. Priests, including Father Edmund Campion, S.J., bore the brunt of brutal torture and execution.

Pope Saint Pius V issued *Regnans in Excelsis* (March 5, 1870), to excommunicate Elizabeth I, thereby instructing Catholics that she was no longer to be considered a legitimate monarch. This was a direct effort on the part of the sainted Dominican, who urged that the Rosary be prayed for the defeat of the Turkish naval forces in the Battle of Lepanto on October 7, 1571, of the temporal power of the papacy in behalf of the Social Reign of Christ the King. It was in this papal bull, as noted before, that he declared the Anglican liturgical books to be heretical, something, of course, that means nothing to the conciliar authorities in our own day:

> Prohibiting with a strong hand the use of the true religion, which after its earlier overthrow by Henry VIII (a deserter therefrom) Mary, the lawful queen of famous memory, had with the help of this See restored, she has followed and embraced the errors of the heretics. She has removed the royal Council, composed of the nobility of England, and has filled it with obscure men, being heretics; oppressed the followers of the Catholic faith; instituted false preachers and ministers of impiety; abolished the sacrifice of the mass, prayers, fasts, choice of meats, celibacy, and Catholic ceremonies; and has ordered that books of

manifestly heretical content be propounded to the whole realm and that impious rites and institutions after the rule of Calvin, entertained and observed by herself, be also observed by her subjects. She has dared to eject bishops, rectors of churches and other Catholic priests from their churches and benefices, to bestow these and other things ecclesiastical upon heretics, and to determine spiritual causes; has forbidden the prelates, clergy and people to acknowledge the Church of Rome or obey its precepts and canonical sanctions; has forced most of them to come to terms with her wicked laws, to abjure the authority and obedience of the pope of Rome, and to accept her, on oath, as their only lady in matters temporal and spiritual; has imposed penalties and punishments on those who would not agree to this and has exacted them of those who persevered in the unity of the faith and the aforesaid obedience; has thrown the Catholic prelates and parsons into prison where many, worn out by long languishing and sorrow, have miserably ended their lives. All these matter and manifest and notorious among all the nations; they are so well proven by the weighty witness of many men that there remains no place for excuse, defense or evasion. (*Regnans in Excelsis*, the decree issued by Pope Saint Pius V on March 5, 1570, excommunicating Queen Elizabeth I.)

The abuses of power by English monarchs, including the subjugating of Ireland and the persecution of Catholics in the Land of Saints and Scholars who refused to defect from the true Church, a persecution that would last until 1921 and still persists in Northern Ireland, led to all manner of social unrest in England, especially as those Anglicans who were followers of John Calvin sought to eradicate all remaining vestiges of Catholicism from Anglican "worship" and "doctrine" (removing Latin from certain aspects of the heretical Anglican liturgy, smashing statues, eliminating high altars in favor of tables, things that have been undertaken in the past forty years in many formerly Catholic churches that are now in the custody of the counterfeit church of conciliarism). This unrest produced the English Civil Wars of the 1640s and the establishment in 1649 of what was, for all intents and purposes, a Calvinist state under the control Oliver Cromwell that became a Cromwellian dictatorship between the years of 1653 to 1660 until the monarchy under the House of Stuart was restored in 1660. Oh yes, King Charles I lost his head, quite literally, in 1649 as the "Roundheads" of Oliver Cromwell came to power in 1649 following seven years of warfare between "parliamentarians" and "royalists." Revolutions always wind up eating their own. The English monarchy itself was eaten up by the overthrow of the Social Reign of the King of Kings by Henry VIII of the House of Tudor in 1534.

King James II, who had converted to Catholicism in France in 1668 while he was the Prince of York under his brother, King Charles II of the restored monarchy, acceded to the English throne o n J u n e 6, 1885, following his brother's death, which occurred after Charles II himself had converted to the Faith on his deathbed. Suspicious that the property that had been acquired and the wealth that had been amassed as a result of Henry VIII's social-engineering land grab of 150 years before would be placed in jeopardy, Protestant opponents of King James II eventually forced him to abdicate the throne in 1688, his rule having been declared as ended on December 11 of that year. The abdication of King James, whose second wife, Mary of Modena, had been assigned Blessed Father Claude de la Colombiere as her spiritual director when she was the Princess of York, is referred to by Protestant and secular historians as the "glorious revolution," so-called because it ushered in the penultimate result   of the Protestant Revolution, the tyranny of the majority.

It was to justify the rise of majoritarianism that John Locke, a Presbyterian (Calvinist) minister, wrote his Second Treatise on Civil Government. Locke believed, essentially, that social problems could be ameliorated if a majority of reasonable men gathered together to discuss their situation. The discussion among these "reasonable men" would lead to an agreement, sanctioned by the approval of the majority amongst themselves, on the creation of structures which were designed to improve the existing situation. If those structures did not ameliorate the problems or resulted in a worsening of social conditions then some subsequent majority of "reasonable men" would be able to tear up the "contract" that had bound them before, devising yet further structures designed to do what the previous structures could not accomplish. Locke did not specify how this majority of reasonable men would form, only that it would form, providing the foundation of the modern parliamentary system that premises the survival of various governments upon the whims of a majority at a given moment.

In other words, England's "problem" in 1688 was King James II. The solution? Parliament, in effect, declared that he had abdicated his throne rather than attempt to fight yet another English civil war to maintain himself in power as the man chosen by the parliamentarians to replace him, his own son-in-law William of Orange, who was married to his daughter Mary, landed with armed forces ready to undertake such a battle. The parliamentary "majority" had won the day over absolutism and a return to Catholicism.

Unfortunately for Locke, you see, social problems cannot be ameliorated merely by the creation of structures devised by "reasonable men" and sanctioned by the majority.

All problems in the world, both individual and social, have their remote causes in Original Sin and their proximate causes in the Actual Sins of men. There is no once-and-for-all method or structure by which, for example, "peace" will be provided in the world by the creation of international organizations or building up or the drafting of treaties.

There is no once-and-for-all method or structure by which, for example, "crime" will be lessened in a nation by the creation of various programs designed to address the "environmental" conditions that are said to breed it.

The only way in which social conditions can be ameliorated is by the daily reformation of individual lives in cooperation with the graces won for men by the shedding of the Most Precious Blood of Our Blessed Lord and Saviour Jesus Christ upon the wood of the Holy Cross and that flow into our hearts and souls through the loving hands of Our Lady, she who is the Mediatrix of All Graces. And to the extent that social structures can be effective in addressing and ameliorating specific problems at specific times in specific places, those who create and administer them must recognize their absolute dependence upon God's graces and that there is no secular, non-denominational or inter-denominational way to provide for social order. Social order and peace among nations depend entirely upon the subordination of the life of every person and the activities of every nation to the Social Reign of Christ the King as it is exercised by the Catholic Church.

The modern state is founded on the specific and categorical rejection of the Social Reign of Christ the King as it is exercised by the Catholic Church. There is thus the need for modern man for find sterile ideologies or philosophies to substitute for the true Faith so as to guide "him" in the course of daily life. The failure of the social structures fashioned after the Lockean model to effect an amelioration of the problems they were intended to address does nothing to deter "true believers" from continuing to persist in the blindness that led them to reject the true Faith and to trust in their own cooked-up schemes.

No, the "true believers" in liberalism or conservatism or capitalism or socialism or communism or fascism or Nazism or utilitarianism or pragmatism or positivism (or any and all other brands of secular "isms") must spend their entire lives searching for a "better way" to realize the goals of their particular ideology or philosophy or economic system. It cannot possibly be, they have convinced themselves, that their initial premises were wrong from the outset. No, the problem must be in the implementation and/or in the communication of their ideas, not in the false nature of the ideas upon which they have based all of their truly delusional hopes.

The Lockean construct for the resolution of social problems is but one part of the Revolution, as it was termed by Popes Pius VI, VII, VIII, Gregory XVI, Pius IX, Leo XIII, and Saint Pius X, against the Faith. The Lockean construct preceded the rise of contemporary Freemasonry in England by twenty-nine years, fitting in nicely with the Judeo-Masonic desire to obliterate the necessity of subordinating all things in personal and social life to the reality of the Incarnation by stressing the conviction that the "universal brotherhood of men" can put aside "denominational differences" to pursue the "common good." Locke's belief that men can resolve their social problems by the creation of structures, in essence the self-redemptive heresy of semi-Pelagianism, also dovetailed into the Judeo-Masonic belief that men can pursue "civic virtue" on their own without belief in, access to or cooperation with sanctifying grace. These false beliefs lead men and their societies into complete and utter chaos, which is the goal of the chief revolutionary, the devil himself, who desires the minds of men to be locked up by the blindness engendered by their narcissism and pride.

The Lockean construct leads to many mutations, all of which have one common theme: the ability of man to better his lot in life on his own without subordinating himself to the Deposit of Faith that the God-Man has entrusted to His true Church.

In the United States, for example, the Lockean construct has produced a situation where liberalism had to give way to the socialism that has been creeping up on us in the past century since the administrations of Presidents Theodore Roosevelt and Thomas Woodrow Wilson.

The failure of incremental, structural "reforms" to improve social conditions led to an increase in the size and the power of government at all levels (state, local, national) and a reduction in the legitimate natural law rights of citizens to be free from the tyranny of governmental leaders possessed of the notion that secular salvation comes from the state.

Thus, the New Freedom of Woodrow Wilson was actually a descent into statism, especially as represented by the creation of the Federal Reserve System, expedited by the New Deal of Franklin Delano Roosevelt (and by many of the policies of his immediate predecessor, Herbert Clark Hoover), and expanded by Lyndon Baines Johnson's "Great Society" and "War on Poverty" programs. The attempts to "engineer" the better society through government programs has reached such a stage that even thought itself is being punished at the state law (and laws are pending on the national level to make criticism of the behavior of certain people a "hate" crime). A land born in the delusional belief that man can ever be "free" without Our Lord and His Holy Church produces all to logically and inexorably a new caste of slaves, most of who are so diverted by bread and circuses that they protest nary a bit as their legitimate freedoms and property are taken away from them bit by bit under one pretext or another. All of this, however, was but a prelude to the socialism of the present moment, including stimulus packages and ObamaCare and the pork-barreling that squanders so many billions of taxpayer dollars (pork-barreling goes by the more commonly-known name of "earmarks" today).

Elsewhere, however, the Lockean construct leads to a degree of violent frustration. That is, the failure of structural reforms to, say, "end" poverty or to "end" wars convinced a number of visionaries that violent, bloody revolutions were necessary to overthrow the remaining vestiges of Catholicism in order to replace it all at once with a man-made paradigm for peace and justice on earth. The French Revolutionaries, the Mexican Revolutionaries, the plotters of the Italian Risorgimento, Otto von Bismarck's Kulturkampf in Germany, the Bolshevik and Maoist Revolutionaries--and scores upon scores of others--believed that their revolutions would bring about a new age for mankind. The failure of even those "once-and-for-all" revolutions, however, to produce their expected results led to attempts to revitalize the revolutionary zeal, a "reform of the reform," if you will. And thus it will ever be with minds that have rejected the simple truth that Catholicism is the one and only foundation of personal and social order as they have been shaped by the demonically inspired naturalistic, religiously indifferentist, semi-Pelagian delusions of Modernity.

The violent street protests in various countries of Europe that have seen overgrown urchins of all ages complain about any threats to their precious entitlements are simply the natural, logical byproducts of a world steeped in the aftermath of one violent revolution after another against the Social Reign of Christ the King as It must be exercised by the Catholic Church, outside of which there is no salvation and without which there can be no true social order. Men must give vent to anger and outrage, yes, even in violent ways, when their immortal souls are not enlightened by the light of the Deposit of Faith and enlivened by Sanctifying Grace. Chaos is the only thing that can result when men believe that they can be "free" of Christ the King and His Holy Church.

The Protestant Revolution that engendered all of the social revolutions of Modernity is indeed a recipe for tyranny. That tyranny can take many forms (one man, a ruling elite, a military junta, a particular political party, popular or legislative or judicial majorities). However, the Protestant Revolution is indeed a recipe for all contemporary forms of statist tyranny, which now includes requiring Catholics and others who oppose sodomy to submit the new order of things or risk some kind of penalty, including the closure of their very businesses.

Catholicism is the one and only foundation of personal and social order:

> Everyone should avoid familiarity or friendship with anyone suspected of belonging to masonry or to affiliated groups. Know them by their fruits and avoid them. Every familiarity should be avoided, not only with those impious libertines who openly promote the character of the sect, but also with those who hide under the mask of universal tolerance,

respect for all religions, and the craving to reconcile the maxims of the Gospel with those of the revolution. These men seek to reconcile Christ and Belial, the Church of God and the state without God. (Pope Leo XIII, *Custodi di Quella Fede*, December 8, 1892.)

From this it may clearly be seen what consequences are to be expected from that false pride which, rejecting our Saviour's Kingship, places man at the summit of all things and declares that human nature must rule supreme. And yet, this supreme rule can neither be attained nor even defined. The rule of Jesus Christ derives its form and its power from Divine Love: a holy and orderly charity is both its foundation and its crown. Its necessary consequences are the strict fulfillment of duty, respect of mutual rights, the estimation of the things of heaven above those of earth, the preference of the love of God to all things. But this supremacy of man, which openly rejects Christ, or at least ignores Him, is entirely founded upon selfishness, knowing neither charity nor self-devotion. Man may indeed be king, through Jesus Christ: but only on condition that he first of all obey God, and diligently seek his rule of life in God's law. By the law of Christ we mean not only the natural precepts of morality and the Ancient Law, all of which Jesus Christ has perfected and crowned by His declaration, explanation and sanction; but also the rest of His doctrine and His own peculiar institutions. Of these the chief is His Church. Indeed whatsoever things Christ has instituted are most fully contained in His Church. Moreover, He willed to perpetuate the office assigned to Him by His Father by means of the ministry of the Church so gloriously founded by Himself. On the one hand He confided to her all the means of men's salvation, on the other He most solemnly commanded men to be subject to her and to obey her diligently, and to follow her even as Himself: "He that heareth you, heareth Me; and he that despiseth you, despiseth Me" (Luke x, 16). Wherefore the law of Christ must be sought in the Church. Christ is man's "Way"; the Church also is his "Way"-Christ of Himself and by His very nature, the Church by His commission and the communication of His power. Hence all who would find salvation apart from the Church, are led astray and strive in vain.

As with individuals, so with nations. These, too, must necessarily tend to ruin if they go astray from "The Way." The Son of God, the Creator and Redeemer of mankind, is King and Lord of the earth, and holds supreme dominion over men, both individually and collectively. "And He gave Him power, and glory, and a kingdom: and all peoples, tribes, and tongues shall serve Him" (Daniel vii., 14). "I am appointed King by Him . . . I will give Thee the Gentiles for Thy inheritance, and the uttermost parts of the earth for Thy possession" (Psalm ii., 6, 8). Therefore the law of Christ ought to prevail in human society and be the guide and teacher of public as well as of private life. Since this is so by divine decree, and no man may with impunity contravene it, it is an evil thing for the common weal wherever Christianity does not hold the place that belongs to it. When Jesus Christ is absent, human reason fails, being bereft of its chief protection and light, and the very end is lost sight of, for which, under God's providence, human society has been built up. This end is the obtaining by the members of society of natural good through the aid of civil unity, though always in harmony with the perfect and eternal good which is above nature. But when men's minds are clouded, both rulers and ruled go astray, for they have no safe line to follow nor end to aim at. (Pope Leo XIII, *Tametsi Futura Prospicientibus*, November 1, 1900.)

Just as Christianity cannot penetrate into the soul without making it better, so it cannot enter into public life without establishing order. With the idea of a God Who governs all, Who is infinitely wise, good, and just, the idea of duty seizes upon the consciences of men. It assuages sorrow, it calms hatred, it engenders heroes. If it has transformed pagan society--and that transformation was a veritable resurrection--for barbarism disappeared in proportion as Christianity extended its sway, so, after the terrible shocks which unbelief has given to the world in our days, it will be able to put that world again on the true road, and bring back to order the states and peoples of modern times. But the return of Christianity will not be efficacious and complete if it does not restore the world to a sincere love of the one Holy Catholic and Apostolic Church. In the Catholic Church Christianity is Incarnate. It identifies itself with that perfect, spiritual, and, in its own order, sovereign society, which is the Mystical Body of Jesus Christ and which has for Its visible head the Roman Pontiff, successor of the Prince of the Apostles. It is the continuation of the mission of the Savior, the daughter and the heiress of His Redemption. It has preached the Gospel, and has defended it at the price of its blood, and strong in the Divine assistance and of that immortality which has been promised it, it makes no terms with error but remains faithful to the commands which It has received, to carry the doctrine of Jesus Christ to the uttermost limits of the world and to the end of time, and to protect it in its inviolable integrity. Legitimate dispenser of the teachings of the Gospel It does not reveal itself only as the consoler and Redeemer of souls, but It is still more the internal source of justice and charity, and the propagator as well as the guardian of true liberty, and of that equality which alone is possible here below. In applying the doctrine of its Divine Founder, It maintains a wise equilibrium and marks the true limits between the rights and privileges of society. The equality which it proclaims does not destroy the distinction between the different social classes It keeps them intact, as nature itself demands, in order to oppose the anarchy of reason emancipated from Faith, and abandoned to its own devices. The liberty which it gives in no wise conflicts with the rights of truth, because those rights are superior to the demands of liberty. Nor does it infringe upon the rights of justice, because those rights are superior to the claims of mere numbers or power. Nor does it assail the rights of God because they are superior to the rights of humanity. (Pope Leo XIII, *A Review of His Pontificate*, March 19, 1902.)

Here we have, founded by Catholics, an inter-denominational association that is to work for the reform of civilization, an undertaking which is above all religious in character; for there is no true civilization without a moral civilization, and no true moral civilization without the true religion: it is a proven truth, a historical fact. (Pope Saint Pius X, *Notre Charge Apostolique*, August 15, 1910.)

This history is very important to understand: that there was indeed quite a contrast between the settlement of the English colonies up and down the Atlantic seaboard of what became the United States of America and the settlement of colonies by Spain and France in the Americas. Although it was not without difficulties and crimes against the indigenous peoples in some instances, the Spanish and the French sought to plant the Cross of the Divine Redeemer, the only true standard of human liberty, deep in the soil of the Americas. And it was within a short time of Our Lady's apparition to Juan Diego in 1531 that a thriving new Christendom had arisen in Mexico and Peru.

The Protestant Revolution thus predestined, if you will, the English-speaking colonies of North America to the social decay and statism of the present time as the only force on earth that can keep people from reverting to barbarism and to keep the civil state from becoming tyrannical is a force that is of Divine origin, direction and sustenance: the Catholic Church.

The history of Catholics in the United States of America is thus shaped by their living in an environment of the rationalism of Protestantism and of the naturalism and religious indifferentism of Judeo-Masonry, which is far, far different from the spirit that permeated the Americas following the landing of Christopher Columbus on the island of San Salvador on October 12, 1492.

Chapter XII
A New Christendom for a New World

Although Christopher Columbus set out on his voyage in 1492 to chart a westerly course to the Indies in the Far East, he was the contemporary discoverer of a new world even though he denied to his dying breath that he found new lands. These new lands became mission fields as priests from Spain and France and Portugal came to evangelize the indigenous peoples of the New World, which were named ultimately for Amerigo Vespucci, a Florentine Italian who sailed under the patronage of Spain and Portugal and concluded that the New World Columbus had discovered was not Asia. The name "America," derived from Vespucci's first name, is itself a variation of the first name of Saint Stephen of Hungary's son, Saint Emeric. While much of North America has been in the control of Protestants and Freemasons from the late-Eighteenth Century to this time, the Americas have been Catholic from the time they were rediscovered by Christopher Columbus and other Catholic explorers, including Amerigo Vespucci.

One can state that the Americans were *rediscovered* as it is most likely the case that Saint Brendan the Navigator made his way in the Sixth Century to what would be considered a "new world" nearly a thousand years later. Here is an account of the voyage of Saint Brendan, an Irish monk, to the Americas that is now supported by the discovery in West Virginia of archeological evidence of Old Irish letters engraved on stones:

> Also known as Brandan and Borodon, Brendan was born about 484 A.D. near Tralee in County Kerry. He was ordained by Bishop Erc and sailed around northwest Europe spreading the Christian faith and founding monasteries — the largest at Clonfert, County Galway. Legend says that the community had at least three thousand monks — their rule dictated to Brendan by an angel. He died at the age of 93 and he was buried at the monastery in 577 A.D.

> Brendan and his brothers figure prominently in Brendan's Voyage, a tale of monks traveling the high seas of the Atlantic, evangelizing to the islands, and possibly reaching the Americas in the 6th century. At one point they stop on a small island, celebrate Easter Mass, light a fire--and then discover the island is an enormous whale!

> Maps of Columbus' time often included an island called St. Brendan's Isle that was placed in the western Atlantic ocean. Map makers of the time had no idea of its exact position but did believe it existed some where west of Europe. It was mentioned in a Latin text dating from the ninth century called Navigatio Santi Brendani Abatis (Voyage of Saint Brendan the Abbot). It described the voyage as having taken place in the sixth century. Several copies of this text have survived in monasteries throughout Europe. It was an important part of folklore in medieval Europe and may have influenced Columbus.

> The account of Brendan's voyage contained a detailed description of the construction of his boat which was not unlike the currachs still made in Ireland today.

> Skeptics could not accept that such a fragile vessel could possibly sail in the open sea. Several passages in the legend also seemed incredible—they were "raised up on the

back of sea monsters", they "passed by crystals that rose up to the sky", and they were "pelted with flaming, foul-smelling rocks by the inhabitants of a large island on their route".

Brendan and his companions finally arrived at the beautiful land they called "Promised Land of the Saints." They explored until they came to a great river that divided the land. The journey of Brendan and his fellow monks took seven years. The return trip was probably the longest part of the odyssey.

In 1976, Tim Severin, a British navigation scholar, embarked from Brandon Creek on the Dingle Peninsula in a currach that he constructed using the details described by Brendan. His goal was to determine if the voyage of Brendan and his fellow monks was possible. Severin and his team tanned ox-hides with oak bark, stretched them across the wood frame, sewed them with leather thread and smeared the hides with animal fat which would impart water resistance.

Examination of nautical charts led Severin to believe that Brendan's route would be governed by the prevailing winds that would take him across the northernmost part of the Atlantic. This   would take him close to Iceland and Greenland with a probable landfall at Newfoundland (St. Brendan's Isle).

Severin and his crew were surprised at how friendly the whales were that they encountered. The whales swam around and even under their boat. The whales could have been even friendlier in Brendan's time, before motorized ships would make them leery of man. So friendly, that they may have lifted the monk's boat in a playful gesture!

After stopping at the Hebrides islands, Severin proceeded to the Danish Faroe Islands. At the island of Mykines, they encountered thousands of seabirds. Brendan called this island "The Paradise of Birds." He referred to the larger island as the "Island of Sheep." The word Faroe itself means Island of Sheep. There is also a Brandon Creek on the main island of the Faroes that the local people believe was an embarkation point for Brendan and his crew.

Severin's route then carried them to Iceland where they wintered, as did Brendan. The volcanoes on the island have been active for many centuries and might well have been erupting when the monks stayed there. This could have accounted for the "pelting with flaming, foul smelling rocks", referred to in the ninth century text.

The monks had never seen icebergs before, so their description of them as "towering crystals" would make sense. Severin's boat was punctured by floating ice off the coast of Canada. They were able to make a repair with a piece of leather sewn over the hole. They landed on the island of Newfoundland on June 26, 1977. This might well have been Brendan's "Land promised to the Saints" referred to in the Navigatio.

Severin's journey did not prove that Brendan and his monks landed on North America. However, it did prove that a leather currach as described in the Navigatio could have made such a voyage as mapped out in the text. There is also no doubt that the Irish were frequent seafarers of the North Atlantic sea currents 900 years before the voyage of Columbus.

More conclusive evidence of Irish exploration of North America has come to light in West Virginia. There, stone carvings have been discovered that have been dated between 500 and 1000 A.D. Analysis by archaeologist Dr. Robert Pyle and a leading language expert Dr. Barry Fell, indicate that they are written in Old Irish using the Ogham alphabet.

According to Dr. Fell, the "West Virginia Ogham texts are the oldest Ogham inscriptions from anywhere in the world. They exhibit the grammar and vocabulary of Old Irish in a manner previously unknown in such early rock-cut inscriptions in any Celtic language."

Dr. Fell goes on to speculate that, "It seems possible that the scribes that cut the West Virginia inscriptions may have been Irish missionaries in the wake of Brendan's voyage, for these inscriptions are Christian. The early Christian symbols of piety, such as the various Chi-Rho monograms (Name of Christ) and the Dextra Dei (Right Hand of God) appear at the sites, together with the Ogham texts."

The lack of any written account of this exploration could be explained by the explorers not being able to return to their homeland. If they indeed did reach what is now West Virginia, it would be extremely doubtful that they could manage to return to Ireland from an embarkation point that far south. The design of their currach required favorable winds and currents in the right direction in order to navigate. Severin discovered that it was extremely difficult to tack as other sailing ships were able to do. Perhaps that is the reason that it took Brendan seven years for his journey. That he was able to return at all is a miracle - or was it all a myth?

Perhaps we'll never know for certain whether or not Brendan's voyage was a medieval fantasy or that he was indeed, among the first to discover the New World. The evidence would indicate that a fantastic voyage across the Atlantic did take place and the stone carvings in West Virginia certainly prove the presence of Irish Christians at just about the right time in history. Whatever you believe, it's a fascinating chapter in Irish folklore and one that should be passed down until such time that the truth can be determined. (*Life of St. Brendan, Irish Heritage Newsletter*, May 2001.)

No, it was not a myth. It was simply not within the Providence of God for the Americas to be evangelized on a permanent basis at that time. Europe itself was still being evangelized. God had other plans for the Americas, and they involved an ambitious Genoan and other equally ambitious explorers, each of whom was being used to prepare the way for the opening of the Age of Mary upon her apparition to Juan Diego in 1531 that was meant to convey that the Indians were to be treated by the Spaniards as their brothers and sisters in her Divine Son, Christ the King.

Christopher Columbus and the Beginning of a Catholic America: Christopher Columbus landed on the island of San Salvador on October 12, 1492. Our Lady herself put the Divine seal of approval on the missionary work that had begun with Columbus's expedition of 1492, appearing to Juan Diego on December 9, 1531, at Tepeyac, Mexico, resulting in the rapid conversion of over nine million indigenous people to the true Faith following within ten years the conquest of the barbaric Aztec system of human sacrifice. Indeed, a thriving Catholic culture emerged in Central and South America within a very short period of time. Saints, both from abroad and those born in the Americas, emerged to propagate the true Faith.

Saint Turibius of Mongrovejo, the first Archbishop of Lima, Peru, founded the first seminary in the newly discovered hemisphere and was a tireless defender of the rights of the native peoples against the Spanish conquerors and colonists. Saint Rose of Lima was a Third Order Dominican who was born six years before the centenary of Columbus's arrival, the first native born saint of the Americas. Her friend, Blessed Martin de Porres, served the poor with tireless love as a Dominican brother in Peru. His friend, Blessed John de Massias, came from Spain to the New World to settle eventually in Peru, where he served as a Dominican lay brother, praying the Rosary every day, especially to release the Poor Souls from Purgatory. Saint Peter Claver came from Spain in 1610 to minister to the Negro slaves who had been brought to Cartagena, Colombia, from various places in Africa, baptizing over 300,000 souls during his priestly service in the New World.

In other words, Christopher Columbus, who thought he was on a mission to find a shorter passage from Europe to the Indies, was responsible for planting the seeds of the replication in the Western Hemisphere at the beginning of the second half of the Second Millennium of what had grown organically in Europe during the First Millennium: Christendom. Catholicism resonated throughout Latin America within a hundred years of Columbus's landing on the island of San Salvador in 1492. Deep devotion to the Mother of God, who had favored the region with her miraculous apparition to Juan Diego, spread throughout the major cities and into the smallest, most remote mountain villages. People lived and worked for the honor and glory of the true God as He has revealed Himself solely through the Catholic Church. They were mindful of frequenting the sacraments and of preparing for a holy death. They raised their children to love the lives of the saints and to strive to imitate them in every aspect of their daily lives.

The Church provided early on for the education of the indigenous peoples (as well as for the colonists and their descendants, many of whom did not want to "mingle" with the Indians). The College of Santa Clara was founded in Tlaltelolco, Mexico, in 1534. The University of Mexico opened in 1553. And the College of San Pablo opened in 1575. The University of San Marcos was established in Lima, Peru, in 1551. The University of Cordoba, which began as the College of Saint Francis Xavier, opened in Argentina in 1611. Other institutions were founded throughout Latin America to foster the natural and supernatural development of the peoples who had been subjected to the superstitions and barbaric practices of demonic "religions" prior to the landing of the first priests with Christopher Columbus in 1492.

Pope Leo XIII issued an Encyclical Letter in 1892, *Quarto Abuente Saeculo*, on the Quadracentenary of the Genoan (all right, all right: all you from Spain who claim Columbus as Spanish have had your objections over the years noted; DNA tests are being done at present, believe it or not, to try to ascertain Columbus's true ethnicity and national origins). Here are a few salient passages testifying to the fact that Catholics should be proud of the work of Columbus and to see in it an inspiration to do the very same in our own day, that is, to Catholicize every single part of our own lives and to shun everything in our popular culture that is hostile to the Catholic Faith (which is, admittedly, pretty much everything):

> For Columbus is ours; since if a little consideration be given to the particular reason of his design in exploring the "mare tenebrosum," and also the manner in which he endeavored to execute the design, it is indubitable that the Catholic faith was the strongest motive for the inception and prosecution of the design; so that for this reason also the whole human race owes not a little to the Church.

> For we have the record of not a few brave and experienced men, both before and after Christopher Columbus, who with stubbornness and zeal explored unknown lands and seas yet more unknown. And the memory of these, man, mindful of benefits, rightly holds, and will hold in honor; because they advanced the ends of knowledge and humanity, and increased the common prosperity of the race, not by light labor, but by supreme exertion, often accompanied by great dangers. But there is, nevertheless, between these and him of whom we speak, a generous difference. He was distinguished by this unique note, that in his work of traversing and retraversing immense tracts of ocean, he looked for a something greater and higher than did these others. We say not that he was unmoved by perfectly honorable aspirations after knowledge, and deserving well of human society; nor did he despise glory, which is a most engrossing ideal to great souls; nor did he altogether scorn a hope of advantages to himself; but to him far before all these human considerations was the consideration of his ancient faith, which questionless dowered him with strength of mind and will, and often strengthened and consoled him in the midst of the greatest difficulties. This view and aim is known to have possessed his mind above all; namely, to open a way for the Gospel over new lands and seas.

> This, indeed, may seem of small likelihood to such as confine their whole thought and care to the evidence of the senses, and refuse to look for anything higher. But great intellects, on the contrary, are usually wont to cherish higher ideals; for they, of all men, are most excellently fitted to receive the intuitions and breathings of Divine faith. Columbus certainly had joined to the study of nature the study of religion, and had trained his mind on the teachings that well up from the most intimate depths of the Catholic faith. For this reason, when he learned from the lessons of astronomy and the record of the ancients, that there were great tracts of land lying towards the West, beyond the limits of the known world, lands hitherto explored by no man, he saw in spirit a mighty multitude, cloaked in miserable darkness, given over to evil rites, and the superstitious worship of vain gods. Miserable it is to live in a barbarous state and with savage manners: but more miserable to lack the knowledge of that which is highest, and to dwell in ignorance of the one true God. Considering these things, therefore, in his mind, he sought first of all to extend the Christian name and the benefits of Christian charity to the West, as is abundantly proved by the history of the whole undertaking. For when he first petitioned Ferdinand and Isabella, the Sovereigns of Spain, for fear lest they should be reluctant to encourage the undertaking, he clearly explained its object: "That their glory would grow to immortality, if they resolved to carry the name and doctrine of Jesus Christ into regions so distant." And in no long time having obtained his desires, he bears witness: "That he

implores of God that, through His Divine aid and grace, the Sovereigns may continue steadfast in their desire to fill these new missionary shores with the truths of the Gospel." He hastens to seek missionaries from Pope Alexander VI, through a letter in which this sentence occurs: "I trust that, by God's help, I may spread the Holy Name and Gospel of Jesus Christ as widely as may be." He was carried away, as we think, with joy, when on his first return from the Indies he wrote to Raphael Sanchez: "That to God should be rendered immortal thanks, Who had brought his labors such prosperous issues; that Jesus Christ rejoices and triumphs on earth no less than in Heaven, at the approaching salvation of nations innumerable, who were before hastening to destruction." And if he moved Ferdinand and Isabella to decree that only Catholic Christians should be suffered to approach the New World and trade with the natives, he brought forward as reason, "that he sought nothing from his enterprise and endeavor but the increase and glory of the Christian religion." And this was well known to Isabella, who better than any had understood the great man's mind; indeed it is evident that it had been clearly laid before that most pious, masculine-minded, and great-souled woman. For she had declared of Columbus that he would boldly thrust himself upon the vast ocean, "to achieve a most signal thing, for the sake of the Divine glory." And to Columbus himself, on his second return, she writes: "That the expenses she had incurred, and was about to incur, for the Indian expeditions, had been well bestowed; for thence would ensure a spreading of Catholicism."

In truth, except for a Divine cause, whence was he to draw constancy and strength of mind to bear those sufferings which to the last he was obliged to endure? We allude to the adverse opinions of the learned, the rebuffs of the great, the storms of a raging ocean, and those assiduous vigils by which he more than once lost the use of his sight. Then in addition were fights with savages, the infidelity of friends and companions, criminal conspiracies, the perfidy of the envious, and the calumnies of detractors. He must needs have succumbed under labors so vast and overwhelming if he had not been sustained by the consciousness of a nobler aim, which he knew would bring much glory to the Christian name, and salvation to an infinite multitude. And in contrast with his achievement the circumstances of the time show with wonderful effect. Columbus threw open America at the time when a great storm was about to break over the Church. As far, therefore, as it is lawful for man to divine from events the ways of Divine Providence, he seemed to have truly been born, by a singular provision of God, to remedy those losses which were awaiting the Catholic Church on the side of Europe.

To persuade the Indian people to Christianity was, indeed, the duty and work of the Church, and upon that duty she entered from the beginning, and continued, and still continues, to pursue in continuous charity, reaching finally the furthest limits of Patagonia. Columbus resolved to go before and prepare the ways for the Gospel, and, deeply absorbed in this idea, gave all his energies to it, attempting hardly anything without religion for his guide and piety for his companion. We mention what is indeed well known, but is also characteristic of the man's mind and soul. For being compelled by the Portuguese and Genoese to leave his object unachieved, when he had reached Spain, within the wall of a Religious house he matured his great design of meditated exploration, having for confidant and adviser a Religious -- a disciple of Francis of Assisi. Being at length about to depart for the sea, he attended to all that which concerned the welfare of his soul on the eve of his enterprise. He implored the Queen of

Heaven to assist his efforts and direct his course; and he ordered that no sail should be hoisted until the name of the Trinity had been invoked. When he had put out to sea, and the waves were now growing tempestuous, and the sailors were filled with terror, he kept a tranquil constancy of mind, relying on God. The very names he gave to the newly discovered islands tell the purposes of the man. At each disembarkation he offered up prayers to Almighty God, nor did he take possession save "in the Name of Jesus Christ." Upon whatsoever shores he might be driven, his first act was to set upon the shore the standard of the holy Cross: and the name of the Divine Redeemer, which he had so often sung on the open sea to the sound of the murmuring waves, he conferred upon the new islands. Thus at Hispaniola he began to build from the ruins of the temple, and all popular celebrations were preceded by the most sacred ceremonies.

This, then, was the object, this the end Columbus had in view in traversing such a vast extent of land and water to discover those countries hitherto uncultivated and inaccessible, but which, afterwards, as we have seen, have made such rapid strides in civilization and wealth and fame. And in truth the magnitude of the undertaking, as well as the importance and variety of the benefits that arose from it, call for some fitting and honorable commemoration of it among men. And, above all, it is fitting that we should confess and celebrate in an especial manner the will and designs of the Eternal Wisdom, under whose guidance the discoverer of the New World placed himself with a devotion so touching. (Pope Leo XIII, *Quarto Abuente Saeculo*, July 16, 1492.)

A beautiful excerpt concerning Christopher Columbus is contained in a book, *Trials and Triumphs of the Catholic Church in America.* Columbus was concerned about the honor and glory of God and the saving of souls, which occupied his mind throughout the course of his initial voyage from Spain to the island of San Salvador:

The sun went down flaming into the vast and solitary ocean. Naught but the horizon on its pure azure appeared to the eye. No vapor indicated that land was near, but suddenly-- as if by inspiration--Columbus changed his course somewhat, and ordered the helmsman to steer due west. As the caravels came together, all joined, according to custom, in singing the Salve Regina--our familiar "Hail, Holy Queen!"--at the conclusion of which the admiral made them a touching discourse. He spoke of the mercy of that good God who had enabled them to reach seas never cut by keel before. He asked them to raise their hearts in gratitude, and vanquish their fears, that the fulfillment of their hopes was near at hand. That very night, he said, would see the end of their memorable voyage. He finally recommended all to watch and pray, as their eyes would behold land before morning.

At two a.m., by the clock of the Santa Maria, a flash came from the Pinta, followed by a loud report--the signal gun. It was no false alarm this time. Roderic de Triana, a sailor on the Pinta, had sighted land. Columbus, at the sound of the gun, fell on his knees and chanted the Te Deum; his men responded with full hearts. Then they went wild with joy. The admiral ordered the sails to be furled, and the ships to be put in a state of defense, for it was impossible to say what the daylight might reveal.

It was Friday, the 12th of October, 1492. Friday--the day of the Redemption--was always a blessed day for Columbus. On Friday he sailed from Palos, on Friday he discovered America; on Friday he planted the first cross in the New World; and on Friday he re-entered Palos in triumph. At dawn of this fateful day there was seen issuing from the mists, a flowery land, whose groves, colored by the first golden rays of the morning sun, exhaled an unknown fragrance, and presented most smiling scenes to the eyes. In advancing, the men saw before them an island of considerable extent, level, and without any appearance of mountains. Thick forests bounded the horizon, and in the midst of a glade shone the pure and sparkling waters of a lake. Green willows and sunny avenues gave half glimpses into these mysteries of solitude,   and revealed many a scattered dwelling, seeming by its rounded form and roof of dried leaves, to resemble a human hive, from which the curling smoke ascended in the air, greeting the glad sunbeams of that early hour.

When all was ready, the anchors were dropped, orders were given to man the boats, and Columbus, with majestic countenance and great recollection--as one who walked in the presence of God--descended into his own cutter. He was richly attired in the costume of his dignities. A scarlet mantle hung from his shoulders, and he held displayed in his hand, the image of Jesus Christ on the royal flag. The captains of the Pinta and Nina, Martin and Vincent Pinzon, likewise put off their boats, each accompanied by a well-armed detachment, and bearing the banner of the enterprise emblazoned with a green cross.

With mute delight, and all the elastic ardor of youth, the admiral stepped on shore. Scarcely had he touched the new land, when he planted in it the standard of the cross. His heart swelled with gratitude. In adoration, he prostrated himself before God. Three times bowing his head, with tears in his eyes he kissed the soil to which he was conducted by the divine goodness. The sailors participated in the emotions of their commander, and kneeling as he did, elevated a crucifix in the air. Raising his countenance towards heaven, the gratitude of his soul found expression in that beautiful prayer which has been preserved by history and which was afterwards repeated by order of the sovereigns of Castile in subsequent discoveries.

"Lord! Eternal and Almighty God! Who by that sacred word hast created the heavens, the earth, and the seas, may Thy name be blessed and glorified everywhere. May Thy Majesty be exalted, who has deigned to permit that by Thy humble servant, Thy sacred name should be made known, and preached in this other part of the world."

Standing up with great dignity, he displayed the standard of the Cross, offering up to Jesus Christ the first fruits of his discovery. Of himself he thought not. He wishes to give all the glory to God, and he named the island San Salvador, which means "Holy Savior." (*Trials and Triumphs of the Church in America*, as quoted in Adsum, a publication of Mater Dei Seminary, Omaha, Nebraska.)

The depth to which the Cross of the Divine Redeemer penetrated the soil of the lands of Latin America was such as to arouse the demonic fury of the adversary. This is why one of the immediate aftermaths of the American Revolution was the sending of Freemasonic emissaries to the countries of Central and South America to disseminate propaganda amongst the Catholics there that the Faith was the enemy of "civil liberty."

The first American ambassador to the independent country of Mexico, Joel R. Poinsset, promoted Freemasonry actively in Our Lady's country. Simon Bolivar, the "Liberator," was a Freemason. There were thus intense efforts to root out the Cross of the Divine Redeemer with violence throughout the lands that had been Catholicized some three centuries before. The United States of America was in the vanguard of exporting its "values" as the means of "liberating" supposedly "ignorant" people from the "tyranny" of "the priesthood and the sword." As was the case in Europe, Freemasonry had to attack the Church with violence head-on in Latin America precisely because of the fact that Christendom had   arisen there and souls were pursuing sanctity, not political ideologies or capitalist dreams of material wealth, as the means by which they would know an unending Easter Sunday of glory in Paradise.

Sadly, even many American Catholics, some of them professing allegiance to the Immemorial Mass of Tradition, believe that people in other countries are truly "liberated" by adopting "American values." The values of the United States of America, however, are not American. American culture is Catholicism. For there was a thriving Catholic America long before English and Dutch Protestants began settling in the land along the eastern seaboard of what became the United States of America.

The "values" of the United States are hostile to Catholicism.

They embrace religious indifferentism, egalitarianism and cultural pluralism as objective goods upon which can be built and maintained a just social order. They reject the necessity of belief in the totality of the Deposit of Faith that Our Blessed Lord and Saviour Jesus Christ has entrusted to His true Church as essential for personal and social order.

They reject the necessity of belief in, access to and cooperation with Sanctifying Grace as indispensable in the pursuit of personal virtue.

The "values" of the United States enslave man to his own disordered passions, convincing him that "civil liberty" defines his existence, not liberation from sin through the Sacrifice of the Cross of the Divine Redeemer, which sacrifice is perpetuated in an unbloody manner at the hands of priests in every offering of the Holy Sacrifice of the Mass.

There is not one part of our lives that is not meant to reflect the glories of the Catholic Faith. Not one.

There is not one aspect of national life (politics, the administration of justice, economics, education, literature, music, science, entertainment) that is meant to be untouched by the Catholic Faith. Not one.

There is never a moment in which we are called to be silent about the Holy Faith. Not one.

There is never a time in which we are called to refrain from exhorting all of those outside of the Catholic Church to convert.

There is never a time in which we are called to refrain from publicly extolling the Holy Name of the Mother of God.

There is never a time in which we can discuss any issue of public policy without mentioning the cornerstone of the Social Teaching of the Church, the Social Reign of Christ the King.

There is never a time in which we are called to do anything other than what the saints have done: profess the Catholic Faith openly and unapologetically at all times in everything we say and do and think.

We must think as Catholics, not as Freemasons or conservatives or liberals or Democrats or Republicans or libertarians or capitalists or socialists or communists or nihilists.

We must pray as Catholics, spending much time before the Blessed Sacrament and pledging ourselves in total consecration to Our Blessed Lord and Saviour Jesus Christ through the Sorrowful and Immaculate Heart of the Blessed Virgin Mary.

Christopher Columbus himself, filled with a bit of pride following his initial discoveries and conquests, implored the help of Our Lady to keep him humble, vowing before undertaking his second voyage to name more places in America after various shrines named in her honor in Spain:

> But before he could go on his voyage, Columbus had first to fulfill the vows made on board the Nina. In June, therefore, he went to the shrine of Guadalupe [in Spain]. He carried a five-pound wax taper and went clad in the simplest garments. For three hours he knelt in the dusk of the shrine, praying, shedding the pride which had come upon him, in homage to the Virgin. "Blessed Mother," he prayed, "intercede in my behalf. Do not let us fail. Pray for us that we shall be the vessels through which the word of God reaches those across the western sea."
>
> One after another Columbus fulfilled the promises he had made to God. Then he turned to Cadiz, that white city down the coast from Palos, from which the second voyage was to start out.
>
> There in the harbor of Cadiz the ships were being assembled. Once more the Nina was among them. And again the biggest ship was named the Santa Maria. Slowly the fleet grew until there were seventeen caravels in all. Seventeen crews were recruited to man the ships. Doctors, soldiers, craftsmen--200 volunteers eager to search for gold--all came to Cadiz to set sail with the Very Magnificent Lord Don Christopher Columbus.
>
> On the morning of September 24 [in 1493] the fleet sailed out of Cadiz into the no longer unknown west. In Columbus humility vied with pride.
>
> Early in the morning of November 3, a lookout sighted land. Columbus immediately named the new island Dominica and called together all hands to offer up a prayer of thanksgiving. The crews sang hymns in their gratitude for an easy, rapid passage across the ocean.

Then there began a journey of exploration among many islands. Columbus named them--at first with devotion to the Virgin Mary and her shrines--Santa Maria de Guadalupe, Santa Maria de Monserrate, Santa Maria de la Nieve, Santa Maria la Antigua; then with other names he thought fitting--Santa Cruz, The Virgins, St. John the Baptist. (August Derleth, *Columbus and the New World*, Vision Books, Farrar, Straus and Cudahy, 1957, pp. 140-142.)

Christopher Columbus made sure that we would know that which Our Lady herself ratified twenty-eight years after that second voyage of Columbus in the year 1493: The Americas Belong to Our Lady. We must never forget this fact. We must proclaim it openly. Every country on the face of this earth must acknowledge Christ as King and Mary as its Immaculate Queen.

The Americas do indeed belong to Our Lady: There is a hideous shrine to the Masonic notion of "liberty" that stands in New York Harbor. It is, of course, called the Statue of Liberty, exalted even today by some traditionally-minded priests as a beacon of "hope" and a sign of the "greatness" of the United States of America as a land of liberty. Sure, this is a land of liberty, a land of false liberties such as "freedom of speech" and "freedom of the press" and "freedom of religion" that have been condemned by true pope after true pope and that helped to pave the way for the triumph of the spirit of the heresy of Americanism at the so-called "Second" Vatican Council, especially in *Gaudium et Spes* and *Dignitatis Humanae*, both of which were issued on the last formal day of that false council, December 7, 1965.

Bishop Donald Sanborn pointed out the Masonic nature of this country's shrine to false notions of liberty in *The Cult of Liberty*:

> One of the many proofs of Freemasonry's cult of liberty, and furthermore of its deep influence upon our culture and mentality, is the Statue of Liberty. This colossus in New York's harbor was conceived by Freemasons, financed by Freemasons, built by Freemasons, and installed by Freemasons in a Freemasonic ceremony.
>
> The maker of the statue was Freemason Frédéric-Auguste Bartholdi. He had already made a statue of the Freemason Marquis de Lafayette for the city of New York, for the occasion of the centenary of the signing of the Declaration of Independence.
>
> Bartholdi sailed to America, at the suggestion of other Freemasons and kindred spirits in France, for the purpose of proposing the project. Although he had no drawings as he set sail, his masonic biographer says that, as he entered New York harbor, "he caught a vision of a magnificent goddess holding aloft a torch in one hand and welcoming all visitors to the land of freedom and opportunity."
>
> Returning to France, he managed to raise, through the help of a great deal of masonic propaganda, the sum of 3,500,000 French francs, a very large sum for the period of the 1870's. For the face of his "Goddess of Liberty" he chose his own mother. The structural framework was provided by Freemason Gustave Eiffel, later to be famous for the 984-foot Eiffel Tower.
>
> Although financial support for the statue was forthcoming in France, America was not willing

to put up the money for the pedestal. It was Joseph Pulitzer, the owner and editor of the New York World, who managed to raise over $100,000 for the project.

On Washington's Birthday in 1877, Congress accepted the statue as a gift from the French people. Bedloe's Island, now Liberty Island, was chosen by General Sherman, the well-known Atlanta-burner. Meanwhile in Paris the work gradually progressed. Levi P. Morton, the then Ambassador to France, drove the first rivet. The statue was finished on May 21, 1884, and presented to Ambassador Levi Morton on July 4th of the same year by Ferdinand de Lesseps, builder of the Suez canal.

On the American side, the chairman of the American committee to receive the statue contacted the Grand Lodge of the Free and Accepted Masons of the State of New York. It had been a tradition in America to have the cornerstone of major public and private buildings and monuments "consecrated" with full Masonic rites, ever since Freemason George Washington, in 1793, had personally laid the cornerstone of the Capitol, with the assistance of the Grand Lodge of Maryland. The cornerstone of the Washington Monument was also laid in a Masonic ceremony.

The ceremony for the laying of the cornerstone was set for August 5, 1884. It poured rain. The decorated vessel Bay Ridge carried about a hundred Freemasons, along with some civil officials to Bedloe's Island. Freemason Richard M. Hunt, the principal architect of the pedestal, handed the working tools to the Masonic officers.

Then Freemason Edward M. L.. Ehlers, Grand Secretary and a member of the Continental Lodge 287, read the list of items to be included in the copper box within the cornerstone: A copy of the United States Constitution; George Washington's Farewell Address; twenty bronze   medals of Presidents up through Chester A. Arthur (including Washington, Monroe, Jackson, Polk, Buchanan, Johnson and Garfield, who were all Freemasons); copies of New York City newspapers; a portrait of Bartholdi; a copy of Poem on Liberty by E. R. Johnes; and a list on parchment of the Grand Lodge officers.

The traditional Masonic ceremony was observed. The cornerstone being found square, level and plumb, the Grand Master applied the mortar and had the stone lowered into place. He then struck the stone three times, and declared it duly laid. Then the elements of "consecration" were presented, corn, wine, and oil.

The "Most Worshipful" Grand Master then spoke a few words. He posed the question: "Why call upon the Masonic Fraternity to lay the cornerstone of such a structure as is here to be erected?" His answer was: "No institution has done more to promote liberty and to free men from the trammels and chains of ignorance and tyranny than has Freemasonry."

The principal address was given by the Deputy Grand Master: "Massive as this statue is, its physical proportions sink into comparative obscurity when contrasted with the nobility of its concept. Liberty Enlightening the World! How lofty the thought! To be free, is the first, the noblest aspiration of the human breast. And it is now a universally admitted truth that only in proportion as men become possessed of liberty, do they become civilized, enlightened and useful."

The statue arrived in dismantled pieces in June of 1885. The statue was dedicated on October 28, 1886. President Grover Cleveland (Freemason) presided over the ceremony and Freemason Henry Potter, Episcopal Bishop of New York gave the invocation. Freemason Bartholdi pulled the tricolor French flag off the statue's face. The main address was given by Freemason Chauncey M. Depew, a United States Senator. (Bishop Donald Sanborn, *The Cult of Liberty*, published originally in the Spring 1995 issue of *Sacerdotium*.)

The Statue of Liberty is indeed a shrine to the false, naturalistic, religiously indifferentist and semi-Pelagian principles of the founding of the United States of America.

The framers of the Constitution of the United States of America believed that it was possible to realize personal and social order absent a due submission in all that pertains to the good of souls to the Deposit of Faith that Our Blessed Lord and Saviour Jesus Christ has entrusted exclusively to His Catholic Church for Its eternal safekeeping and infallible explication.

The framers of the Constitution of the United States of America believed that it was possible for men to be virtuous on their own without any belief in, access to or cooperation with Sanctifying Grace.

Many of the men who founded this nation had great contempt for Our Blessed Lord and Saviour Jesus Christ and for His Most Blessed Mother, Mary our Immaculate Queen, and for our Holy Mother Church. No one who hates Our Lord and His Most Blessed Mother is a person we can exalt and praise. The "ideas" of such agents of the devil are meant to convince men that "they" can organize themselves and their nations without reference to Christ the King and His true Church. This is a lie, and anyone, priest or layman, who does not recognize this is surrendering himself to nationalistic myths that are the antitheses of the authentic Social Teaching of the Catholic Church and of genuine notions of patriotism that are, after all, to prompt us to seek the good of our nation, the ultimate expression of which is her complete conversion to the Catholic Church by means of recognizing and submitting to the Social Reign of Christ the King.

What should be standing in New York Harbor? You know, don't you? Don't you? Of course you do. Think about it.

What should be standing in New York Harbor is a beautiful, glorious statue of Our Lady of Guadalupe, she who is the Patroness and the Empress of the Americas.

The Americans truly belong to Our Lady. This does not simply mean that we are to have a pious devotion to Our Lady of Guadalupe as the Patroness and Empress of the Americans and to Our Lady under the title of her Immaculate Conception as the Patroness of the United States of America. No! A thousand times no! This means that we are to attempt to plant the seeds for what Our Lady wants, namely, the conversion of each nation in the Americas to the Catholic Faith, and the United States of America is not an exception to the work that began when she appeared to a simple fifty-five year-old Indian man named Juan Diego four hundred seventy-nine years ago now. The conversion of between nine and thirteen million indigenous peoples what in we call Latin America now within a short time after Our Lady left that miraculous image of herself on Juan Diego's tilma on this very day in the year 1531 was meant to presage the conversion of all peoples and all nations of the Americas to the Catholic Faith without any exception whatsoever.

We need to ask Our Lady to be made as simple and as trusting as Juan Diego, the mere peasant to whom she condescended to appear to bring about the conversions of millions upon millions of Indians in the Americas at the same time as millions upon millions of Catholics in Europe were abandoning the Holy Faith to plunge themselves headlong into the demonic errors of the Protestant Revolution. It is indeed the case that Our Lady chooses the lowly and those who count for nothing in this world to show forth her Divine Son's bountiful mercy for the race He redeemed by the shedding of every single drop of His Most Precious Blood on the wood of the Holy Cross.

Juan Diego was chosen to be the human instrument through which Our Lady could replicate the spirit of Christendom in the Americas that was in the process of disintegrating in Europe.

Who is this Juan Diego? It is necessary to focus on this simple peasant who had a deep and abiding humility and sense of lowliness to understand why Our Lady chosen to appear to him and to leave on one of his few possessions, his tilma, her miraculous image to effect the conversion of the Americas:

> Long, long ago, there dwelt in a little Mexican village, Cuautitlan, a poor Aztec Indian whose name was Juan Diego. At least, that is what the Spaniards, who had then recently come to Mexico for the first time, always called him, and it is the name by which he has been known ever since. It is much easier to remember and to pronounce than his Indian name, which was Cuatitlatuoatzin. So it is the name I shall use in telling his story.

> The situation in Cuautitlan, his birthplace, is beautiful. In the distance, misty blue mountains rise toward the soft blue sky and green hills slope upward from the green plains to meet them. The growth of cactus is luxuriant on these slopes, and it furnishes both solid and liquid nourishment to the people who live among it. They have always been hard-working people, and in the time of Juan Diego they had no beasts of burden to help them with their work. When the Spaniards first came to Mexico there were no cows in the country, no sheep or horses, they brought all these useful domestic animals with them. But at first they had barely enough for themselves, and they had no dispensation to share them with the Indians in any case. It did not trouble them to think that the Indians worked hard and that the only animals the conquerors discovered in the villages were queer dogs, unlike any they had ever seen before.

> Juan Diego was one of the most hard working men of Cuautitlan. He belonged to the class known as mazohuales, the poorest and humblest of all the Indians. So his little home was poor and humble like himself. Its walls were made of dried mud and its roof was thatched with cornstalks and there was one small windowless room in it. In the daytime, the door was uncovered, so that the warm Mexican sun might stream in, but at night Juan Diego hung a straw mat called a petate in front of it to keep out the cold, which in this country comes quickly after the brief twilight.

> Though he had few possessions, there were several petates among them. They could be put

to various useful purposes besides keeping the cold from the door. For instance, they could be laid on the ground as a rug or a mattress; they were akin to the cloaks, also made of straw, which could be wrapped about the person, as an outer garment, when the rain pelted down or the wind blew fiercely. The other garments which Juan Diego had did not suffice to shield him from the wind and rain. He wore trousers and a shirt made of coarse colorless cotton, and over these, sometimes, two long pieces of cloth called ayate--woven from ichti, the fiber of the cactus plant--which were joined in a straight seam and together called a tilma. The ends of this tilma were knotted together at the back of the neck, and when not in use, it hung straight down in front, like an apron or a scapular. When Juan Diego held it up, it served as a bag in which to carry food and wood and tools, and when he twisted it and wrapped it around his shoulders, it served as a cloak, which shrouded his slight figure. He was a small man and his features were far less fierce than those of the Indians whom the French and Indian settlers found farther north. His habits were not warlike, either. His bronzed face was friendly and his harmless ways were trustful toward others. There was reserve and resignation in his look. His bearing was humble, and when he walked he was inclined to stoop and shuffle.

The garments worn by Juan Diego's wife, whom the Spaniards called Maria Lucia, were gayer than his. She was clever in the use of cochineal, and with the juice extracted from this insect she colored her full petticoats a beautiful clear red. Sometimes she used other dyes, blue and green, which were made with vegetables instead of insects and which gave a fine color, too. She embroidered the blouses that hung straight down over her skirts and the square pieces of cloth with which she covered her head. She wore her hair in two long braids, with the part between them running all the way from her forehead to the nape of her neck. The braids were glossy and thick, for her hair, like her eyes, was beautiful. In manner she was gentle and there was dignity in her carriage and her movements. When she carried a jar on her head, it seemed to become a part of her figure. When she was still, she gave repose to her surroundings. It is the way of Indian women.

Because she and Juan Diego were so poor, Maria Lucia would not have as many ornaments as most of her neighbors, only earrings and a necklace, instead of many chains and beads. Her ornaments were made of a green stone, not unlike jade in color and texture, and shaped to form tiny figures strung together. But she was satisfied with these and with the bright garments which she wove and dyed and embroidered herself. Her loom stood in the corner of her little home, near the pots where she kept her dyes. She had other pots, too, which she used for containers and cookery--large round jarros and cazuels, besides the shallow comales, in which she made tortillas. Even when the times were at their hardest, Maria Lucia made tortillas, taking the dough into which maize had been ground, after boiling, and patting this dough between her palms before baking it on her clay griddle. If times were better, she folded meat and red peppers into the tortillas, changing their shape from flat cakes into turnovers, wrapped them in corn husks, and boiled them. When they were thus transformed, they were called tamales and were considered a great treat. Maria Lucia could cook frijoles, too, so that they tasted better than any beans in the village. At least her husband told her so, and it pleased her to believe him.

Juan Diego himself raised the beans and the corn and the chili which Maria Lucia prepared with such skill. It was on these foodstuffs that they lived, for the most part, through sometimes they had venison and wild turkey, too, when Juan Diego had time to hunt these, for both were abundant. So was a specimen of wild pig, that this did not have flesh that was toothsome, and it was covered with quills, like a porcupine. After he and his wife had eaten the flesh of a deer, Juan saved the skin for sandals, which he called huaraches. He was clever in fashioning these, and he wore them when he walked on rough ground, though Maria Lucia went barefoot about the house and the terrain on which it stood.

Though they lived so simply, Juan Diego and Maria Lucia were cleanly in their habits. Near their home was a little hut used as a bathhouse. It was called a temazacal. In this hut was a large pile of stones which they heated until it was almost red hot, then they placed sweet-smelling herbs which had been crushed among the stones and poured water over the whole. A vapor rose after that, filling the little hut with steam and scent, and this vapor formed the bath which the Indians loved and used. In villages like Cauatutilan they do so to this day.

The life of Juan Diego and Maria Lucia was very uneventful. Occasionally, ritualistic or popular dances took place to the accompaniment of a tambour called a teponaxtle, and to strains of singing and wailing. But these celebrations, in a village as poor as Cuatutitlan, were infrequent, and there were few others, except at weddings. So when the missionary brothers, who were called Frailes, appeared among the inhabitants, this marked a great occasion in their lives. The Frailes celebrated Mass on the tops of Aztec pyramids and other high places where the people could look up to see the ceremony, for such elevations were impressive and aroused admiration. They also made free use of music, which they knew the Indians loved. Furthermore, they gathered men and boys together in groups and taught them. The taught them Spanish first of all, and themselves learned the different Indian dialects so that there might be mutual understanding. Then they taught many useful arts and crafts, to help the Indians in the cultivation of their land and the care of their homes and the fashioning of their garments. The Frailes were practical in their purposes no less than lofty, and by such means they tried to prepare the Aztecs for the Gospel they ardently desired to preach.

Among the very first of the Indians who dared to signify this desire was Juan Diego and Maria Lucia. The Spaniards had been in Mexico only three years when they were baptized. And after this they went regularly to Mass, though it was not easy for them to do so. There was no church in Cuautitlan. The nearest was the one built by the Franciscans in connection with the Convent at Tlaltelolco, which was fifteen miles away even by the short cut over the hills which made up the range of Tepeyac. Although they walked rapidly, like all Indians, and were adroit in finding their way across stony land and marsh ground, it took them two hours or more to make the trip. They had to rise long before dawn, in order to reach Tlaltelolco in time for Mass. They were not allowed to be late for this. They were required to be in their seats before the services began, for it was the habit of the priests to count their congregations and call upon each worshiper to answer to his name. This was in order that they might be sure there were no backsliders, that none was missing from his appointed place.

For a long time Juan Diego and Maria Lucia were never missing. But at last the time came when Juan followed the rough road and answered the brief roll call alone. Maria Lucia had died, leaving no child behind her. There was no one with Juan now in the little hut and the dye hardened in the pots. There was silence in the room, instead of the pleasant sound that a woman makes when she moves quietly about on her appointed tasks. And there was silence in Juan's heart, instead of the music that had been there for so long. He was very lonely, and his life was empty of tenderness and love and all that had given it beauty.

If he had been a young man, this would not have been so hard for him to bear. There is a hopefulness which is a part of the heritage of youth and which neither death nor desolation can wholly kill. Even when it seems crushed, it rises again, it is a wellspring. But with maturity, this hopefulness becomes less vital; and with advancing years, it altogether declines, unless something happens to give it new strength.

The years passed, and nothing gave new strength to the hope of regained happiness which Juan had almost lost. He had reached the age of fifty-five and he saw only more loneliness and more silence stretching out before him: no renewal of beauty, no prospect of reward. And still he did not fail to keep his tryst and cling to his faith. He continued to rise, before the starlight had faded, and make his way over the hills, in order that he might worship God in spirit and in truth and pay the tribute of his deep devotion to the Queen of Heaven.

It was increasingly difficult for him to make the journey, although he did not have as far to go as he had in the beginning. He had left Cuautitlan, where the silences had become unbearable to him, and had gone to live in another village, called Tolpetlac, which was closer to Tlaltelolco. He had an uncle living in Tolpetlac, whose name was Juan Bernardino, and near this uncle's home he built himself another little hut, under the shadow of a hill. The countryside was less wide and open here than in the place where had had lived before, but it was green and friendly and productive, too. It took him only a short time, not more than five minutes, to reach his uncle's home from his own, so it was possible for them to be a great deal together. He was fond of Juan Bernardino, who always made him welcome and who was a good man, a believer, like himself, in the teaching of the Frailes. In a way his uncle took the place of a father in his life. But no one took the place of Maria Lucia.

He dwelt on this sadly, as he went painfully over the hills to Mass one Saturday in early December. The stones on the path hurt his feet, piercing through his leather sandals; the cold wind penetrated his coarse clothing. He wrapped his tilma more and more closely about him. But it was not enough. He could not control his shivering by the time he reached the summit of Tepeyac.

It was always a bleak and barren place. But never before had it seemed as bleak and as barren as it did now, when he reached it with heaviness in his heart and sorrow in his soul. Then he stopped, suddenly astounded. For the silences were filled with music. The darkness was flooded with light, and out of the distance came a gentle voice, calling him tenderly by name. (Frances Parkinson Keyes, *The Grace of Guadalupe*, published in 1941 by Julian Messner, Inc., pp. 17-29.)

This is quite a portrait of our seer, a simple, humble peasant who loved to go to the Holy Sacrifice of the Mass, a man who walked with his wife a total of thirty miles round trip just to do so. Juan

Diego was a man who moved closer to the Holy Sacrifice of the Mass once his dear wife, Maria Lucia, had died.

Quite apart from Juan Diego's humble bearing as he went about his business on a daily basis to give honor and glory to God, there is a very salutary lesson to be learned from Juan Diego's devotion to the unbloody re-presentation of Our Blessed Lord and Saviour Jesus Christ's Sacrifice of Himself to the Father in Spirit and in Truth on the wood of the Holy Cross in atonement for our sins.

Juan Diego's example teaches us that nothing is more important than assisting at Holy Mass. Nothing. Why is this lesson so difficult for Catholics to take to heart today? Why are we encumbered by attachment to a certain place or to certain conveniences? Why do we care so much about earthly possessions and our familiar surroundings. Everything around us is dust. It will perish just as surely as our bodies will turn back after our deaths into the elements from which they were made until they are resurrected and reunited with our souls on the Last Day at the General Judgment of the living and the dead. Why not make the same kind of sacrifices to move to where true priests offer Holy Mass, the perfect prayer? Imagine the merit that is lost today as Catholics who ought to know better make one excuse after another as to why it is "impossible" for them to rearrange their lives to be near Holy Mass. After all, a parent with grown children can do more for his children and grandchildren, if any, by assisting at Holy Mass and praying for them there than they can by their physical presence. Juan Diego teaches us that a simple heart yearns for the eternal joys that are contained within and foreshadowed by every true offering of Holy Mass.

The beautiful music that Juan Diego heard as he walked to Holy Mass on Saturday, December 9, 1531, was just a prelude to meeting the most beautiful creature he had ever seen, the very fairest flower of our race, Mary our Immaculate Queen, just a day after the Feast of her Immaculate Conception (which was celebrated variously as the Feast of her Immaculate Conception or as the Feast of her Conception, depending upon the local tradition in the centuries leading up to the solemn definition of this doctrine by Pope Pius IX in the Papal Bull *Ineffabilis Deus* on December 8, 1854). The late Frances Parkinson Keyes described the scene for us as it was recorded by contemporaries at the time it took place:

"It was Saturday very early in the morning"--the ancient chronicler relates--"and Juan went in search of Christian learning, as revealed through divine doctrine. When he reached the top of the hillock called Tepeyac, dawn was breaking; and thence he heard strains of music coming. It sounded like the song of rare and wonderful birds. For an instant the singing ceased, and then it seemed as if the mountains echoed with response. The song, very suave and delicate, resembled that of the Coyoliteototl and the Tzinizcan and other beautiful birds.

"Juan Diego stopped to look about him and said to himself, 'How can I be worthy of what I am hearing? Am I dreaming? Have I ceased to sleep? Where am I? Am I in the terrestrial Paradise, of which our elders told us? Am I already in Heaven?'

"He gazed about, looking toward the east, beyond the hillock, whence came the celestial song; and when suddenly this ceased and there was silence, this was followed by the sound of a voice which called to him, saying, 'Juanito, Juan Dieguito.' Then he ventured to pursue the sound.

"He was not in the least frightened. On the contrary, he was filled with gladness, as he went on up the hill to discover who was standing there serenely, and who motioned to him that he should approach. Once arrived within the radius of her presence, he greatly marveled at this, for there was something supernatural about it. Her garments were shining like the sun. The cliff on which she stood glittered with glory, like an anklet of precious stones, and illumined the earth like a rainbow. The mesquite, the prickly-pear trees, and the other scrubby plants growing there took on an emerald hue. Their foliage changed to turquoise and their branches and thorns glistened like gold.

"He bowed before her and hearkened to her words, which were gentle and courteous, spoken after the manner of those addressed to one greatly esteemed. She said, 'Juanito, the least of my sons, where art thou going?'

"He replied, 'My Lady and my Child. I must needs go to the church at Tlaltelolco, to study divine mysteries, which are taught us by our priests, the emissaries of our Lord and Saviour.' Immediately she resumed her discourse and revealed her sublime will.

"'Know and take heed, thou, the least of my sons, that I am Holy Mary, Ever Virgin Mother of the True God for whom we live, the Creator of all the world, Maker of Heaven and Earth. I urgently desire a temple should be built to me here, to bear witness to my love, my compassion, my succor and protection. For I am a merciful Mother to thee and to all thy fellow people on this earth who love me and trust me and invoke my help. I listen to their lamentations and solace all their sorrows and their suffering. Therefore, to realize all that my clemency claims, go to the palace of the bishop in Mexico and say that I sent thee to make manifest to him my great desire; namely, that in the valley a temple should be built to me. Tell him word for word all that thou hast seen and heard and admired. Be assured that I shall be grateful and that I will reward thee, for I will make thy life happy and cause thee to become worthy of the labor thou hast taken and the trouble thou performest to do that which I enjoin thee. Now thou hast heard all my bidding, least of my sons. Go and do thy utmost.'

"At this point he bowed before her and said, 'Lady, I go to do your bidding. As your humble servant, I take my leave of you.' Then he went on to accomplish her will, taking the causeway that leads directly to Mexico City. (Frances Parkinson Keyes, *The Grace of Guadalupe*, published in 1941 by Julian Messner, Inc., pp. 31-32.)

"Juanito, the least of my sons, where art thou going?" Doesn't this bring tears to your eyes?

Our Lady, the very Immaculate Mother of God, called Juan Diego the "least of her sons." This is what everyone in the Americas should desire to be called by Our Lady.

Where are we going with our lives? To strive for Heaven with every beat of our hearts, consecrated to the Most Sacred Heart of Jesus through the Sorrowful and Immaculate Heart of Mary? Or to immerse ourselves headlong in the midst of the world and its false attractions? Where are we going? Do we want Our Lady's help to make us as simple and trusting and humble as the Indian peasant named Juan Diego? Are we desirous of undertaking the work that Our Lady desires of us to sanctify our souls as members of the Catholic Church as we seek to spread devotion to her, particularly by means of her Most Holy Rosary and Brown Scapular of Mount Carmel and the Miraculous Medal and the Green Scapular and True Devotion to Mary as taught by Saint Louis Grignion de Montfort?

Juan Diego was desirous to do the bidding of Our Lady, determined to set out for Mexico City, which was as intimidating in his day as it is now to those who are visiting it for the first time. And he discovered, of course, that he was to be tested in his determination to obey Our Lady once he arrived at the palace of Fray (Bishop) Juan de Zumarraga:

> The causeway which Juan Diego took was the one by which the travelers entered from the north, and though there were few of these abroad at this early hour, their appearance was alien to him and added to his sense of strangeness. The looks which they cast in his direction, sometimes curious and sometimes condescending, discomforted him also. He was only too well aware of his coarse clothing and his shuffling gait. Only the conviction that he was charged with a sacred trust gave him the courage to persevere. He had no more hesitated to undertake his mission than he had doubted the reality of his blessed and beautiful vision. The Queen of Heaven, whom he had so long and so devotedly venerated from afar, had left the realm of Paradise, and on a rocky mountaintop had condescended to come close to him, heralded by song and surrounded by glory. She had done even more; she had made him her chosen messenger to approach a great dignitary and express her will. He could not fail her in so high a purpose.

> Having conquered his abashment and entered the city, he made his way without undue difficulty to the episcopal palace, which was located near the Zocalo and was not hard to find. Concealing his inner trepidation, he asked the servants whom he found stationed at the portal to take him at once to see the Bishop. He was told, not too discourteously, to sit down in the patio and wait; and presently a messenger returned, saying that His Excellency would deign to receive him. . . .

> From the beginning of his career in Mexico, he [Don Fray de Zumarraga] was outstanding for his apostolic zeal and for his sympathetic attitude toward the Indians. He became one of their warmest defenders against the forces which sought to exploit, oppress, and abuse them. If Juan Diego had only known how warm and tender a heart was beating under the brown robes of this personage whose penetrating eyes were fixed firmly upon him, his own frightened and fluttering heart would have been instantly calmed.

> As it was, the whole experience was terrifying to him. Mexico City, with its impressive size and incipient splendor, was unfamiliar ground. He had never before gone beyond Tlaltelolco, which stood on the outskirts and had remained essentially an Indian settlement; there when he left his own people he moved only among the friendly Friars, whose cool conventual corridors were as bare as his own home and whose hands were active in healing hurts. He was the element product of a small village, accustomed only to this and

to other villages akin to it, to the simple folk that peopled them, to the open plains that lay about them and the rugged hills that rose above them. The blue and distant mountains, the still bluer and more distant skies, seemed less remote to him than did this capital of the Conquistadores. The episcopal palace, with its high walls and its succession of stately apartments, was overpowering, too. Never before had he beheld such furnishings, such draperies, and such adornments as were there. The servants who were lounging about the entrance, eying him suspiciously from the first and taking no trouble to conceal the scorn in which they beheld him, made him conscious of their mockery and their contempt. He smarted under it. In the audience chamber itself, the Bishop's entourage regarded him with condescension and the Bishop with courteous incredulity. He quailed before it. And still he persisted, thinking of the Lady he had seen and the goodness which shone through her glory.

He bowed and knelt before the Bishop. Then lest fright should overcome him before he could   accomplish his mission, he began, without preamble, to deliver the message with which he had been entrusted. He told everything that he had seen and heard, and, in his simple way, he tried to express his amazement and his admiration.

"I saw a great light shining behind the summit of the hill. I thought it was the sunrise. Instead, it was the Blessed Virgin."

The expression on the Bishop's face did not soften when Juan said this, as the Indian had hoped that it would. He felt instinctively that the prelate did not believe him, and he stumbled on, striving to clarify and convince. But he would not change the purport of his words, no matter how much he repeated them. Zumarraga had heard him, though. But when he stopped, inwardly and shamefacedly, the bishop raised a deprecating hand.

"You must come again, sometime, my son, when I can hear you more at my leisure. I will reflect on what you have told me, and I shall not fail to take into careful consideration both the good will and the earnest desire that caused you to come to me."

The Bishop made a gesture which the Indian realized was one of dismissal. He rose from his knees and turned away, sad in the knowledge that he had utterly failed in his mission. On his way out, he passed the condescending courtiers and the mocking servants again. Though he turned away his head, he could feel their scornful gaze upon him. He continued to feel it as he made his way slowly out of the city, sunk in the bitterness of defeat, and took again the causeway that led across the marshes north to Tepeyac. (Frances Parkinson Keyes, *The Grace of Guadalupe*, published in 1941 by Julian Messner, Inc., pp. 34-36, 37-38.)

Juan Diego thought that he had failed the Queen of Heaven. He had not done so. He did what he was instructed to do with proper fear and respect of the clerical authority possessed by Fray Don Juan de Zumarraga and the knowledge of his low social station. Do we stop to reflect, yes, if even for a moment, how we do indeed fail Our Lady by refusing to keep our promises to her? How many extra Rosaries that we promised to pray never get said? How many faults that we have asked her help to correct remain as ingrained in our lives now as they have been in the past because we have not sought to cooperate with the graces that she sends us. Juan Diego was shamefaced although he was on a mission given him by the very Mother of God herself. Are we ever ashamed of our interior lukewarmness or of our inconstancy in prayer and mortification and self-sacrifice? Ever? Just a little bit ashamed?

Juan Diego thought that he had failed Our Lady after his first visit to Fray Juan de Zumarraga in Mexico City to submit her request that a temple be built in her honor on Tepeyac Hill. Our Lady consoled him, telling him to persevere in the mission that she, the Queen of Heaven and of Earth, had entrusted to him, the most lowly of her sons:

> He went doggedly on until he reached the top of the hill. Throughout his misery, he never doubted that he would find the Queen of Heaven waiting for him in the same place that he had seen her before. It was this certainly which had upheld him throughout his hard climb. When he caught sight of her again, clad in her radiant robes and standing serenely above the rocks which she transformed, he quickened his pace and flung himself down before her.

> "Nina mia," he breathed. It was the greeting that he had used the first time, the same greeting that she had used in speaking to him. The literal meaning of it is "my child," but it is the form of address which for centuries in Mexico was customary for servants and other humble folk to employ in addressing their superiors, especially in rural regions. It denotes tenderness as well as respect. "My Lady, least of my Daughters and my Child," he continued, "I went where you sent me and obeyed your orders. I entered into the place which is the seat of the Bishop, though I did this with difficulty. I saw him and I delivered your message, exactly as you told me. He received me kindly and listened to me, but when he answered me, it seemed that he did not believe me. He said to me, 'You must come again sometime, my son, when I can hear you more at my leisure. I will reflect on what you have told me, and I shall not fail to take into careful consideration both the good will and the earnest desire that caused you come to come to me.' I understood perfectly, by the manner in which he replied, that he thinks that I am inventing the story of your wish to have a temple here, and that it is not a real order from you. So I beg you most earnestly, my lady and my Child, to send someone of importance, well known, respected, and esteemed, in order that he may be believed. For I am everything that is   mean and lowly, and you, my Child, the least of my Daughters and my Lady, you have sent me to a place where I have caused you great annoyance and disappointment as your messenger,   my Lady and my Mother."

> He was overcome with the sense of his own unworthiness. Now, having poured out his whole heart, there was nothing more he could say, and he waited with bowed head for her reply. But even before she answered him, he could feel the compassion of the Virgin, as it encompassed him with tenderness and healing.

> "Listen, the least of my sons," she said to him gently, "thou must try to understand that I have many messengers and servants whom I could charge with the delivery of my message and cause to do my will. But it is altogether necessary that that thou myself shouldst undertake this entreaty and that through thy own mediation and assistance my purpose

should be accomplished. I earnestly implore thee and definitely command thee to go again tomorrow to   the Bishop. Give orders in my name and let him know my whole will, which is that he should undertake the erection of the temple for which I ask. And go on to tell him that I, in person, Holy Mary, Ever Virgin, Mother of God, am she who sends thee."

Juan had begun to feel strength and courage flowing back into his brain and body like a warm flood. He was able to answer with a new ring of determination in his voice.

"My Lady and my Child, I will not cause you affliction. I will gladly go to accomplish your will. I will not cease from striving nor will I find the way too hard to do your bidding. But perhaps I shall not be graciously heard, and if I am heard, perhaps it will be without belief. I do not know. So tomorrow afternoon, when the sun is setting, I will come to give you a report concerning the reception of your message, together with an account of the Bishop's answer. With this assurance let me take my leave of you, my little Daughter, my Child, and my Lady. Rest quiet in the meanwhile, until I come again."

He bowed himself out of her presence. Then without looking back, he resumed the rough road over the mountains that led to Tolpetlac. When he reached the village, he went straight to his own home and himself laid down to rest.

He had need of this rest, for as usual it was very early in the next morning when he left his house the next day. The force of habit was too strong for him to break, and he first went directly to Tlaltelolco, to be present at the "count" to remain for Mass, and to receive instructions in Christian doctrine. But immediately afterward, he started in the direction of Mexico City. It was almost ten o'clock before he was under way, for on Sundays the "count" took longer than it did on weekdays. More people came to church, and when Mass was over they did not disperse immediately, but lingered around the great stone cross dominating the walled courtyard in front of the church. Here they exchanged greetings and items of interest w i t h   their neighbors before going to their separate homes, after the custom of church-goers the world over from time immemorial. In one way, Juan regretted his delay, for he had been sincere in saying that he would be proud in continuing to do the Virgin's bidding. Yet in a sense the delay was a respite. He had no delusions concerning the sort of reception that would be given him, and he could not wholly suppress his sense of dread at the prospect of seeing the Bishop's servants again.

As he anticipated, he experienced more difficulty in penetrating to the presence of this functionary than he had the first time. The servants put him off. "The Bishop was busy, they said" - he had retired for prayer and meditation, he was taking counsel with his advisers. The courtiers came and went, casting careless glances in the direction of the Indian as he waited patiently, hour after hour, in the patio, his tilma wrapped around him. But he declined to be cowed. And finally his persistency was rewarded. Grudgingly he was told that the Bishop had consented to see him briefly a second time.

He stood up well under the order of waiting. But when his vigil was over, something vital within him snapped. He did not have complete command of himself when tried to talk. Tears choked him, making him incoherent. Finally he cast himself at the Bishop's feet, wringing his hands imploring as he stammered out the hope that this time his message might be believed and that the will of the Immaculate might be accomplished through the erection of a temple in the place which she had designated.

"God grant that this may be done!" he cried over and over again.

The Bishop, who instinctively disliked undisciplined behavior, was less favorably inclined toward Juan than he had been the first time. Somewhat sternly he told the Indian that incoherency and importunity would avail him nothing; if he were to make himself believed, he must state facts briefly and answer questions meticulously.

Juan made a supreme effort. He understood the manner of his approach had prejudiced his cause and that he must manage to adapt his untutored ways to the formality of his surroundings and suppress his overflowing emotion in the presence of dignity and decorum. Forcing himself to assume at least the appearance of self-control, he waited respectfully for the Bishop to speak to him; then, he answered without evasion or hesitation. In the quiet repetition of his narrative, he retracted nothing that he had said before and was not confused by the cross-questioning. He steadfastly continued to repeat that he had seen the Virgin and had talked to her. In detail he described her appearance and the place where she stood. He reiterated that she had sent him to the Bishop to deliver a message and that he felt duty bound to do so. And again he insisted that the message related to the erection of a temple which must be built on Tepeyac.

Zumarraga, seeing him so unshaken, was inclined to temper his severity. But he was still disposed to believe that the Indian, though sincere, was suffering from some kind of delusion. He suggested, not unkindly, that Juan should return once again, and that on the occasion of his next visitation he should bring with him some kind of sign from the Queen of Heaven as proof that he was speaking the truth.

The Indian did not seem in the least disturbed by the suggestion. Indeed, he seized upon it with eagerness. His only query concerned the form that the Bishop desired to have it take.

"Sir, consider what this sign for which you ask should be, that I may go and ask it of the Queen of Heaven who sent me here."

It was Zumarraga's turn to be slightly nonplused. He had given no time to the considering of this aspect of the case and he was not prepared to say exactly what sort of sign would serve to convince him. He indicated that Juan was dismissed without giving him a definite answer. Then he ordered some of his people, in whom he had confidence, to follow after the Indian, carefully observing where he went, whom he saw, and with whom he talked. He spoke to them in Spanish lest Juan might be lurking close enough to overhear; presumably, an Indian would not regard eavesdropping as an indelicacy.

The Bishop's servants obeyed him with pleased alacrity. Their own curiosity was piqued, and as Juan retraced his footsteps and hurried along the causeway leading to the north, they followed closely after him. Indeed, for a long distance they kept at his heels. Then suddenly something inexplicable happened. As they neared the ravine beneath the bridge of Tepeyac, they were aghast at finding that he had vanished from their view.

They hunted far and wide, at first incredulously, then with the mounting anger of defeated purpose. There was, to be sure, a slight mist rising from the ravine and enveloping the road. Such a vapor was rare in a place where, as a rule, the air was clear as crystal under a bright blue sky. But it could not account, at least to them, for Juan's disappearance. Like many other men, before and since that time, they tried to put the blame for their own failure on the alleged trickiness of someone else.

They began by telling each other that the Indian was a charlatan and a fraud and that they had known it all the time; they could not understand why His Excellency should bother about such a low creature. Then they went trudging back along the causeway to Mexico City, hot and tired, dirty and disgusted, and said much the same thing to the Bishop. They told him that they were sure that the Indian was bent on deceiving him, that Juan had invented his story or based what he had told as true upon a dream; in either case he was merely a nuisance. In their opinion, if he returned, the Bishop should permit them to seize him and beat him, in order that he might learn better than to lie and cheat again.

Zumarraga, who was more and more inclined to reserve judgment, dismissed them without commitment, which added to their discomfiture. This would have been greater still if they had known how unperturbed the object of their displeasure was by their angry contempt. He did not doubt that the cloud which concealed him from his persecutors had been sent to envelop him by the Virgin, that they had once formed part of the aura which surrounded her, and that when he had ceased to have need of them, they would again be wafted away to celestial heights. Meanwhile, without obscuring his accustomed path, they veiled it in ethereal beauty. He reached the summit of the hill speedily and in safety, and once again told his story to the Radiant Lady who awaited him there.

Her answer came calmly and reassuringly, like everything else she had said to him. "So be it my son. Return here tomorrow, in order that thou mayest secure for the Bishop the sign for which he has asked. When this is in thy possession, he will believe thee; he will no longer doubt thy word and suspect thy good faith. Be assured that I shall reward thee for all that thou hast undergone. Go now. Tomorrow I shall await thee here again." (Frances Parkinson Keyes, *The Grace of Guadalupe*, published in 1941 by Julian Messner, Inc., pp. 39-44.)

We must believe that Our Lady will reward each of her consecrated slaves who must undergone hardship in her behalf in this passing, mortal vale of tears. The difficulties of the present moment--whether they be personal, social or ecclesiastical--will pass. Our Lady will reward even poor sinners such as us if we persevere until the point of our dying breaths in a state of Sanctifying Grace as members of the Catholic Church, outside of which there is no salvation and without which there can be no true social order. Those who may not believe us now about the necessity of referring all things to the true Faith or about the true state of the Church Militant during this time of apostasy and betrayal will believe us in the end. Our Lady will make right all of our stammering and stuttering efforts to defend the truth.

We must trust in her to do the bidding of her Divine Son, Christ the King. We cannot worry about who will not believe us in this life. It is enough that we attempt to maintain the Faith without making any concessions to conciliarism and its false doctrines and its offensive liturgical rites.

Our Lady came to Guadalupe to effect the conversion of peoples to the true Church, a goal that has been abandoned by the conciliarists in favor of "dialogue" and the "inculturation" of the very superstitious rites of pagan and barbaric peoples that Our Lady wanted eradicated in the Americas. It should teach us something about the state of apostasy and betrayal that is upon us at this time that the conciliarists exalt what Our Lady sought to eradicate; they forbid what Our Lady come to do, that is, to seek with urgency the unconditional conversion of non-Catholics to the true Faith.

The path on which we must trod to serve Our Lady is the same one that we must trod to save our immortal souls, that is, the rocky road that leads to the Narrow Gate of Life Himself, her Divine Son, Our Blessed Lord and Saviour Jesus Christ. And it was quite literally a rocky road that Juan Diego trod when he went to visit Our Lady atop Tepeyac Hill.

Anxious to care for his beloved uncle, Juan Bernardino, who appeared to be dying, Juan Diego could not keep his promise to visit Fray Juan de Zumarraga for yet a third time so that he could be informed of the specific sign that would be proof of Our Lady's apparition. He wanted to secure the Sacrament of Extreme Unction for his dying uncle, and thus tried to evade Our Lady as he did so on Monday, December 11, 1531:

> In his desperation, he felt that there was not a moment lost. If he went to the top of the hill, in accordance with his promise to the Lady, he felt that she would detain him by talking to him about the sign for the Bishop; she might even insist upon sending him to Mexico City with such a token, according to their original plan. And meanwhile Juan Bernardino lay dying. It seemed to Juan Diego that his duty was clear. He took a side road, skirting the hill at the east, his mind distracted by the sense of his uncle's extremity, his eyes fixed on the path that led to the home of the brothers with healing hands.
>
> "In his ignorance he thought that by taking a roundabout route he would be unobserved by her who sees everything," Valeriano [the contemporary chronicler of these events] tells us at this crucial point of the story. (How many there are, far less ignorant and far less conscientious, too, who have made this same mistake!) "But he saw her descend from the summit--where he had beheld her before. She came to meet him on the side of the hill and said to him, 'What is the matter, least of my sons? Where art thou going?' "
>
> He had failed her, but she did not fail him. Since he had not sought her on the heights, she had sought him in the depths. Shame and grief overwhelmed him, and with his shame and grief, fright was intermingled. In an endeavor to cloak this, he tried to speak to her lightly, using the familiar form of greeting in addressing her, asking if the morning found her well, and exclaiming, "God grant that you be content with me!" But the moment was too solemn for pleasantry, and almost instantly Juan was aware of this. He steadied himself and spoke more soberly.

"I am going to cause you grief," he said, "for I must tell you that a poor servant of yours, my uncle, is seriously ill. He has the plague and is about to die. I am now hurrying to your house to call one of the priests beloved by Our Saviour, in order that he may absolve my uncle after confession, for in the midst of life we are in death. But if I first succeed in doing this duty, I will return here later, to go and deliver your message. Forgive me, my Lady and my Child. Be patient with me, for the moment. I am not deceiving you, least of my Daughters. Tomorrow I will come in good season."

He saw that while he was laying his troubles before her and beseeching her sympathy and understanding she regarded him with infinite compassion, even greater than she had shown before. He knew that she needed no words of his to explain that he had been torn between two loyalties and that he had tried to do what was right, in so far as he knew what this was. She answered him, with supreme gentleness.

"Listen and take heed, least of my sons," she said quietly. "There is nothing which thou needst dread. Let not thy heart be troubled. Do not fear this illness, neither any other illness or affliction. Am I not here beside thee; I, thy Merciful Mother? Am I not thy hope and salvation? Of what more dost thou have need? Let nothing distress or harass thee. As to the illness of thy uncle, he will not die of it. Indeed, I ask thee to accept as a certainty my assurance that he is already cured." (Frances Parkinson Keyes, *The Grace of Guadalupe*, published in 1941 by Julian Messner, Inc., pp. 47-48.)

We are not to fear any illness or affliction. There is no suffering that we can bear in this life that is the equal of what one of our least Venial Sins caused Our Blessed Lord and Saviour Jesus Christ to suffer in His Sacred Humanity during His fearful Passion and Death as those Seven Swords of Sorrow were plunged through and through the Immaculate Heart of Mary.

Why do we fear a particular illness?

Why are we so upset about what others think about us or what they might think if we admitted to them that the conciliarists are imposters who do not hold their ecclesiastical offices legitimately?

Why do we fear the likes of Barack Hussein Obama or Harry Reid or Nancy Patricia D'Alesandro Pelosi?

Why?

How many people alive today know the names of Trajan or Valerian or even Diocletian, men who persecuted Catholics with particular ferocity?

Do we not know that the petty caesars of today will be consigned to the dustbin, the trash heap of history, that they will be mostly forgotten as pawns of the devil, who uses his minions in this life only to discard them as he mocks them for all eternity if they do not convert to the true Faith and repent of their crimes before God and men?

Why do we fear when Our Lady is so near? Why? Why believe in the absolute farce that is the naturalistic farce called partisan politics as the means to retard various social evils, including chemical and surgical baby-killing and the advances being made by the exponents of perversity? Can't Our Lady effect miracles today the way that she has done in the past? Indeed, haven't you--each of you--been the beneficiaries of abundant miracles of grace worked in your own lives and those of your family in members or acquaintances?

Shouldn't we be fortified by these words that Our Lady spoke to Juan Diego? He was! Why not us?

Again, he felt strength and courage coming back to him as he listened. Even his deep concern for his uncle was assuaged. If the Queen of Heaven told him that all was well with the old man, who was he to question that this was so? Penitently, he sought to prove that he believed her: he renewed his offer to go at once to the bishop, without stopping at Tlaltelolco, taking with him any sign which she might designate.

> She gave her instructions instantly. "Go my son, to the summit of the hill where I gave thee thy first orders. There thou wilt find a large variety of flowers. Gather them and assemble them. Then fetch them hither."
>
> "Juan Diego went immediately up the hill," Valeriano tells us. (Again I feel that it is his narrative that I should follow from afar, rather than attempt one of my own. For how could I hope to clothe such a lovely story in such lovely language?) "And when he arrived at the summit, he was astounded to find that quantities of exquisite Castilian roses had blossomed there, out of season, for at this time of year everything was frozen. They were very fragrant and covered with dewdrops, which looked like precious pearls. He began at once to pick them, making them into a cluster and taking them into his tilma. It was the more strange that he could do this, for the summit was strewn with rocks, thistles, thorns, prickly pears, and mesquite; and what vegetation there was did not flourish in the month of December, when all was destroyed with cold.
>
> "As soon as he had picked the flowers, he went down the hill again, taking to the Queen of Heaven the roses which he had gathered. When she saw them, she took them in her own hands, and rearranged them in her own hands, and rearranged them in his tilma, saying as she did so, 'Least of my sons, this cluster of roses is the sign which you are to take the Bishop. You are to tell him, in my name, that in them he will recognize my will and that he must fulfill it. You will be my ambassador, wholly worthy of my confidence. I enjoin you only that in the presence of the Bishop shall you unfold your mantle and disclose that which you carry. Omit nothing in the telling. Say that I ordered you to go to the top of the hill and that there you found flowers in abundance for gathering. And, furthermore, repeat the story of all you have seen and admired, so that you may induce the prelate to give his help, so that in the end that temple for which I have asked may be built.

"After the Queen of Heaven had given him these her orders, Juan took the road toward the causeway which leads directly to Mexico City. He was already tranquil and confident of a happy outcome, and he carried with great care the contents of his tilma, being watchful that nothing should slip from his hands and meanwhile rejoicing in the fragrance of the beautiful flowers.

"When he arrived at the palace of the Bishop, the prelate's major-domo and other servants came out to meet him. He asked them to say that he desired to see the Bishop. But none of them wished to do so. They acted as if they could not hear him, perhaps because they knew already that he would only annoy them with his importunities, and, furthermore, their companions had already told them that they had had the misfortune of losing him from view when they had gone to follow him. Accordingly, they made him wait for a long time. But when they saw how patiently he stood there, with hanging head, waiting to be called, and how closely he was guarding something that he seemed to be holding in his robe, they approached him, in order to find out what he had and satisfy their curiosity.

"When Juan Diego saw that he could not conceal the fact that he was carrying something and that on account of this burden the servants intended to molest him, shoving him about and striking him, he gave them a glimpse of what he had. Seeing that this was a great variety of Castilian roses and knowing that this was not the time when such flowers normally blossomed, the servants were greatly astonished, and all the more so because the flowers were in such full bloom and were so fragrant and so beautiful. Avidly they tried to snatch them away. But they met with no success, though three times they attempted to wrest them form him. Each time they sought to size the roses these no longer seemed to be growing flowers, but only something that had been sewn or embroidered or painted on the tilma of Juan Diego.

"Discomfited, they went to tell the bishop what they behold and to say that the Indian who had been there so many times before again wished to see him. When he heard this, the Bishop was convinced that they must have seen something of the sign which in its entirety would bear witness to that for which the Indian had asked. So he immediately ordered that Juan Diego should be brought into his presence.

"As soon as the man entered the room, he bowed down, as he had done before, and told the Bishop again everything that he had seen and heard, besides delivering his message. 'Your Excellency,' he said, 'I did that which you asked. I told my Mistress, the Queen of Heaven, Holy Mary, Mother of God, that you required a sign in order that you might believe what I had told you regarding the temple she enjoins you to build in the place she asks that you should erect it. And, furthermore, I said that I had given my word to bring here some sign and proof of her will, as you asked. She met your request and with graciousness accepted your condition concerning the sign you needs must have before her will might be accomplished. Very early this morning she told me to come to see you again. So I asked for the sign which would make you believe and which she has said she would give me. Instantly she complied with my petition. She sent me to the top of the hill where I had previously seen her point to pick Castilian roses. Although I well know that the summit of the hill is not a place where flowers grow, nevertheless I doubted nothing. And when I arrived at the top, I saw that I was in a terrestrial paradise, where every variety of exquisite flowers, brilliant with dew, flourished in abundance. These I gathered and carried back to her. With her own hands she arranged them and replaced them in my robe in order that I might bring them to you. Here they are. Behold and receive them.'

Until that moment, Juan had kept the folds of his tilma closely drawn, guarding his roses zealously. Now, with a sudden movement, he released them. They fell on the floor in a colorful cascade, scattering perfume about them. Looking down at them, he felt waves of exultation sweep over him. He had delivered his burden, he had accomplished his mission, he had fulfilled his trust. Like Saint Paul, he could declare with conviction, "I have kept the faith." It seemed the supremely glorious moment of his dreary and heavy-laden life.

But his triumph had not yet reaches its pinnacle. As he stood still, his heart pounding and his eyes fixed on the flowers, still bright with drew, that lay at his feet, he was suddenly aware that the Bishop had been moved by some miracle even greater than that of the roses. Zumarraga descended form his throne and dropped on his knees. His lips were parted in prayer, and in his eyes glistened tears, as bright as the dewdrops on the roses. His transfigured gaze was turned not downward but upward, and with astonishment that knew no bounds. Juan saw that this was fixed with fervor upon his own humble person. Increasingly bewildered, he himself glanced toward the tilma from which the mass of brilliant bloom had so recently been released.

Its coarseness was completely concealed. On it, in glorious tones, was painted the image of the Blessed Virgin, exactly as she had appeared to him on the heights of Tepeyac. (Frances Parkinson Keyes, *The Grace of Guadalupe*, published in 1941 by Julian Messner, Inc., pp. 48-52.)

Juan Diego was rewarded for the simple trust he put in the words of the Mother of God. Why do we doubt that that the words that Our Lady spoke so recently to the seers at Fatima are not going to be fulfilled? Do not we not realize that her Immaculate Heart will indeed triumph in the end? Again, I ask a simple question: why do we live in so much fear? Our Lady wins! Christ the King will be victorious through the Triumph of the Immaculate Heart of Mary. We just have to overcome our fallen natures, which are prone to worry in the midst of troubles, and ask Our Lady to make us as simple and trusting as Juan Diego himself. It's really that simple.

Perhaps a note of speculation is in order concerning the role that Juan Diego's deceased wife, Maria Lucia, may have played in these remarkable events.

To wit, I am prone to think that it was no accident that this great miracle that was made manifest on Tepeyac Hill occurred on December 12, 1531, the day before the feast of our dear Saint Lucy, that immovable foe of religious liberty. Our Lady, Mary of Nazareth, came to Tepeyac Hill to bring the light of the Holy Faith to the Indians of the Americas just as Saint Lucy, virgin and martyr, helps us to see our own lives and the events of the world more clearly by the light of that same Holy Faith. Perhaps--just perhaps, mind you--it was to honor the long years of devotion that Maria Lucia paid to her, the Mother of God, that Our Lady chose to manifest the great miracle of the Castilian roses and of her image on Juan Diego's tilma the day before the feast of Saint Lucy. Perhaps. Just perhaps.

Fray Juan de Zumarraga had a proper sense of awe and wonderment upon seeing the miraculous image of Our Lady on Juan Diego's simple tilma. Deo gratias! Here was a bishop willing to admit his errors and to repent of them! Deo gratias!

Only the ignorant and vainglorious assume that they are incapable of error; only the ignoble and the ungenerous are reluctant to acknowledge mistakes. Don Fray Juan de Zumarraga was a great gentleman as well as a great statesman and a great ecclesiastic. The revelation which had given such impetus to his faith and such force to his fervor did not render him oblivious of his obligations to the man whom he had humiliated by delay and wronged by distrust. His first act, when he rose from his knees, was to approach Juan Diego with outstretched hands and with every mark of courtesy make manifest his contrition for the ordeal for which his own incredulity has subjected the Indian. In the tone of one addressing an honored guest he asked Juan Diego to remain overnight at the palace. Early the next day, he said, they would go together to inspect the place where the temple should be built; meanwhile, he must insist that his visitor have rest and refreshment.

Having made his apology, extended his invitation, and given his essential promise, Zumarraga leaned over and, adroitly untying the knots of Juan's tilma with his long flexible fingers, lifted the transfigured garment from the Indian's neck and bore it away to his oratory, in order that he might contemplate it in prayerful seclusion. Juan himself was still too stunned to stir from the spot where he stood. It had been hard enough for him to grasp and absorb the miracle of the roses; confronted by another miracle, infinitely greater, he was stupefied with the shock. The fleeting sight of the Queen of Heaven had, in itself, been enough to beatify his life. The lasting imprint of her Sacred Image upon his own humble garment suffused his soul with such wonder and such awe that he could neither move nor speak nor collect his dazzled thoughts.

The followers of the Bishop had been swift to follow His Excellency's example. They too had fallen on their knees at the sight of the radiant painting; they too had shed tears and offered up prayers as they gazed at it. Indubitably, their amazement was genuine and their adoration spontaneous, but Juan would have been more than human if he had not felt a pang of pleasure at the consciousness that there was an element of fright in their astonishment, and if there had not been some secret scorn in his heart from the change in their attitude toward him. Only two days before they had not been content to deride and torment him; they had been bent on beating him before they chased him away. Now they fawned about him, desiring that he would deign   to notice them and striving to insinuate themselves into his good graces. Only his own essential humility and unfailing loving-kindness kept him from revealing the contempt they might logically have aroused.

Still bemused, he suffered himself to be led away from the audience chamber and to accept the accommodations and entertainment so prodigally offered him. But though his clarity of conscience eventually prevailed over his confusion of mind, he still did not feel reconciled to his resting place or at ease in his heart. His surroundings were too strange and his anxiety for his uncle was too great for that. Even if he had experienced no other emotional upheaval, these elements would have sufficed to disturb him; and, as it was, there was also too the supreme manifestation of the Virgin's grace to pervade and preoccupy his mind. He longed to consider it in private and at untroubled length, as the Bishop was now considering the tilma which had once been the Indian's own.

All this being so, Juan was thankful beyond measure when the morrow came and Zumarraga gave the signal for departure. Though he shrank before the size and importance of the gathering which had assembled to accompany them, there was relief in action and the recovery of familiar ground. Today no mist obscured his progress: the sun shone brightly and the mountains were white in the distance. Still, the crossing of the causeway was not rapid enough to suit him and the very barrenness of Tepeyac was beautiful in his sight. For this was the beginning of the road that would take him home, to the village which he knew and the uncle whom he loved, after his eyes had rested once more on the desert where he had gathered roses and the rocky ground which had served as a footstool for the Queen of Heaven.

Unhesitatingly, he pointed out the place where the glorious Lady had stood. The Bishop accepted the designation without question. Some sort of shrine, His Excellency assured the Indian, would be built there are once. Probably only a chapel or something of that sort, for the time being; possible a hermitage would best answer the purpose at first. Later on, of course, more elaborate plans could be made and executed.

This part of the program, as far as Juan was concerned, seemed relatively unimportant. It was not for him to decide what form the sanctuary should take. That must be left to the enlightened knowledge of those who were wiser than he. His own task, as he saw it, was ended. He had revealed the place of the Virgin's choosing, and he had received the assurance that her will should be accomplished there. This done, he humbly asked for permission to depart.

The Bishop graciously gave it. But he did not suffer the Indian to go alone. Instead, he designated other persons to accompany him, as an escort of honor. Juan Diego's arrival in Tolpetlac savored of a triumphal entry. Wondering crowds collected to hail, to stare at the strange Spaniards who followed in his train, and then to salute them. But he uncle was not only alive but also convalescent. The old man was sitting up in bed, and everything about his appearance indicated a substantial improvement in health and a lively interest in all that was happening about him. He was unfeignedly impressed by the company in which his nephew had returned; like most men living in small villages and in a simple fashion, it gratified him to see personages of importance congregating around his home. But he could hardly take time to listen to an explanation of the presence of these magnificent strangers before he launched upon an exciting narrative of his own.

Juan Diego had scarcely left him, he said, to fetch the priest who was to confess and absolve him than his painful stupor had been glorified by a miraculous vision: the Queen of Heaven, splendidly appareled, had appeared before him, and from the moment of her arrival he had felt himself cured. More than this: she had spoken words of comfort and encouragement to him. She had told him that she had sent his nephew into Mexico City, and why. He knew the whole story of the marvelous apparitions and the beautiful roses that had appeared in glowing colors on the coarse tilma. He knew that a temple was to be built at Tepeyac in honor of the Blessed Lady who wrought all these wonders. Yes, and there was still something. The same Blessed Lady had confided to him, Juan Bernardino, no less, the name which her image was to bear when it was suitably enshrined. It was to be called Santa Maria de Guadalupe Siempre Virgen.

So now he also had a message to give the Bishop. With his own lips he must tell His

Excellency about the benign visitation and above all about this important title. Unperturbed by any of the qualms which had caused his nephew to quail, he demanded to be borne to the episcopal palace.

Zumarraga, having taken due note of the significant situation at Tepeyac, had not gone on to Tolpetlac with the followers whom he had designated to accompany Juan Diego. Instead, with the rest of his retinue, he had returned to Mexico City, in order to put his plans for some sort of sanctuary into immediate execution. But the servants who had so impressed Juan Bernardino were, in their own turn, more and more awed. Far from trying to discourage the old man, they agreed with alacrity to take him to the Bishop's palace. A litter was improvised on which he could rest easily during the course of his journey. He was lifted into it with solicitude and carried away by careful stretcher bearers. With his nephew at his side and the Bishop's suite bearing up in the rear, he left his native village with even more pomp and far greater self-satisfaction than Juan Diego had anxiously entered it a few hours earlier.

There was no waiting about in the portal or the patio this time. The old man was promptly carried into the audience chamber and the Bishop rose to the occasion with complete savoir-faire. He expressed himself as being delighted to see them and assured both nephew and uncle that they were more than welcome. Indeed, he hoped that they would be his guests for several days--until such time, as a matter of fact, as he could complete the arrangements for the transfer of the miraculous image to Tepeyac. He listened with great attention to all that Juan Bernardino had to say and seemed especially impressed with the name which the Virgin had revealed as her choice. Juan Bernardino left the episcopal presence and retired to rest filled with gratification and heartfelt pleasure.

The Bishop's own reveries, however, were prolonged far into the night. He had already decided that he should not keep the miraculous painting concealed in his own private oratory any longer. Instead, he proposed to transfer it to the Cathedral where everyone could inspect it at will. There were many details about it which should be remarked. The seam that divided the two parts of the tilma, for instance, was still plainly visible. It ran straight through the Virgin's robe and along the sides of her folded hands, but it altogether escaped her blessed and beautiful face. The texture of the tilma was another matter of moment. Coarse material of this type, under normal circumstances, did not take or hold colors well, as any craftsman skilled in their use would readily testify, but these colors were fast and shining on both sides of the fabric. It was significant that the Virgin stood in the center of the crescent moon, but surrounded by the sun's rays, with clouds behind her and the firmament beneath her; it gave the symbolic effect of her sovereignty over both day and night, over both the heavens and the earth. Even the expression of the cherub with rainbow-tinted wings, who supported the figure of the Virgin, repaid scrutiny. It could be seen, upon investigation of this fortunate angel, that his happiness in bearing such a burden was amply apparent. The Bishop was confident that the populace would be much moved by the sight of such a picture and that great devotion would come of it. Indeed, in his opinion, it might mark the beginning of a new cult.

What a strange coincidence it was that Guadalupe should have been designated as the name for the image! Juan Bernardino was an ignorant man. It was beyond the realm of possibility, as the Bishop well knew, that he could ever have heard of the shrine by the same name so greatly revered in Spain and thus have drawn upon his own imagination in attempting to interpret a supernatural message. There might be other explanations for the designation. In the Nahuaatal language, Coatl was the word for serpent, Tlaloc was the one for goddess, and tlalpia the expression for watching over. By sliding the words together, as one naturally did in speaking, thus suppressing the sound of the tla, the three together became Coatalocpia, which had almost exactly the same sound as Guadalupe in Spanish. And in the churches which he frequented with his nephew, Juan Bernardino had certainly seen images of the Blessed Virgin in which she was represented as crushing a snake under her feet. It was not unnatural that she might have appeared to him as a "goddess watching over a serpent."

But after all, the name, like everything else, was part of an inexplicable but sublime pattern. Why seek for its sources? Was it not enough to know that it was settled and to go on from there?

Don Fray Juan de Zumarraga, first Bishop of Mexico, decided that it was. (Frances Parkinson Keyes, *The Grace of Guadalupe*, published in 1941 by Julian Messner, Inc., pp. 53-60.)

Yes, there is a lot to reflect upon in these passages from the late Frances Parkinson Keyes's *The Grace of Guadalupe*.

First, of course, there is the humility of Fray Juan de Zumarraga, the first Bishop of Mexico, in admitting that he was wrong, that he had dealt harshly with a chosen soul. He did not stand on the privileges that are those of one who possesses the fullness of the Holy Priesthood by taking refuge in the assertion that he had to be harsh with Juan Diego in order to test whether he was fabricating the story of having seen Our Lady atop Tepeyac Hill. No, there was instant repentance as he sought to do justice to Juan Diego by according him honors here on earth that he, Juan Diego, did not seek but were fitting for one who had been so honored by the very Mother of God herself.

Second, the processions that accompanied Juan Diego from Tepeyac to Tolpetlac and that took him back to Mexico City with his uncle, Juan Bernardino, are but foretastes of the processions that accompany the souls of the elect to Heaven after their deaths or after they have paid back the debt they owed God for their sins by being purified by the torments and fires of Purgatory.

These processions are also symbolic of the fact the all the souls of the Church Triumphant in Heaven and the Church Suffering in Purgatory are present with each of the nine categories of angelic spirits (Seraphim, Cherubim, Thrones, Dominions, Virtues, Powers, Archangels, Principalities and Angels) at every true offering of Holy Mass. Imagine being escorted by a company of angels as you receive Holy Communion! Actually, you don't have to imagine. They accompany us up to the Communion rail, a thought that should send shivers up our spines and cause us to reflect on how privileged we are to be Catholics.

Third, the miraculous nature of the image left by Our Lady on Juan Diego's tilma still defies scientific explanation. If you think about it, however, many scientists, especially those who believe in the junk science represented by the ideology of evolutionism, have yet to figure out that the world was created by God and is ordered down to its last detail by His own willing it so. Why should it amaze us that the miraculous image of Our Lady of Guadalupe on the tilma of her chosen soul, Juan Diego, is so rich and exquisite in the details of its beauty and brilliance to such an extent that rationalists in the various fields of science cannot accept the simple fact that God worked this miracle through His Most Blessed Mother?

Perhaps it is pertinent to note at this juncture that the public honor that Bishop Juan de Zumarraga knew had to be given to the Mother of God stands in stark contrast to the unwillingness of most Catholics in public life, including most of the conciliar "bishops," to mention anything about Our Lady in "mixed company." A lot of these "bishops," starting with the non-bishop who lives in the Casa Santa Marta, Jorge Mario Bergoglio/Francis, even omit references to Our Lady's Divine Son, Our Blessed Lord and Saviour Jesus Christ, in "mixed company." This has emboldened the forces of rank secularism to push ahead in their efforts to eliminate even the generic Judeo-Masonic references to God that have survived in popular culture, no less references to Our Lord Himself and/or to His Most Blessed Mother.

We are living through a period similar to the French Revolution or the Bolshevik Revolution or the Mexican Revolution or the Spanish Revolution wherein any public reference to or visible display of Christian symbolism is considered to be "offensive" to unbelievers. The difference between those revolutions and what is happening before our very eyes is that most Catholics are not in the least bit bothered by the removal of Christian symbolism or by the failure to reference Christ the King and Mary our Immaculate Queen in popular culture or social discourse on the issues of the day as they have been so brainwashed by the ethos of conciliarism that they cannot see the plain truth that the lords of Modernity have won them over to naturalism because of the counterfeit church of conciliarism's hypersensitivity to "inter-religious dialogue" and "diversity" as essential to "peace" within and among nations.

As noted before, the miracles wrought by Our Lady atop Tepeyac Hill on Tuesday, December 12, 1531, effected the conversion of between nine and thirteen million indigenous people in the Americas in a relatively short period of time. Our Lady has been intent in seeking the conversion of non-Catholics to the Faith. She is an enemy of the false ecumenism proclaimed and practiced by the conciliar "popes" and their "bishops."

The late Father Maximilian Kolbe, a Conventual Franciscan who became the founder of the Knights of the Immaculata whose cause for legitimate canonization will be, I believe, advanced rapidly after the restoration of the Church Militant on earth as he was a militant foe of all forms of naturalism as he promoted total Marian Consecration as the means to build up the City of Mary Immaculate (which w a s w hy, after all, the Nazis had imprisoned him in Auschwitz), explained the enmity that exists between false ecumenism and the Immaculata:

> "Only until all schismatics and Protestants profess the Catholic Creed with conviction, when all Jews voluntarily ask for Holy Baptism – only then will the Immaculata have reached its goals."

> "In other words" Saint Maximilian insisted, "there is no greater enemy of the Immaculata and her Knighthood than today's ecumenism, which every Knight must not only fight against, but also neutralize through diametrically opposed action and ultimately destroy. We must realize the goal of the Militia Immaculata as quickly as possible: that is, to conquer

the whole world, and every individual soul which exists today or will exist until the end of the world, for the Immaculata, and through her for the Most Sacred Heart of Jesus." (Father Karl Stehlin, *Immaculata, Our Ideal*, Kansas City, Missouri, Angelus Press, 2007, p. 37.)

Any questions? No one who supports false ecumenism, no less practices it in the form of "inter-religious dialogue" and "inter-religious prayer services" is a friend of Christ the King and Mary our Immaculate Queen.

Our Lady wants the conversion of men and their nations to the Catholic Faith, outside of which there is no salvation and without which there can be no true social order.

It was one hundred seventeen years, four months after the miracles wrought by Our Lady atop Tepeyac Hill to effect the conversion of the Americas to the true Faith that she appeared in France to a Catholic who had apostatized by becoming a member of the hideous, demonic sect known as Calvinism. Why did she appear to this man, Pierre Port-Combet? To engage in "dialogue" with him. No! A thousand times no! She came to tell him that he would go to hell if he did not convert back to the Faith of his baptism:

> Many years ago in the village of Plantees, France, there lived a farmer named Pierre Port-Combet, who used to work on Sundays and Feast Days. At one time he had been a Catholic, but he had fallen away from the truth Faith and joined a Protestant religion called Calvinism. He had a great dislike for Catholics and anything about the Catholic Faith.
>
> Pierre had married a devout Catholic woman named Jeanne. They had six children and Jeanne tried to raise them as good Catholics. But even though Pierre had made a vow to allow his wife to raise their children as Catholics, he gradually led their six children into the Calvinist religion! Jeanne was brokenhearted about this because it meant that her husband and children were in great danger of losing their souls. And since Pierre would not listen to her pleadings, the best she could do was to go to Mass, pray, and make sacrifices.
>
> This area of France was very Catholic at the time. There was a law that all people should not work on Sundays and on special Holy Days, so that they could go to Mass and spend the rest of the day in prayer and holy reading. But Pierre loved to break this law, especially on Our Lady's Feast Days, because he did not like the Catholic religion!
>
> On March 25, 1649, the Feast of the Annunciation, Pierre showed his dislike for the Catholic Church by working near a road where villagers could see him, as they traveled on their way to Mass. He pretended to work, by using his knife to cut into a willow tree, which grew beside the road. But as soon as he cut into the willow, the tree bled! Pierre was shocked as the blood flowed out of the tree and splashed onto his hands and arms. At first Pierre thought he was wounded, but finding that he was not injured, he stabbed the willow tree another time, and again the tree bled!
>
> Around this time, Pierre's wife passed by on her way to church. Seeing that her husband's arms

were covered with blood, she rushed over to help him. While she was looking for the wound, Pierre tried to explain to his wife what had just taken place. Jeanne tried to calm her husband and cut the tree with his knife, but nothing happened. When Pierre noticed that no blood came from the tree, he grabbed the knife from his wife and cut off a willow branch. The blood came gushing out of the tree!

By now Pierre was terribly frightened! He called to Louis, a neighbour who was just passing by, and begged him to come and see what happened. But when Louis took the knife and tried to cut the tree, no blood came out. As the other villagers passed by they began to realize that the blood from the tree was a warning from God to Pierre, so that he would come back to the Catholic Faith and not work on Sundays.

Before long, Pierre was brought to court for working on this special Feast Day and he had to pay a fine. And when the Bishop heard about the miracle of the bleeding willow tree, he ordered some priests to look into the matter. Pierre and others who saw the miracle were questioned. In the end it was decided that this miracle was a stern warning from God to Pierre, so that he would mend his ways!

Pierre had a change of heart and realizing that he was wrong, he would often go to pray near the willow tree. But when some of his Calvinist friends saw him, they threatened to hurt him if he left the Calvinist religion. Because of this Pierre refused to go back to the Catholic Church.

Heaven was watching over Pierre and after seven years, on March 25, 1656, Our Lady appeared to him. On that day, Pierre was working in the field and saw a Lady standing far away on a little hill. The Lady wore a white dress, a blue mantle and had a black veil over her head, which partly covered her face. As the Lady came toward Pierre, she suddenly picked up speed and in a flash, she stood beside him. With her beautiful, sweet voice, the Lady spoke to Pierre, "God be with you my friend!"

For a moment, Pierre stood in amazement. The Lady spoke again, "What is being said about this devotion? Do many people come?"

Pierre replied, "Yes many people come."

Then the Lady said, "Where does that heretic live who cut the willow tree? Does he not want to be converted?"

Pierre mumbled an answer. The Lady became more serious, "Do you think that I do not know that you are the heretic? Realize that your end is at hand. If you do not return to the True Faith, you will be cast into Hell! But if you change your beliefs, I shall protect you before God. Tell people to pray that they may gain the good graces which God in His mercy has offered to them."

Pierre was filled with sorrow and shame and moved away from the Lady. Suddenly realizing that he was being rude, Pierre stepped closer to her, but she had moved away and was already near the little hill. He ran after her begging, "Please stop and listen to me. I want to apologize to you and I want you to help me!"

The Lady stopped and turned. By the time Pierre caught up to her, she was floating in the air and was already disappearing from sight. Suddenly, Pierre realized that the Most Blessed Virgin Mary had appeared to him! He fell to his knees and cried buckets of tears, "Jesus and Mary I promise you that I will change my life and become a good Catholic. I am sorry for what I have done and I beg you please, to help me change my life…"

On August 14, 1656, Pierre became very sick. An Augustinian priest came to hear his confession and accepted him back into the Catholic Church. Pierre received Holy Communion the next day on the Feast of the Assumption. After Pierre returned to the Catholic Faith, many others followed him. His son and five daughters came back to the Catholic Church as well as many Calvinists and Protestants. Five weeks later on September 8, 1656, Pierre died and was buried under the miraculous willow tree, just as he had asked.

Fr. Fais, the parish priest from the nearby town of Vinay, helped a lady to buy the field where Pierre had spoken to Our Lady. In time the chapel of Our Lady of Good Meeting was built on the spot where Our Lady had spoken to Pierre. Soon, a large church was built over the spot of the miraculous tree, and named in honour of Our Lady of the Willow. Some good person also carved a statue of Our Lady similar to the way Pierre had described the Blessed Virgin Mary. When this statue was placed in the church, many people came to honour Our Lady of the Willow.

But alas, because of the sinfulness of man, this beautiful shrine did not last and was ruined by members of the horrible French Revolution. These wicked men took the statue of Our Lady of the Willow and chopped it to pieces! Oh, what a terrible way to treat Our Lady's image! However, all was not lost! A good lady gathered up the pieces of the statue and hid them until the French Revolution was over. A piece of the willow tree was also saved from the hands of these wicked men.

After the horrible French Revolution, people came again to honour Our Lady of the Willow at this sacred spot. The statue of Our Lady was repaired and in time the shrine was placed in the hands of the Oblates of Mary Immaculate. Now some priests were caring for the shrine and could help the many people who came there.

In 1856, two hundred years after the apparition of Our Lady to Pierre, Blessed Pope Pius IX decreed that the statue of Our Lady should be crowned on September 8 of that year. More than 30,000 people were present at the shrine for the crowning of Our Lady of the Willow, and at least four hundred priests were also present at the ceremony. And this same Pope ordered that another crowning should take place in 1873!

On March 17, 1924, Pope Pius XI declared that Our Lady of the Willow Church was now a minor basilica. Here the statue of Our Lady of the Willow is venerated. A box containing a piece of the old willow tree lies under her altar and Pierre's grave is at the foot of the altar.

Many people come to honour Our Lady of the Willow at this shrine and many have left little plaques in thanksgiving to Our Lady, for some special grace which she has given them. Also more than a hundred miracles are reported to have taken place at this shrine. Thank-you Jesus and Mary for your great mercies.

Our Lady of the Willow, Pray for Us! (Our Lady of the Willow Tree)

Our Lady did this for just one soul. One soul, mind you, one soul, that of Pierre Port-Combet, who was privileged to witness no less than two miracles take place within seven years of each other on the Feast of the Annunciation before he did on the Feast of the Nativity of the Blessed Virgin Mary. Just one soul. That's how important one soul is to Our Blessed Lord and Saviour Jesus Christ and His Most Blessed Mother.

Our Lady's love of the lost sheep of the Jews, her very own people, is such that she appeared to one soul, Alphonse Ratisbonne, on January 20, 1842, in the Church of San Andrea delle Fratte in Rome, Italy, in the same image that she appears on the Miraculous Medal that this Catholic-hating Jewish man had placed around his neck. Just one soul. One soul, that of Alphonse Ratisbonne, who went on, of course, to become a priest to work amongst his own people for their conversion to the true Faith, something that is now forbidden by the counterfeit church of conciliarism. Sure, Jews can convert to the conciliar church if they want to do so. Any "missionary" activity to seek their conversion, such as that undertaken by Father Marie-Alphonse Ratisbonne, is forbidden (see the appendix for proof). Please tell me what is Catholicism and what is but a precursor of Antichrist.

The fact that millions of pagans, steeped as they were in the barbaric practices of the Aztecs and Mayans, converted to the Catholic Faith within a short period of time following the miracles that Our Lady wrought atop Tepeyac Hill on Tuesday, December 12, 1531, did not go unnoticed by authorities in Rome:

> It is not enough for a great lady that she should be welcome among her friends in their homes and that she should be able to receive them suitably in her own. With proper pride, she desires general recognition of this fact. Her entourage is duly aware of this and sees to it that her will in such a respect is accomplished. She is not obliged to take any initiative herself; she has only to wait until her wishes are fulfilled. Then the acclamation with which she is hailed is not only abundant but also universal.

> Thus it had been in the case of the Great Lady of Guadalupe. By the end of the sixteenth century, the cult of the Miraculous Image had extended beyond Mexico City and environs, and within the next hundred years it had spread so far that it was no longer limited by the boundaries of New Spain. This penetration, and the reasons for it, did not escape the watchful eyes of the alert authorities in Rome. Indeed, we find that Gregory XIII--the brilliant Bolognese reigning between 1572 and 1585, to whom the education of the masses of all nations became a passion, and who is universally immortalized by his reformation of the calendar--extended the benefits derived from indulgences granted in previous years to the Guadalupan Hermitage.

The document testifying to this is one of extreme importance, since it proves that within an almost incredibly short time after its foundation the Sanctuary of Our Lady of Guadalupe had been recognized by the Holy See as the repository of Special Grace. Innocent X--the Roman aristocrat whose great preoccupation was for the poor--was apparently the first to receive a representation of the Sacred Image. In a sermon preached by Vidal de Figueroa in December 1660, he states that "the Supreme Pontiff had a copy of the Sacred Image in the Apostolic   Chamber, and today we see medals depicting it." Four years later Alexander VII--the learned Sienese responsible for the condemnation of Jansenism and the canonization of St. Francis de   Sales--granted plenary indulgences to all those who visited the Sanctuary on the fourteenth of December, having apparently been slightly misinformed as to the exact date of the apparitions,   which as we know, took place between the ninth and the twelfth. Later, however, he received a petition asking that the twelfth might be proclaimed a feast in the Church Calendar, so the original mistake, if one occurred, was promptly rectified. And it was during this same epoch, according to one report, that Guadalupan medals appeared, bearing the inscription, "Non fecit   taliter omni nationi" ("This has been grated to no other nation"), which is, incidentally, a quotation from Psalm 107.

It was not until the time of Benedict XIV, who reigned between 1740 and 1758, however, that this was uttered as a pronouncement, which has since spread all over the world, and the masses have always subscribed to the belief that it was spontaneous as well as official. The truth of the matter is that the Pope, while certainly well aware of the source of this saying--since he was one of the most learned of all Saint Peter's successors--was moved to adapt words of the Psalmist to fit the occasion which had so deeply stirred his own sensibilities.

It was certainly dramatic in the extreme: The clergy and laity of Mexico had for some time been clamoring at the gates of Rome, so to speak, for more signal recognition of the Sacred Image than had so far been accorded. They were convinced that the Virgin of Guadalupe alone had saved them from the frightful plague with which their land had recently been ravaged. And their urgency was no longer limited to the desire, long since expressed, that the twelfth of December should be proclaimed an Obligatory Feast, with its proper Mass and Ordinary; they also desired the proclamation of a general Canonical Patronage, in which the Virgin of Guadalupe should be solemnly declared the principal Patroness of New Spain. With extreme care they chose an appropriate envoy and dispatched him to Rome, entrusting to him "the complete documentary process of the nation's demand."

The envoy in question, a Jesuit by the name of Francisco Lopez, was in every way worthy of their confidence. He was a native of Venezuela who at the age of eleven had gone with his father first to Veracruz and then to Jamaica, where they had both been thrown into prison. After extricating themselves from this unpleasant predicament, they had gone on to Mexico, where the boy had received an excellent education in a Jesuit college. When his course of instruction was completed, he had become consecutively Professor of Human Letters at San Louis Potosi and in Veracruz, Professor of Philosophy in Zacatecas and Mexico City, and Professor of Theology in Merida; Prefect of Divine Doctrine at the Mother House in Mexico City; and Provincial Procurator in Madrid and Rome. He fulfilled all these duties with ability   and tact and learned how to associate himself on terms of ease and intimacy with the members of the Hierarchy and with other personages of importance. All in all, the Mexicans were justified in assuming that if anyone could meet with success, this was the man.

Lopez was well aware that his task would not be an easy one, for Benedict XIV, a canonist and liturgist of note, was inclined to be cautious and conservative when it came to a question of innovations. With the canniness characteristic of the Order to which he belonged, Father Lopez had supplemented his documents by an offering which was even more appealing and arresting--a copy of the Sacred Image made by Miguel Cabrera, a native Oaxaca, who was one of the greatest painters of his time and the author of a treatise on the technical attributes of the miraculous picture, which, according to him, could not have been given by human hands. Cabrera had achieved innumerable notable paintings, among them several portraits of Sor Juana Ines de la Cruz, the famous Mexican poetess, and scenes from the lives of San Ignacio de Loyola and Santo Domingo, but he had never accomplished anything comparable in beauty to this copy of the Sacred Image which Father Francisco Lopez took with him to Rome.

The manner of its presentation has been graphically described by the historian Davila and admirably translated by Father Lee in Our Lady of America. When Father Lopez had been admitted in audience to the presence of His Holiness, "The Father Procurator, holding a rolled canvas, came before Benedict XIV, and having obtained permission to speak, gave briefly but eloquently the narrative of the Miracle of the Guadalupan Apparition. And while the Pope was listening attentively and wonderingly, the speaker suddenly stopped and cried hold: 'Holy Father, behold the Mother of God who deigned to be also the mother of the Mexicans!' Thereupon taking the canvas in both hands, as did once the happy Juan Diego before the venerable Bishop Zumarraga, he unrolled it on the platform occupied by His Holiness. Benedict, who was already moved by the narration, at this unexpected action and at sight of the beauty of the figure, cast himself down before it with the exclamation that has since been the distinctive motto of our amiable and venerable Patroness: "Non fecit taliter omni nationi."

The success of the Lopez mission seemed assured at the end of this portentous audience. But at the last moment a technicality threatened the happy outcome of the good Father's endeavor after all. The Congregation of Rites was satisfied in a general way with the evidence he submitted, but was inclined to rule that no distinctive liturgy should be sanctioned for the time being, because the archives of the Congregation lacked specific documents to prove that the Guadalupan cause had already been formally introduced at Rome. Father Lopez knew that documents had been submitted in both 1663 and 1667, which should furnish every required proof, and he also knew that these must be somewhere in Rome. But his every effort to locate them proved fruitless. From the archives he went to the libraries, where his search was equally vain. But at last, though no valuable volumes came to light, he discovered an entry in a catalogue which gave him a clue to what he sought. For this catalogue listed the "Historical Relation of the Admirable Apparition of the Most Holy Virgin Mother of God, under the title of Our Lady of Guadalupe, which occurred in Mexico, in the year 1531. Its author, Anastasio Nicoselli; dedicated to the R.P.M.F. Raymundo Capisucchi, Master of the Sacred Palace; printed in the Italian tongue, at Rome in the year 1581."

Father Lopez was well aware that Nicoselli, a Roman prelate of great learning, had transcribed the Mexican documents sent to the Holy See during the seventeenth century in preparing his work on Guadalupe. Therefore, the entry represented the lost treasure which he sought. But the entry, alas, was not the book itself, nor did it even prove conclusively that the book still existed. Given time, Father Lopez believed that he might be able to track this down; but time, unfortunately, was lacking. Limits had been set to the period which he might spend on his mission, and he began to believe that it was doomed to failure, like those of its predecessors. Discouragement overwhelmed him, and in his dejection he began to range the streets, preoccupied by distracted thoughts. It took nothing less than an outcry to rouse him from these, but at last such an outcry arose. An itinerant vendor pursued him relentlessly and Father Lopez turned toward the man, bent only on silencing his noise. Then the unawaited, the unhoped for, the utterly amazing happened: Outstanding among the old books which constituted the vendor's dilapidated wares, its title leaping out toward the Jesuit as if had been written in flame, was Nicoselli's Relation!

"God moves in a mysterious way. His wonders to perform"--and so does the Mother of God, the Virgin of Guadalupe. There was no question, after this astonishing discovery, of Father Lopez' success. The Congregation of Rites approved both the Special Office and the Mass which he had sought; and in 1754 the Holy Father issued one of his most memorable briefs.

"For the greater glory of Almighty God and the furtherance of His Worship, and for the honor of the Virgin Mary," he wrote, "We by these letters approve and confirm with apostolical authority the election of Most Holy Virgin Mary under the invocation of Guadalupe, whose Sacred Image is venerated in the splendid collegiate and parochial church outside the city of Mexico, as Patroness and Protectress of New Spain, with all and every one of the prerogatives due to principal patrons and protectors according to the rubrics of the Roman Breviary; an election which was made by the desire, as well of Our Venerable Brothers, the bishops of that Kingdom, as of the Clergy secular and regular, and by the suffrages of the people of those States. In the next place We approve and confirm the preinserted Office and Mass with the Octave; and We declare, decree and command that the Mother of God called Holy Mary of Guadalupe be recognized, invoked, and venerated as Patroness and Protectress of New Spain. Likewise, in order that henceforth the solemn commemoration of so great a Patroness and Protectress may be celebrated with the more reverence and devotion, and with due worship of prayer by the faithful of both sexes who are bound to the Canonical Hours, by the same apostolic authority We grant and command that the annual feast of the twelfth of December, in honor of the Most Holy Virgin Mary of Guadalupe, be perpetually celebrated as a day of precept and as a double of the first class with Octave; and that the preinserted Office be recited and the preinserted Mass be celebrated. . . . Given at Rome, in St. Mary Major, under the Fisherman's Ring, twenty-fifth of May, 1754, in the fourteenth years of Our Pontificate."

Besides issuing this brief, Benedict XIV authorized the establishment of Guadalupan Congregations, already widespread in Mexico, outside of that country, and gave to the Guadalupan Sanctuary--already raised to the states of Collegiate Church, with a

Special Chapter of Canons, by Benedict XII--the rank of a Lateran Basilica.

"I have done more for the Mexicans in honor of the Virgin of Guadalupe than I have done for the Italians in honor of the Holy House of Loreto," Benedict XIV remarked more than once in the days to come. But there is nothing to indicate that he ever regretted the stand he had taken and his successors, one after another, continued along the same lines, which he had begun. But it was not until the time of Leo XIII, however, that the name of another Pope was as closely linked with that of Guadalupe as Benedict XIV had been. (Frances Parkinson Keyes, *The Grace of Guadalupe*, published in 1941 by Julian Messner, Inc., pp. 123-131.)

As we know, of course, Popes Saint Pius X, Pius XI and Pius XII each were very devoted to Our Lady of Guadalupe. It was Pope Pius XII who, in 1945, proclaimed Our Lady of Guadalupe as the Queen of Mexico and the Empress of the Americas, declaring her a year later to be the Patroness of the Americas. Four hundred fifteen years had passed since the miracles that Our Lady worked atop Tepeyac Hill and the time that Pope Pius XII declared that Our Lady of Guadalupe was the Patroness of the Americas.

Even with that, however, there have been skeptics, especially as the years advanced and some of the clergy in Mexico deemed themselves to be more "sophisticated" than the peasants who believed in the story of Our Lady of Guadalupe as it had been handed down to them. Oh, I am not referring here to the dastardly efforts of Abbot Guillermo Schulenburg, the director of the Shrine of Our Lady of Guadalupe for over three decades, in 1996 to debunk belief in the existence of Juan Diego, mind you, and in the miraculous nature of the image left by Our Lady herself on Juan Diego's tilma. Oh no. I am referring to efforts made by clerics in the Seventeenth Century, just a little over one hundred years after Our Lady's apparitions, to debunk belief in the miracle of Our Lady of Guadalupe, paralleling efforts in our own day to attempt to discredit or to debunk the messages of Our Lady in La Salette, France, in 1846, and near Fatima, Portugal, in 1917.

We know the truth. Our Lady appeared to the simple, humble Indian peasant named Juan Diego, effecting miracles of grace in the Americas that must cause us to redouble our own efforts to spread devotion to her so that the Americas can be reconverted to the Catholic Faith that once permeated the entirety of Latin America and substantial parts of what are now the countries of Canada and the United States of America. We do indeed need to pray to Our Lady of Guadalupe to ask her to help us to be made as humble and simple and trusting as Juan Diego, who never lost those qualities even though he had been favored by the Queen of Heaven herself:

It had been the Bishop's idea that Juan Diego might find gladness and fulfillment in consecrating the remainder of his life at the service of the Queen of Heaven, and Juan's humble face and trustful eyes had been illumined with gratitude and pride as he accepted the mission.

His home, since the death of Maria Lucia, had been at best a makeshift. The cultivation of the land had lost its meaning. His uncle, for whose sake he had moved to Tolpetlac, would find far more gratification in visiting at the hermitage than in trotting around the corner to see him in his humble house. There was every reason why he should go and none why he should stay. He disposed of his few possessions and took up his abode in the little hut close beside the hermitage which the faithful built for him.

His primary privilege was one of worship. In an era of infrequent Communion for the laity, he was given special permission from the Bishop to receive this thrice a week. Fortified by this holy food, he undertook his simple duties with quiet zest. The little sanctuary where the Virgin was enshrined shone with the beauty of cleanliness, for it was swept and scoured each day and garnished with fresh flowers. It was merely a small rectangular room--in size and shape probably very like the tiny chapel into which Juan Bernardino's house had been converted--with the altar, approached by a short flight of stone steps, at one end and the basin for holy water at one side. But above the altar was the miraculous picture and above the holy water was the Cross. For Juan, and for the ever-increasing throngs of worshipers, these sufficed. What more did they need to show them the way to salvation?

In giving no thought to the morrow, as to what he should eat or what he should drink or wherewithal he should be clothed, Juan had followed a Biblical injunction, never doubting that His Heavenly Father knew that he had need of all these things. The friendly and fecund earth did not fail to furnish food; a spring of water, gushing out of the ground near the hermitage, gave clear and sparkling water, and coarse cotton garments sufficed, as they had always done, for raiment. Nor was it only in such ways as these that all was well with Juan; his craving for companionship, so long unfulfilled, was wholly realized now. Communing as he had with the Sacred Image, how could his life be lonely? Moreover, his neighbors loved him and revealed this affection. He was a prophet with honor among his own people. It was their belief that he received instruction as to his way of life from God Himself, and often they came to him, asking that he intercede for them at the throne of Divine Grace. When they spoke of him, they referred to him with respect as the "Pilgrim." More than once, the Bishop, passing through the streets of Tepeyac on his way to visit the hermitage, heard a fond mother exclaiming, as she clasped her child to her breast, "God grant that you may become such a man as Juan Diego!" In that heartfelt cry, Zumarraga could interpret the degree of favor which Juan had found in their sight.

The Bishop also remarked the change which had been wrought in Juan himself. Without losing his essential humility, the Indian's face and form had taken on a new dignity. Because he had been found worthy to serve God and the Mother of God, he had learned to meet his fellow men as an equal. The discipline and frugality of his life were likewise revealed in his person; he had the refinement which marks the ascetic. Contemplation had stood him in the stead of learning and prayer had given him understanding. He had become a man of culture because he was a man of ordered living and lofty thinking.

The Bishop did not fail to dwell on all this thoughtfully and ardently. In the course of the sermon which he had preached at the close of the great procession, he had asked for funds with which to build a great temple, and little by little these were coming in. But while envisioning from afar the glorious sanctuary of the future at Tepeyac, his mind was at rest concerning the immediate custody of the unique treasure enshrined at the hermitage. This was the more fortunate, since he could not, himself, spend as large a portion of his time there as he would have wished. His required journeys took him to many parts of New Spain and sometimes to Old Spain itself. But secure in the knowledge that wherever he himself might be, Juan Diego never left the hermitage, all his travels were tranquil. . . .

But, as the Archbishop had divined, it was his last journey. After that he did not leave his place any more, and his friend, Fray Domingo [a Dominican priest from Spain], did not leave him. And though every day they talked together, according to their old familiar habit, they spoke more and more of celestial things, and less and less of the things of the earth. Although Zumarraga did not disregard what was happening around him, much of which he knew was important, he withdrew from it. It ceased to concern him or to spur him on to fresh action. And, finally, it seemed as if a veil had fallen, so that he saw none of it clearly any more, but only through a heavenly haze, which kept him from being troubled at the sight of anything.

And so it came about that he was not troubled when his people came to him and told him Juan Diego had died. He listened with no change of expression, while they said that far and wide it was being rumored that the Virgin had appeared to Juan again, first to tell him that the hour of his death was approaching, and then, or concern, when the hour came. He did not doubt the truth of what they were saying in this regard, nor was he doubtful, either, when he was told that in Tepeyac Juan's own friends and neighbors were acclaiming him as a saint. But he felt no grief because Juan had died, for, through the heavenly haze that surrounded him, he was able to see that death was only the beginning of life.

He did not wonder what would happen to the Sacred Image now that Juan was longer in the hermitage watching over it. He knew that somehow it would be safeguarded through the ages, and that in the time to come its sanctuary would be worthy of it. He only wondered how long it would take before he, like Juan, would see the Queen of Heaven, not as an image, but in her own intrinsic glory.

When the Archbishop's people saw that he did not answer while they spoke to him of Juan, they did not understand. It had been very different when they spoke to him about the death of Heran [Hernando] Cortes, which had occurred six months earlier. He had listened with absorbed attention when he had heard that the Conqueror of Mexico died with a prayer to Our Lady of Guadalupe on his lips. But in speaking of Cortes, they had also spoken of Seville, for it was there that the Conqueror had died. So his people thought it might be more pleasing to the Archbishop if they spoke to him about other places in Spain rather than about people--about the sights he had loved as a young man, like the gate at Avila and the twin towers of the Cathedral at Burgos, or of the deeds he had accomplished in Mexico, such as founding the university and bringing the printing presses to the people. So they tried to rouse his memories and to praise his great deeds and they were discouraged when he only smiled and shook his head and turned away. Only Fray Domingo understood that these things did not matter any more, and that the reason that Archbishop was not interested in them, or concerned about Juan's death and the fate of the sanctuary, was because the veil had been drawn away and many things, not only about Juan, but about all else, were now clear that had never been known before.

Fray Domingo leaned over, folding the beautiful fingers around the crucifix they had so long supported. Then very gently he closed the Archbishop's eyes. Don Fray Juan de Zumarraga had survived Juan Diego by only two days. It had been as if his hold on life had not been strong enough to endure beyond the Indian's, in whose fate his own had become so strangely intertwined and in whose fame his own was to be mysteriously submerged. (Frances Parkinson Keyes, *The Grace of Guadalupe*, published in 1941 by Julian Messner, Inc., pp. 72-74, 77-80.)

The simple, trusting and humble Juan Diego died on June 1, 1548, two days before Archbishop Juan de Zumarraga, who had indeed accomplished much during the time of his service to Holy Mother Church in Mexico. The simple Indian, who was met with disbelief by a Spanish Basque, and his Archbishop were united for all eternity after having promoted the cult of Our Lady of Guadalupe with unfailing fidelity and joy.

The story of the Faith in the New World was marked for a long time by conflicts between the Spanish conquistadores and the missionaries sent to evangelize the Indians. The miracle of Our Lady of Guadalupe helped to attenuate those conflicts over time to such an extent that the Spaniards and their descendants intermarried with the Indians, creating a new race of people in the process as a new Christendom arose in Latin America. Bishops and priests and missionaries fought for rights of the indigenous peoples. While the subject of the blight of the African slave trade that made possible the mining of the riches of Brazil, a Portuguese colony, and the Spanish colonies is outside of the scope of this book, suffice it to say that Holy Mother Church sought to end slavery and the unjust treatment of the indigenous people, although slavery remained entrenched in Cuba until 1863 and the Dominican Republic until 1865.

Although the barbaric peoples of Africa and the Americas had for centuries enslaved numbers of their own people, Holy Mother Church sought at first to bring spiritual comfort to the slaves and then to make it possible for the institution to be abolished over the course of time. Saint Peter Claver personally baptized over 300,000 people, most of them Africans who had been brought over to serve as slaves in Colombia, and Saint Francis Solano baptized an entire cargo hold full of slaves on the ship that was taking him to Peru from Spain before the ship sank after he had escaped. He spared those slaves from enslavement to the devil and God then spared them from chattel slavery by taking them unto Himself soon after their Baptism.

Robert Leckie, a journalist and novelist who died in 2001, wrote a book, *American and Catholic*, that was published in 1970. Leckie is undeniably an Americanist, that is, one favorably disposed to the American influence upon the practice of the Faith. As will be seen later in this book, Leckie was confused by the appearance of the so-called "new Mass" and the changes ushered in by the "Second" Vatican Council. His book, however, contains great nuggets of information, including an excellent description of the spread of the Faith in the land that became the United States of America. I cannot improve upon this description, which is why it is being provided here:

It was not until 1513, however, that the American mainland was reached. On Easter Sunday (Pascua Florida), Ponce de Leon came ashore on the vast peninsula he named Tierra Florida. That same year, Balboa crossed the isthmus to look upon the vast Pacific from his "peak in Darien." Now was begun the glorious period of discovery and exploration that is irrevocably associated with the names of Catholics. In the south, Ponce de Leon, who was *not* seeking the Fountain of Youth, returned to Florida in 1521 to take possession for Spain and was mortally wounded by Indians. Two years before Alvarez de Pineda came upon the mouth of the Mississippi and named it the River of the Holy Ghost. In 1541, de Soto crossed the Mississippi to explore the Southwest, coming back in 1542 to die on the great river's banks and to be buried in her waters to prevent the Indians from mutilating her body. That same year, the seeds of the American Church were nourished by the blood of her first martyr: Father Juan de Padilla, murdered by Indians on the Kansas plain. And to the northeast, Vasquez de Ayllon visited the Cape Fear district in 1521, and in 1526 he settled on the Chesapeake. Eight-one years before the first settlement of English Protestants was made at nearby Jamestown, Holy Mass was celebrated among Ayllon's six hundred settlers on the Chesapeake. Their colony did not last, however, and within another year it was abandoned.

Not so St. Augustine in Florida, the oldest settlement in North America, which Pedro Menendez founded in 1565, and at which today the Mass is still celebrated and the sacraments administered. So also survived Sante Fe–the City of the Holy Faith–the oldest capital city in the United States. It was founded around 1605 by that very Juan de Onate whose great gift to the United States was a Southwest populated by domesticated cattle and horses. Today's Texas longhorns are descended from the cattle Onate turned loose, and his horses are the ancestors of the wild mustang.

Paramount though the religious motive might be, the friars had far from a free hand in the New World. They wished to convert and civilize the Indians whom the conquistadors often wished to exploit and enslave; and because of the extremely close union of the Spanish Church and state, there was almost unending conflict between the political and ecclesiastical arms of the empire. The friars, of course, were not always in the right. A priest who believes he has God on his side can often be a most unreasonable critic of an administrator, who is, after all, only trying to enrich his master, the king. Still, the friars were fired by a deep compassion for the Indians and it was because of the protests of Father Bartholomew de las Casas that Pope Paul III in 1537 declared: "The said Indians and other people who may later be discovered by Christians, are by no means to be deprived of their liberty or the possession of property, even though they be outside the faith of Jesus Christ." If it is too much to suggest that this protest and admonition place a priest and a pope in the position of being the first advocates of racial justice in America, it is nevertheless true that it was chiefly because of the efforts of the Catholic Church that the Indians under Spanish rule were not destroyed and dispossessed.

On the contrary, here and in South America they were converted by the millions. Where possible, they were organized in peaceful pueblos by Jesuit and Franciscan missionaries, many of whom were gifted scholars who had sacrificed the comfort of the universities to come to the New World. These were the Emperor Charles's "religious persons," and they taught the Indian men to plant, build and tend cattle, while instructing the women in sewing, cooking, spinning and weaving. Theirs were the missions that the American historian Herbert Eugene Bolton described as "a force" which made for the preservation of the Indians, as opposed to their destruction, so characteristic of the Anglo-American frontier. For more than two centuries, they continued in this way, until they were destroyed by a secularizing Mexican government and then left to the tender mercies of the Yankee settlers and gold miners who followed in the wake of the American victory in the Mexican War.

All of their labors may seem to have been in vain, but to men dedicated to the God who died ignominiously on the cross and who celebrated martyred comrades with a Te Deum, success is measured with another yardstick. And of the temporal glory of the Spanish conquest, the historian Samuel Eliot Morrison has said: "Our forebears in Virginia and New England, the pathfinders of the Great West, and the French pioneers of Canada, were indeed stout fellows; but their exploits scarcely compare with those of brown-robed Spanish friars and armored conquistadors who hacked their way through solid jungle, across endless plains, and over snowy passes of the Andes, to fulfill dreams of glory and conversion; and for whom reality proved even greater than the dream." Finally, the American nation, which was born nearly three centuries after Spain discovered the New World, became the chief heir to the Spanish legacy. Americans of California and the Southwest are proud of a "mission" style of architecture as distinctive and as apposite of the white colonial of New England or the red brick of Virginia, and as the American Catholic historian John Tracy Ellis has observed: "This old Christian civilization of the borderlands endured far beyond the age of Spanish greatness, and when the Americans arrived in those areas in the mid-nineteenth century, it afforded a link entirely absent from the plains and valleys to the north, with which to bind the old with the new order. It was facts such as these that Herbert Ingram Priestly had in mind when he said, "It is of prime importance to the life of America today that the first white men to settle on these   western shores were Spaniards and Roman Catholics, representatives of a powerful nation that was the citadel of a united faith."

After the Spaniards came the French, and they were also Catholics. As early as 1524, King Francis I sent the Italian navigator Verrazano to explore the North Atlantic coast, and ten years later the doughty Jacques Cartier entered and named the St. Lawrence River, sailing up that mighty stream as far as present day Montreal. More than the Spaniards, the French were the true explorers of North America. The limitations of sailing ships and horses had confined the Spaniards to the rim of the continent, but the unfettered French penetrated the interior. On foot following the forest trails or paddling along the silent primeval rivers in bobbing birchbark cockleshells, they traversed the lake-and-water chain linking the St. Lawrence to the Hudson; they broke out into the Great Lakes and into the Illinois country beyond; they reached the Rockies; they descended the Mississippi to its mouth, cleaving a continent in two. Their names are immemorial and commonplace: Cartier, Champlain, Joliet and the most illustrious, and after them in a swelling anonymous flood, came those curious and dedicated missionaries,   those Capuchins, Recollects, diocesan clergy and especially those black-robed sons of Loyola, of whom Bancroft had written: "Not a cape was turned, or a river entered, but a Jesuit led the way."

More than the Spanish again, the French seemed to understand that the key to America was not in its coasts, but in its mighty forests and fertile plains, in its intricate network of rivers. So they built a chain of forts and trading posts stretching from Quebec to New Orleans, and when they had done this, they seemed to have blocked the westward movement of the struggling little cluster of English colonies on the Atlantic seaboard and to have checked Spanish ambition in the east. And because they also understood the Indians, neither forcibly converting like the Spanish or eventually attempting to exterminate them like the English, but treating them like brothers, it would have appeared that the destiny of America was to be French–and Catholic. It is possible that this French penchant for exploration and fortification, together with their more humane approach to the Indians, might have sprung from a basic economic difference among the three colonizing powers. The Spanish, seeking gold, wanted the labor of the Indians as much as their salvation; the English, wishing to settle, cared chiefly for the Indian land and little for their souls; but the French, looking for wealth in furs, needed the Indian hunters as commercial partners and Indian warriors as allies–in a word, as equals.

Whatever the reason, on the political side the French set themselves to charm the savages; and on the spiritual, their missionaries proposed to convert them by adapting themselves to the red man's primitive way of life. To do so meant a life of appalling hardship and intellectual degradation for these polished products of what was then the highest civilization of the age, and yet, they accepted it willingly, even eagerly, so ardent was their desire to serve and to suffer in the cause of Christ and His Virgin Mother. They were a noble and dedicated band, these Black Robes, and no one seems to have appreciated and understood them better than the Protestant historian Francis Parkman. Although far from being in sympathy with the objectives of Jesuits such as Pere Marquette, Parkman could nevertheless write of him:

> He was a devout votary of the Virgin Mary, who, imagined to his mind in shapes of the most transcendent loveliness with which the pencil of human genius has ever informed the canvas, was to him the object of an adoration not unmingled with a sentiment of chivalrous devotion. The longings of a sensitive heart, divorced from earth, sought solace in the skies. A subtle element of romance was blended with the fervor of his worship, and hung like an illuminated cloud over the harsh and hard realities of his daily lot. Kindled by the smile of his celestial mistress, his gentle and noble nature knew no fear. For her he burned to dare and to suffer, discover new lands and conquer new realms to her sway. [Leckie added a footnote to this passage from Francis Parkman: "Like many non-Catholic writers before and since, Parkman confused Catholic 'veneration" of Mary and the saints with the 'worship' which is given to God alone.]

Idealists and visionaries that they were, the Black Robes were nevertheless practical men. They realized that the Indians they sought to convert were among the most mulish and perverse savages in the world. They were men of noble bearing and great courage, true, whose oratory had a movingly simple dignity encountered nowhere else on the globe and whose language was, as one astonished Jesuit father wrote, "richer than the French in its complex shades of meaning"; but the Indian was nonetheless a savage, a dirty, crafty savage whose high qualities were all but obscured by his brutal sexuality, his obscenity, his cruelty and his nature- worshiping superstition which led him to believe that he must do whatever his *manitou* or *oki* (spirit) had suggested to him in his dreams. (Robert Leckie *American and Catholic*, Doubleday, 1970, pp. 2-8.)

There were vast distinctions between the work of the Spanish and French settlement of the New World with that of the English who came here. The work of the missionaries, including the Spanish Jesuit Martyrs of Virginia, who died for the Faith in 1571, was quite different from that of the English settlers who founded Jamestown, Virginia, in 1607, as the first permanent English settlement in North America, and that of the Dutch who came to explore and then colonize what they called New Amsterdam (New York) in 1626. Most of the English who came to North America had a profound and abiding hatred of Catholicism, none more so than the Pilgrims who founded the Plymouth Bay Colony in 1620.

The difference was simple: Catholics were guided by the true Faith. The Protestants were guided by the devil, who desires to mock Our Lord by presenting a corruption of His teaching as being an "authentic" means of personal salvation. And thus is the difference between Catholic America, including New Spain and New France, and the America of Protestantism and of Judeo-Masonry.

Chapter XIII

Claiming for the Devil What Belongs to Christ the King and Mary our Immaculate Queen

The Pilgrims were nothing but the wretched disciples of John Calvin, people who believed that their fellow Calvinists, the Puritans, were wrong in seeking to "purify" the Anglican sect of its remaining Catholic trappings, desiring a total separation from anything to do with even the slightest trace of England's warped vestiges of the true Faith, Catholicism. Their Mayflower Compact, signed aboard the ship that was bringing them to the New World, was an embodiment of Calvinism, providing future colonists and the framers of the American constitution with a road map to the heralding of the "sovereignty of the people" rather than of the rights of Christ the King. These poor, misled, deluded people believed that they had settled in a land that was "pure" of the filth of the "whore of Babylon," the Catholic Church, a place where there had been no Catholic Masses offered. And it is their hatred of the Holy Mass that caused them to make the celebration of Christmas, "Christ's Mass," illegal.

It is not without reason that the incomparable English essayist Gilbert Keith Chesterton wrote the following about the wretched band of people known as "the Pilgrims" who came to the New World to escape from Catholicism even though Catholic martyrs had already sanctified its soil with their blood and that the very Mother of God whose very name they abhorred had appeared to effect its conversion to the Social Reign of her Divine Son, Christ the King:

> "The Americans have established a Thanksgiving Day to celebrate the fact that the Pilgrim Fathers reached America. The English might very well establish another Thanksgiving Day to celebrate the happy fact that the Pilgrim Fathers left England." (Gilbert Keith Chesterton, quoted in Father Denis Fahey, *The Mystical Body of Christ in the Modern World*, p. 16.)

Calvinist preachers in the Plymouth Colony and the Massachusetts Bay Colony and Connecticut and elsewhere in New England spoke of their new land as a "shining city set on a hill," imagery invoked constantly by President Ronald Wilson Reagan, himself a Calvinist by virtue of his being raised by a Presbyterian mother, and by an endless succession of naturalist politicians in the United States of America, including in September of 2011 by New Jersey Governor Christopher Christie. These poor, pathetic people, no matter the four hundred years that separate the Puritans of Plymouth Bay and their contemporary rhetorical spear carriers, reject the simple truth that the shining city set on a hill is the Catholic Church. She alone is the standard-bearer of true liberty that comes from the Cross of the Divine Redeemer, Christ the King, her founder and Invisible Head.

The first Catholics who came to the English colonies arrived in Maryland in 1634, where they could, at least for a time, practice their faith. These Catholics were content simply to have the Mass and the sacraments without appearing to be a "threat" to their Protestant neighbors.

Catholics came to the New World for a variety of motives. With them, however, were always to be found missionaries who desired to convert souls to the true Faith as the precondition for establishing a new Christendom, something that was far from the minds of the Catholics who settled in Maryland in 1634 after they and their immediate ancestors had suffered through a century of intense persecution at the hands of the bloodthirsty Protestant revolutionaries in England and Ireland, starting with King Henry VIII and his son, Edward VI, resuming during the reign of Elizabeth I and thereafter.

In this the devil had set up a truly clever trap. The ancient adversary raised up bloodthirsty Protestant revolutionaries in the German states, Switzerland, the Low Countries and England and Ireland to root out the Faith with violence in these thoroughly Catholic lands. Catholics by the thousands died. The late Dr. Warren Carroll, the founder of Christendom College, wrote that, "according to a contemporary estimate," Henry VIII "had executed 72,000 persons during his reign, some three percent of the population of England (Warren Carroll, *The Cleaving of Christendom: A History of Christendom*, Volume 4, Christendom Press, 2000, p. 203.) The Catholics who came to Maryland in 1634 at the invitation of Cecil Calvert, Lord Baltimore, simply wanted to practice the Faith "quietly," thus accustoming future generations of Catholics in what became the United States of America to accept what Pope Pius VI called a "monstrous doctrine" and Pope Pius VII termed a heresy, "religious liberty," as the best means to protect their ability to worship as they desired.

Although Catholics suffered much in the English colonies that became the first thirteen states of the United States of America, including at times in Maryland as the years progressed, and although they were to face more suffering and bigotry and persecution in the Nineteenth Century, all they really wanted was to be "accepted" by their Protestant and "freethinking" countrymen. There was no thought of converting the land to the Catholic Faith and thus to the Social Reign of Christ the King.

This is evident from the instructions that the future Second Lord of Baltimore, Cecil Calvert, gave to his brother Leonard prior to the departure of the ship Ark and the Dove that was to take Catholics to settle in the Colony of Maryland that had been chartered under their father, the First Lord of Baltimore, George Calvert. These passages from Robert Leckie's *American and Catholic* explain the origins of what Leckie believed was a virtue, "religious freedom," but which was from the beginning a trap to keep Catholics silent about the Faith in exchange for the "right" to worship privately as "quietly as possible":

> Ten days before the ships [taking Catholics to the Colony of Maryland] sailed, Baron [Cecil, later to be the Second Lord of Baltimore] handed his brother [Leonard] instructions enjoining the Catholics aboard the Ark and the Dove to be careful "that they suffer no scandal or offence be given to ay of the Protestants," and that they hold their own services **"as privately as may be,"** remembering **"to be silent upon all occasions of discourse concerning matters of Religion."** Baltimore not only sought "unity and peace amongst all the passengers on Shipp-board," but ashore as well, and thus he gave orders that upon landing the Catholics should immediately make a public oath of allegiance to the king, that when a messenger was sent to Virginia he should be "such a one as is conformable to the Church of England," and that throughout their governance of Maryland "the said Governor and Commissioners [who were all Catholic] treat the Protestants with as much mildness and favor as Justice will permit."

In these famous instructions, then Cecilius Calvert wrote the blueprint for religious freedom in America. His father had conceived of a colony in which Protestants and Catholics might live side by side in amity, each respecting the rights of the other, and he himself had put it into execution. True as it undoubtedly is that the Calverts were motivated by expediency, that they desperately desired to obtain religious freedom for their persecuted brethren, and that there is no reason to believe that they would have been offered it had the Catholic party, rather than the Protestant been in power, the fact remains that the Maryland Colony was tolerant at a time when all others were intolerant, and in this it was unique. As John Tracy Ellis has observed: "Two years before Roger Williams fled the Puritan wrath of Massachusetts Bay to establish religious tolerance in Rhode Island, Baltimore had laid the groundwork for such a policy in Maryland." (Robert Leckie, *American and Catholic*, Doubleday, 1970, p. 25.)

Catholics are not baptized to be "silent upon all occasions of discourse concerning matters of Religion." They are baptized and confirmed to bear witness to the truths of the true Faith. The process of "conversion in reverse" had begun. The state of apostasy and blasphemy and sacrilege and betrayal that is so prevalent today among Catholics in the United States of America and elsewhere in the world is traceable, at least in large measure, to the "relief" that Catholics, who ought to rejoice in being persecuted for the Holy Faith as Our Lord Himself promised a great reward for those who are persecuted for His Name's sake, felt at being able to practice their Faith without persecution upon arrival in Maryland in 1634. It is no wonder that some of the descendants of those first Catholics, including the Shrivers of Maryland, have been so supportive of a "quiet" and "respectable" Catholicism as the precondition for good citizenship and "peace" with those who belong to false religions.

Protestants did not return the gift of "toleration" that Catholics had extended to them in Maryland, especially when Puritans were in control of the colony during the years when the bloodthirsty Puritan named Oliver Cromwell had overthrown and then had beheaded King Charles I, making him, Cromwell, England's stern, Catholic-killing dictator between 1649 and the time of his death on September 3, 1658. Maryland's "Toleration Act", which established toleration for "Trinitarian Christians" in a vote taken by the colonial assembly on April 21, 1649, was revoked by Cromwell's colonial commissioner, William Clairbone, in 1654, before being reinstated again after the Calverts regained control of Maryland in 1658 but abolished permanently in 1692 following the "Glorious Revolution" that had overthrown King James II, the last Catholic to have reigned in England.

Catholics fared even worse in the rest of the colonies, something that historian Dr. Marian T. Horvat related in a very fine article on the subject:

In the 16th century, the English began their long, violent and cruel attempt to subdue the Catholics of Ireland. (5) The English were able "to resolve" any problem of conscience by convincing themselves that the Gaelic Irish Catholic Papists were an unreasonable and boorish people. Maintaining their false belief that they were dealing with a culturally inferior people, the English Protestants imagined themselves absolved from all normal ethical restraints. This attitude persisted with their settlers in the American colonies. (6)

To these factors should be added the role of the Puritan sect. Its relationship with Catholics in colonial America represented the apotheosis of Protestant prejudice against Catholicism. Even though the so-called Anglican church had replaced the Church of Rome, for many Puritans that Elizabethan church still remained too tainted with Romish practices and beliefs. For various reasons, those Puritans left their homeland to found new colonies in North America. A major Puritan exodus to New England began in 1630, and within a decade close to 20,000 men and women had migrated to settlements in Massachusetts and Connecticut. (7) They were principal contributors to a virulent hatred of Catholicism in the American colonies.

Evidence of this anti-Catholic attitude can be found in laws passed by colonial legislatures, sermons preached by colonial ministers, and various books and pamphlets published in the colonies or imported from England. (8)

For example, even though no Catholic was known to have lived in Massachusetts Bay in the first 20 years or more of the colony's life, this did not deter the Puritan government from enacting an anti-priest law in May of 1647, which threatened with death "all and every Jesuit, seminary priest, missionary or other spiritual or ecclesiastical person made or ordained by any authority, power or jurisdiction, derived, challenged or pretended, from the Pope or See of Rome." (9)

When Georgia, the thirteenth colony, was brought into being in 1732 by a charter granted by King George II, its guarantee of religious freedom followed the fixed pattern: full religious freedom was promised to all future settlers of the colony "except papists," that, is Catholics. (10)

Even Rhode Island, famous for its supposed policy of religious toleration, inserted an anti-Catholic statute imposing civil restrictions on Catholics in the colony's first published code of laws in 1719. Not until 1783 was the act revoked. (11)

To have an idea of how this prejudice against Roman Catholics was impressed even among the young, consider these "John Rogers Verses" from the New England Primer: "Abhor that arrant whore of Rome and all her blasphemies; Drink not of her cursed cup; Obey not her decrees." This age of penal restriction against Catholics in the colonies lasted until after the American Revolution.

Someone recalling a lesson from his Catholic history classes might pose the objection: But what about the exceptions to this rule, that is, the three colonial states of Maryland, New York, and Pennsylvania, where tolerance for Catholics existed in the colonial period? Once again, this impression comes from a very optimistic and liberal writing of History rather than the concrete reality.

Catholicism in Maryland

The "Maryland Experiment" began when Charles I issued a generous charter to a prominent Catholic convert from Anglicanism, Lord Cecil Calvert, for the American colony of Maryland. In the new colony, religious tolerance for all so-called Christians was preserved by Calvert until 1654. In that year, Puritans from Virginia succeeded in overthrowing Calvert's rule, although Calvert regained control four years later. The last major political uprising took place in 1689, when the 'Glorious Revolution" of William and Mary ignited a new anti-Catholic revolt in Maryland, and the rule of the next Lord Baltimore, Charles Calvert, was overthrown.

Therefore, in 1692 Maryland's famous Religious Toleration Act officially ended, and the Maryland Assembly established the so-called Church of England as the official State religion supported by tax levies. Restrictions were imposed on Catholics for public worship, and priests could be prosecuted for saying Mass. Although Catholics generally maintained their social status, they were denied the right to vote or otherwise participate in the government of the colony their ancestors had founded. (12) This barebones history is the real story of the famous religious liberty of colonial Maryland.

The Religious Toleration Law of 1649 establishing toleration for all religions in early Maryland has generally been interpreted as resulting from the fact that Cecil Calvert was a Roman Catholic. Catholic American histories commonly presented the foundation of Maryland as motivated by Calvert's burning desire to establish a haven for persecuted English Catholics.   On the other side are Protestant interpretations that present Calvert as a bold opportunist driven by the basest pecuniary motives. (13)

More recent works have provided a much more coherent analysis of the psychology behind the religious toleration that Calvert granted. That is, Calvert was only following a long-standing trend of English Catholics, who tended to ask only for freedom to worship privately as they pleased and to be as inoffensive to Protestants as possible.

A directive of the first Lord Proprietor in 1633 stipulated, for example, that Catholics should "suffer no scandal nor offence" to be given any of the Protestants, that they practice all acts of the Roman Catholic Religion as privately as possible, and that they remain silent during public discourses about Religion. (15) In fact, in the early years of the Maryland colony the only prosecutions for religious offenses involved Catholics who had interfered with Protestants concerning their religion.

As a pragmatic realist, Calvert understood that he had to be tolerant about religion in order for his colony, which was never Catholic in its majority, to be successful. It was this conciliatory and compromising attitude the Calverts transplanted to colonial Maryland in the New World. Further, the Calverts put into practice that separation of Church and State about which other English Catholics had only theorized.

Catholicism in New York

Neither the Dutch nor English were pleased when the Duke of York converted to Roman Catholicism in 1672. His appointment of Irish-born Catholic Colonel Thomas Dongan as governor of the colony of New York was followed by the passage of a charter of liberties and privileges for Catholics. But the two-edged sword of Dutch/ English prejudice against the "Romanists" would soon re-emerge from the scabbard in which it had briefly rested.

After the "Glorious Revolution" of 1688, the virulently anti-Catholic Jacob Leisler spread rumors of "papist" plots and false stories of an impending French and Indian attack upon the English colonies, in which the New York colonial Catholics were said to be aligned with their French co-religionists. Leisler assumed the title of commander-in-chief, and by the end of the year he had overthrown Dongan and taken over the post of lieutenant governor of the colony as well. His government issued orders for the arrest of all reputed "papists," abolished the franchise for Catholics, and suspended all Catholic office-holders. (16) The government after 1688 was so hostile to Catholics, noted Catholic historian John Ellis, "that it is doubtful if any remained in New York." (17)

That very fact made all the more incongruous the severity of measures that continued to be taken against Catholics, which included the draconian law of 1700 prescribing perpetual imprisonment of Jesuits and "popish" messengers. This strong anti-Catholic prejudice persisted even into the federal period. When New York framed its constitution in 1777, it allowed toleration for all religions, but Catholics were denied full citizenship. This law was not repealed until 1806. (18)

The myth of religious toleration of Catholics in New York relies concretely, therefore, on that brief 16-year period from 1672 to 1688 when a Catholic was governor of the colony.

Catholicism in Pennsylvania

Due to the broad tolerance that informed William Penn's Quaker settlements, the story of Catholics in Pennsylvania is the most positive of any of the original 13 colonies. William Penn's stance on religious toleration provided a measured freedom to Catholics in Pennsylvania. The 1701 framework of government, under which Pennsylvania would be governed until the Revolution, included a declaration of liberty of conscience to all who believed in God. Yet a contradiction between Penn's advocacy of liberty of conscience and his growing concern about the growth of one religion – Roman Catholicism – eventually bore sad fruit.

To replace the liberal statutes that provided almost unrestricted liberty of conscience and toleration for those who believed in Christ, officials were required to fulfill the religious qualifications stated in the 1689 Toleration Act, which allowed Dissenters their own places of worship, teachers and preachers, subject to acceptance of certain oaths of allegiance. The act did not apply to Catholics, who were considered potentially dangerous since they were loyal to the Pope, a foreign power. Catholics were thereby effectively barred from public office. (19)

Despite the more restrictive government imposed by Penn after 1700, Catholics were attracted to Pennsylvania, especially after the penal age began in neighboring Maryland. Nonetheless, the Catholic immigrants to Pennsylvania were relatively few in number compared to the Protestants emigrating from the German Palatinate and Northern Ireland. A census taken in 1757 placed the total number of Catholics in Pennsylvania at 1,365. In a colony estimated to have between 200,000 and 300,000 inhabitants, the opposition against the few Catholics living among the Pennsylvania colonists is testimony to an historic prejudice, to say the least. (20)

Even in the face of incessant rumors and several crises (e.g. the so-called "popish plot" of 1756), no extreme measures were taken and no laws were enacted against Catholics. A good measure of the prosperity of the Church in 1763 could be attributed to the Jesuit farms located at St. Paul's Mission in Goshehoppen (500 acres) and Saint Francis Regis Mission at Conewago (120 acres), which contributed substantially to the support of the missionary undertakings of the Church. (21) The history of the Jesuits has been called that of the nascent Catholic Church in the colonies, since no other organized body of Catholic clergy, secular or regular, appeared on the ground till more than a decade after the Revolution. (22)

Relaxation of anti-Catholicism in the revolutionary era

This phase of strong, blatant persecution of Catholicism came to a close during the revolutionary era (1763-1820). For various reasons, the outbreak of hostilities and the winning of independence forced Protestant Americans to at least officially temper their hostility toward Catholicism. With the relaxation of penal measures against them, Catholics breathed a great sigh of relief, a normal and legitimate reaction.

However, instead of maintaining a Catholic behavior consistent with the purity of their Holy Faith, many of them adopted a practical way of life that effectively ignored or downplayed the points of Catholic doctrine which Protestantism attacked. They also closed their eyes to the evil of the Protestant heresy and its mentality. Such an attitude is explained by the natural desire to achieve social and economic success; it is, nonetheless, a shameless attitude with regard to the glory of God and the doctrine that the Catholic Church is the only true religion.

As this liberal Catholic attitude continued and intensified, it generated a kind of fellowship that developed among Catholics with Protestants as such. And so, an early brand of an experimental bad Ecumenism was established, where the doctrinal opposition between the two religions was undervalued and the emotional satisfaction of being accepted as Catholics in a predominantly Protestant society was overestimated. These psychological factors help to explain the first phase of the establishment among our Catholics ancestors of that heresy which Pope Leo XIII called Americanism. (Dr. Marian T. Horvat, "Let None Dare Call it Liberty: The Catholic Church in Colonial America," Tradition in Action website.)

No Catholic should exalt for a single moment about colonial life in the English colonies that became the first thirteen states of the United States of America. The seeds were indeed being planted for an ethos that has taken deep root in the American Catholic soul, an ethos that considers it a virtue to speak only of the natural and to leave the "controversial" matters of the supernatural as "divisive" to national unity, personal success and national material prosperity. False ecumenism began in colonial America, and it flowered in the Nineteenth and Twentieth Centuries long before the fathers of the "Second" Vatican Council convened in Rome on October 11, 1962.

In other words, Catholics in colonial America were being accustomed to accept the Masonic spirit of religious indifferentism that would, along with Puritanism, play its own role in shaping the

American national soul and thus of how Catholics in the United States of America view the Holy Faith and Its role in public life. It is the spirit of "religious freedom" born of the Calverts' desire for "peace" with the Protestants and the Masonic spirit of religious indifferentism that has made Catholics either entirely hostile to any discussion of the necessity of converting the United States to the true Faith or wholly ignorant that it is indeed the teaching of the Catholic Church that Our Blessed Lord and Saviour Jesus Christ must reign as the King of both men and their nations, including the United States of America..

The Catholics of the English colonies had a spirit that was the antithesis of that which was demonstrated by the North American Martyrs, who were willing to die for the Holy Faith, to sanctify the northern reaches of North America for the conversion of the Indians and of their land. And those Catholics of the English colonies had a spirit that was far, far removed from Our Lady of Guadalupe's desire to have the entirety of the Americas converted to the Social Kingship of her Divine Son, Christ the King.

The Antithesis of English America: New France and the North American Martyrs--The North American Martyrs (Saints Isaac Jogues, Rene Goupil, Jean Lalande, Gabriel Lalemant, Noel Chabanel, Anthony Daniel, Charles Garnier, and John de Brebeuf) shed their blood in the fifth decade of the Sixteenth Century to hallow the land of the northern part of North America, to make it possible for there to be here on this continent the same Social Reign of Christ the King that had overtaken the peoples of Central and South America following Our Lady's apparition to Juan Diego in 1531. The establishment of a new Christendom in Latin America helped to eradicate most of the pagan superstitions and barbaric practices that characterized this land of savagery. Some of those barbaric practices included the brutal murders of millions of people in ritual sacrifices.

The North American Martyrs left the comforts of France and the remnants of Christendom in Europe to seek the conversion of souls, understanding that there was a need to do in the northern part of North America what had been done in the southern part of North America and throughout South America in the one hundred thirty-three years between the time of the arrival of Christopher Columbus on the Island of San Salvador in 1492 and the arrival of Father John de Brebeuf in North America in the year 1625.

As noted earlier in the previous chapter of this book, a remarkable, truly miraculous flowering of a new Christendom had taken place in Latin America during those one hundred thirty-three years. Mexico City, Mexico, and Lima, Peru, had become thriving centers of Catholicism and Catholic learning. Lima produced no fewer than five Catholics renowned for their sanctity (Rose Flores, Archbishop Turibius, Martin de Porres, John Massias, Francis Solano). It was to try to plant the seeds for such glorious fruit for Christ the King and Mary our Immaculate Queen that the French missionaries came to the upper reaches of the North American continent (Mexico, of course, is part of North America, as is every country north of the Isthmus of Panama and the Panama Canal).

A fundamental zeal for souls motivated the Jesuit missionaries from France who came to the shores of what was then called New France at the beginning of the Sixteenth Century, just a few years after the Catholic-hating Calvinists had arrived at Plymouth Rock in what is now called Massachusetts. The contrast between the Jesuit missionaries and the Catholic-hating Calvinists could not be more clear. The Jesuit missionaries came here to convert souls to the true Faith, to convert the heathens out of their barbaric practices. The Catholic-hating Calvinists of the Plymouth Colony were giving thanks to God, as they saw it, that they were in a land where there were no Catholics and no offering of the Catholic Mass, which they hated with a particular fury and rage (which is why they abolished the celebration of Christmas Day!). If we lived in a Catholic nation, you see, our true Thanksgiving Day would be this day, September 26, the Feast Day of the North American Martyrs.

Father John de Brebeuf wrote to his superior in Quebec on December 28, 1637, of the inhospitable nature of the savages among whom he was working. His description of the nature of the savages he found in the upper reaches of North America nearly four hundred years ago could pass for a description of the savages found throughout North America today, the descendants of those Catholic-hating Calvinists whose rejection of the true Faith has plunged them into the darkness of naturalism and all of the savagery that is produced thereby:

> We are perhaps upon the point of shedding our blood and of sacrificing our lives in the service of our good Master, Jesus Christ. It seems that His Goodness is willing to accept this sacrifice from me for the expiation of my great innumerable sins, and to crown from this hour forward the past services and the great and ardent desires of all our priests who are here....But we are all grieved over this, that these barbarians, through their own malice, are closing the door to the Gospel and to Grace.... Whatever conclusion they reach, and whatever treatment they accord us, we will try, by the Grace of Our Lord, to endure it patiently for His service. It is a singular favor that His Goodness gives us, to allow us to endure something for love of Him...."

The sad truth is, of course, that the very barbaric practices that the North American Martyrs sought to eradicate by converting the Indians to the true Faith have become part of "mainstream" law and culture in the supposedly "civilized" United States of America.

Human sacrifice?

We have that, don't we? Over four thousand babies a day are sacrificed on the altar of the lie of the autonomy of man from the binding precepts of the Divine positive law and the Natural Law as the foundation of personal and social order. Countless other babies are dispatched "invisibly" by means of chemical abortifacients.

The horrible, demonic drum beat of the Indian tribes, which were meant to conjure up evil spirits, can be heard booming out of automobile radios, sometimes as far as a half a mile away from where the automobile is positioned (there should be a bumper sticker printed up that reads: "Future Deaf People of America" for those who drive under such demonic conditions).

All manner of people walk around as naked as the barbaric peoples of North America, some displaying the various ways in which they have mutilated their bodies by means of tattoos. People speak in the most vile, crude manner imaginable, harkening back to the horrors that pierced the ears of the Jesuit missionaries as they spent long winters in the same quarters as the Indians.

Let's just amplify this point a bit.

A woman at a bank in Spring Hill, Florida, on Monday, September 24, 2007, the Feast of Our Lady of Ransom, was displaying a tattoo of Minnie Mouse! Minnie Mouse. And it was about a month earlier there in Florida that we had encountered elderly women, who were in their late-seventies, who were talking in the most vile, vulgar, degrading, profane manner at a dinner table in public within earshot of children.

Get a grip on reality, you people out there in cyberspace who think that we are going to get some kind of "respite" from this barbarism. A land where women, who are supposed to carry themselves with the feminine dignity and grace of the Mother of God, can kill their own children and mutilate their bodies to display their affection for Minnie Mouse--or for Betty Boop--and speak in profane, scatological terms is not going to get any kind of "respite" from God, Who is going to permit this land to degenerate more and more until she turns to Him through His true Church and by honoring His Most Blessed Mother publicly. A country that does not recognize Christ the King as He has revealed Himself through His true Church and that does not honor His Most Blessed Mother must degenerate more and more into savagery. There is no naturalistic way to stop this. None.

Silvio Cardinal Antoniano wrote about this less than one hundred years before the martyrdom of the North American Martyrs:

> The more closely the temporal power of a nation aligns itself with the spiritual, and the more it fosters and promotes the latter, by so much the more it contributes to the conservation of the commonwealth. For it is the aim of the ecclesiastical authority by the use of spiritual means, to form good Christians in accordance with its own particular end and object; and in doing this it helps at the same time to form good citizens, and prepares them to meet their obligations as members of a civil society. This follows of necessity because in the City of God, the Holy Roman Catholic Church, a good citizen and an upright man are absolutely one and the same thing. How grave therefore is the error of those who separate things so closely united, and who think that they can produce good citizens by ways and methods other than those which make for the formation of good Christians. For, let human prudence say what it likes and reason as it pleases, it is impossible to produce true temporal peace and tranquillity by things repugnant or opposed to the peace and happiness of eternity.

The North American Martyrs were willing to endure all manner of tortures and martyrdom itself for the sake of the honor and glory of God and thus of the eternal good of the souls for whom He shed every single drop of His Most Precious Blood on the wood of the Holy Cross. Brother Rene Goupil, S.J., was the first to suffer the blows of the savages, dying on September 13, 1642. He was martyred in the ravine to the west of the main grounds of the Shrine of Our Lady of the North American Martyrs in Auriesville, New York, preceding his friend Father Isaac Jogues to the ultimate crown of glory for the Catholic Faith by forty-nine months, six days. Anyone who walks down to that ravine will be filled with a sense of wonder and awe at the courage exhibited by Rene Goupil as he was treated so cruelly by men whose immortal souls were in the grips of the devil, who is consumed, as we know, with a hatred of the true God and the Catholic Church and thus for each of our immortal souls that are made in the image and likeness of the One he, the devil, hates.

Saint Rene Goupil showed courage in the face of hostility to the Faith. We must do no less.

Father Isaac Jogues, S.J., was mutilated by these savages at the same time and at the same place, Sennen, now called Auriesville, being rescued after a period of cruel slavery to the Indians by Dutch Calvinists, who took pity on him but nevertheless did not exactly feed him well during the time that he was in their "care" before he left the City of New Amsterdam to return to France. The scene of his touching return to France was described by Milton Lomask in *St. Isaac and the Indians*:

> Off the coast of England, while waiting to change ships, he had been set upon by thieves. He had lost the fine cloak the Dutch had given him in New Amsterdam and the fine beaver hat. The ragged garments he now wore were the gift of a French fisherman.

> A winter dawn lighted the streets of Rennes as Pere Isaac knocked at the door of the Jesuit College. One hand clutched an official-looking paper. It was a letter written by the director-general of New Netherlands and stamped with his seal. It identified Pere Isaac. It related how he had escaped from the Mohawks and how the Dutch had taken him under their protection.

> Pere Isaac knocked again on the thick oak door. He found it hard to believe that he was actually home. To think that in a few minutes he would once more clasp the hands of his fellow Jesuits!

> In the drafty community room at the rear of the college building, Brother Porter was laying a fire on the hearth. He heard the pounding on the street door and frowned.

> Brother Porter was feeling his years and his rheumatism this cold winter morning. He grumbled under his breath as he limped down the long, damp hallway. Decent people, he told himself, didn't come visiting at this early hour.
> He opened the street door and peered with distaste at the bedraggled figure on the

> steps. "I wish to see Father Rector," said Pere Isaac.

> "Sorry," said Brother Porter in a high, shaking voice. "Father Rector is about to say Mass. If you care to wait, you may do so here." He led Pere Isaac into a small parlor. "If you're in a great hurry," he added, "I'll call one of the other priests."

> "I do not wish to see one of the other priests," said Pere Isaac firmly. "I wish to see Father Rector--now!"

> Brother Porter hobbled from the room, shaking his head. "These beggars," he muttered to himself. "Bold as kings, some of them!"

> He pushed open the door to the sacristy and called to Father Rector. "A poor man to see you, I asked him to wait but he insists on seeing you now."

> Father Rector was vesting for Mass. "A poor man?" he inquired.

"Poor in material things," squeaked Brother Porter, "but very rich in boldness."

Father Rector smiled. Brother Porter, he reflected, was never at his best on these cold winter mornings. "A poor man," he repeated, half to himself and half to Brother Porter.

"His need must be great to bring him here so early."

He removed his vestments. He swung down the hall into the parlor.

It was very dark there behind the thick window draperies. Father Rector took the letter that Pere Isaac thrust into his hand. He glanced at it in the gleam of a single candle. His eyes picked up the opening words only: "We, William Kieft, Director-General, and the Council of the New Netherlands, to all . . ."

He lay the letter on the table beside him. He examined the face of his visitor, a worn and tired face under a peasant's cap.

"What is it we can do for you?" he asked gently.

"I come from Canada," said Pere Isaac, "and I -"

He was not allowed to finish his sentence. "From Canada!" cried Father Rector. "From Canada, you say?"

"Yes, I have been there many years."

"Do you know any of our missionaries there?" "I know practically all of them."

"Good!" cried Father Rector. "Perhaps then you can tell me what everyone in France is longing to know. What of Pere Isaac? Do the savage Iroquois still hold him? Is he alive?"

"He is alive. Indeed, he is free." Pere Isaac's voice broke. He flung himself to his knees, grasping the older Jesuit's hands. "Father Rector," he cried, "it is he who speaks to you!"

Father Rector gasped. His eyes went from the letter on the table to the heavily lined face below him. With a cry that rang through the house, he pulled Pere Isaac to his feet and embraced him.

He ran down the room. His voice echoed down the long corridor as he summoned the other priests.

They came quickly, filling the little parlor. They could not believe it at first; then they were amazed and delighted. They shouted. They laughed and cried at the same time as, one by one, they embraced Pere Isaac. Brother Porter was called. Open mouthed, he received the news. Then he hurried, squeaking down the corridor--willingly this time--to procure a clean cassock for the welcome guest.

After Mass and breakfast, the Jesuits crowded into the community room. For hours they talked. Or rather, Pere Isaac talked. The others listened with wonderment and reverence. (Milton Lomask, *St. Isaac and the Indians*, Vision Books, 1956, pp. 158-161.)

Father Isaac's zeal for souls was such, however, that he did not want to remain in the safety of his native France for long. He desired to return to the very land where the tips of his two thumbs and forefingers had been chewed off by the savage Indians. Pope Urban VIII, who recognized Father Jogues as a "living martyr," gave him special permission to offer the Holy Sacrifice of the Mass with his mutilated fingers. Carrying the Crucifix which he received when making his profession as a member of the Society of Jesus, Father Isaac Jogues, S.J., returned to Canada to continue his missionary work there. So many Catholics today blanche at the prospect of speaking as Catholics to their own family members, mind you! Saint Isaac Jogues was willing to return to the land where savages had chewed off his fingers as they killed his lay associate, Brother Rene Goupil, in a most brutal manner.

We can do no less as we bear witness to the Faith and as we continue to denounce apostasy and betrayal by their proper names, never once, under any pretenses, making any concessions to the conciliarism or to its false shepherds who mock the honor and glory of God by praising false religions and who spit in the faces of true popes by deconstructing the very meaning of truth so as to justify their own embrace of one absolutely condemned proposition after another.

Saint Isaac Jogues wrote the following letter shortly before he began his last journey from New France to Ossernenon, not realizing that he would be captured en route thereto, the place of his first sufferings and the place of his own martyrdom:

> The Iroquois have come to make some presents to our governor, ransom some prisoners he held, and treat of peace with him in the name of the whole country. It has been concluded, to the great joy of France. It will last as long as pleases the Almighty.
>
> To maintain, and see what can be done for the instruction of these tribes, it is here deemed expedient to send them some father. I have reason to think I shall be sent, since I have some knowledge of the language and country. You see what need I have of the powerful aid of prayers while amidst these savages. I will have to remain among them, almost without liberty to pray, without Mass, without Sacraments, and be responsible for every accident among the Iroquois, French, Algonquins, and others. But what shall I say? My hope is in God, who needs not us to accomplish his designs. We must endeavor to be faithful to Him and not spoil His work by our shortcomings....
>
> My heart tells me that if I have the happiness of being employed in this mission, Ibo et non redibo, I shall go and shall not return; but I shall be happy if our Lord will complete the sacrifice where He has begun it, and make the little blood I have shed in that land the earnest of what I would give from every vein of my body and my heart.
>
> In a word, this people is "a bloody spouse" to me (Exodus iv, 25). May our good Master, who has purchased them in His blood, open to them the door of His Gospel, as well as to the four allied nations near them.

Adieu, dear Father. Pray Him to unite me inseparably to Him. Isaac Jogues, S.J.

The story of Saint Isaac's demise--and of the conversion of his killer--should inspire us all to remain steadfast in the true Faith at all times and to pray for our persecutors, forgiving them their offenses against us as we are forgiven our many sins by Our Blessed Lord and Saviour Jesus Christ in the Sacred Tribunal of Penance at the hands and with the lips of an *alter Christus* acting *in persona Christi*:

Pere Isaac and his two companions talked. Occasionally, and for short spells, they slept. Toward evening, as the autumn dusk closed in, they prepared their supper.

Hearing footsteps outside the cabin, Pere Isaac hurried to the door. He was eager to hear what had been decided at the council fire. But it was not his [Mohawk] Aunt. A young brave stood on the porch.

The Mohawk lifted his arm. "Welcome again to the Mohawk villages, Ondessonk," he said. "I bring you an invitation. There is a feast at my house. You will follow me."

"One minute." Pere Isaac went to a corner of the cabin. From among some belongings he lifted a small rosary.

As he turned to leave, young La Lande leaped to his feet. The French youth placed himself at the door, barring the way.

"Mon Pere," he begged, "do not go! The old woman said we must remain here till she returns. How do you know this is not some trick?" "It may be," said Isaac quietly."

"All the same, I will go."

"But, mon Pere!"

"As a missionary," said the Jesuit, "I must respect the Indians' customs. To refuse an invitation to a feast is to make an enemy for life."

He dropped his hand on the youth's shoulder. Gently pushing the lad aside he lifted the door flap and went out.

The Indian was still on the porch. They walked together, in silence, through the dark streets, stopping before a large longhouse decorated with the roughly carved figure of a bear. It was not a cold night, only brisk. Clean-cut stars glistened in the darkening sky. The tangy fragrance of frostbitten apples hung in the air.

The Mohawk pulled aside the deerskin covering the door. "Enter, Ondessonk," he said, indicating that Pere Isaac was to go first.

The door was low. The Jesuit was not a tall man. Even so, he was forced to bow his head.

Inside, in the shadows, a Mohawk brave waited--a tall, handsome man with a slanting black scar along his left cheek.

As Pere Isaac entered, the tall Mohawk lowered his tomahawk. Pere Isaac knew only a single, fleeting flash of pain before becoming God's own. It was about six o'clock in the evening. The date was October 18, 1646.

Ondessonk was dead.

The news drifted through the Indian villages like a sad breeze.

There was mourning in the Huron cabins, and in Iroquois cabins too, for many Mohawks had come to love and admire the brave blackrobe.

Pere Isaac's Aunt gathered together his few belongings and carried them to Rensselaerswyck. When she handed them to the Dutch minister, the dominie wept.

No one, anywhere, was more grieved than a sturdy young man named Jean Amyot--the same Jean, who, as solemn, freckle-faced las of ten, had gone with Pere Isaac to the Huron country ten years before.

Jean had grown to manhood among the Indians, first in the Huron cabins and later among the Algonquins near Quebec. In the fall of 1647, he led a band of Algonquins near Quebec on a scouting expedition. The Iroquois had dug up the war hatchet. They had broken the peace. All summer, along the St. Lawrence, they attacked and robbed.

In a forest clearing, not far from Quebec, Jean Amyot and the Algonquins met and defeated an Iroquois war party. Seven Iroquois were slain. As the victors were about to depart, Jean Amyot discovered an enemy brave hiding in the hollow trunk of a tree.

The captive was a Mohawk--a tall, handsome man. The Algonquins promptly nicknamed him the "Scarred One" because of the slanting black scar running across his left cheek.

They took him to Quebec. Living there were several Hurons who had been in the Mohawk capital, as captives, at the time of Pere Isaac's death. When these Hurons saw the Scarred One, they muttered among themselves.

Soon a strange rumor was heard on all sides. The Scarred One, people said, is Pere Isaac's murderer!

Word of the rumor reached the French governor. He called the tall Mohawk and questioned him. "Were you in the Mohawk capital on the night of Pere Isaac's death?" he asked.

"Yes," said the Indian. "I was there."

"Was Pere Isaac's death ordered by your chieftains?"

"No. It was not."

"Whey then was he killed?"

"Because some Mohawk braves were determined to destroy all Frenchmen."

The governor conferred with his aides. He turned back to the scarred Mohawk. "Some Hurons," he said," "say that you yourself killed Pere Isaac. Did you?"

The Indian did not answer. He had answered all the other questions forthrightly. Now he was silent.

The French governor conferred again with his aides. "We cannot execute this man," he said. "The Hurons say he is guilty. I myself believe he is. But no one here actually saw the murder committed. We must let this man go."

Leaving the fort, the Mohawk brave went at once to the Jesuit Mission house in Quebec. Several of the priests were present.

"I am here," he told them, "to request of you the waters-of-importance." He spoke in the Indian manner. "Waters-of-importance" was their phrase for the waters of baptism.

The Jesuits looked at one another, amazed. They too believed that this was the Indian who had killed Pere Isaac.

He noted their expressions. "I speak in earnest," he assured them. "I wish to go to Heaven. I am sorry to have offended Him-Who-Made-All. We must all appear before Him, according to your saying. At that time you may say I have been false if my heart has not now the belief which my mouth declares to you."

His words moved the Jesuits. They instructed him. They found that he knew the beliefs of their faith and was wholly sincere. On September 16, 1647, the tall Mohawk was baptized and given the Christian name of Isaac Jogues. Soon after, the Algonquins took him away to one of their villages. There, sometime the following month, they executed him.

News of this reached Quebec in the late winter. There were several versions of what had happened. Some said that the Scarred One had admitted his guilt just before he died. Others said that he had remained silent to the end. One thing all agreed. The Indian Isaac Jogues had died, as the Jesuit Isaac Jogues had died before him, in the faith and like a man.

The name did not die with him. On June 29, 1930, Pope Pius XI raised Pere Isaac Jogues to the Altars of the Church. Today, he who was known to all the Indians of his time and place as Ondessonk, is known to all the world as Saint Isaac. (Milton Lomask, *St. Isaac and the*

Indians, pp. 175-181.)

Each of the eight Jesuits who were martyred in the northern reaches of North America died manfully in behalf of the Holy Faith. They did make converts to the Faith, although it was not within God's Holy Providence for the lands they evangelized to be as permeated with the Faith as were the lands from the parts of what are now the southeastern and southwestern United States of America south to Mexico and down to Argentina and Chile.

This is indeed quite a contrast with the spirit of "religious freedom" that has existed amongst Catholics in the United States of America dating back to colonial days. Every Catholic in every age is supposed to demonstrate the exact same courage in the face of modern-day pagan savages as that exhibited by the North American Martyrs between 1642 and 1649. It does not matter that we may not make many converts or that the United States of America and Canada may not be converted to the true Faith anytime soon. What matters is our fidelity to the cause of Christ the King and to Mary our Immaculate Queen without making any concessions at all to the lies of civil and religious liberty that are the foundation of the modern, anti-Incarnational civil state that was destined for its very perverse beginnings to degenerate to the base level of savagery that characterizes it in our days.

Each of the eight North American Martyrs of the Society of Jesus were men of profound Eucharistic piety and deep and tender devotion to the Mother of God, especially by means of her Most Holy Rosary, which they taught their converts to pray. Saints Isaac Jogues, Rene Goupil, Jean de Brebeuf, Jean Lalande, Gregory Lalemant, Noel Chabanel, Anthony Daniel and Charles Garnier spent many hours in earnest prayer before the King of Kings in His Real Presence in the Most Blessed Sacrament. And it is upon such Eucharist piety and Total Consecration to Our Lady and fidelity to her Most Holy Rosary and to the conditions associated with her Brown Scapular that the entirety of personal and social order rests.

All of this was very far from the minds of those who were steeped in one falsehood after another in   the English colonies of what became the United States of America. Content with the pursuit of material prosperity and social peace at all costs, justifying themselves in the mantle of various heresies passing for Christianity and in liturgical rites that were inspired by the devil himself, the colonists sought to have a "land of plenty" rather than to make sure to have plenty of Sanctifying Grace in their immortal souls. These victims of the Protestant Revolution and its aftermath were thus primed and ready for the importation and transplantation of various naturalistic "philosophies" that were being "developed" in Europe by the sons and daughters of the so-called "Enlightenment" (or "Age of Reason") that, far from   being any kind of "enlightening" upon man, was the beginning of the true Dark Ages of human barbarism under the cover of the "rights of man" and the "sovereignty of the people." And it would be these false, interrelated and multifaceted naturalist "philosophies" that even Catholics in what became the United States of America would become indistinguishable in their beliefs and actions from the adherents of Judeo-Masonry.

Chapter XIV

The Rise of the Lodge and Its Influence in the Anglo-American Colonies

Although there are some who like to dismiss the influence of Judeo-Masonry in the United States of America by claiming that "American Masonry has been different than European Masonry," the truth of the matter is that every form of Masonry exists to promote the false belief that it is possible for men to live together as "brothers" while they disagree about matters of religion and philosophy in order to   pursue "civic virtue" as the fabric of social order. In other words, it matters not to personal and social order that there is a true God, the Most Blessed Trinity, or that the Second Person of the Most Blessed Trinity became Incarnate in the Virginal and Immaculate Womb of His Most Blessed Mother by the power of the Third Person of the Most Blessed Trinity, God the Holy Ghost, or that He created a true   Church, the Catholic Church, to be the infallible teacher and eternal guardian of His Sacred Deposit   of Faith as well as providing men with the sole means of sanctification He won for them by His Redemptive Act on the wood of the Holy Cross.

Pope Leo XII, writing in *Ubi Primum*, May 5, 1824, explained the essence of the Masonic ethos nearly one hundred seven years after the forming of the Grand Lodge of England from the "Free and Accepted Masons" and the "Alchemical Society of the Rosicrucians" on June 24, 1717:

> But at what are these remarks aimed? A certain sect, which you surely know, has unjustly arrogated to itself the name of philosophy, and has aroused from the ashes the disorderly ranks of practically every error. **Under the gentle appearance of piety and liberality this sect professes what they call tolerance or indifferentism. It preaches that not only in civil affairs, which is not Our concern here, but also in religion, God has given every individual a wide freedom to embrace and adopt without danger to his salvation whatever sect or opinion appeals to him on the basis of his private judgment.** The apostle Paul warns us against the impiety of these madmen. "I beseech you, brethren, to behold those who create dissensions and scandals beyond the teaching which you have learned. Keep away from such men. They do not serve Christ Our Lord but their own belly, and by sweet speeches and blessings they seduce the hearts of the innocent."

> Of course this error is not new, but in Our days it rages with a new rashness against the constancy and integrity of the Catholic faith. Eusebius cites Rhodo as his source for saying that the heretic Apelles in the second century had already produced the mad theory that faith should not be investigated, but that each man should persevere in the faith he was raised in. Even those who put faith in a crucified man were to be saved, according to Apelles, provided that they engaged in good works. Rhetorius too, as We learn from St. Augustine, used to claim that all the heretics walked on the right road and spoke truth. But Augustine adds that this is such nonsense that he cannot believe it. **The current indifferentism has developed to the point of arguing that everyone is on the right road. This includes not only all those sects which though outside the Catholic Church verbally accept revelation as a foundation, but those groups too which spurn the idea of divine revelation and profess a pure deism or even a pure naturalism. The indifferentism of Rhetorius seemed absurd to St. Augustine, and** rightly so, but it did acknowledge certain limits. But a tolerance which extends to Deism and Naturalism, which even the ancient heretics rejected, can never be approved by anyone

who uses his reason. Nevertheless -- alas for the times; alas for this lying philosophy!- such a tolerance is approved, defended, and praised by these pseudophilosophers.

Certainly many remarkable authors, adherents of the true philosophy, have taken pains to attack and crush this strange view. But the matter is so self-evident that it is superfluous to give additional arguments. **It is impossible for the most true God, who is Truth Itself, the best, the wisest Provider, and the Rewarder of good men, to approve all sects who profess false teachings which are often inconsistent with one another and contradictory, and to confer eternal rewards on their members. For we have a surer word of the prophet, and in writing to you We speak wisdom among the perfect; not the wisdom of this world but the wisdom of God in a mystery. By it we are taught, and by divine faith we hold one Lord, one faith, one baptism, and that no other name under heaven is given to men except the name of Jesus Christ of Nazareth in which we must be saved. This is why we profess that there is no salvation outside the Church**.

But Oh! the depth of the riches of the wisdom and knowledge of God! How incomprehensible His judgments! God, who destroys the wisdom of the wise, has clearly given the enemies of His Church, who despise supernatural revelation, a perverted mind corresponding to the symbol of iniquity which was written on the forehead of the wicked woman in the Apocalypse. For what greater iniquity is there than for those proud men not only to abandon true religion, but also to seek to ensnare the imprudent by criticisms of every sort, in speech and writings filled with all deceit! Let God arise and restrain, make futile and destroy this unbridled license in all its manifestations. (Pope Leo XII, *Ubi Primum*, May 5, 1824.)

It is of the very heart and soul of the heresy of Americanism that took root in one hundred sixty-nine years between the founding of Jamestown, Virginia, in 1607 and the promulgation of the Declaration of Independence on July 4, 1776, to promote the belief that it is necessary to reduce all things to the merely natural level. Catholics have been forewarned by their true popes that they cannot approve or defend the religious indifferentism that is the foundation of the anti-Incarnational civil state of Modernity, including that of the United States of America.

Some defenders of all things American who seek to defend the "founding principles," if not try to reconcile them to the truths of the Holy Faith, as this writer sought to do for the first ten to twelve years of his college teaching career, focus on what is asserted to be the "small number" of the founders who were Freemasons. Such a defense, however, was exploded by Poe Leo XIII in *Humanum Genus*, April 20, 1884, as he explained that it is the ethos of Freemasonry that matters, not the identities of those who are formal members of Masonic lodges:

For, from what We have above most clearly shown, that which is their ultimate purpose forces itself into view -- namely, the utter overthrow of that whole religious and political order of the world which the Christian teaching has produced, and the substitution of a new state of things in accordance with their ideas, of which the foundations and laws shall be drawn from mere naturalism.

What We have said, and are about to say, must be understood of the sect of the Freemasons taken generically, and in so far as it comprises the associations kindred to it and confederated with it, but not of the individual members of them. There may be persons amongst these, and not a few who, although not free from the guilt of having entangled themselves in such associations, yet are neither themselves partners in their criminal acts nor aware of the ultimate object which they are endeavoring to attain. In the same way, some of the affiliated societies, perhaps, by no means approve of the extreme conclusions which they would, if consistent, embrace as necessarily following from their common principles, did not their very foulness strike them with horror. Some of these, again, are led by circumstances of times and places either to aim at smaller things than the others usually attempt or than they themselves would wish to attempt. **They are not, however, for this reason, to be reckoned as alien to the masonic federation; for the masonic federation is to be judged not so much by the things which it has done, or brought to completion, as by the sum of its pronounced opinions**. (Pope Leo XIII, *Humanum Genus*, April 20, 1884.)

It is a mistake to bogged down in the "trees" of trying to identify which of the "founders" of the United States of America were Freemasons. What matters is that they were influenced by its naturalistic, semi-Pelagian, religiously indifferentist and anti-Incarnational tenets that were summarized quite precisely by Pope Leo XIII in numerous encyclical letters, including in *Humanum Genus*:

But the naturalists go much further; for, having, in the highest things, entered upon a wholly erroneous course, they are carried headlong to extremes, either by reason of the weakness of human nature, or because God inflicts upon them the just punishment of their pride. Hence it happens that they no longer consider as certain and permanent those things which are fully understood by the natural light of reason, such as certainly are -- the existence of God, the immaterial nature of the human soul, and its immortality. The sect of the Freemasons, by a similar course of error, is exposed to these same dangers; for, although in a general way they may profess the existence of God, they themselves are witnesses that they do not all maintain   this truth with the full assent of the mind or with a firm conviction. **Neither do they conceal that this question about God is the greatest source and cause of discords among them; in fact, it is certain that a considerable contention about this same subject has existed among them very lately. But, indeed, the sect allows great liberty to its votaries, so that to each side is given the right to defend its own opinion, either that there is a God, or that there is none; and those who obstinately contend that there is no God are as easily   initiated as those who contend that God exists, though, like the pantheists, they have false   notions concerning Him: all of which is nothing else than taking away the reality, while retaining some absurd representation of the divine nature.**

When this greatest fundamental truth has been overturned or weakened, it follows that those truths, also, which are known by the teaching of nature must begin to fall -- namely, that all things were made by the free will of God the Creator; that the world is governed by Providence; that souls do not die; that to this life of men upon the earth there will succeed another and an everlasting life.

When these truths are done away with, which are as the principles of nature and important for knowledge and for practical use, it is easy to see what will become of both public and private morality. We say nothing of those more heavenly virtues, which no one can exercise or even acquire without a special gift and grace of God; of which necessarily no trace can be found in those who reject as unknown the redemption of mankind, the grace of God, the sacraments, and the happiness to be obtained in heaven. We speak now of the duties which have their origin in natural probity. That God is the Creator of the world and its provident Ruler; that the eternal law commands the natural order to be maintained, and forbids that it be disturbed; that the last end of men is a destiny far above human things and beyond this sojourning upon the earth: these are the sources and these the principles of all justice and morality.

If these be taken away, as the naturalists and Freemasons desire, there will immediately be no knowledge as to what constitutes justice and injustice, or upon what principle morality is founded. And, in truth, the teaching of morality which alone finds favor with the sect of Freemasons, and in which they contend that youth should be instructed, is that which they call "civil," and "independent," and "free," namely, that which does not contain any religious belief. But, how insufficient such teaching is, how wanting in soundness, and how easily moved by every impulse of passion, is sufficiently proved by its sad fruits, which have already begun to appear. For, wherever, by removing Christian education, this teaching has begun more completely to rule, there goodness and integrity of morals have begun quickly to perish, monstrous and shameful opinions have grown up, and the audacity of evil deeds has risen to a high degree. All this is commonly complained of and deplored; and not a few of those who by no means wish to do so are compelled by abundant evidence to give not infrequently the same testimony.

Moreover, human nature was stained by original sin, and is therefore more disposed to vice than to virtue. For a virtuous life it is absolutely necessary to restrain the disorderly movements of the soul, and to make the passions obedient to reason. In this conflict human things must very often be despised, and the greatest labors and hardships must be undergone, in order that reason may always hold its sway. But the naturalists and Freemasons, having no faith in those things which we have learned by the revelation of God, deny that our first parents sinned, and consequently think that free will is not at all weakened and inclined to evil. On the contrary, exaggerating rather the power and the excellence of nature, and placing therein alone the principle and rule of justice, they cannot even imagine that there is any need at all of a constant struggle and a perfect steadfastness to overcome the violence and rule of our passions.

Wherefore we see that men are publicly tempted by the many allurements of pleasure; that there are journals and pamphlets with neither moderation nor shame; that stage-plays are remarkable for license; that designs for works of art are shamelessly sought in the laws of a so-called verism; that the contrivances of a soft and delicate life are most carefully devised; and that all the blandishments of pleasure are diligently sought out by which virtue may be lulled to sleep. Wickedly, also, but at the same time quite consistently, do those act who do away with the expectation of the joys of heaven, and bring down all happiness to the level of mortality, and, as it were, sink it in the earth. Of what We have said the following fact, astonishing not so much in itself as in its open expression, may serve as a confirmation. For, since generally no one is accustomed to obey crafty and clever men so submissively as those whose soul is weakened and broken

down by the domination of the passions, there have been in the sect of the Freemasons some who have plainly determined and proposed that, artfully and of set purpose, the multitude should be satiated with a boundless license of vice, as, when this had been done, it would easily come under their power and authority for any acts of daring.

What refers to domestic life in the teaching of the naturalists is almost all contained in the following declarations: that marriage belongs to the genus of commercial contracts, which can rightly be revoked by the will of those who made them, and that the civil rulers of the State have power over the matrimonial bond; that in the education of youth nothing is to be taught in the matter of religion as of certain and fixed opinion; and each one must be left at liberty to follow, when he comes of age, whatever he may prefer. To these things the Freemasons fully assent; and not only assent, but have long endeavored to make them into a law and institution. For in many countries, and those nominally Catholic, it is enacted that no marriages shall be considered lawful except those contracted by the civil rite; in other places the law permits divorce; and in others every effort is used to make it lawful as soon as may be. Thus, the time is quickly coming when marriages will be turned into another kind of contract -- that is into changeable and uncertain unions which fancy may join together, and which the same when changed may disunite.

With the greatest unanimity the sect of the Freemasons also endeavors to take to itself the education of youth. They think that they can easily mold to their opinions that soft and pliant age, and bend it whither they will; and that nothing can be more fitted than this to enable them to bring up the youth of the State after their own plan. **Therefore, in the education and instruction of children they allow no share, either of teaching or of discipline, to the ministers of the Church; and in many places they have procured that the education of youth shall be exclusively in the hands of laymen, and that nothing which treats of the most important and most holy duties of men to God shall be introduced into the instructions on morals.**

Then come their doctrines of politics, in which the naturalists lay down that all men have the same right, and are in every respect of equal and like condition; that each one is naturally free; that no one has the right to command another; that it is an act of violence to require men to obey any authority other than that which is obtained from themselves. According to this, therefore, all things belong to the free people; power is held by the command or permission of the people, so that, when the popular will changes, rulers may lawfully be deposed and the source of all rights and civil duties is either in the multitude or in the governing authority when this is constituted according to the latest doctrines. It is held also that the State should be without God; that in the various forms of religion there is no reason why one should have precedence of another; and that they are all to occupy the same place.

What, therefore, sect of the Freemasons is, and what course it pursues, appears sufficiently from the summary We have briefly given. Their chief dogmas are so greatly and manifestly at variance with reason that nothing can be more perverse. To wish to destroy the religion and the Church which God Himself has established, and whose perpetuity He insures by His protection, and to bring back after a lapse of eighteen centuries the manners and customs of the pagans, is signal folly and audacious impiety. Neither is it less horrible nor more tolerable that they should repudiate the benefits which Jesus Christ so mercifully obtained, not only for individuals, but also for the family and for civil society, benefits which, even according to the judgment and testimony of enemies of Christianity, are very great. In this insane and wicked endeavor we may almost see the implacable hatred and spirit of revenge with which Satan himself is inflamed against Jesus Christ. -- So also the studious endeavor of the Freemasons to destroy the chief foundations of justice and honesty, and to co-operate with those who would wish, as if they were mere animals, to do what they please, tends only to the ignominious and disgraceful ruin of the human race.

The evil, too, is increased by the dangers which threaten both domestic and civil society. As We have elsewhere shown, in marriage, according to the belief of almost every nation, there is something sacred and religious; and the law of God has determined that marriages shall not be dissolved. If they are deprived of their sacred character, and made dissoluble, trouble and confusion in the family will be the result, the wife being deprived of her dignity and the children left without protection as to their interests and well being. -- . Human society, indeed for which by nature we are formed, has been constituted by God the Author of nature; and from Him, as from their principle and source, flow in all their strength and permanence the countless benefits with which society abounds. As we are each of us admonished by the very voice of nature to worship God in piety and holiness, as the Giver unto us of life and of all that is good therein, so also and for the same reason, nations and States are bound to worship Him; and therefore it is clear that those who would absolve society from all religious duty act not only unjustly but also with ignorance and folly. . . .

Would that all men would judge of the tree by its fruit, and would acknowledge the seed and origin of the evils which press upon us, and of the dangers that are impending! We have to deal with a deceitful and crafty enemy, who, gratifying the ears of people and of princes, has ensnared them by smooth speeches and by adulation. Ingratiating themselves with rulers under a pretense of friendship, the Freemasons have endeavored to make them their allies and powerful helpers for the destruction of the Christian name; and that they might more strongly urge them on, they have, with determined calumny, accused the Church of invidiously contending with rulers in matters that affect their authority and sovereign power. Having, by these artifices, insured their own safety and audacity, they have begun to exercise great weight in the government of States: but nevertheless they are prepared to shake the foundations of empires, to harass the rulers of the State, to accuse, and to cast them out, as often as they appear to govern otherwise than they themselves could have wished. In like manner, they have by flattery deluded the people. Proclaiming with a loud voice liberty and public prosperity, and saying that it was owing to the Church and to sovereigns that the multitude were not drawn out of their unjust servitude and poverty, they have imposed upon the people, and, exciting them by a thirst for novelty, they have urged them to assail both the Church and the civil power. **Nevertheless, the expectation of the benefits which was hoped for is greater than the reality; indeed, the common people, more oppressed than they were before, are deprived in their misery of that solace which, if things had been arranged in a Christian manner, they would have had with ease and in abundance. But, whoever strive against the order which Divine Providence has constituted pay usually the penalty of their pride, and meet with affliction and misery where they rashly hoped to find all things prosperous and in**

conformity with their desires. (Pope Leo XIII, *Humanum Genus*, April 20, 1884.)

The generic kind of Christianity that existed within the English colonies up and down the Atlantic seaboard in the Seventeenth and Eighteenth Centuries is what almost all Catholics today believe is "acceptable" to God as a means of personal salvation and thus for some kind of "common ground" social order. This is simply not so.

Pope Pius XI, writing in *Mit Brennender Sorge*, March 17, 1937,

> **Beware, Venerable Brethren, of that growing abuse, in speech as in writing, of the name of God as though it were a meaningless label, to be affixed to any creation, more or less arbitrary, of human speculation. Use your influence on the Faithful, that they refuse to yield to this aberration. Our God is the Personal God, supernatural, omnipotent, infinitely perfect, one in the Trinity of Persons, tri-personal in the unity of divine essence, the Creator of all existence. Lord, King and ultimate Consummator of the history of the world, who will not, and cannot, tolerate a rival God by His side.**

> No faith in God can for long survive pure and unalloyed without the support of faith in Christ. "No one knoweth who the Son is, but the Father: and who the Father is, but the Son and to whom the Son will reveal Him" (Luke x. 22). "Now this is eternal life: That they may know thee, the only true God, and Jesus Christ whom thou has sent" (John xvii. 3). Nobody,   therefore, can say: "I believe in God, and that is enough religion for me," for the Savior's words brook no evasion: "Whosoever denieth the Son, the same hath not the Father. He that confesseth the Son hath the Father also" (1 John ii. 23) (Pope Pius XI, *Mit Brennender Sorge*, March 17, 1937.)

Generic references to "God" and "Supreme Being" and to the "Supreme Judge of the Universe" do not please God, Who has revealed Himself to be a Trinity of Divine Persons and has created a true Church, that Catholic Church, to teach and sanctify men. And it is these generic references to some kind of "supreme being" that began to proliferate in the colonies, especially among the class of men among whom came many of those who signed the Declaration of Independence, in the 1730s and thereafter following the merger of the Free and Acceptance Masons with the Rosicrucians in 1717. Error spreads like wildfire. The devil sees to that fact.

The "ideas," such as they were, of one naturalistic philosopher (Thomas Hobbes, who was influential in Seventeenth Century England but who remained somewhat influential during the "Age of Reason;" John Locke, discussed earlier in this book; Immanuel Kant; Isaac Newton; and, among others, David Hume), began to take root in the minds, hearts and souls of men who had been set adrift by the lies of the Protestant Revolution. Mere contingent beings, men who did not create themselves and whose bodies were destined for the corruption of the grave, reinvent the wheel, so to speak, constantly in order to discover the "meaning" of human existence and how man is to view himself, his nature, liberty, the civil state, society, politics, governance, education and the arts. This work was a logical extension of the "humanism" of the Renaissance that had given a "rebirth" to the moral relativism and the sophistry of Athens in the Fifth Century before Christ. "Educated" and "refined" "gentlemen" of means and influence looked to these naturalist philosophers rather than to the teaching of Holy Mother Church for their guidance on human existence. The names listed above are just several of the legion of writers who served as champions of "man," therefore, whether wittingly or unwittingly, doing the work of the adversary, who lured Adam and Eve into thinking that they could have the same knowledge, power and authority of God.

There were various French "philosophes" whose writing helped to plant the seeds for the French Revolution, which began on July 14, 1789. Among those, of course, were Francois-Marie Arouet, better known as Voltaire; Charles Louis Montesquieu, who had a profound influence upon some of the American "founding fathers," especially James Madison; and, among others, Jean-Jacques Rousseau. Although Alexis de Tocqueville, whose *Democracy in America*, which was published in two volumes (in 1835 and 1840), was an elegy of praise in behalf of the Puritans for their promotion of the ethos of "equality" that de Tocqueville saw taking root in the United States of America, makes a strong case that Rousseau had great influence upon the mind of Alexis de Tocqueville.

Father Denis Fahey summarized Rousseau's false beliefs very well in *The Mystical Body of Christ in the Modern World*:

> [Jean-Jacques] Rousseau carries on the revolution against the order of the world begun by Luther. Luther's revolt was that of our individuality and sense-life against the exigencies of the supernatural order instituted by God. It was an attempt to remain attached to Christ, while rejecting the order established by Christ for our return to God. Rousseau's revolt was against the order of natural morality, by the exaltation of the primacy of our sense-life.
>
> The little world of each one of us, our individuality, is a divine person, supremely free and sovereignly independent of all order, natural and supernatural. The state of Liberty or of sovereign independence is the primitive state of man, and the nature of man demands the restoration of that state of liberty. It is to satisfy this-called exigency that the 'Father of modern thought' invented the famous myth of the Social Contract.
>
> The Social Contract gives birth to a form of association in which each one, while forming a union with all the others, obeys only himself and remains as free as before. Each one is subject to the whole, but he is not subject to any man, there is no man above him. He is absorbed in the common Ego begotten in the pact, so that obeying the law, he obeys only himself. Each citizen votes in order, that by the addition of the number of votes, the general will, expressed by the vote of the majority, is, so to say, a manifestation of the 'deity' immanent in the multitude. The People are God (no wonder we have gotten used to writing the word with a capital letter). The law imposed by this 'deity' does not need to be just in order to exact obedience. In fact, the majority vote makes or creates right and justice. An adverse majority vote can not only overthrow the directions and commands of the Heads of the Mystical Body on earth, the Pope and the Bishops, but can even deprive the Ten Commandments of all binding force.
>
> To the triumph of those ideals in the modern world, the Masonic denial of original sin and the Rousseauist dogma of the natural goodness of man have contributed not a little. The dogma of natural goodness signifies that man lived originally in a purely natural paradise of

happiness and goodness and that, even in our present degraded state, all our instinctive movements are good. We do not need grace, for nature can do for what grace does. In addition, Rousseau holds that this state of happiness and goodness, of perfect justice and innocence, of exemption from servile work and suffering, is natural to man, that is, essentially demanded by our nature. Not only then is original sin nonexistent, not only do we not come into the world as fallen sons of the first Adam, bearing in us the wounds of our fallen nature, is radically anti-natural. Suffering and pain have been introduced by society, civilization and private property. Hence we must get rid of all these and set up a new form of society. We can get back the state of the Garden of Eden by the efforts of our own nature, without the help of grace. For Rousseau, the introduction of the present form of society, and of private property constitute the real Fall. The setting up of a republic based on his principles will act as a sort of democratic grace which will   restore in its entirety our lost heritage. In a world where the clear teaching of the faith of Christ about the supernatural order of the Life of Grace has become obscured, but where men are still vaguely conscious that human nature was once happy, Rousseau's appeal acts like an urge of homesickness. We need not be astonished, then, apart from the question of Masonic-Revolutionary organization and propaganda, at the sort of delirious enthusiasm which   takes possession of men at the thought of a renewal of society. Nor need we wonder that men work for the overthrow of existing government and existing order, in the belief that they are not legitimate forms of society. A State not constructed according to Rosseauist-Masonic principles is not a State ruled by laws. It is a monstrous tyranny, and must be overthrown in the name of "Progress" and of the "onward march of democracy.' All these influences must be borne in mind as we behold, since 1789, the triumph in one country after another of Rousseauist-Masonic democracy. (Father Denis Fahey, *The Mystical Body of Christ in the Modern World.*)

Rousseau's ideas would influence the likes of the radical American pamphleteer, Thomas Paine, who is responsible for coining the phrase "the United States," and would serve to influence politics from the period of Andrew Jackson's ascent in American politics in the 1820s and thereafter, playing a critical role in the contemporary "left's" view of how their leaders represent the "general will" of the people, thus enabling them to impose their statist prescriptions to "improve" the world by enslaving the people whose interests they claim to serve to their ideological predilections.

Not to be overlooked in the admixture of errors that influenced the intellectual elites in the English colonies were those of the homegrown variety, including those of Thomas Paine, who blasphemed Our Blessed Lord and Saviour Jesus Christ and His Most Blessed Mother in *The Age of Reason*, who mocked all religions, especially Christianity, with great glee, presaging the day when such mockery would become part of the "mainstream" of American educational and cultural life. Here is an excerpt from Paine's "The Age of Reason" that could be found today in any number of popular textbooks and commentaries.

The excerpts from Thomas Paine's scandalously blasphemous writing are being provided to demonstrate to Catholics that it is morally wrong to praise such a man or to quote him favorably on any topic. An unbelieving blasphemer is to be mocked, not praised or quoted favorably.

Here is just one brief except from the work of the "freethinking" Paine that should offend every

Catholic without question:

> When also I am told that a woman, called the Virgin Mary, said, or gave out, that she was with child without any cohabitation with a man, and that her betrothed husband, Joseph, said that an angel told him so, I have a right to believe them or not: such a circumstance required a much stronger evidence than their bare word for it: but we have not even this; for neither Joseph nor Mary wrote any such matter themselves. It is only reported by others that they said so. It is hearsay upon hearsay, and I do not chose to rest my belief upon such evidence.
>
> It is, however, not difficult to account for the credit that was given to the story of Jesus Christ being the Son of God. He was born when the heathen mythology had still some fashion and repute in the world, and that mythology had prepared the people for the belief of such a story. Almost all the extraordinary men that lived under the heathen mythology were reputed to be the sons of some of their gods. It was not a new thing at that time to believe a man to have been celestially begotten; the intercourse of gods with women was then a matter of familiar opinion. Their Jupiter, according to their accounts, had cohabited with hundreds; the story therefore had nothing in it either new, wonderful, or obscene; it was conformable to the opinions that then prevailed among the people called Gentiles, or mythologists, and it was those people only that believed it. The Jews, who had kept strictly to the belief of one God, and no more, and who had always rejected the heathen mythology, never credited the story.
>
> It is curious to observe how the theory of what is called the Christian Church, sprung out of the tail of the heathen mythology. A direct incorporation took place in the first instance, by making the reputed founder to be celestially begotten. The trinity of gods that then followed was no other than a reduction of the former plurality, which was about twenty or thirty thousand. The statue of Mary succeeded the statue of Diana of Ephesus. The deification of heroes changed into the canonization of saints. The Mythologists had gods for everything; the Christian Mythologists had saints for everything. The church became as crowded with the one, as the pantheon had been with the other; and Rome was the place of both. The Christian theory is little else than the idolatry of the ancient mythologists, accommodated to the purposes of power and revenue; and it yet remains to reason and philosophy to abolish the amphibious fraud. (Thomas Paine, *The Age of Reason*, Chapter II.)

Consider also this telling passage in Paine's *Of The Religion of Deism Compared With the Christian Religion*, that heaps further insults upon Our Lord, the Blessed Mother, Saint Joseph and the entirety of the Catholic Faith:

> Certain books in what is called the New Testament tell us that Joseph dreamed that the angel told him so, (Matthew I, 20): "And behold the angel of the Lord appeared to Joseph, in a dream, saying, Joseph, thou son of David, fear not to take unto thee Mary thy wife, for that which is conceived in her is of the Holy Ghost."
>
> The evidence upon this article bears no comparison with the evidence upon the first article, and therefore is not entitled to the same credit, and ought not to be made an article in a creed, because the evidence of it is defective, and what evidence there is, is doubtful and suspicious. We do not believe the first article on the authority of books, whether called

Bibles or Korans, nor yet on the visionary authority of dreams, but on the authority of God's own visible works in the creation.

The nations who never heard of such books, nor of such people as Jews, Christians, or Mahometans, believe the existence of a God as fully as we do, because it is self-evident. The work of man's hands is a proof of the existence of man as fully as his personal appearance would be.

When we see a watch, we have as positive evidence of the existence of a watchmaker, as if we saw him; and in like manner the creation is evidence to our reason and our senses of the existence of a Creator. But there is nothing in the works of God that is evidence that He begat a son, nor anything in the system of creation that corroborates such an idea, and, therefore, we are not authorized in believing it. . . .

But though this is the creed of the Church of Rome, from whence the Protestants borrowed it, it is a creed which that Church has manufactured of itself, for it is not contained in nor derived from, the book called the New Testament.

The four books called the Evangelists, Matthew, Mark, Luke and John, which give, or pretend to give, the birth, sayings, life, preaching, and death of Jesus Christ, make no mention of what is called the fall of man; nor is the name of Adam to be found in any of those books, which it certainly would be if the writers of them believed that Jesus was begotten, born, and died for the purpose of redeeming mankind from the sin which Adam had brought into the world. Jesus never speaks of Adam himself, of the garden of Eden, nor of what is called the fall of man.

But the Church of Rome having set up its new religion, which it called Christianity, invented the creed which it named the Apostles's Creed, in which it calls Jesus the only son of God, conceived by the Holy Ghost, and born of the Virgin Mary; things of which it is impossible that man or woman can have any idea, and consequently no belief but in words; and for which there is no authority but the idle story of Joseph's dream in the first chapter of Matthew, which any designing imposter or foolish fanatic might make.

It then manufactured the allegories in the book of Genesis into fact, and the allegorical tree of life and the tree of knowledge into real trees, contrary to the belief of the first Christians, and for which there is not the least authority in any of the books of the New Testament; for in none of them is there any mention made of such place as the Garden of Eden, nor of anything that is said to have happened there.

But the Church of Rome could not erect the person called Jesus into a Savior of the world without making the allegories in the book of Genesis into fact, though the New Testament, as before observed, gives no authority for it. All at once the allegorical tree of knowledge became, according to the Church, a real tree, the fruit of it real fruit, and the eating of it sinful.

As priestcraft was always the enemy of knowledge, because priestcraft supports itself by keeping people in delusion and ignorance, it was consistent with its policy to make the acquisition of knowledge a real sin.

The Church of Rome having done this, it then brings forward Jesus the son of Mary as suffering death to redeem mankind from sin, which Adam, it says, had brought into the world by eating the fruit of the tree of knowledge. But as it is impossible for reason to believe such a story, because it can see no reason for it, nor have any evidence of it, the Church then tells us we must not regard our reason, but must believe, as it were, and that through thick and thin, as if God had given man reason like a plaything, or a rattle, on purpose to make fun of him.

Reason is the forbidden tree of priestcraft, and may serve to explain the allegory of the forbidden tree of knowledge, for we may reasonably suppose the allegory had some meaning and application at the time it was invented. It was the practice of the Eastern nations to convey their meaning by allegory, and relate it in the manner of fact. Jesus followed the same method, yet nobody ever supposed the allegory or parable of the rich man and Lazarus, the Prodigal Son, the ten Virgins, etc., were facts. (Thomas Paine, *Of The Religion of Deism Compared With the Christian Religion.*)

Thomas Paine is treated with reverence by many today as a champion of "liberty" and "reason" and "common sense" when he was nothing other than a naturalist of the Deistic variety who mocked the true Faith, which is the true mother and guardian of the reason with which man has been endowed. Such men as Thomas Paine are unworthy of admiration as no one is a "patriot" to his country if he mocks its King and Queen. Our Lord is the King of the United States of America. Our Lady of Guadalupe is the Empress of the Americas and she is the Queen of the United States of America under the title of her Immaculate Conception.

Not to be overlooked, of course, is another home grown naturalist of the Deistic variety. He was also a Freemason who was looked upon with great fondness as an "intellectual" by the Carrolls of Maryland, including the first American bishop and archbishop, John Carroll. Franklin was a libertine, who, like many of his contemporaries in the Eighteenth Century, was impressed with himself as a paragon of "reason" and virtue. The truth is, of course, that men such as Benjamin Franklin were pseudo-intellectuals. Far from being a "Christian" as many apologists have attempted to portray him, Franklin was a Deist who believe that his "deity' needed no worship or praise, rejecting the entirety of Divine Revelation to invent a "god" of his own imagining:

I believe there is one Supreme most perfect Being, Author and Father of the Gods themselves.

For I believe that Man is not the most perfect being but One, rather that as there are many Degrees of Beings his Inferiors, so there are many Degrees of Beings superior to him.

Also, when I stretch my Imagination thro' and beyond our System of Planets, beyond the visible fix'd Stars themselves, into that Space that is every Way infinite, and conceive it fill'd with Suns like ours, each with a Chorus of Worlds for ever moving round him, then this little Ball on which we move, seems, even in my narrow Imagination, to be almost Nothing, and my s e lf less than nothing, and of no sort of Consequence.

When I think thus, I imagine it great Vanity in me to suppose that the Supremely Perfect, does in the least regard such an inconsiderable Nothing as Man. More especially, since it is impossible for me to have any positive or clear Idea of that which is infinite and incomprehensible, I cannot conceive otherwise, that He, the Infinite Father, expects or requires no Worship or Praise from us, but that he is even INFINITELY ABOVE IT.

But since there is in all Men something like a natural Principle which inclines them to DEVOTION or the Worship of some unseen Power;

And since Men are endued with Reason superior to all other Animals that we are in our World acquainted with;

Therefore I think it seems required of me, and my Duty as a Man, to pay Divine Regards to SOMETHING.

I CONCEIVE then, that the INFINITE has created many beings or Gods, vastly superior to Man, who can better conceive his Perfections than we, and return him a more rational and glorious Praise. As among Men, the Praise of the Ignorant or of Children, is not regarded by ingenious Painter or Architect, who is rather honour'd and pleas'd with the Approbation of Wise men and Artists.

It may be that these created Gods, are immortal, or it may be that after many Ages, they are changed, and Others supply their Places.

Howbeit, I conceive that each of these is exceeding, wise and good, and very powerful; and that Each has made for himself, one glorious Sun, attended with a beautiful and admirable System of Planets.

It is that particular wise and good God, who is the Author and Owner of our System that I propose for the Object of my Praise and Adoration.

For I conceive that he has in himself some of those Passions he has planted in us, and that, since he has given us Reason whereby we are capable of observing his Wisdom in the Creation, he is not above caring for us, being pleas'd with our Praise, and offended when we slight him, or neglect his Glory.

I conceive for many Reasons that he is a good Being, and as I should be happy to have so wise, good and powerful a Being for Friend, let me consider in what Manner I shall make myself most accepted to him.

Next to the Praise due, to his Wisdom, I believe he is pleased and delights in the Happiness of those he has created; and since without Virtue Man can have no Happiness in this World, I firmly believe he delights to see me Virtuous, because he is pleas'd when he sees me Happy.

And since he has created many Things which seem purely design'd for the Delight of Man, I believe he is not offended when he sees his Children solace themselves in any manner of pleasant Exercises and innocent Delights, and I think no Pleasure innocent that is to Man hurtful.

I love him therefore for his Goodness and I adore him for his Wisdom.

Let me then not fail to praise my God continuously, for it is his Due, and is all I can return for his many Favours and great Goodness to me; and let me resolve to be virtuous, that I may be happy, that I may please Him, who is delighted to see me happy. Amen. (Benjamin Franklin, *Articles of Belief*, November 20, 1728.)

The *novus ordo seculorum* (the new world order) that sprang from these false beliefs in the Eighteenth Century became the basis of the modern civil state and of modern "culture," thus finishing off the job that the devil had undertaken by means of the Protestant Revolution to eradicate Catholicism as the driving force of men and their nations. To make this new world order more possible in the United States of America, therefore, the devil uses the naturalists who propagated ideas such as those discussed above to befriend and ingratiate themselves to leading Catholics, who in turn were flattered by the attention paid to them. After all, of course, these Catholics were grateful for the "liberty" of practicing their religion. Why not make the "best" of the environment in which they found themselves?

Mrs. Solange Hertz, writing in *The Spar Spangled Heresy: Americanism: How the Catholic Church in America Became the American Catholic Church*, provided her readers with a explanation of how Freemasonry in North America as found in *The Mystery of Freemasonry Unveiled*, which was written by Jose Maria Cardinal Cano y Rodriguez, the Archbishop of Santiago, Chile, from August 28, 1939, to December 4, 1958:

"The hatred of North American Masonry against religious teaching, especially Catholic teaching, is the same as that of all the lodges of the world. Because of it they have dictated the law of only public and compulsory teaching; and of course it is atheistic in several states . . . However, this does not mean that the campaign does not go on, to prepare the land, to transform the Constitution too, that according to the explanation given by the most noted Masons in the United States, the god of Masonry is not the God worshiped by the Christians, or the Mohammedans, or the Jews; it is a pagan god; any god, Nature, sun, flesh, etc., anything except the real God, the personal God, different from the world, and the Creator of Christianity.

"It is true that the Grand Lodge Masons of New York have declared that they do not want affiliations with lodges which do not acknowledge God or the Bible, but that does not mean an absolute breach at all." And he quotes William A. Rowan who in *The Builder* wrote, "There is only one God, Father of human race; there is rock over which we build; the Holy Bible is the Great Cross in Masonry. . . On these principles, I dare say, our Great Jurisdiction will be in union with all the Great Jurisdictions of the Universe, with a view to better reciprocal understanding, closer relations, and a common action to realize the Masonic unity and make the spirit of Brotherhood progress." All types of Masonry, says the Cardinal, "are serving as a base . . . to that mysterious pyramid, in which at the top, Satan is worshiped and Jesus Christ and God are renounced, and where there is taught as an ideal, universal rebellion and absolute licentiousness." (As found in Solange Hertz, *The Spar Spangled Heresy: Americanism: How the Catholic Church in America Became the American Catholic Church*, Veritas Press: Santa Monica, California, 1992, pp. 44-45.)

Although Bishop John Carroll was forced by the Vatican in 1810 to issue a pastoral letter to remind Catholics that they were forbidden to join Freemasonry, his own brother, Daniel Carroll, was a Freemason. Moreover, a benign view of "American Freemasonry" being different from "European Freemasonry" was shared by a number of leading Americanist bishops in the Nineteenth Century, including James Cardinal Gibbons, the Archbishop of Baltimore from 1877 to 1921, who believed, contrary to the truth of the matter:

Of record is Cardinal Gibbons' trip to Rome to defend the American secret societies, for he shared the prevailing Americanist view of American Masonry and its affiliates are "different" from continental varieties and essentially benign. He was even known to preach in Masonic lodges. He would have agreed with San Francisco's Archbishop Riordan, who believed "we should treat such organizations in as large a spirit as the discipline of the Church will permit us," and with Archbishop Ireland, who favored allowing Catholics "as much liberty" as is at all consistent with Catholic principles in their contacts with the fraternities. One of the group coups of the Gibbons regime was his successful reversal of the Vatican's condemnation of the Knights of Labor, a union two-thirds Catholic, largely modeled on Irish political secret societies of Masonic inspiration, and even in that day known to be heavily larded with Communists. Its approval opened the Catholic working class in the U.S. to the machinations of the left.

Such complaisance would seem to be nothing new, however, for a number of the Carrolls had never seen any conflict between Masonry and Catholicism. William J. Whalen, in *Christianity and American Freemasonry*, says, "Daniel Carroll, brother of the first American bishop, was active in Masonry, and apparently Bishop Carroll did not consider the papal ban applicable to this country until some time after 1800. For example, the bishop discussed the various censures of the Holy See on the lodge question in a letter to a layman in 1794. He added, "I do not pretend that these decrees are received generally by the Church, or have full authority in this diocese . . .' Masons laid the first cornerstone for St. Mary's Church, the first Catholic Church in Albany [New York] and first cathedral in that diocese.' Catholic sightseers in Baltimore should find Bishop Carroll's first cathedral worthy of notice, for it was designed by the Masonic architect of the Capitol, Benjamin Latrobe, and is an especially fine example of the "Enlightenment" style then being popularized by the sons of Hiram Abiff. (Solange Hertz, *The Spar Spangled Heresy: Americanism: How the Catholic Church in America Became the American Catholic Church*, Veritas Press: Santa Monica, California, 1992, pp. 88-89.)

Many Catholics in Eighteenth Century colonial America, having become so used to the religious indifferentisim wrought by the practical concessions that they needed to make to practice the Faith "as quietly as possible", saw "toleration" of Freemasonry as just a logical extension of the tolerance that had been granted to them by their Protestant neighbors, seeing absolutely nothing wrong in the Masonic references to God that were made at the time, references that continued to be made by one American president after another. Here are just a few examples that some of them lived long enough to experience in their own lifetimes after the inauguration of the first president, George Washington, on April 30, 1789:

Having thus imparted to you my sentiments as they have been awakened by the occasion which brings us together, I shall take my present leave; but not without resorting once more to the benign Parent of the Human Race in humble supplication that, since He has been pleased to favor the American people with opportunities for deliberating in perfect tranquillity, and dispositions for deciding with unparalleled unanimity on a form of government for the security of their union and the advancement of their happiness, so His divine blessing may be equally conspicuous in the enlarged views, the temperate consultations, and the wise measures on which the success of this Government must depend. (First Inaugural Address, April 30, 1789; there was no reference to God at all in his second inaugural address, March 4, 1793.)

The Nation's first chief executive took his oath of office in April [1789] in New York City on the balcony of the Senate Chamber at Federal Hall on Wall Street. General Washington had been unanimously elected President by the first electoral college, and John Adams was elected Vice President because he received the second greatest number of votes. Under the rules, each elector cast two votes. The Chancellor of New York and fellow Freemason, Robert R. Livingston administered the oath of office. The Bible on which the oath was sworn belonged to New York's St. John's Masonic Lodge. The new President gave his inaugural address before a joint session of the two Houses of Congress assembled inside the Senate Chamber. (A description of Washington's First Inaugural.)

Let us unite, therefore, in imploring the Supreme Ruler of Nations to spread his holy protection over these United States; to turn the machinations of the wicked to the confirming of our Constitution; to enable us at all times to root out internal sedition and put invasion to flight; to perpetuate to our country that prosperity which his goodness has already conferred, and to verify the anticipations of this Government being a safeguard of human rights. (George Washington, State of the Union message, 1794.)

I trust I do not deceive myself when I indulge the persuasion that I have never met you at any period when more than at the present the situation of our public affairs has afforded just cause for mutual congratulation, and for inviting you to join with me in profound gratitude to the Author of all Good for the numerous and extraordinary blessings we enjoy. (George Washington, State of the Union message, 1795.)

If an unshaken confidence in the honor, spirit, and resources of the American people, on which I have so often hazarded my all and never been deceived; if elevated ideas of the high destinies of this country and of my own duties toward it, founded on a knowledge of the moral principles and intellectual improvements of the people deeply engravened on my mind in early life, and not obscured but exalted by experience and age; and, with humble reverence, I feel it to be my duty to add, if a veneration for the religion of a people who profess and call themselves Christians, and a fixed resolution to consider a decent respect for Christianity among the best recommendations for the public service, can enable me in any degree to comply with your wishes, it shall be my strenuous endeavor that this sagacious injunction of the two Houses shall not be without effect.

With this great example before me, with the sense and spirit, the faith and honor, the duty and interest, of the same American people pledged to support the Constitution of the United States, I entertain no doubt of its continuance in all its energy, and my mind is prepared without hesitation to lay myself under the most solemn obligations to support it to the utmost of my power.

And may that Being who is supreme over all, the Patron of Order, the Fountain of Justice, and the Protector in all ages of the world of virtuous liberty, continue His blessing upon this nation and its Government and give it all possible success and duration consistent with the ends of His providence. (John Adams, First Inaugural Address, March 4, 1797.)

John Adams had a "decent respect" for Christianity even though he placed it alongside his rationalistic "god." Adams blasphemed Christ the King very frequently in his private letters:

"And the day will come when the mystical generation of Jesus by the supreme being as his father in the womb of a virgin will be classed with the fable of the generation of Minerva in the brain of Jupiter. But we may hope that the dawn of reason and freedom of thought in these United States will do away {with} all this artificial scaffolding..." (11 April, 1823, John Adams letter to Thomas Jefferson, Adams-Jefferson Letters, ed. Lester J. Cappon, II, 594).

Can a free government possibly exist with the Roman Catholic religion? (John Adams, Letter to Thomas Jefferson, May 19, 1821)

I almost shudder at the thought of alluding to the most fatal example of the abuses of grief which the history of mankind has preserved -- the Cross. Consider what calamities that engine of grief has produced! (John Adams, Letter to Thomas Jefferson, quoted in 200 Years of Disbelief, by James Hauck)

Although the Deistic views of Thomas Jefferson will be discussed in the next volume of this trilogy, suffice it to say for present purposes that the Eighteenth Century colonial America saw the rise and acceptance of liberalism and the liberal spirit by many Catholics, a spirit that led directly to the "Second" Vatican Council and is enshrined in the Protestant and Masonic *Novus Ordo* service. Father Felix Sarda y Salvany, a Spanish priest, explained in *What Is Liberalism?*, which was translated and published in the United States of America in 1899, that the spirit of Protestantism leads to the toleration of error. And it is precisely this toleration of error which has possessed the minds of and hearts of many Catholics in the United States of America, presaging the toleration of error and falsehood that has exited in the minds of the conciliar revolutionaries, including Joseph Ratzinger/Benedict XVI himself and Jorge Mario Bergoglio/Francis:

Protestantism naturally begets toleration of error. Rejecting the principle of authority in religion, it has neither criterion nor definition of faith. On the principle that every individual or sect may interpret the deposit of Revelation according to the dictates of private judgment, it gives birth to endless differences and contradictions. Impelled by the law of its own impotence, through lack of any decisive voice of authority in matters of faith, it is forced to   recognize as valid and orthodox any belief that springs from the exercise of private judgment. Therefore does it finally arrive, by force of its own premises, at the conclusion that one creed is as good as another; it then seeks to shelter its inconsistency under the false plea of liberty of conscience. Belief is not imposed by a legitimately and divinely constituted authority, but springs directly and freely from the unrestricted exercise of the individual's reason or caprice upon the subject-matter of Revelation. The individual or the sect interprets as it pleases–rejecting or accepting what it chooses. This is popularly called liberty of conscience. Accepting this principle, Infidelity, on the same plea, rejects all Revelation, and Protestantism, which handed over the premise, is powerless to protest against the conclusion; for it is clearer that one who, under the plea of rational liberty, has the right to repudiate any part of Revelation that may displease him, cannot logically quarrel with one who, on the plea of rational liberty, on the same plea, no creed is as good as any. Taking the field with this fatal weapon of Rationalism, Infidelity has stormed and taken the very citadel of Protestantism, helpless against   the foe of its own making.

As a result, we find amongst the people of this country [Spain] (excepting well formed Catholics, of course) that authoritative and positive religion has met with utter disaster and that religious beliefs or unbeliefs have come to be mere matters of opinion, wherein there are always essential differences, each one being free to make or unmake his own creed–or to accept no creed.

Such is the mainspring of the heresy constantly dinned into our ears, flooding our current literature and our press. It is against this that we have to be perpetually vigilant, the more so because it insidiously attacks us on the grounds of a false charity and in the name of a false liberty. Nor does it appeal to us only on the ground of religious toleration.

The principle ramifies in many directions, striking root into our domestic, civil, and political life, whose vigor and health depend upon the nourishing and sustaining power of religion. For religion is the bond which unites us to God, the Source and the End of all good; and Infidelity, whether virtual, as in Protestantism, or explicit, as in Agnosticism, severs the bond which binds men to God and seeks to build human society on the foundations of man's absolute independence. Hence we find Liberalism laying down as the basis of its propaganda the following principles:

> The absolute sovereignty of the individual in his entire independence of God and God's authority.

> The absolute sovereignty of society in its entire independence of everything which does not proceed from itself.

> Absolute civil sovereignty in the implied right of the people to make their own laws in entire independence and utter disregard of any other criterion than the popular will expressed at the polls and in parliamentary majorities.

Absolute freedom of thought in politics, morals, or in religion. The unrestrained liberty of the press.

Such are the radical principles of Liberalism. In the assumption of the absolute sovereignty of the individual, that is, his entire independence of God, we find the common source of all others. To express them all in one term, they are, in the order of ideas, Rationalism, or the doctrine of the absolute sovereignty of human reason. Here human reason is made the measure and sum of truth. Hence we have individual, social, and political Rationalism, the corrupt fountainhead of liberalist principles [which are]: absolute worship, the supremacy of the State, secular education repudiating any connection with religion, marriage sanctioned and legitimatized by the State alone, etc; in one word, which synthesizes all, we have Secularization, which denies religion any active intervention in the concerns of public and of private life, whatever they be. This is veritable social atheism.

Such is the source of liberalism in the order of ideas; such in consequences of our Protestant and infidel surroundings, is the intellectual atmosphere which we are perpetually breathing into our souls. Nor do these principles remain simply in the speculative order, poised forever in the region of thought. Men are not mere contemplatives. Doctrines and beliefs inevitably precipitate themselves into action. The speculation of today becomes the deed of tomorrow, for men, by force of the law of their nature, are ever acting out what they think. Rationalism, therefore, takes concrete shape in the order of facts. It finds palpable expression and action in the press, in legislation, and in social life. The secular press reeks with it, proclaiming with almost unanimous vociferation, absolute division between public life and religion. It has become the shibboleth of journalism, and the editor who will not recognize it in his daily screed soon feels the dagger of popular disapproval. In secularized marriage and in our divorce laws, it cleaves the very roots of domestic society; in secularized education, the cardinal principle of our public school system, it propagates itself in the hearts of the future citizens and the future parents; in compulsory school laws, it forces in the entering wedge of socialism; in the speech and intercourse of social life, it is constantly asserting itself with growing reiteration; in secret societies, organized in a spirit destructive of religion and often for the express purpose of exterminating Catholicity, it menaces our institutions and places the country in the hands of conspirators, whose methods and designs, beyond the reach of the public eye, constitute a tyranny of darkness.

In a thousand ways does the principle of Rationalism find its action and expression in social and civil life, and however diversified be its manifestation, there is in it always a unity and a system of opposition to Catholicity. Whether concerted or not, it ever acts in the same direction, and whatever special school within the genus of Liberalism professes it or puts it into action–be it in society, in domestic life, or in politics–the same essential characteristics will be found in all its protean shapes–opposition to the Church–and it will ever be found stigmatizing the most ardent defenders of the Faith as reactionaries, clericals, Ultramontanes [See p. 92, par. 1], etc.

Wherever found, whatever its uniform, Liberalism in its practical action is ever a systematic warfare against the Church. Whether it intrigue, whether it legislate, whether it orate or assassinate, whether it call itself Liberty or Government or the State of Humanity or Reason, or whatnot, its fundamental characteristic is an uncompromising opposition to the Church.

Liberalism is a world complete in itself; it has its maxims, its fashions, its art, its literature, its diplomacy, its laws, its conspiracies, its ambuscades. It is the world of Lucifer, disguised in our times under the name of Liberalism, in radical opposition and in perpetual warfare against that society composed of the Children of God, the Church of Jesus Christ. (Father Felix Sarda y Salvany, *Liberalism Is A Sin*, republished by TAN Books and Publishers, pp. 8-13; translated and adapted by Conde B. Pallen, Ph.D., LL.D., and published originally by B. Herder Book Company, St. Louis, Missouri, in 1899 under the title of *What Is Liberalism?*)

The Catholics of colonial America suffered much at the hands of Protestants. They did, however, find a degree of "liberty" in some places to practice their Faith quietly while those of means, such as the Carrolls, made money, which is how they became "respectable" in the eyes of the Deists and Freemasons and freethinkers who were more than happy to use them to lend credibility to their own schemes to inaugurate a new world order that was premised upon a hatred of the Catholic Faith. Eager to be part of this new world order and failing to see that their supposed friends amongst the intelligentsia in the colonies were just as opposed to the Faith as were the English who had oppressed their ancestors so cruelly, the leading Catholics of colonial America failed to realized that their own openness to "progress" and "enlightenment" made them enablers of the Liberalism that would destroy the fabric of the Faith just as surely as it was destined to result in the rise of statism in own time.

The problems of Modernity in the world and Modernism in the counterfeit church of conciliarism are thus intertwined. The Americanist roots of these problems played just as an important a contributing role in the rise of conciliarism as did the ideas and consequences of the French Revolution.

Chapter XV
Adapting the Faith So As to Prevent Anti-Catholicism

Catholics who are imbued with the mythology of the American founding, a mythology that has been propagated in one history book after another written by Catholic authors, including those who wrote textbooks for Catholic elementary and secondary schools students, believe that the colonial break from the United Kingdom was caused by the abuse of royal authority in the colonies that resulted in the British Parliament's imposition of taxes, imposts and duties that the colonists considered unfair and unjust, especially since the colonists had no representation in the world's oldest civil legislature. Most Catholics who accept the nationalistic mythology of the American founding do not realize the extent of anti-Catholicism that existed in the colonies in the Seventeenth and Eighteenth Centuries, failing also to realize that the cumulative percent of taxation that the British crown had imposed upon the colonists amount to the grand total of seven percent of a colonist's annual income. This pales into insignificance in comparison to the heavy burden of taxation imposed by the Federal, state and local governments in the supposedly "free" United States of America at the present time.

Prelude to the American Revolution

The British began to increase taxation and other revenue-raising measures after the end of the Seven Years' War in Europe in 1763. The North American extension of that war was known as the French and Indian War (1756-1763), during which New France was lost to Great Britain after the defeat of the French forces in the Battle of Quebec, fought on the Plains of Abraham (and also known, therefore, as the Battle of the Plains of Abraham) on September 13, 1759 (the French surrendered New France on September 8, 1760 after the British had captured Montreal). There would be no Christendom in New France as had developed in New Spain. Although the vestigial remnants of Catholicism would remain in New France as rivers and cities would continue in most, although not in all, cases to retain names given in honor of Our Lord and Our Lady and Saint Joseph and of the Holy Faith, the Faith itself would no longer be the foundation of social life.

The British eventually decided to extend religious "toleration" to the Catholics of Quebec in the Quebec Act, which was approved by King George III on June 22, 1774. Being unwilling to see the denizens of the recently captured New France show any allegiance to the English colonists to their south who had been complaining about excessive taxation and royal measures that were believed to curb legitimate human liberties, the British government wanted to secure the cooperation and allegiance of the Catholics in Quebec. It is necessary to contrast the Quebec Act, which was made as a matter of sheer political expediency, with the forcible breakup of families and the cruelty visited upon them as occurred with the faithful Catholics of Acadia in 1775.

Acadia, when it was part of New France until was captured by the British in 1710, was renamed Nova Scotia (New Scotland, the home of John Knox's Scottish brand of Calvinism, Presbyterianism). Governor Charles Lawrence of Nova Scotia ordered the forcible deportation of those Acadians who would not swear allegiance to the British Crown and also renounce the Catholic Faith. This exercise in English social engineering, which had been employed in Ireland to kill and repress Catholics in the island of saints and scholars, occurred without complaint or protest by the colonists in the territory that became the United States of America, including by the Catholics living there at the time.

Here is an account of the terrible story of the Grand Derangement:

> The British "Final Solution" for the Acadians was deportation. It all started at 3 PM on September 5, 1755 at the Catholic Church in Grand Pre. Following the orders and plan of the Lieutenant General, Governor Lawrence, following the decree of the King of England, the British Council at Halifax unanimously decided to begin deporting the Acadians immediately to various British Colonies outside of Canada. The vessels needed for this were to be commandeered in the King's name. By this time, the Acadians numbered some 13,000 on the Acadian peninsula alone. More and more British troops had been arriving and the Acadians were acutely aware that big trouble was brewing.
>
> A proclamation was issued accordingly to "all the inhabitants of the district of Grand Pre, Minas, River Canard, etc. ..... to attend the Church at Grand Pre on Friday the fifth instant, at three of the clock in the afternoon, that we may impart to them what we are ordered to communicate to them; declaring that no excuse will be admitted, on any pretense whatever, on pain of forfeiting goods and chattels, in default of real estate. - Given at Grand Pre 2d September, 1755."
>
> That Friday, 418 of the residents presented themselves at the Church as ordered. Colonel John Winslow, having tricked them into this assembly, announced to them that they were to be immediately deported outside of the Province and that all their properties and goods with the exception of their cash monies and personal belongings were hereby confiscated by and to the benefit of the British Crown. Soldiers surrounded the church to prevent any escapes.
>
> The news of this spread quickly and those who could escaped to the woods, but in vain. Their country was laid to waste. Deported from Grand Pre alone were 2,242 Acadians. The Acadians were lined up and driven to the transport ships. Women and children were loaded on boats as fast as could be provided. As if to deprive the exiles of even the hope of return, the British burned to the ground 255 of their homes, 276 barns, 11 mills, and one church while the transport vessels were still in sight. Despite the promises of Colonel Winslow to keep families together, most families were separated immediately - parents from their children, wives from their husbands, children from their siblings - many to never see each other again. The Acadians were placed under arrest and were loaded on the ships with no choice in the manner. They took only what they were wearing and what little monies they had on their person at the time. Some of the ships used as transports were not seaworthy. Consequently, two of the ships, the Violet and the Duke William, with two groups of 650 Acadians went to a watery grave in the icy mid-Atlantic on December 10 of that year. Only one lifeboat with 27 survivors lived to tell what happened. "I do not know," observes 19th century American historian George Bancroft, "if the annals of the human race keep the record of sorrows so wantonly inflicted, so bitter and so lasting as fell upon the French inhabitants of Acadia."

How ironic it must seem for the living descendants of those expelled Acadians who now live in the town of Winslow - a town so named in honor of the same British officer, General John Winslow, who was directly responsible for carrying out those dastardly deeds in the darkest hour in the history of the Acadians.

About 2,000 Acadians managed to escape arrest and they wandered through the woods like hunted animals, half-clad and half-starved, in ever search of some near relative. Some made it safely into Quebec where they established new lives in such towns as l'Acadie, Becancour, Nicolet, and others. Of those escapees was one of my own 6th generation paternal ancestors, Laurent Doucet, son of Paul Doucet (a direct descendant of Acadia's first governor, Germain Doucet) and Anne LeBrun. How they survived this terrible ordeal is almost miraculous. Today, the direct descendants of these escaped Acadians number over 230,000 souls, including one-third of the present population of New Brunswick.

The deportation continued unabated over a period of 8 years. Between 1755 and 1763, Governor Lawrence kept unloading the Acadians along the American coast - over 2,000 to Boston, where the Bostonians treated them like slaves, 700 from Grand Pre and Port Royal to Connecticut, and about 250 poor, naked, and destitute to New York. New York rid the major part of her Acadian exiles by persuading them to emigrate to Santo Domingo, where most of them perished miserably from the torrid sun. Lawrence exiled 754 to Philadelphia where, being held captive aboard the ships in the harbor for three months, smallpox killed 237 of them. Some 2,000 more were removed to Maryland where several hundred of them escaped to Louisiana, Quebec, and the West Indies. To North Carolina, Lawrence sent 500, and to South Carolina, 1,500 Acadians. The Carolinians cleverly enticed them to leave in some old boats for Acadia. Of these, only 900 arrived at the River St. John. Another 400 were banished to Georgia where, preferring death anywhere in the tropics to slavery with the blacks in the cotton fields and sugar plantations, they fled. Wherever they went, the Acadians were unwanted, shunned, cheated, despised, and heartlessly allowed to die without even the care and affection given to pet animals. Only Connecticut was prepared to receive the exiles sent to her and treated them as a group humanely. In all, nearly 3,700 Acadians were dispersed along the coast in the British colonies of America. There is no doubt that every Acadian would have preferred exile in France to banishment to any other place.

The method of dispersing the Acadians has scarcely an equal in history. Said Edmund Burke, "We did, in my opinion, most inhumanely, and upon the pretenses that, in the eye of an honest man, are not worth a farthing, root out this poor, innocent, deserving people, whom our utter inability to govern, or to reconcile, gave us no sort of right to extirpate." How right was his judgement. There were many pitiful separations in families. One case is particularly well-known. Due to the small number of transports, Rene Leblanc, notary-public of Grand Pre, his wife, and their two youngest children were put on one ship and landed in New York, but their eighteen other children and 150 grandchildren were loaded aboard different ships and dispersed among the colonies. There were deliberate separations of husbands from their wives and fathers from their children. Men would come back home from their work in the woods or fishing boats only to find their families gone, their homes burned to the ground, and the British soldiers waiting to arrest them and force them aboard ships for permanent banishment from their lands. Yet others were taken to various ports in England as prisoners of war and placed in concentration camps such as at Liverpool. (Acadia and the Acadians, by Robert Chenard.)

Readers will notice that the men noted for their devotion to "liberty" in the thirteen colonies of what became the United States of America did not believe that "liberty" extended to the Catholic refugees from Acadia, enslaving some and persecuting the rest. It was this hatred of Catholics that caused colonists to consider the Quebec Act as "intolerable" as it was a sign, at least to them, that the British were beginning to slacken in their resolve against "popery" when the truth of the matter was the act demonstrated British pragmatism in the face of a populace more numerous and prosperous than were the Acadians who were dispersed in Nova Scotia.

Robert Leckie described the flames of hatred that were fanned by anti-Catholic propagandists in the colonies in the immediate aftermath of the Quebec Act:

> This piece of legislation had not only confirmed the French in the free exercise of their religion and the practice of their native law, it had also granted the Quebec government those lands in the west which the English colonies claimed. Now, the colonists fancied themselves surrounded by French-speaking Catholics, the old enemy of former years, and their rage was so unbounded that on October 21, 1774, the [First] Continental Congress addressed a letter to the British people admonishing them for tolerating in America a religion which "has deluged your island in blood, and dispersed impiety, bigotry, persecution, murder and rebellion through every part of the world."

> One again, it was popular to quote Samuel Adams, who had said six years earlier [that is, in 1768]: "I did verily believe, as I do still, that much more is to be dreaded from the growth of popery in America, than from the Stamp Act or any other acts destructive of civil rights. . . ." Once again, the popular press picked up the old anti-Catholic cudgels, and one journal went so far as to predict: "We may live to see our churches converted into mass houses and our lands plundered by tythes for the support of the Popish clergy. The Inquisition may erect her standard in Pennsylvania and the city of Philadelphia may yet experience the carnage of St. Bartholomew's Day." Others, misrepresenting the truth of the Quebec Act, insisted that it actually established Romanism as an official religion, and warned: 'If Gallic Papists have a right To worship their own way Then farewell to the liberties Of poor America.'

> Ministers, of course, were in full voice once more, but so also were John Adams, apparently recovered from his momentary lapse into tolerance, Patrick Henry, Richard Henry Lee, the inevitable Samuel Adams, and none other than Washington's protégé and confidante, Alexander Hamilton, who thundered: "If [Parliament] had any regard to the freedom and happiness of mankind they would not have done it. If they had been friends to the Protestant cause, they would never have provided such a nursery for its greatest enemy . . . They may as well establish Popery in New York and the other colonies as they did in Canada!"

> More than the Stamp Act, perhaps more than any other act by Parliament or any British minister, the Quebec Act was a direct cause of the American Revolution. It so inflamed colonial hatred of the mother country that even that staunch and solid Protestant, King George III, was accused of being a Jesuit in disguise, and his statues, from which the rebels later were to melt so many serviceable bullets, were adored with mocking rosaries.

Meanwhile, patriots   such as Paul Revere did a brisk business in scurrilous engravings which depicted His Majesty and his Ministers clothed in the livery of the Pope of Rome. To the Catholics of colonial America–who actually represented no more than 1 per cent of the total population of three million persons–it appeared that it was time to pull tight the shutters again, and it was this furor of anti-Catholic sentiment that rose about the ears of Father John Carroll when he returned to   his native Maryland in 1774. (Robert Leckie, *American and Catholic*, Doubleday, 1970, pp. 45-47.)

Look at those names. John Adams. Samuel Adams. Alexander Hamilton. Paul Revere. These are not men to admire. They hated Our Blessed Lord and Saviour Jesus Christ and His true Church, she that is the one and only means of personal salvation and social order.

They had little to fear, however. Eager to be accepted by their fellow colonists, the leading Catholics of the colonies did not want to convert them to Catholicism. They simply desired the "freedom" to practice their Faith without persecution which is the only thing that the Quebec Act had guaranteed French Catholics in Quebec. Indeed, one could say that the Quebec Act was an incubator of the heresy of "religious liberty" just as much as had been the approach taken by the first Catholics who had arrived in Maryland in 1634 and the pragmatic tack taken by William Penn, who was no friend of Catholicism, in the Colony of Pennsylvania.

Caught in the Devil's Trap

To be sure, Catholics in the colonies, few in number though they were in the eighth decade of the Eighteenth Century, were in a very untenable situation. Indeed, they were in a trap that had been laid for them by the devil, finding themselves torn in a situation where they were not being killed, as had been the case for so long in England, but were still a hated minority in the land where some of their   ancestors had lived for over one hundred forty years. A very small number of Catholics remained loyal to the British Crown as the first shots in the Revolutionary War were fired in Lexington and Concord, Massachusetts, on April 19, 1775. Most Catholics, however, were to be found on the side of the self- styled "patriots," that is, colonists who desired to break from the mother country, Great Britain.

The "religious liberty" desired by Catholics came at quite a price: their fidelity to the Social Teaching of Holy Mother Church. There was never a time in the one hundred eighty-six years between the Declaration of Independence and the beginning of the "Second" Vatican Council on October 11, 1962, that the American "bishops" sought to teach the necessity of converting their land to the true Faith. To do so, obviously, would be to jeopardize their own acceptance and to disturb civil peace, they believed. Rather than seek to convert their fellow countrymen to the true Faith, the American bishops presided over the conversion of their fellow Catholics to the "republican spirit" of "freedom" and "democracy" and "independent thinking" that would lead most Catholics in the United States of America to come   to view Holy Mother Church over the course of time through the lens of republicanism, "freedom" and "democracy."

Such a spirit of independence from Roman "interference" had developed amongst Catholics in the colonies that Father John Carroll defied Bishop Richard Challoner (after whom the Challoner Douay-Rheims Bible is named) after he had been assigned to oversee the dismantling of the Society of Jesus following its suppression by Pope Clement XIV on July 21, 1773:

> Although shocked by the enmity which passage of the Quebec Act had unleashed against his faith, Father Carroll nevertheless sided with the Patriots in their dispute with England. He proudly followed the career of his famous cousin, Charles, sympathizing with his republican convictions and becoming so independence-minded himself that he refused his obedience to Father John Lewis, acting as Bishop Challoner's vicar-general. By this act, like so many of his fellow priests in America, he made it clear that he had no wish to submit to ecclesiastical authority based in England. Nevertheless, John Carroll was far from enthusiastic when his cousin Charles approached him with the astounding invitation to help win the Catholics of Canada to the Patriot cause (Robert Leckie, *American and Catholic*, Doubleday, 1970, p. 48.)

Anti-Catholics though the leading colonists may have been, they were also as pragmatic as their British overlords. Some of those leading colonists believed that a way could be found to win over Catholics to the "patriot" cause, an invitation that suited the purposes of the Carrolls of Maryland in order to win acceptance and thus general "tolerance" for their co-religionists in each of the colonies when they became states in an independent United States of America.

Mrs. Solange Hertz described the Masonic background of Charles Carroll, one of the signers of the Declaration of Independence, who had enlisted his cousin, Father John Carroll, to accompany the libertine Freemason Benjamin Franklin and Samuel Chase on a mission to Canada to win over the very people who had been the object of such hatred after the Quebec Act to the cause of American independence:

> Charles Carroll, born in Annapolis in 1737, had become very active politically on completing his education abroad. He served 23 years in the Maryland legislature as well as in the U.S. Senate until it became illegal to hold both offices simultaneously. At the t i m e of the Revolution he was probably the richest man in America, owning some 80,000 acres in Maryland alone. Enjoying a reputation as a somewhat eccentric, but affable money-grubber, he was invaluable in managing the finances of the Continental Army. It has been pointed out that he stood most to lose should the Revolution fail: "There go a few millions!" exclaimed one onlooker who watched him sign the Declaration of Independence. But this was to lose sight of the fact that he also stood the most to gain if the Revolution succeeded and English taxes thereby abolished. His gamble paid off gloriously.

> He was the only Catholic to sign the Declaration, whose language a true son of the Church would have held under the deepest suspicion. Although he never denied the Faith and was sober and disciplined in his personal habits, he was not noted for any outbursts of piety. His birth may have been illegitimate, inasmuch as his parents' marriage certificate bears a date some twenty years after he was born. His wife died young, a victim of opiates, and he never re-married. All his children died out of the Church, his only son Charles of Homewood renouncing the Faith, taking to drink and never holding any position worth mentioning.

The Masonic builders of liberty had the utmost confidence in Charles Carroll. He not only helped win Maryland to the Articles of Confederation and later to the hotly resisted Constitution, but through his connections abroad, smoothed Franklin's path in Paris to seal the French Alliance whereby France threw her weight against the English king. In February 1776 the Continental Congress resolved "that a committee of three–two of whom to be members of Congress–to be appointed to repair to Canada, there to pursue such instructions as shall be given them by that body." Those named were the dean of American Masonry, Benjamin Franklin, together with the Maryland Protestant Samuel Chase–and Charles Carroll. This despite the fact that he was only an observer at the Congress, Catholics being barred from serving as delegates. (Solange Hertz, *The Spar Spangled Heresy: Americanism: How the Catholic Church in America Became the American Catholic Church*, Veritas Press: Santa Monica, California, 1992, pp. 36-37.)

The mission to Quebec that Father John Carroll undertook with his cousin, a Master Mason, and the chief of the Masons in the English colonies, Benjamin Franklin, began the official co-opting of leading Catholics by men who had no use for the Faith other than to use Its adherents for their purposes of promoting the "new science of politics" represented by their false ideas. This is not an exaggeration. Leading American "patriots" sought to do this very explicitly, something that Robert Leckie demonstrated (without understanding that he was doing so) in *American and Catholic*:

After its first outburst against the Quebec Act, Congress [the First Continental Congress] had second thoughts about Canada. On the very same day that it had excoriated King George for tolerating in America a religion which "has deluged your land in blood," they addressed a quite dissimilar letter to the people of Quebec, inviting them to join the fight against tyranny and declaring:

We are too well acquainted with the liberality of sentiment distinguishing your nation, to imagine, that difference of religion will prejudice you against a hearty amity with us. You know, that the transcendent nature of freedom elevates those, who unite in her cause, above all such-low minded infirmities.

The Canadians, however, were also "too well-acquainted" with the true religious sentiments of the Protestants to the south, and they angrily spurned the overtures of what they called "the perfidious Congress." Moreover, Bishop [Jean-Oliver] Briand of Quebec deeply distrusted the Americans, and forbade any of his flock to join them under penalty of excommunication. Thus, Canada remained loyal to the British crown, and in 1775 Congress, despairing of diplomacy, authorized a two-pronged military assault on Montreal and Quebec under Richard Montgomery and Benedict Arnold. Although this expedition ultimately ended in failure, Congress flip- flopped back to diplomacy again. Already aware that the traditional American hatred of Catholicism was going to have to be muted during the war against England, it authorized a diplomatic mission to Canada charged with impressing upon the Canadians its new-found tolerance of Popery. Benjamin Franklin was the obvious choice to lead the embassy, along with Samuel Chase, known to have Catholic friends, and the Catholic Charles Carroll. A few weeks later the British-born General Charles Lee wrote to his friend John Hancock: "I should think that if some Jesuit of Religieuse or any other Order (he must be a man of liberal sentiments, enlarged mind and a manifest friend of Civil Liberty) could be found out and sent to Canada, he would be worth battalions to us." The same idea had occurred to John Adams, who wrote to a friend: "We have empowered the Committee to take with them, another gentleman of Maryland, a Mr. John Carroll, a Roman Catholic priest, and a Jesuit, a gentleman of learning and Abilities." Obviously, John Adams, could he swallow his hatred of priests, and especially Jesuits, to the extent that he could praise one, Catholicism was once again in good odor in Philadelphia. (Robert Leckie, *American and Catholic*, Doubleday, 1970, pp. 48-49.)

Only a corrupted version of Catholicism displays "liberal sentiments" with an "enlarged mind" and is a "manifest friend" of "Civil Liberty." In other words, the Catholicism desired by Charles Lee and his fellow anti-Catholics was a "safe Catholicism." Although it took much time and many struggles of one sort or another, the "safe," "acceptable" brand of Catholicism that emerged after the Revolutionary War was a prophetic harbinger of the "safe Catholicism" that now exists in the entire world. It is called the counterfeit church of conciliarism that most people in the world believe is the Catholic Church but is in fact her counterfeit ape.

It was on that mission to Quebec in 1774 that the colonial elite began to realize that they could neutralize "popery" by extending leading "papists" some baubles of recognition, thus convincing them that they could all live together in peace and brotherhood while they, the Catholics, surrendered any claim to seek the conversion of the country to the true Faith. Furthermore, the colonial elite believed that the Catholics could be convinced to "stand up" to any kind of "Roman interference" in their "internal affairs" in an independent American nation the way that they were standing up to King George III and the military might of the British Empire.

It was a year after the Treaty of Paris that formally ended the Revolutionary War and resulted in concessions by England to France and Spain that Father John Carroll was selected to be the *de facto* superior of the approximately 25,000 Catholics who lived in the new country, the United States of America. Benjamin Franklin personally recommended his old friend from the Quebec mission to Pope Pius VI's papal nuncio to France for the position. Some of the American priests, having worked for so long without a superior, were resentful at the mere notion of the sudden appearance of a hierarchy, no less one established by "Rome." Father Carroll himself was so concerned about the appearance of "foreign interference" that he wrote to Leonardo Cardinal Antonelli, the Prefect of the Congregation for the Propagation of the Faith from May 2, 1780, to June 25, 1784, to request him to phrase his appointment in such a way so that Protestants would not be frightened:

> In the official letter to Carroll, Cardinal Antontelli confirms that he was chosen because "it is known that your appointment will please and gratify many members of that republic, and especially Mr. Franklin, the eminent individual who represents that republic at the court of the Most Christian King [Louis XVI of France]. Accepting the appointment, Carroll urged the Cardinal to find some method whereby in future it would not appear that the American Church was receiving its authority from a foreign power! He had petitioned the Pope not to leave American Catholics under the jurisdiction of their prelate in England, alleging that this could not be done "without open offense at this supreme magistracy and political government." (Solange Hertz, *The Spar Spangled Heresy: Americanism: How the Catholic Church in America Became the American Catholic Church*, Veritas

Press: Santa Monica, California, 1992, p. 38.)

Father John Carroll was sincerely concerned about the growth of the Faith in the United States of America. He simply believed that a way could be found to do this without appearing to threaten the Protestants.

An admirer of Father Carroll, Jay P. Dolan, quoted Carroll at length on the matter:

> I consider powers issued from the Propaganda not only as improper, but dangerous here. The jealously in our Governments of the interference of any foreign jurisdiction is known to be such that we cannot expect, and in my opinion ought not to wish, that they would tolerate any other, than that which being purely spiritual, is essential to our Religion, to wit, an acknowledgment of the Pope's spiritual Supremacy, and of the see of S. Peter being the center of Ecclesiastical unity. The appointment therefore by the Propaganda of a Superior for this Country appears to be a dangerous step, and, by exciting the jealousy of the governments here may lend much to the prejudice of Religion, and perhaps expose it to the reproach of encouraging a dependence on a foreign power, and giving them an undue internal influence by leaving with them a prerogative to nominate to places of trust and real importance, and that ad scum beneplacitum [at their own pleasure]. (Quoted in Jay P. Dolan, *The American Catholic Experience*, Doubleday, 1985, p. 106.)

The future proto-bishop and archbishop in the United States of America, John Carroll, also believed passionately in what Pope Saint Pius X would term a thesis absolutely false, separation of Church and State, a thesis that was condemned repeatedly by pope after pope in the Nineteenth Century. No matter Archbishop John Carroll's becoming a bit more "conservative" in his later years, especially concerning the necessity of Church discipline and the retention of Latin in the Sacred Liturgy despite having supported the use of the vernacular thirty years previously (in the 1780s), he remained a champion of the falsehoods of "separation of Church and State" and "religious liberty" until the day he died on December 3, 1815. This was no mere pragmatic concession to the reality of the situation in which Catholics found themselves. This was a complete and total commitment to these insidious falsehoods as a matter of firmly rooted principle, thus preparing the way for the triumph of conciliarism in our own days:

> In addition to being independent and American, a third dimension of the republican blueprint of Catholicism was an insistence on the separation of church and state. In the seventeenth century, Lord Baltimore had implemented this practice when he refused to allow the Jesuits any special privileges; at the time, it was a pragmatic decision rooted in the necessity for religious toleration in a Catholic colony populated by Protestants. With the Protestant takeover in Maryland, religious toleration became an orphan. Only with the [American] Revolution, did this republican idea became actualized once more. This time it emerged not as a pragmatic concession to a religiously plural environment, but as a fundamental human right endorsed by the Revolution. Catholics accepted this rights-of-man philosophy and enthusiastically supported the concept of a free church in a free society. Such thinking placed American Catholics squarely in the mainstream of Catholic Enlightenment thought. (Jay P. Dolan, *The American Catholic Experience*, Doubleday, 1985, p. 108.)

Such a description could have been written by Joseph Ratzinger/Benedict XVI himself, who does indeed see the events of the American Revolution as decisive in shaping the ethos of the "Second" Vatican Council:

> In the meantime, however, the modern age had also experienced developments. People came to realize that the American Revolution was offering a model of a modern State that differed from the theoretical model with radical tendencies that had emerged during the second phase of the French Revolution. (Benedict XVI, Christmas Greetings to Members of the Roman Curia, December 22, 2005.)

The model of the "modern State" "offered" by the American Revolution was no less radical than the one that emerged during the "second phase of the French Revolution." Although many Catholic apologists of the American founding have sought to portray it as different than the radicalism of the French Revolution, the differences are matters of degree, not of kind, as the principle root is the same: the belief that men and their nations could be well-organized absent a due subordination to the Sacred Deposit of Faith as It has been entrusted by Our Blessed Lord and Saviour Jesus Christ exclusively to the Catholic Church in all that pertains to the good of souls, upon which is hinged the totality of social order. The devil had to attack France with the violence and bloodshed that began to be unleashed on July 14, 1789, as the Cross of the Divine Redeemer had been planted firmly into the French soil; he used more subtle–and hence more insidious–means to co-opt American Catholics into becoming just as hostile to the Social Reign of Christ the King as were the Jacobins of the French Revolution.

There are others who claim that the "independent" spirit that has long characterized Catholicism in the United States of America is the reason that the traditional movement had a much larger following, relatively speaking, than in Europe. One may concede that point, only to note, however, that there would be no need for any kind of traditional movement anywhere in the world if the virus of Americanism had not incubated during colonial days and then began to spread following the end of the American Revolution and the ratification of the Constitution of the United States of America, which, as will be seen in volume two of this book, would later infect the entirety of the world and become the very foundation of the conciliar church's embrace of separation of Church and State and religious liberty and of false ecumenism itself.

Jay P. Dolan came to this conclusion in an admiring, not critical, way in *The American Catholic Experience*:

> For Roman Catholics, modernism is a term generally associated with a theological controversy that surfaced in the late-nineteenth and early-twentieth centuries. But the rise of historical-mindedness, or what can be called the modernist mentality, clearly predated this controversy. As regards European Catholicism, the evidence for this is extensive. Even though the evidence is not so extensive for American Catholicism, a definite modernist impulse can be discerned in some leading American Catholic thinkers. Though they did not call themselves modernists, nor did the self-conscious think of themselves as such, they were thinking and acting according to a modern perspective that theologically viewed the church as historically conditioned–unlike the classicist or

neo-Scholastic mentality, which viewed it as unchanging and immune to the influence of history.

John Carroll was an intellectual heir of the Enlightenment, and his thinking on the nature of the church leaned in the modern direction. As previously noted in the chapter on republican Catholicism, John Carroll wanted to adapt certain practices of the church to the American environment. These included the training of priests, an English liturgy, friendly relations and cooperation with Protestants, and a church independent of foreign interference. In this manner he envisioned a church in the United States distinct from Roman Catholic churches in other countries. Such a program of adaptation to the American cultural situation clearly pointed in   the modernist direction. Though these types of adaptation were more external and would not alter the intrinsic meaning of the church, Carroll did go further. He advocated the separation of Church and state, and promoted the idea of religious liberty. This touched on the very meaning of the church. According to the institutional model, the church was the one perfect society, and the state or civil society was subject to the rule of the church. Carroll promoted a different point of view, and in doing so modified the institutional model of the church as the one perfect visible society. Though he never fully explained how church and state would be separated and the consequent relationship between the two, his advocacy of the general concept of separation according to the American model clearly put him at odds with the prevailing model of the church as the one perfect society. In addition, Carroll celebrated religious liberty, not as a pragmatic concession to a religiously pluralist society, but as a natural human right. This, too, challenged the prevailing Roman Catholic position that said error had no rights and false religious beliefs could not be tolerated. The logic of Carroll's position suggested that, in a religiously pluralist society, Roman Catholicism could not claim to be the one and only visible church.

In advocating these positions on religious liberty and the separation of Church and state, Carroll was implying that the understanding of the church should be adapted to the cultural context, in this case the United States. Such thinking reflected a historical consciousness, a modern mentality in other words, when it came to defining the meaning of the church. This   does not mean that Carroll self-consciously was adopting a historical, modern perspective in place of the classicist point of view. Nor was Carroll alone. During the Republican era, other American Catholics advocated religious liberty and separation of church and state. Unlike in Europe, such thinking did not result in a new school of thought or a new theology, but it did set a precedent. The precedent was the need of the church to adapt itself to the American context, not just in externals, but even in its very definition. (Jay P. Dolan, *The American Catholic Experience*, Doubleday, 1985, pp. 304-305.)

The process of "conversion in reverse" began with the arrival of Catholics in Maryland in 1634. It became institutionalized in the decades thereafter, anchoring itself upon the mooring provided by the Constitution and the "founding principles." The process of adaptation used by John Carroll has become that of the conciliar church. Unfortunately, for John Carroll, however, his desire to adapt the Faith to the American experience resulted in the precise thing he feared: Catholics becoming more and more Protestant in their mentality over the course of time:

Obviously, American Catholicism did not seem to have a promising future [in 1785], and Father Carroll's report reflects his deep concern for its chief problem of "leakage." By then, the country contained an estimated quarter-million lapsed Catholics, ordinary people who, unlike the wealthy planters of Maryland, and farmers of Pennsylvania, had found it exceedingly difficult to practice their religion. With the shortage of priests continuing, and the immigrant tide rising daily, many more were to be lost irrevocably. Even today [1970], the presence of so many Protestant Irish in the South testifies to the mass defection of their ancestors. They lost their faith, wrote Father Carroll, not only because they found no place to practice it or found hostility to the public profession of it too much to bear, but also because of "unavoidable intercourse with non-Catholics." This produced moral laxness, or at least a relaxing of comparatively stricter Catholic morality, and what the prefect apostolic considered a greater danger: mixed marriages. Again and again, Carroll was to complain of this problem and his helplessness against it. In 1798 he wrote to a friend in England: "Here our Catholics are so mixed with Protestants in all the intercourse of civil society and business public and private, that abuse of intermarriage is almost universal and it surpasses my ability to devise an effectual bar against it. No general prohibition can be exacted without reducing many of the faithful to live in a state of celibacy." In other words, if one Catholic family was set down in a community of, say, thirty Protestant families, where would the Catholic children find partners? And if they accepted reality and chose them from among the Protestants, would it be very likely that the offspring of the dominant majority would embrace an abhorred minority faith? If one is to judge from so distinguished a Catholic as Charles Carroll of Carrollton, here is the answer: all of Carroll's children married non-Catholics; and apparently none of his grandchildren were raised as Catholics. Another outstanding Catholic, Dominick Lynch of New York, one of the pillars of the Church who signed the letter to Washington, fathered a family of thirteen children, but within a few generations almost all of his descendants were lost to the faith. (Robert Leckie, *American and Catholic*, 1970, p. 64.)

Archbishop John Carroll found himself in a quandary as he never wavered in his support for the very thing that made it possible for the pluralism about which he complained to flourish and thus to take hold of the minds, hearts and souls of Catholics in the United States of America: the founding principles expressed in the Declaration of Independence and the very framework of the American Constitution that enshrined the principles of separation of Church and State and religious liberty without ever using those exact words. And it would be the rotten fruit of those principles that was to plant insidious seeds for the rise of a counterfeit ape of the Catholic Church headed by men who believed that the expression of Church teaching is indeed historically conditioned and must be adapted to the circumstances of time and place.

Behold the results that are upon us today, both in the United States of America and the rest of the world.

Behold.

The second volume of this book will examine the founding principles and the Constitution in great detail, explaining how leading Catholics embraced the framework of the American regime in the belief that the Faith could prosper in spite of pluralism and that, far from being an offense to God and hindrance to the salvation of souls, the separation of Church and State and religious liberty were beneficial both to the Faith and thus to society.

It was not the spirit of the Catholic Middle Ages that informed John Carroll, not even as a model after which to pray could be realized in the United States of America one day. It was the spirit of Modernity that had taken root during the Renaissance, began to sprout during the Protestant Revolution and came to flower with the "enlightenment" that darkened the minds of the American founders and, so sadly, of the Carrolls themselves.

Our Lady of Guadalupe, pray for us.

ABOUT THE AUTHOR

Dr. Thomas A. Droleskey, who was born in Jamaica, Queens, New York, on November 24, 1951, received a Bachelor of Arts, *cum laude*, from Saint John's University, Jamaica, New York, on January 31, 1973, a Master of Arts from the University of Notre Dame, Notre Dame, Indiana, and his Doctor of Philosophy from the State University of New York at Albany, Albany, New York, on August 5, 1977.

Droleskey taught as a full-time faculty member at numerous colleges and universities between September of 1976 and January of 2007, starting with Mohawk Valley Community College in Utica, New York, in the 1976-1977 academic year, and including Illinois State University (1977-1979 and 1986-1987), Allentown College of Saint Francis de Sales (1979-1980), Nassau Community College (1980-1983), Saint Francis College, Brooklyn, New York (1985-1986), Morningside College (1992-1993) and the C. W. Post Campus of Long Island University (1994-1995). Droleskey also served as an adjunct professor of political science at Saint John's University (1982-1992), the C. W. Post Campus of Long Island University (1991-2007) and New York Institute of Technology (1991-1993).

Formerly a pro-life activist and candidate for public office, Dr. Droleskey ran for the office of lieutenant governor of the State of New York on the Right to Life Party line in 1986, running also for the office of Supervisor of the Town of Oyster Bay in 1997 and in a primary for the United States senatorial nomination of the Right to Life Party in 1998. He also served as a volunteer surrogate speaker in two different presidential campaigns in the 1990s.

Committed to the restoration of the Social Reign of Christ the King and of Mary our Immaculate Queen, hundreds of Droleskey's articles appeared in *The Wanderer* (1992-2001) and later *The Remnant* (2002-2006) and *Catholic Family News* (2004-2006). A few of his articles appeared in *Celebrate Life* and *The Latin Mass: A Journal of Catholic Culture*. This writing led to numerous invitations to speak to groups of Catholics across the nation in the 1990s and into the first decade of the Twenty-first century.

Droleskey's online publication, www.ChristorChaos.com, is the continuation of a printed journal that began in September of 1996 and continued until June of 2003. Over two thousand articles have appeared online since the debut of the website on February 20, 2004.

Married since June 7, 2001, to the former Sharon Collins, Droleskey and wife live with their daughter, Lucy Mary Therese Norma, who was born on March 27, 2002, within the United States of America.

Made in the USA
Monee, IL
07 July 2026

56550050R00173